MEDIA AND MEDIATION

Communication Processes

Series Editors: Bernard Bel, Jan Brouwer, Biswajit Das,
Vibodh Parthasarathi, Guy Poitevin

Other Books in the Series

Volume 2: Domination and Appropriation
Volume 3: Culture and Confrontation

Communication Processes Vol. 1

MEDIA AND MEDIATION

Editors
Bernard Bel, Jan Brouwer,
Biswajit Das, Vibodh Parthasarathi,
Guy Poitevin

SAGE Publications
New Delhi/Thousand Oaks/London

Copyright © Centre for Cooperative Research in Social Sciences, Pune, 2005

All rights reserved. No part of this book may be reproduced or utilized in any form or by any means, electronic or mechanical, including photocopying, recording or by any information storage or retrieval system without permission in writing from the publisher.

First published in 2005 by

Sage Publications India Pvt Ltd
B–42, Panchsheel Enclave
New Delhi 110 017
www.indiasage.com

Sage Publications Inc
2455 Teller Road
Thousand Oaks
California 91320

Sage Publications Ltd
1 Oliver's Yard
55 City Road
London EC1Y 1SP

Published by Tejeshwar Singh for Sage Publications India Pvt Ltd, typeset in 10/12 Georgia at InoSoft Systems, Noida, and printed at Chaman Enterprises, New Delhi.

Library of Congress Cataloging-in-Publication Data

Media and mediation/editors Bernard Bel ... [et al.].
    p. cm.–(Communication processes; v. 1)
Includes bibliographical references.
    1. Communication—Political aspects—India. 2. India—Politics and government. I. Bel, Bernard. II. Series.

P95.82.I4M43   324'.01'4–dc22   2005   2005023327

ISBN: 0-7619-3428-6 (Hb)   81-7829-576-8 (India-Hb)

Sage Production Team: Vineeta Rai, Swati Sahi, Sanjeev Sharma and Santosh Rawat

To Guy
who brought many of us together
and, as quietly, left us

CONTENTS

List of Tables and Figures — 11

List of Abbreviations — 13

Preface — 15

Overture: Excavating 'the Political' — 17
Bernard Bel, Jan Brouwer, Biswajit Das, Vibodh Parthasarathi, Guy Poitevin

1. The Quest for Theory: Mapping Communication Studies in India — 35
   Biswajit Das

2. Investigating Communication: Remooring the Contours of Research — 66
   Biswajit Das, Vibodh Parthasarathi, Guy Poitevin

Part 1: CONSTRUCTIONS AND CONFIGURATIONS

Introduction — 93
Editors

1.1 Fulcrums of Administration

3. 'Beyond the Reach of Monkeys and Men'? O'Shaughnessy and the Telegraph in India, c.1836–1856 — 105
   Deep Kanta Lahiri Choudhury

4. Information Society as if Communication Mattered: The Indian State Revisited — 135
   Dipankar Sinha

1.2 Landscapes of Commerce

5 Construing a 'New Media' Market: Merchandising the Talking Machine, c.1900–1911   165
Vibodh Parthasarathi

6 A Question of Choice: Advertisements, Media and Democracy   199
Maitrayee Chaudhuri

1.3 Arenas of Assimilation

7 Mediating Modernity: Colonial Discourse and Radio Broadcasting, c.1924–1947   229
Biswajit Das

8 In Search of Autonomy: The Nationalist Imagination of Public Broadcasting   255
Shanti Kumar

Part 2: ANATOMIES OF ARBITRATION

Introduction   283
Editors

2.1 Invasion and Intrusion

9 State, Market and Freedom of Expression: Women and Electronic Media   295
Uma Chakravarti

10 Forging Public Opinion: The Press, Television and Electoral Campaigns in Andhra Pradesh   315
G. Krishna Reddy

2.2 Interaction and Appropriation

11 Personal and Social Communication: Two Instances of Electronic Mail   349
Bernard Bel

12 Communication for Socio-Cultural Action: 'Is the Discourse "on", "for" or "of"?' *Jitendra Maid, Pandit Padalghare, Guy Poitevin*	371

2.3 Interrogation and Contestation

13 The Political Meaning of a River: Intellectuals and the Economy of Knowledge around the Narmada *Joël Ruet*	405
14 That Persistent 'Other': The Political Economy of Copyright in India *Pradip N. Thomas*	436
In Lieu of an Epilogue: Beyond Disciplinary Elusiveness *Editors*	465
About the Editors and Contributors	469

List of Tables and Figures

Tables
10.1 Population Changes in Andhra Pradesh and Newspaper Change in Telugu, 1961–91 — 321
10.2 Agencies and Circulation of *Eenadu* Daily Newspaper — 326
10.3 Aiming Sky-high! Advertisement Rates and Airtime Utilization (1999) of Regional Channels — 332

Figures
5.1 Profile of Calcutta's Retail Market — 183
5.2 GTL/GC in the Advertisement Markets of Calcutta and Madras — 185
10.1 The Rapid Growth of Cable Television in India — 329
10.2 Advertising Revenues of Doordarshan — 330

LIST OF ABBREVIATIONS

AIADMK	All India Anna Dravida Munnetra Kazhagam
BBC	British Broadcasting Corporation
BJP	Bharatiya Janata Party
BSP	Bahujan Samaj Party
CAS	conditional access system
CEO	chief executive officer
CMC	computer-mediated communication
CBD	Convention on Biological Diversity
CRISP	Computerized Rural Information Systems Project
DISNIC	District Information System of National Informatics Centre
DMK	Dravida Munnetra Kazhagam
DTH	direct to home
GATT	General Agreement on Tariffs and Trade
GATS	General Agreement on Trade in Services
GC	The Gramophone Company
GMT	Greenwich mean time
GNP	gross national product
GTL	Gramophone and Typewriter Limited
IBC	Indian Broadcasting Company
ISBS	Indian State Broadcasting Service
IRDP	integrated rural development programme
IT	information technology
IPR	intellectual property rights
MKSS	Mazdoor Kisan Shakti Sangathan
MNC	multinational corporation

List of Abbreviations

NAM	Non-Aligned Movement
NIC	National Informatics Centre
NICNET	National Informatics Centre network
NIEO	New International Economic Order
NWICO	New World Information and Communication Order
PAR	participatory action research
RJD	Rashtriya Janata Dal
RTI	Right to Information
SP	Samajwadi Party
TDP	Telugu Desam Party
TWI	Transworld Image
TRIPS	Trade-related Intellectual Property Rights
UNESCO	United Nations Educational, Scientific and Cultural Organization
UPA	United Progressive Alliance
USTR	United States Trade Representative
VBAC	vaginal birth after a caesarean
VSNL	Videsh Sanchar Nigam Limited
NDA	National Democratic Alliance
WTO	World Trade Organization

PREFACE

This triptych on *Communication Processes* is dedicated to our colleague Guy Poitevin whose sudden demise deprived us to share the results of the mammoth editorial work that he was so passionately part of. Without his sharp mind, multidisciplinary erudition and extraordinary strength and patience, this task would never have been completed.

Many of the contributions in the three anthologies emerged from the interdisciplinary seminars organized by the Centre for Cooperative Research in Social Sciences (CCRSS), Pune in January 1996, the Centre for Human Sciences (CSH), New Delhi and the Department of Sociology, Jamia Millia Islamia (New Delhi) in April 1997, and by the CCRSS again in January 1998. The first and the third meets were generously supported by the Charles Leopold Mayer Foundation for the Progress of Humankind (FPH), Paris, and the second by the CSH. These extensive dialogues, the longest extending to nine days, sought to foreground and sharpen our understanding of the field of communication in India. The following years saw us reaching out to many others in different parts of the country and abroad and vice versa. These discussions further refined and enhanced the engagement with common concerns, albeit from intellectual domains and different walks of life that were not strictly, or even conventionally, rooted in 'communication'.*

Disciplinary, professional, social and linguistic divides were what Guy Poitevin incessantly sought to transcend. His lifelong involvement in cooperative action research among oppressed communities will remain exemplary. Born in Mayenne

---

*Andriene Bel, Jan Brouwer, Bruno Dorin, Sheena Jain, Deepak Kem, Neshat Quaiser, Hema Rairkar and Michel Sauquet remained ardent supporters and constructive critics throughout this endeavour.

(France) in 1934, he graduated in philosophy from the Sorbonne (University of Paris) and taught philosophy for 12 years in a seminary in western France. During his early years in Pune (1967–72), he came into close contact with Indian students through the Students' Welfare Association. He obtained his Ph.D. in social sciences from Paris University, with his research on attitudes and aspirations of Indian students from lower social sections. He settled in Pune in 1972 and later became a naturalized citizen. He was involved in two theoretically related activities carried out through two small associations set up for this purpose with his wife Hema Rairkar, friends and associates. The Village Community Development Association (<http://vcda.ws>) for sociocultural action in remote rural areas was founded in 1978 and the Centre for Cooperative Research in Social Sciences (<http://ccrss.ws>) in 1980. Together with Rairkar and the team of social animators of the Garib Dongari Sanghatna, he conducted research on a wide variety of interventionist and innovative themes. He published extensively in English, French and Marathi, including translations.

In July 2004 he was admitted to a hospital in his hometown, Pune, with extreme fatigue and encephalic pain. He had just given the finishing touches to the manuscript of his last book, *Le chant d'Ambedkar, mémoire de soi de paysannes intouchables* (Ambedkar's Song—Social Memory of Untouchable Women Peasants).

Guy Poitevin passed away in Pune on 29 August 2004.

At the onset of the gigantic exercise leading to the *Communication Processes* anthologies, Guy wished that this series should constitute critical educational research material with the much needed focus on India. We hope that his wish will be fulfilled and furthered by many others in the near future.

Bernard Bel, Biswajit Das, Vibodh Parthasarathi
New Delhi, Paris, Pune

OVERTURE:
Excavating 'the Political'

BERNARD BEL, JAN BROUWER, BISWAJIT DAS,
VIBODH PARTHASARATHI, GUY POITEVIN

This volume is engaged in understanding the politics in and of communication. Politics in general and communication in particular have been challenged, critiqued and contested from varying perspectives over the last decade. Today communication, informed by the projects of both universality and enlightenment, is suspect. As a result, there is a growing realization of a mismatch between the theory and practice of communication. The present task is to engage with the unresolved questions of the past and also address the emerging challenges in the area of communication.

The very foundation of modern politics was invested with ideas pertaining to the implementation of universal goals such as justice, equality and freedom. Based on the project of enlightenment, it critiqued and challenged anything that was not guided by reason so that the distinction between sense and common sense of communication could be established. It sought to ensure a healthy communicative environment for democratic thinking, discussion, free speech, interventions in the realms of public life, and provided a guarantee of basic rights for a better citizenry.

The classical vision of politics rested on a model of communication that was constituted of dialogue, interpersonal sharing, debates, discussions and consensus—a procedural aspect for politics to grow and sustain. This vision of politics also ensured a fixed sense of territory and populace. In contemporary times, while the procedural aspects of the classical vision of politics continues, its representation has proved to be problematic. This is precisely because the operation of the media has never really confronted this problem of representation. Our thinking about communication still remains largely trapped within a paradigm of direct face-to-face communication. On the contrary, the spatial frameworks of communication that remained under the rubric of state structured and territorially bound public life are threatened with a multiplicity of networked spaces of communication.[1] The restructuring of communicative space arrests our attention to revise our understanding of terms such as public life and public good.[2] As a result, our mode of governance, human life, body politic, boundaries of nation state and capital are challenged. The new technologies of communication have intervened in every domain of human life to link the global with the local. Local, too, takes on a new meaning and becomes a site where global is contested.[3] Politics remains affected with its renewed form and content. Thus the boundaries of political, economic and social processes are shifting, as are the channels of intervention and governance.

This is the context which sets the tone for our excavation of the term politics. It requires the identification of new areas of communication activity that need to open up to the democratic idea, as well as the invention of new ways of instituting the idea. For a long time, many independent researchers and collectives, engaged in a combined perspective of research and action and taking a direct part in new social and political movements, have helped fill the gaps left by institutional research and have opened new fields of investigation.

However, the new turn in politics is still suspect.[4] It is not our intention here to revisit the site of this debate, nor to settle scores over what is or is not the politics and poetics of communication; rather, in the light of the recent developments we examine the 'body politik' that inflicts communication. While protractors of the 'new' view it as reconstructed politics,[5] the detractors look at these changes as anti-politics.[6] The outcome leads to alliances and fragmentation; the collapsing of class to identity politics and the replacement of macropolitics by micropolitics.[7] The latter rejects a global politics of systemic change in favour of modifications at the local level designed to enhance individual freedom and progressive change. What is important is to verify and examine the extent to which the renewed political configurations pose a coherent and systemic explanation.[8]

This new turn in politics also politicizes all spheres of social and personal existence, which were ignored as legitimate spaces earlier. Simultaneously, it redefines the term 'political' in light of changes in society, technology and economy within the last two decades. It presumes that due to these changes, we live in a culture colonized by neoliberal capitalism which shapes and guides our experience of sights and sound. What it underscores is that the consciousness regained may lead to seductive pleasures of music videos, popular films, Internet, fashion and advertising, and commodity consumption of all kinds.[9]

There is no doubt that the new politics provides new ways of seeing and thinking. It is an equally slippery path. What we need to study at this juncture is how affective structures and modes of experience can act as catalysts, and the condition of the possibility of cognitive and broader social transformations.

Whither 'Communication'?

In India the study of communication processes does not seem to be critically engaged with political developments. Its lack of disciplinary concern and scholarly rigour has made the field sometimes abstruse, other times unidimensional. A certain apolitical and ahistorical notion of communication does not allow a creative engagement with the realms that communication affects and is affected by. While the academia lack forum to engage with such developments, many intellectuals and activists raise pressing concerns about communication in everyday life. We need to question communication from the dimensions of an aggressive political modernity, namely, the faith in progress and the will to transform an old world of traditions. While scholars who have broken away from the promise of modernity have much more to say, our enquiry needs to move beyond it. We need to move out of this impasse since communication cannot create politics; politics creates communication. Further, the present development of communication technologies is prompting utopian hopes of a new era in developing societies. It promises a new dimension of the modern religion of progress and commits itself to transforming both levels of reality, material and symbolic. The purpose cannot but appear as power in the hands of a few—those with the means to monitor the desired transformations. Communication means, technologies and forms become particularly strategic assets to the ends of a few. Communication operates as an ideology in their hands with the sanction and authority of modernity. It is instrumentalized towards ends of domination, hegemony, globalization, power, forced social restructuring and cultural control. In the process, culture itself is at stake insofar as it becomes a mere means for various ends. Our concern therefore is with a critique of communication as dominance, and consequently with an overall attempt to turn it into an instrument of interactive processes of cooperation or dialectic encounter.

This anthology is about communication as a political process. It engages with the dynamics of communication implied in political practice, and equally with the political configurations of communication processes. In this sense, we seek to doubly excavate 'the political'. To address the first—which is primarily an analytical challenge—we need to grasp the political terrain within which various processes of communication unfold and upon which they are deployed. In addressing the second—which is a methodological challenge—we ought to revisit our understanding of institutions of communication and ways in which they have been apprehended.

Interestingly enough, in pursuing both sets of investigations we stumble upon an impasse that has characterized communication theory. For, preoccupied with the 'deployment' of technology and the 'impact' of mass media, critical thinking in this sphere has engaged rather thinly with the dynamics of communication processes, both the historical contours and the emergent political economy specific to India. The foremost reason for this, we believe, lies in the amorphous character of 'communication' as an intellectual quest in India. Consequently, through a series of engagements in this volume we seek to overcome an impasse in the shaping of communication as a domain of inquiry in India. The urgency of pursuing this path has been compounded by the expansion and explosion in all spheres of activity clubbed under the term communication. We have seen changes not merely in the contours of the 'mass media' and the varieties of its technologies—both systemic and consumer oriented—but in their economic and jural regimes as well. However, all this is indicative of transformation underway; it is neither as extensive as in the industrialized countries, nor as rapid as in other industrializing countries of Asia, nor, for that matter, is it as widespread within India as its commercial and intellectual advocates may claim. But it has ushered in a set of dynamics in certain spheres of our lives, and in pockets of the country, similar to those visible in the more dense media environments of the individual countries.

The roots of the disciplinary myopia in communication as the early years of the twenty-first century reveal, seem to lie in the unduly media-centred concerns of research. Without a broader social theory in which to locate the concerns of the communication researcher, we are bound perennially to lament the inconclusiveness of our research. The kinds of questions arising from such wider concerns include the growing interest in the contribution of the media to the quality of democratic processes. The twin processes of media conglomeration (with the concomitant reduction in the range of political and cultural discourses widely available) and political centralization create the conditions for a distinct and ominous concentration of power over political communication. This has been notably evident in India where radical conservatism in government has been widely endorsed in the editorial stance of large parts of the media, and buttressed by a growing sophistication and investment in political public relations. The pessimism—quite reasonable—which might flow from such observations can, if unchecked, lead down a conceptual cul-de-sac in which political defeatism simply walks hand in hand with the theoretical determinism of the all powerful media commentator.

Reinstalling 'the Political'

Our emphasis on the political is concerned with the contest of social, cognitive and economic relations upon communication processes—in everyday life, media representations and institutional practices. Changes in national regimes may follow as a result of the chemistry of ideological contestations or the arithmetic of political compulsions. This is also true for changes in public policy where international chemistry and arithmetic play an additional, often dominant, role. But 'the political' is not confined to the activities of electoral parties, business lobbies or the fourth estate. They are dominant, and even overwhelmingly so, but not the sole fulcrums of politics; rather, politics is a potential in social life itself.

The redefinition of politics is a result of both empirical and theoretical changes. Theoretically, it depends on a reconceptualisation of power. In recent times the understanding of power is shifting from institutions, groups or classes to subjectivity or identity. Politics involves the contestation of subjection or, alternately, the repression of a confrontation in which subjection is contested. It is therefore a possibility in any social relation and may take place in any social context. The characterization of culture, and the prominent place of poststructuralism in redefining concepts of power and politics, mean that it is appropriate to think of newer dimensions of politics as participating in the postmodern turn. This links it to the rethinking which has been going on in all disciplines in recent years. In relation to the study of politics it is important for two reasons. First, politics may be cultural—where social life is based on signification, the manipulation of symbols is itself political. Politics in this sense involves the contestation of meanings, the repression of certain possibilities and the realization of some others. Second, if culture is taken to be unstable and fluid, cultural politics is the principle of social change. People no longer follow traditional ways and social structures are taken to be insufficiently fixed to do any more than constrain their activities. Social life is being endlessly remade through lifestyle choices, value judgements, and changing definitions of self interest which individuals and groups bring to bear upon themselves. In this respect, not only is politics a potentiality in every aspect of social life, it is also increasingly important. It is the continual contestation and reformation of social identities and institutions in cultural politics which make possible the reproduction of relatively stable but fluid forms of contemporary social life. The wider definition of politics developed is now more concerned with meaning and the interpretation that social actors give events and practices than with structure and the causes of social behaviour. The understanding of culture exemplified in the new dimension of politics is better seen as involving disparate and diverse signifying practices which do not necessarily form an easily identifiable, bounded totality, 'a society'.

Further, empirical changes have contributed to the change in the focus of politics by de-centring the state as the centre of political activity. There are two main changes in this respect. First, processes of globalization have drawn attention to the reduced autonomy of the state. Given, however, that its dependence on socio-economic relations was an issue, this would not be sufficient in itself to require a rethinking of the field. More importantly such processes have called into question the very idea of society as a bounded entity, uncovering the traditional sociological assumptions that a society is equivalent to the physical territory of a nation state. Once the extent to which economic activities, groups of people, ideas, media images and so on cut across territorial borders is acknowledged, it is more difficult to think in terms of any particular society. Furthermore, global processes call into question the scope of political decisions. If we are affected by processes which the nation state cannot control, questions arise concerning where and how decisions about those processes should be made.

Last, we believe that the ideological euphoria of the 'communication revolution' is essentially a mirage, if not a complete denial, of the political. It is no coincidence that such discursivities have been unleashed in tandem with the dismantling and disorientation of welfare. The concerns of distributive justice are now to be looked after by, for the liberal, an emphasis on corporate social responsibility, and in more critical circles, a renewed centrality of civil society. In current debates on the nature and role of 'civil society', efforts to create an ideology of civil society as a separate social institution, superior to political parties and organizations seem to be made. The state is being portrayed as the personification of all negative trends like Fascism, Nazism, Stalinism and so on. Civil society is presented as the sane and democratic opposite, and represents the aspirations of the marginalized and of public good in general. But civil society certainly cannot exclusively assume the role of safeguarding public interest. The state has to be evoked; that is the reason why the more critical section of civil society invokes the state to tame the market, and the more conservative to shield the market. What is required is building up the power of resistance and pluralism to check and balance the state-market complex.

It is this promise of political insight that we want to examine. First, communication deeply affects the conditions of possibility of human experience as it is inextricably linked with both space and time. Spatially it links the local, the regional and the global. Due to the interlinking of both intensive and extensive spaces, time is experienced differently. This new space-time coordinate is yet to be explored, described and understood in communicative practices.

Second, in terms of modalities, communication comprises of both early industrial and postindustrial forms of social interaction, starting with orality and literacy to the audiovisual and now informatic forms. But these modes do not replace each other. Rather, there is an interface between them, a sophisticated blending of forms as in technomusic. Such developments provide a new lease of life to old forms with the help of storing and retrieving information, and networking beyond conventional space boundaries.

It is this terrain that we want to explore through a series of conceptual articulations, theoretical constructs, empirical experiences and free debates. How fruitful is communication as a concept? What types of insights does it yield? Do the latter emanate primarily from academic colportage or from the practices within society?

Taking stock of commentaries on these expansions and explosions, and critically assuming their explanatory powers, we arrive at a set of startling observations. We realize that 'communication' as a field of investigation has a long intellectual history, and a richer set of biographical and chronological landmarks. But, amazingly enough, a closer glance at its intellectual contours indicates that the notion of communication itself has been rather elusive.[10] By this we imply that its subject matter remains to be constructed as a constituent of the social sciences, or even more fundamentally, as a set of investigative concerns. Gaining institutional recognition as a 'scientific field'—most readily reflected in Communication Research being taught at colleges, patronized by other disciplines, and often being treated as a subdiscipline—however, does not blur the existence of the longstanding crisis. For one, such recognition has been historically associated with courses on journalism, public relations, management, advertising, marketing, etc. Herein, for pedagogues and administrators alike, emphasis was on production and management of human resources, without necessary investment in even the most rudimentary theoretical and conceptual inputs. More recently, its emergence as a vocational field has only attenuated this, governed as this sector is by the requirements of the communication industry. Although an increasing number of scattered meetings, conferences, symposia and workshops are held outside formal academia, rarely has attention been paid to longstanding epistemological assumptions on 'communication'—a phenomenon which, paradoxically, both 'dominant' and 'alternative' standpoints have in common. The more highbrow efforts have shied away from debating methodological challenges/alternatives, which has adversely affected the possibilities of moulding communication as a scientific interpretative enterprise.

Tracking an Elusive Discipline

A cursory glance at the evolution of this field of research in India reveals the following trends. In the initial period, the studies were mostly descriptive and documentary. They were contributed by journalists, artists and media professionals due to their association with the field. The studies during this period were mainly related to circulation of newspapers, the analysis of the impact of modern innovations such as cinema, radio and records, and finally legislation regulating the workings of such media. In the late 1950s, the expansion of mass media throughout the country heightened the need for communication research. But the thrust of the research was to study the audience and public opinion for obtaining data orientated towards the commercial decisions of the advertising industry or of the mass media. These research activities concerned themselves with the direct bearing or impact of mass media on the people's mind.

From the 1960s onwards, communication research was extended UNESCO support to foster the spread and growth of national networks through mass media for educational development. The motive was to democratize educational opportunities on the presumption that electronic media could bring about low cost mass literacy and continuing education among sociocultural and educational minorities. Many initiatives were taken to import communication technologies. Furthermore, scientific models and administrative systems were developed to cater to the needs and the human capital able to manage the goods acquired. Various institutes, sponsored by the governments as well as private, emerged during this period, developing professionals for the above requirements. These institutions also contributed research findings for the growth and expansion of communication technologies.

We observe that two models of research were widely disseminated by such organizations, namely, studies of the structure and content of the press, and studies on public opinion and audience for mass media. Almost overlapping with these, two methodological watersheds were specific to the above periods. First, the research operated within the orbit of power structure whereby the techniques of bibliographical compilation and the analysis of documents predominated. It reduced the understanding of the reality of facts registered by privileged contemporaries. Second, opinion research picked up the other end of the communication process by confining itself to the study of reactions and preferences of the audience, or in other words, the consumers. Research into public opinion was based upon clients' responses in numbers, rather than looking for qualitative datum on audience characteristics within the social structure and the effect of communication within that structure. Alongside traditional market and audience surveys, university research was developing in India in the 1960s.

In the 1970s, the term 'extension' became a catchword both for planners as well as departments undertaking research on agriculture, family planning and rural development. This new approach was adopted rapidly during this time with the quantitative expansion of studies relating to the diffusion of innovation in developmental projects—a superimposition of scientific motives, commercial interests and various ideologies related to growth and development. These studies directed attention towards the dynamics of communication in rural India, until then little explored by social scientists. It revealed unknown facets of regional cultures and peasant world views. But it had enormous inadequacies in terms of explaining and interpreting them. The social conditions were purported through research tools based on models designed for the study of societies far removed from the lived reality of Indian peasants. The major lacunae of these studies were hasty generalizations and prediction of useless outcomes, and ingenuous solutions unable to overcome contradictions inherent in the social structure.

Furthermore, most studies were informed by models of social innovation borrowed from diffusionist theories, which rest on the assumption that 'modern' communication by itself can stimulate innovation and generate development independent of political and socio-economic conditions. These studies emphasized the behavioural attributes of the beneficiaries, their reluctance or otherwise to welcome 'modern' technology and accordingly change their traditional values and adopt 'modern' attitudes. These studies were significantly influenced by the modernization theorists. They overlooked the dimension of power relations, which precisely explains that those people most inclined to innovate and adopt new technologies were the privileged ones in terms of land, educational status and access to the means of communication, traditional or modern.[11] Due to the aforementioned reasons, communication research provided little insight to properly understand the working of developmental programmes in India. It could not escape the larger questions linked to the power structure nor realize the outcome of such research, which might lead to branding the poor and those at the subsistence level as enemies of 'progress' and 'development'. By their sheer resistance to the automation of such modernization programmes, they are merely securing their own conditions of survival in a structure already unfavourable to them. In spite of people's resistance, the state-sponsored projects have expanded immensely and circulated communication technologies in the name of developmental programmes.[12] The failures or perverse successes of many of them stand as a sad denial of the validity of the communication assumptions made by their planning and implementing agents.

In the 1970s, most of the research legitimized state-sponsored projects and justified the technocratic solution for communication and social change. Indeed, in some quarters there was a critique of such interventions as transfer of technology and knowledge by an alien culture and society. Although these critiques subscribed their argument to the thesis of 'cultural imperialism', these voices did not reach the forefront, nor could they develop an alternative perspective to study communication in the Indian context. Most significant was the fact that debates on the New World Information and Communication Order (NWICO) received 'stepmotherly treatment' by the academia, which was more interested with the New International Economic Order (NIEO).[13] This, despite the fact that NWICO had a very important place in the charter of the Non-Aligned Movement (NAM) and of the UNESCO, and that the NWICO had a very comprehensive charter covering issues like communications infrastructure, transborder data flow, satellite communication, technology transfer—issues that have resurfaced, albeit within an altered scenario from the mid-1990s onwards. Considering that the struggle for the NWICO itself was directly concerned with the inequitable nature of the emergent global information order, particularly its implications for the South, the fact that little interest was shown by academia only showed the inability of Indian scholarship to pay due attention to and come to terms with what can be called the pre-history of the information order in our times. It may be pointed out that this was unlike their western counterparts, from both within and outside universities, who took part in the NWICO debate, some arguing in favour and most against it. All in all, trends during the 1970s continued to broadly reflected concerns for national reconstruction as well as national integration.[14] A sense of urgency directed research about the processes of mass communication and their effects upon society, which required explanations and solutions to a variety of social, political and economic problems for a growing nation. In this sense, perspectives on communication studies echoed those of mainstream social science research: both relied on a pragmatic model of society, advocated modern individualistic values and were guided by instrumental efficiency.

The early 1980s projected an epistemic shift with the decline of state monopoly and the rise of market forces. Communication appeared less as a cultural proposition and became more as a commodity for sale. While the consequence was a reinforcement of a technocratic conception of communication, many intellectuals still doubt whether mass mediated technology has any relation to culture whatsoever. The commercialization of Indian communications radically questions the autonomy of a nation state communication system. At the same time, the idea of a public service closely linked to that of public monopoly was called into question. Furthermore, the emergence of new technologies projects the apparatus of communications into much more complex communication network systems. Such network systems are directly affected, on the one hand, by the structural transformation of international exchanges and, on the other hand, by the constant transformation and renewal of communication technology. As a result, communication becomes increasingly dependent on technological innovation, professional training and ideological control.

Failures of development policies brought attention to the particular inadequacy of their development theories and related methodologies in development communication. Development strategies were called by the International Commission for the Study of Communication Problems to 'incorporate communication policies as an integral part in the diagnosis of needs and in the design and implementation of selected priorities'.[15] This points to important characteristics of communication theory at that time in the West, namely, its interdisciplinary and holistic approach[16] and its involvement in policy and planning.[17]

In the 1990s, even if the emergent explosion in communication provided a fertile terrain to explore the complexities of communication processes more rigorously and in an urgent manner, mainstream Indian academics hardly showed a rigorous, historical and empirically grounded interest in it. The explosion of an intense set of writing largely focusing on television and cinema, often characterized by a sophisticated language thanks to their intimacy with cultural studies, helped in addressing the relationship between textuality and subjectivity and of everyday practice.[18] These, at best, remain excellent 'inward-looking' media studies; while they familiarized us with the very rich repertoire of image-centred, narrative-based accounts, they were unable to, and in some cases chose not to, integrate the dynamics of the media with the broader political and historical contours within which it was unfolding. This can perhaps be attributed to the postmodern influence in which any attempt to look for a broader process might be construed as an effort to construct and reinforce the grand narrative.

This decade also saw renewed emphasis on an older theme: participation. Thus, 'participatory communication' became the new *avataar* in which the traditional debates on communication and/for development reemerged.[19] Although some of these realized that incorporating a critique of development itself forms an appropriate entry point in making this crucial link,[20] the need remains of a theoretically specific approach of communication itself in human sciences. And in this sense too, 'communication' as a social science constituency remains elusive.

Reinstilling Communication

The history of communication is a story of theoretical antagonisms and binary oppositions such as culture versus technology, discourse versus media, micro versus macro, local versus global, tradition versus modernity, individual versus society, actor versus system, etc. Biswajit Das in his essay 'The Quest for Theory' locates the disciplinary growth of communication studies in India. Das argues that communication has always remained topical and vibrant in Indian society. It is an irony that it rarely received attention and approval from scholars to allow grow it to as a discipline like other social sciences. It did not encounter the trajectories as in the West which subsequently led to the establishment of communication as a science, nor did it take into account the historicity or learnt lesson from the role and importance of communication in the anticolonial struggle in India. Communication received due significance in the postcolonial context in India when the architects of a modern nation state realized its importance and invested in it as an input in the development process. Thus, developmentalism caught the attention of Indian communication studies in the early years. On the contrary, scholars who have broken away from this project have a great deal to say about the constitutive role of communications in contemporary life. Although there has been a tradition of social criticism, it remained as a peripheral intellectual activity. The neoliberal claims regarding the fiscal necessity of privatizing public media institutions and deregulating trade and industry, and the imperatives of technology and globalization have rapidly become the privileged categories and added to the vocabulary of communication studies. Further, cultural studies and studies on information society have added new dimensions and made the field more complex. These developments cannot be sufficiently captured by a pluralist approach to communication. Critical communication theory has an edge over the pluralist approach. However, the critical position is not free from contest; the division between political economists and ideologists have created ferment in the field. We need to blend both so that political economy and production do not remain alien to cultural texts and audiences; the latter would be incorporated within its analysis and thereby produce an environment within which cultural production and reception takes place.

We are not only concerned with scrutinizing conceptual issues of communication but with a relevant analytical understanding of its ongoing dynamics and practices. In this sense, our effort consists in experimenting with communication as a source of knowledge through exchanges on the basis of one's particular competence and knowledge—hence the need to study its method. The study of method helps us to overcome handicaps erected by a detrimental hierarchy of knowledge, which then facilitates fruitful exchanges between partners of different forms of experience and knowledge. We want to bridge the distance which separates image and reason, concept and experience, emotion and objective truth, event and theory, observation and categorization, practice and insight. Both the poles should be kept together. The essays in the volume attempt to portray the nature of concrete analyses of experiments by social scientists and reflexive accounting of experiences by social actors. Biswajit Das, Vibodh Parthasarathi and Guy Poitevin in 'Investigating Communication' trace the political contexts and contours of communication research in India. Right from its diffusionist origins, the authors highlight how communication research in India has been governed by dominant trends of positivistic traditions in the name effect, impact and reception studies, and outside the positivist tradition, by interpretative writings in the 1990s. In the first phase until the mid-1970s, communication research became autonomous and hardly collaborated or benefited from social science research tradition in India—resulting in studies that were ahistorical and decontextualized to the Indian society. In the second phase, led by scholarship incubated amidst the media boom of the 1990s, latest trends in social theory were deployed by simply adjusting suitable empirical material to arguments. Clearly, there is a gaping hole between the earlier traditions and the present ones; while the former highlighted the importance of communication technology, the latter celebrated all technology and derived 'pleasure' out of it. What is totally missing in both traditions is an appreciation of the context(s) of technology and the structures that enable it. The authors end with preliminary thoughts on apprehending 'communication' by situating it as a form of social agency and a phenomenon of social relation.

If redefining the subject matter of communication concerns the disciplinary preoccupation of this anthology, then the desire to reinstall 'the political' within communication theory informs its analytical preoccupations. The ensuing contributions build on these opening perspectives through a 'dialogue in multiple voices'—a dialogue demonstrating the varied paths to overcome the epistemological and methodological impasse in communication. With a view to steer clear of conceptual dichotomies in the structure of the volume itself, we find it more beneficial to focus on levels of analysis[21] concerning communication processes. Accordingly, the essays have been grouped under a variety of recurring themes and subthemes, which together point out to the general concerns suggested in the title of this first volume of 'communication processes'—*Media and Mediation*. It is in this sense that we stress that an understanding of communication denotes political processes, as much as 'the political' implies a mode of communication.

Notes

1. David Held, *Democracy and the Global Order: From the Modern State to Cosmopolitan Governance* (Cambridge: Polity Press, 1995).
2. John Keane, *The Media and Modernity* (Cambridge: Polity Press, 1991).
3. Steven Best and Douglas Kellner, *The Postmodern Turn* (New York: Guilford Press, 1997).
4. Steven Best and Douglas Kellner, *Postmodern Theory: Critical Interrogations* (London/New York: MacMillan/Guilford Press, 1991).
5. Ernesto Laclau and Mouffe Chantal, *Hegemony and Socialist Strategy: Toward a Radical Democratic Politics* (London: Verso Books, 1985).
6. Jean Baudrillard, 'The Year 2000 Has Already Happened', in Arthur Kroker and Marilouise Kroker (eds), *Body Invaders: Panic Sex in America* (Montreal: The New World Perspectives, 1988), p. 44.
7. Steven Best, *The Politics of Historical Vision* (New York: Guilford Press, 1995).
8. Herbert Marcuse, *Negations* (Boston: Beacon Press, 1968).
9. Herbert Marcuse, *Counterrevolution and Revolt* (Boston: Beacon Press, 1972).
10. Vibodh Parthasarathi, 'The Problem', *Seminar*, 455 (*Alternatives in Communication*), 1997 (July), pp. 12–15.

11. J. V. Vilanilam, *Science, Communication and Development* (New Delhi: Sage, 1993), pp. 104–222.
12. K. Sadanandan Nair and Shirley A. White (eds), *Perspectives on Development Communication* (New Delhi: Sage, 1996).
13. For an elaboration on this point see, Dipankar Sinha, 'The NWICO and the NIEO in the Seventies', in *Understanding Development in the New World Order: A Critical Analysis* (New Delhi: Kanishka, 1999), pp. 22–82.
14. S. R. Melkote, *Communication for Development in the Third World* (New Delhi: Sage, 1991). J. V. Vilanilam (1993), pp. 142–164.
15. Sean MacBride (ed.), *Many Voices, One World* (Paris: UNESCO, 1980), p. 258.
16. George Gerbner, 'Ferment in the Field', *Journal of Communication* (special issue), 33(3), 1983; Dennis MacQuail, *Mass Communication Theory* (London: Sage, 1983); James Lull, *Media Communication, Culture: A Global Approach* (Oxford: Basil Blackwell, 1995), Andrew A. Moemeka, *Communication for Development: A New Paradisciplinary Perspective* (Albany: State University of New York Press, 1994).
17. J. Servaes, 'Development Communication—for Whom and for What?' *Communicatio* 21(1) pp. 39–49.
18. C. Brosius and M. Butcher (eds), *Image Journeys: Audio-Visual Media and Cultural Change in India* (New Delhi: Sage, 1999); Amrita Shah, *Hype, Hypocrisy and Television in Urban India* (New Delhi: Vikas, 1997); Ananda Mitra, *Television and Popular Culture in India: A Study of Mahabharata* (New Delhi: Sage, 1993).
19. Shirley A. White, K. Sadanandan Nair and Joseph Ascroft (eds), *Participatory Communication: Working for Change and Development* (New Delhi: Sage, 1996); Jan Servaes, Thomas L. Jacobson and Shirley A. White, *Participatory Communication for Social Change* (New Delhi: Sage, 1996).
20. Servaes et al., *op. cit.*
21. Armand Mattelart and Michele Mattelart, *Theories of Communication. A Short Introduction* (New Delhi: Sage, 1998), p. 3.

1

THE QUEST FOR THEORY:
Mapping Communication Studies in India

BISWAJIT DAS

In recent years, the field of communication[1] has witnessed an increasing divergence in the way communication is perceived and studied in India. Communication has always remained topical and vibrant in Indian society; it engaged scholars, intellectuals, leaders and the masses in the polemics of day-to-day life. It is an irony that it rarely received scholarly attention and approval to grow as a discipline like other social sciences in India. It did not encounter trajectories like in the West which subsequently led to the establishment of communication as a Science,[2] nor did it take into account the history of experience from the role and importance of communications in the anticolonial struggle in India.[3] While the architects and founding fathers of the Indian nation state, themselves were brilliant communicators, they did not place communication at the centre of scientific enquiry during the post independence period. Although, Communication did emerge as an area of study, it was studied as a 'resource' to cater to the professional requirements of a growing nation or as a 'means' for overall development in society. Thus, communication as a science did not receive any intellectual attention so that it could be studied in its own right.[4]
However, communication as an area of study developed and is growing day by day in applied courses such as journalism,

advertising, public relations, market research and various audio-visual production oriented courses. Although, these courses do have a pretension of providing theoretical insights, invariably they cater to the demands of market—by focussing on short-term attitudinal and behavioural changes in limited segments of society. Such an approach also helps policy makers in legitimizing their administrative interventions and reforms. These courses do not provide sufficient intellectual resources for self-introspection and critical self-reflection so as to contribute towards theory building exercises and growth of knowledge.[5]

Communication did receive attention in social sciences like sociology, psychology, education, political science and agriculture, but remained as a subfield or optional course to these disciplines.[6] It is quite astonishing that although a series of meetings, conferences, workshops and symposia are held every year by various institutions in the country, the deliberations are mostly based on issues and problems at hand. Rarely have scholars paid attention to the methodological challenges and the epistemological impasse affecting communication.

Studies on communication becomes an extremely difficult interpretative enterprise keeping in view the ethical and moral concerns, programmatic thrust and lack of scholarly interventions and theoretical inputs. While I consider the concept of discourse a necessary element of any interpretation of communication, I find that a great deal of writing on discourse of communication fails to grasp this field's dispersed and conflicted character. However, there have been signs of change in recent times. Besides, the broader social and ideological context within which communication research is conducted and exchanged altered significantly in the past two decades or so. Hence, there is a need to situate the study of contemporary communications where it belongs—among a set of disciplines concerned with the emergence, development and structural characteristics of contemporary society and its futures.[7]

Much writing in the field has contributed to issues related to communication of institutions[8] rather than in the area of communication of knowledge. This essay focuses on one area which seems to be in need of further explanation, namely the basic assumptions and tenets of the theoretical approach to understand communication studies in India. It begins by mapping the major developments and assumptions in Indian society. By exploring these assumptions, this essay hopes to contribute to the development of an increased understanding of the theoretical premises and approaches in Indian communication.

Mapping the Field

In the Indian context, we witness that communicative concerns embrace issues of enlightenment and progress, morality and good order, justice and equality, social identity and cohesion, cultural quality, the working of democratic political institutions, development and underdevelopment and many others. With the process of national reconstruction and development, communication embraced developmentalism, a view that registered social progress and equated social growth with the expansion of communication in order to sustain its logic of growth. The emphasis was placed on the development of social reform policies that demanded the widespread diffusion of new knowledge and techniques. In the late 1950s, the expansion of mass media throughout the country heightened the need for communication research. Thus, our understanding of communication emerged through an atmosphere of certainty.[9] In order to realize its developmental venture, it resorted to a pluralistic perspective of the relationship between state and society. The policies to bring about radical social, economic and cultural or ideological changes were implemented with much fervour since independence. The emphasis remained on centralized planning and the relevance of decentralization and self-rule. Communication became a mediating factor between state and society.

At the operative level of social, economic and cultural processes of change, however, these institutions manifested a new vigour during the past six decades. Of course, their adaptive responses to policies of modernization have now assumed an entirely new ideological flavour. On the contrary, scholars who have broken away from this project have a great deal to say about the constitutive role of communications in contemporary life. Although there has been a critical tradition, which emerged as social criticism, it remained a peripheral intellectual activity. Neoliberal claims regarding the fiscal necessity of privatizing public media institutions and deregulating trade and industry, and the imperatives of technology and globalization have rapidly become the privileged categories and added to the vocabulary of communication studies.[10] Further, cultural studies and studies on information society and globalization have added new dimensions and made the field more complex.[11] With the advent of new information technologies, the established powers are strengthened, new dependencies are created and new social discrepancies are brought about. This is because the ethical questions have been subsumed under the banners of science, progress and development.

Given the increasing proliferation of research traditions in communication, it would be useful to document and analyse these traditions to map the contours and their contributions to the field of communication in India.

My starting point is that the discussions and debates within social and political theory and communication studies in particular have a similar yearning (for example, the ongoing debate between 'common good' and 'class struggle' conception forms the basis in communication studies as well). I would like to discuss various positions organized into two larger categories or approaches namely, 'Pluralist' and 'Critical'. These positions have been developed in response to historical conditions and events as well as through theoretical arguments.[12] The need for such a distinction arises because the theoretical and methodological distinctions are inadequate and fallacious. Yet some other scholars are of the view that the distinction is not real, that it is rather an identification on the basis of method alone.[13] On the contrary, there is no inherent incompatibility between empirical methods and theory. Besides the differences in methodology and procedure, profound ones remain in theoretical perspective and political calculations. This shift is essentially from a behavioural to an ideological one.[14]

The Pluralist Approach

Here I would like to discuss two different positions which share a number of assumptions: Effect Research and Developmentalism. Both these positions assume that communication is transparent and visible, while the critical approach assumes that communication is multidimensional, rarely transparent in any direct sense and, in fact, often invisible. This substantive distinction on the basis of how communication is defined (implicitly or explicitly) also helps to explain why scholars cling more to positivist scientific methods (if communication is visible, then it is observable and can be documented and quantified). Besides a positivist orientation, scholars also prefer more interpretative analytical methods that attempt to reach into several layers of decreasing visibility where communication cannot always be observed.

The pluralist approach broadly refers to a structure of society where communication is based on the equilibrium of forces, with complex layers of checks and balances for social control. For maintaining social control, this approach is built up with an assumption of consensual unity and it reduces complex social and political issues of communication and authority to an examination and legitimation of the dominant social system.[15] Since the pluralist theses have provided the dominant working assumptions of mainstream social sciences in the past decades, communication studies have also shared the basic tenets of the prevailing paradigms (the belief that the world is knowable through the application of scientific techniques and objectivity of observations and the power of empirical explanations).

As a theoretical perspective and research, there appears to be limited scope for the range of pluralist studies of communication.[16] McQuail, however, attempts to identify and isolate some of the key features of the pluralist approach in communication.[17] In his view, pluralists tend to approach communication production as something creative, free and original. Such a view of communication can be derived from the notion and model it adopts, which is paradigmatically empiricist and its main focus and formulation centre on the individual.

Effect Research

The effect research tradition can be assessed from the communication studies concerned with the application of cybernetics[18] to society. Through the application of cybernetics and information theory, the attempt was to study the effects of communication on behaviour, emotions, attitudes and knowledgeability. This research tradition grew up along with twentieth century social sciences. To a large extent, this tradition shared the social sciences' particular vision of scientific enquiry based on the interconnection of theory, hypothesis and experiment. The central argument in this tradition is that communication has its effects which show up empirically in terms of a direct influence on individuals.

Communication studies in this paradigm presuppose the values of individualism and operate on the strength of efficiency and instrumental value. Most scholars make distinctions between the structures of processes of human social systems from the structure created strictly by humans (that is, technology).[19] Scholars have endeavoured to demonstrate these complications diagrammatically. The skeleton provided by the original model is Source/Receiver (S-R). It was used further by behavioural psychology as Stimulus-Response; both cases involved an assumption that human social behaviour can be adequately explained in terms of independent, environmentally isolated, discrete social chains. In fact, more conceptual components have been added to the original assumptions. Thus, the Stimulus-Response model has enjoyed a quasi-hegemonic existence. Since communication is treated as a series of specific and isolated social phenomena, what results is a narrow understanding of communication. Such studies fail to appreciate the importance of the historical environment.

The growing interest in socialization and construction of a social reality provides another significant challenge to the static behavioural model of pluralism. One of the major concerns about the role that communication has in structuring thoughts, ideas and images of the world is found in the focus on comprehension and interpretation of reality, that is, communication content, a focus that is found primarily in studies of children and media in India.[20] Unlike the explicit, behavioural decision-making model of pluralism, the focus on comprehension also draws attention to non-behavioural processes and outcomes. This general area of interest also assumes a more complex dynamic model than does the static pluralist formation, as it considers media effects within a developmental framework and considers the effects of communication to be largely interaction effects.

Further, studies in social identity extend the concern with the construction of social reality to include more of the external influences found in the social structure, and make an explicit attempt to tie together internal and external processes at different levels of analysis. Most of these scholars explicate socialization as a process of integrating individuals into larger legitimate social structures. Legitimation—a way of explaining and justifying a given actual structure and ideas that support it—helps to reify that role structure by preventing people from recognizing the conventional (that is, not natural) basis of such a social creation. There is, however, a tendency to seek actual evidence for the exercise of power in more manifest forms of conflict, as is evidenced at the individual level or aggregated outcomes.

Consequently, communication research delves into the relationship among individuals, investigates questions of social identity and, broadly speaking, raises some doubts about the stability of individuals in their social relations. At the same time, however, there is a marked absence of investigating the structure of society, the location of authority and the distribution and transmission of power, as well as a lack of articulation of larger, more fundamental questions about the failure of the liberal-pluralist vision of the social whole, including the failure of its own theoretical and conceptual foundation. Although reform minded, in the sense of understanding itself as contributing to the betterment of society, communication research remains committed to a traditionally conservative approach to the study of social and cultural phenomena in which instrumental values merge and identify with moral values.

This position tends to consider mediated, conditioned, effect variables to be more informative than overt decision-making behaviours. Also, non-decision making, or the exercise of power through the suppression of interests as in 'gatekeeping', is important in itself. It extends the concept of communication to include less visible forms. Usually operating at the individual level of social analysis, this position tends to seek most of its evidence in observable (directly or indirectly) conflict and behaviour.

A host of studies assume the a priori existence of open, rational, informed debate and tend to prefer a vision of communication consistent with the ideals of participatory democracy. The scholars working with such a vision are concerned with the integrative functions of media.[21] This integrative orientation in the functional approach is particularly evident in uses and gratification research, which has remained a popular approach over the years in communication studies.[22] Such research uses communication to help explain connections between individuals and social environment.

Similarly, Goode had long criticized the functionalist perspective for its conservative view that forces are static, and for ignoring the extent to which the larger social system of alternatives and opportunities has actually inhibited or prevented people from behaving as they otherwise might have.[23] This restriction of opportunity tends to maintain and reproduce the existing structure of power and functionalism is not able to provide a critique of existing communication structures within society. In general, the functionalist perspective is criticized for neglecting process, historical change and conflict. It prefers a rather one-sided, optimistic view of society as an exclusively positive force with its individual elements working autonomously but cooperatively for the benefit and enhancement of the system. Further, functionalism is criticized for its lack of theoretical explanation in its common use as a descriptive analytic tool. Functionalist sociology has made us too accustomed to viewing the study of effects within a therapeutic and operational context because any disfunctioning of a means of communication is established according to the existing institution's schemes.[24] It is characterized by its potential danger to the balance of the existing social forces and never by any dynamic qualities, which might engender another system. Another difficulty with such analysis is that it does not perceive the possibility of rupture within the system. Thomas argues that the functional perspective entails technical and mechanical reasoning in its presumption of system stability or the trend toward the maintenance of system equilibrium.[25] There is an emphasis on functional unity and activism within the system, which is seen as functional equivalence for every individual's lot in society is in his or her own hands. It thus obscures the roles of communication played out through organizational, institutional and social arrangements. Eliott notes similar problems in uses and gratifications research, arguing that it has all the problems associated with functionalism and more because it is a highly individualistic version of social theory.[26] The 'uses and gratifications' approach treats communication as an isolated process, somehow autonomous from the larger social context. It considers how media gratifies basic human needs (or functions for society as a whole) while considering neither the source of those needs nor the differential distribution of power and social opportunity. Since needs develop within the existing social structure, the 'uses and gratifications' approach based on identifying and describing needs inevitably tends to support the existing structure. This approach assumes an aware and active audience that cannot only make and report its choices, but also identify its reasons for those choices. Politically, such an assumption could provide justification for an existing system as neither communication content nor its production need to be questioned or subjected to critical policy decisions—after all the audience can take care of itself.

Studies on communication interaction resulting in changes in social structure, communication patterns and culture shift the focus of communication as social control to communication as integral to sociocultural change.[27] More research is required in this area to demystify the dominance of behaviourism in communication research. Critics of behaviourism have not only argued that its research methods are unscientific, but that these impose overtly simplistic and narrow ways of thinking about the relation between the environment and the individual. On the one hand, communication's effects are formulated in psychobehavioural terms in ways which belie the complexity of human experience; on the other, communication, as part of the environment, is treated in isolation and in terms of stimulus properties, which again distort its complexity. The dynamic interpretations of need, motivation, intent, values, interest and so on relevant to the interpretation of experience must figure in any attempt to understand communication exercises over people. The methods of behaviourism are unable to grasp more complex communication—people-society relationships—and it is primarily for this reason that scholars of communication turn towards critical theory for a more adequate understanding of communication and power.[28]

What is peculiar to behaviourist research on effects of communication is not so much the particular kind of effects studied, but the scientific methods and related techniques used. Researchers employing these methods are convinced that they are producing evidence about the consequences of communication. The conviction is based upon the assumption that only scientific research methods and techniques are capable of discovering realities about communication and power, which include the politics within communication as also the politics of communication. The evidence comes in a scientific mantle which belies the unscientific manner in which it has been produced. At each stage in the production of scientific knowledge, via the methods of behaviourist psychology, the researcher draws objective inferences. The observed differences between experimental and control groups are made by means of psychological and behavioural measures which actually evaluate the relevant psychological variable in question.

The inferences which are routinely structured into behaviouristic methods, and which are intended to produce scientific evidence, are the products of an underlying theoretical behaviourism itself.[29] Further, evidence obtained is used to give scientific credibility to the researcher's theoretical ideas, thus raising the status of these ideas above mere speculation. At the broader level, communication is held to be largely reflective or expressive of an achieved consensus. It raises questions concerning the social role and responsibility of media where it simply reproduces those definitions of situations which favour and legitimize the existing structure of things.

What seems at first a merely reinforcing role has now to be reconceptualized in terms of communication's role in the process of consensus formation. The quest for neutral objectivity in the study of social beings is a corollary of the scientific approach to social affairs. An analytic reductionism necessarily takes place in the process of this positivist approach. Such scientific studies propose that man should be manipulated in the service of a system, which treats them mechanically.[30] As a result, most of the contemporary mainstream work in communication is critiqued for continuing to cling uncritically to Lazarsfeld's 'limited effects' thesis. This thesis implicitly assigns ultimate responsibility for individual political behaviour to the individual since communication merely reinforces predispositions to behave.[31]

Developmentalism

The field of development communication research is almost coterminous with communication research in India. So much energy has been invested in this field ever since the inception of communication research in India that most of the policies, institutions and research priorities were geared towards the role of communication in development.[32] What is peculiar about this field is it is routed through planned intervention with a programmatic thrust. The underlying belief was that the more the nation engages with communicative resources, the better communication in society.

Broadly, two factors can be identified as potentially productive lines of inquiry into how communication might be characterized within development studies in India: first, the development of mass mediated technologies and the resulting adaptation of communication networks for wider dissemination across spatial dimensions; second, the emphasis placed on the development of social reform policies that demanded the widespread diffusion of new knowledge and techniques. These social measures included modest agrarian and rural reforms, which attempted to stimulate modern attitudes in agriculture, rural and community development as well as birth control policies. Further, rapid diffusion of ideas through mass media into less developed countries has made social scientists consider the media as possible engines of cultural diffusion and economic development. Here, the term 'development' is held to be a source of change with principles of progress and growth and the processes of development become the basis for the transition or transformation of societies, cultures and even personalities of individuals.[33]

Most of the image derived to measure development are based on poverty, standard of living, gross national product (GNP), per capita income, quality of life and so on. These quantitative measurements problematized the term development as evident in the works of first generation scholars[34] and questioned its universal validity at the cost of particular experiences. Wherever information on development and communication were available, it made a point to justify the international comparisons but did not make any effort to reveal cross-cultural or even intranational settings. Such a commonsensical understanding of development drew attention to its gross negligence of social inequity and the dominance of a country's affairs by external influences and international capital.

What is underlined here, in short, is an alien but self-imposed definition of development. Rarely is the term development is conceptualized in terms of collective expressions and concern within society. While this field received its purchase by various extension education departments, specially in agriculture and population studies, rarely did these disciplines interact with social sciences where the concept of 'development' was debated by the academia. The lack of critical input from the academia coupled with the programmatic thrust made the field function with a technomanagerial approach, so that development and underdevelopment were viewed as technical malfunctions. These malfunctions, it was thought, could be evaded by technical solutions and communication became the rescue for such underdevelopment.

These efforts pretended to reduce inequality by involving people in their own development, giving them independence from central authority, and employing 'small' and 'appropriate' technologies. Their emphasis shifted from economic growth to meeting basic needs. Sometimes scholars working within the discipline have also discussed the limitation of their past approaches.[35] Rogers and Kinkaid note the passing of the older persuasion behaviour paradigm with its built-in assumption that development results in the equitable distribution of resources. In its place, a growing concern with inequitable gaps in knowledge and effects has emerged. The simple unilinear effect models in development communication are being replaced by more complex integrated theoretical models of effectivity. The old science of communication has embraced new modalities and needs. One of the most significant examples is the evolution of the theory of 'diffusionism'. Also the new model of 'convergence' defines 'communication' as a process of information exchange between two or more people who try to give a common meaning to symbolic events, thereby accommodating unilateral communication into the old model of development.

The 'convergence' model better fits the theoretical conception of development as perceived by participation, self-fulfilment and justice. Such studies proclaim that social efficacy and technical efficiency of dialogic communication, as well as the installation of participatory communication, ought to enable more producers and local groups to determine their needs and formulate their demands for techniques and technologies themselves. These studies forge the new concept of 'feed-forward', to indicate that messages must be elaborated on the basis of the needs expressed by peasants and producers with an emphasis on self-management and self-maintenance.[36]

Thus, development communication as a field developed a distinct idea about development which can be better understood by its managers and practitioners. Today, the field has almost reached a point of saturation, although not the discipline and its professionals. There have been voices of dissent and resistance; for instance, in the late 1970s and 1980s, a new paradigm of development communication emerged which better recognized the process of deliberate underdevelopment as a function of colonialism, dependency between the North and the South, technology transfers without knowhow and so on. All these discussions remained confined to the academia. Instead of addressing these issues, the practitioners and managers of development communication developed a sense of suspicion and distrust between the field view and book view of development communication. As a result, an alternative conception of development communication emerged. Although the term 'alternative' sounds fascinating, keeping in view the saturation and therefore stagnation in the field, requires close scrutiny and constant reexamination.[37] But the power of mass media technologies always remained a 'magic multipliers' of development benefits.

Be it in a SITE experiment or various video experiments at the grass roots level, the managers of development communication have scripted with success stories about alternative communication. No doubt some changes in beliefs and behaviours did occur, but there is little indication that technologies were the best means to that end. The project did lead to India's development of its own satellite network but some of the findings require close scrutiny; for example, programmes are best viewed in small groups with a teacher to introduce them and to lead a discussion afterwards.[38] But communication technology per se cannot replace the age old practice of classroom teaching in the countryside; at best it can become an aid to the ongoing education system. Similarly the various video experiments undertaken by grassroot agencies celebrated the notion of alternative by taking control of communication gadgets. It gave them a sense of feeling of decentralization and an absence of hierarchy. Such naïve understanding of the term alternative made the field and 'practice' a fetish. The recent entry of community radio—in the wave of liberalization of the state media—for empowerment is an addition to the list.[39]

Further, the premise that the decentralizing technologies can lead to decentralized networks and social relations which can escape from the authoritarian heaviness and constraint of centralized media, avoid larger questions on social power exercised either by mediators or by the whole of the social structures in which they operate. By abstaining from questioning the political context of their interventions and studying the necessary relation between decentralized communication and the decentralized network of social organizations, these media reduce to nothing the original notion of self-reliance, a notion indissociable from that of political mobilization.[40] However, scholars continue to resort to the motivations and methods of market studies and marketing campaigns to bring out the needs of local populations and project them as authentic. Seen in this perspective, the new legitimizing discourses, which rely on the demand for participation[41] and dialogue, cannot hide the fact that what is new is not the promotion of self-management and self-development but rather the promotion of self-exploitation. Further, these new forms exploitation are perfectly in keeping with the low-profile strategies of transnational capital, which is also obliged to maintain a decentralizing, participative and localist discourse.[42]

The confusion regarding the conceptual issues on development is similar to that of current communication studies. Wherever communication is linked with development, it is always viewed as an external source or aid used to provide messages pertaining to development. Communication provided the opportunity to expand the capacity of development services. Development by communication explored the capacity of communication provisions. On the contrary, the development for communication might be interpreted to mean empowerment and dialogic communication between the state and the civil society so that public policy decisions are based on communicative rather than instrumental rationality. But how far are such communicative means dialogical in nature? To what extent are the agencies deploying such means open and receptive to empowerment?

While such questions remain to be settled, further breakthroughs in new information and communication technologies have subsequently added new dimensions and made the field more complex.[43]

Critical Approach

Within this approach we will discuss a number of positions that are based on a complex conceptualization of communication operating as an invisible form of domination.[44] Most of the theoretical constructs within this approach emerge from the continuing intellectual exchange of social and political ideas located within the Marxist perspective.[45] Further, the continuing political and direct confrontation between pluralism and 'Marxism' as the two competing theories was reflected on the quality and intensity of the intellectual commitment to study communication.

Communication theory has immensely benefited from these ongoing polemics. The prominence of these ideas resulted in a rigorous introspection within western European Marxism, French structuralism, Gramscian Marxism and Althusserian structuralism. Their scholarly contributions served as the intellectual and theoretical resource for alternative, political response to the problems of society including production, distribution and transmission of economic and political power through and within the determinant domains of communication. A critical approach can indeed initiate a number of significant changes in the definition of society, social problems and the role of communication as well. These changes are rooted in radical ideas and are innovative in their creation of appropriate methodologies and theoretical propositions.

In spite of their differences, the critical approach is based on the premise of conflicting class interest. In general, Marx and Engels' view of domination has endured in some form or the other, through various theoretical formulations within critical communication research.

> The ideas of the ruling class are in every epoch the ruling ideas, i.e., the class which is the ruling material force of society, is at the same time its ruling intellectual force. The class which has the means of material production at its disposal, has control at the same time over the means of mental production, so that thereby, generally speaking the

ideas of those who lack the means of mental production are subject to it. The ruling ideas are nothing more than the ideal expression of the dominant material relationships grasped as ideas hence of the relationship which make the one class the ruling one, therefore the ideas of its dominance (Marx and Engels 1970: 69).[46]

According to the critical review, communication is exercised at several levels, including the often opaque and unconscious level of ideas, producing and reproducing relations of material and symbolic production. This realm of ideas is conditioned by material base, the economic structure of the society. The emphasis on political structures, however, assumes different forms and locations depending upon the specific theoretical perspective employed. Despite variations in the overall theoretical models adopted by the critical approach, what is common to all is the implicit conception of communication as located not on the surface of society's structure but as deeply woven into a complex contextual social web.

Political Economy

In communication studies, this position emphasizes and asserts that modes of communication and cultural expression are determined by the structure of social relations and power relations. The underlying power structure and its impact on the communication media and the production of power within communication are the primary focus of the political-economic approach. The material influences and imperatives are not necessarily direct but rather complex and hidden, taking the form of a multiplicity of pressures and limits that structure power relationships of domination and subordination.[47] Golding and Murdock had pointed out: 'The task of mass communication research is not to explore the meanings of media messages, but to analyse the social process through which they are constructed and interpreted and the contexts and pressures that shape and constrain these constructions'

(p. 72).⁴⁸ They view 'social process' as essentially involved in economic practices, which guarantee production and reproduction of social life. Communication, as an institution of that broader social process, is directly involved in economic practices. Further, it secures a relationship between the modes of economic forces and the relations between systems of production and distribution.⁴⁹

Communication as an apparatus is integrally linked to the practice of class domination for determining the social structure and the social conditions in which people live. Some works from the Frankfurt school's project address the relationship between such mass production and the domain of consciousness, imagination and thought. Communication becomes a conduit through which practices of production determines practices of consumption.⁵⁰ Economic and technological practices not only determine the cultural superstructure but also insert them into pre-existing social relations of power.⁵¹ Works of Dorfman and Mattelart and Gitlin also highlight this when they refer to the relationship which exists between the producer and the text, implying that consumers are not always aware and conscious of the ways in which messages act upon them and impinge upon their consciousness.⁵²

Such a multilayered relationship between the practices of production and assumption can be theoretically traced to Marx's earlier humanistic writings. Capitalism, according to Marx, 'created false needs so that the modern experience is primarily built upon standardisation, the sensationalisation of every day life, dehumanisation, escapism and a fragmented, if not false, understanding of the world'. Both economic interests and processes of production are projected as hidden.

Contemporary critiques of political economy represent one major category of critical approach and echo an ongoing critique of orthodox Marxist positions or economic determinist positions as simplistic and crude. Instead, they prefer theoretical models that consider complex mediating processes and interdependent relationships. The emphasis throughout these works is weighed heavily towards economic pressures (both direct and indirect), rather than toward a cultural or ideological domination of communication.

Garnham establishes the political-economic approach to communications very aptly when he says that it provides a more direct explanation of the dynamics behind the production of ideas, as opposed to explaining only their content or effects.[53]

We can outline certain characteristics of this approach to communication. It identifies the determining moment of social life with economic forces and relations. This approach establishes a correspondence between production and power of communication. Culture is not considered as the site of struggle for power unless there exist radically alternative and competing political and economic systems of media production. The medium, however, is never questioned. It is assumed to be transparent or a conduit through which a relationship is established between producer and consumers of the message.

Such types of analyses assume that the consumers are passive and unaware of the ways in which communication acts upon them. Thus, communication becomes a process of self-colonization of the individual. Here, cultural production operates as an ideological mystification in the service of the existing structures of communication.

Ideology

Keeping in view the inadequacy of the political-economic approach, scholars have explored the area of 'ideology'. Such a position assumes that cultural practices play a very active but ideological role in the construction of communication relations. This approach is guided by two central questions: (a) how does the ideological process work and what are its mechanisms? (b) how is the 'ideological' to be conceived in relation to other practices within a social formation?

The main thrust here is to examine in detail the media messages and to justify the media as a part of the historical dialectical process. An analysis of such an aspect could further throw light on the dominant social interests represented within the state and the various forces responsible for shaping the class consensus.

However, such an analysis entails an eclectic mixture of different traditions. Most of these have close ties to the humanities rather than social sciences, including linguistics, semiotic theory, film semiotics, structural anthropology and postmodernism. Cultural studies also draw upon and retain the Frankfurt school's emphasis on culture, incorporating in addition Gramsci's[54] concept of ideological hegemony and Althusser's structural Marxism.[55] Hall argues that this integrated cultural perspective combines two views of culture: culture as a symbolic form and culture as a productive force (that is, social relation). Although Hall's attempt to theorize on ideology is stimulating, the questions poised by him cannot be resolved within existing theoretical frameworks. Hence media is represented as a 'key terrain where a contest is won or lost.' In other formulations, it is conceived of as signifying a crisis, which has already occurred both in economic and political terms.[56]

Studies in India in the recent years have shown much interest to analyse the effects of newspapers,[57] radio,[58] television,[59] film,[60] and other popular cultural forms[61] on audiences; they also focused on how various audiences interpret and use media culture differently, analysing the factors that made different audiences respond in contrasting ways to various media texts.[62] These studies insist that culture must be studied within the social relations and system through which culture is produced and consumed, and that this study of culture is intimately bound up with the study of society, politics and economics. These studies show how media articulates the dominant values, political ideologies and social developments and novelties of the era. It conceives of Indian culture and society as a contested terrain with various groups and ideologies struggling for dominance. Television, film, music and other popular cultural forms are the sites of contestation and conflict. Although there is richness in these studies, in terms of multimethodologies and nature of the questions raised, some of them merge the distinction between media based reality and social reality. Wherever attempts are made to combine both, there is either a flaw in theorization or in terms of the empirical material collected to prove a point.

However, studies on ideology are valuable because they provides us perspectives that would enable us to read and interpret our culture critically as there are cultural assertions by various groups. The earlier understanding of culture and communication remained primarily literary and delved into its aesthetics. It rejected media culture as a fetish and trash. Studies on ideology provide a significant entry point to demystify the politics of culture, cutting across disciplinary boundaries and normative potential. It also provides us research tools to examine and critically assess the whole range of cultures, artefacts, text, institution and practice.[63]

Although considerable literature has been generated in this regard, further examination is required by situating culture and communication historically in the context of its societal origins and effects. We need to emphasize culture and communication within a theory of social production and reproduction, specifying the ways that cultural forms serve either to further social domination or to enable people to resist and struggle against domination. Such an analysis would shed light on unequal social relations in the social structure. The idea behind such analysis is to locate social transformation by specifying forces of domination and resistance in order to aid the process of political struggle and emancipation from oppression and domination. Studies on ideology would further help us to develop a media pedagogy for critical intervention to demystify the hidden motif behind encoding and decoding of text and the art of resistance to such text. But the ideological reading devoid of cultural context and the system of production and distribution would not provide much insight; instead it would undermine the seriousness of reading such text. In recent times, the onslaught of globalization has brought with it a torrent of fleeting images, popular music, talk shows, game shows and genres that are alien to our society. It is essential to study not only the ideological dimensions but also the production dynamics of these images. The economic dimension would unmask the politics of control, purpose, logic of distribution, homogeneity of products, repeats and crossovers and the constituency for such products. A political-economic reading of such products would help us to understand the interplay of various political and ideological discourses. It would further highlight the hidden interest of national and global media conglomerates. Thus, mere emphasis on media and ideology exaggerates the power of the media in shaping the society. Murdock and Golding comment that 'the proposition "modes of communication" determine the "modes of society" is a kind of media centeredness with the sole concern of studying the impact of communication on society through content or effects'.[64]

Conclusion

In conclusion, we can reiterate that in the pluralist conception communication is first assumed to be structurally diffused and equitably dispersed through society. Second, it is assumed to be transparent to all parties—in other words, overt and observable. Conflict represents competing interests and conflict is examined in terms of overt tensions, which ultimately motivate the self-regulating system as a whole towards a state of stability, equilibrium, integrity and homeostasis via converging individual behaviours. Decision making is assumed to be a positive force, evident in the long-lived spirit of reformists found in 'common good' conceptions of communication.

Most criticisms of the pluralist thesis focus on its conservative bias. Such criticisms challenge the pluralist assumption that society is composed of a wide variety of equally powerful groups reflecting the interests of most people so that while in society pluralism exists, in political reality this is so only among the most powerful business related social groups. That is, the ideal abstract conception of communication in the pluralist perspective does not match up with the more concrete current historical and material moment. The pluralist thesis obscures the asymmetrical distribution of communication in society and tends to support inequitable distribution. On the contrary, the underlying assumptions about communication shared by the diversity of critical positions discussed above are numerous. First, communication is viewed as a relationship of domination and related subordination within the class struggle perspective. Second, communication is assumed to take a relatively invisible form, either as hegemony or complex conflict relationships manifest and latent within a complex, highly contextual model of effectivity. Due to the traditionally shared concern with class struggle, critical approach generally views communication as a dynamic relationship. Critical positions' sustained criticism of pluralist approach, its methodologies and lack of critical reflexivity provides a better insight and quest for theory building exercise. However, the critical position is not free from contest. Within it, the division between political economists and the ideologists have created foment in the field. Neither ideological reading nor political economists alone can contribute for a radical social theory of media. We need to blend both so that political economy and production do not remain alien to cultural texts and audiences but incorporate both within its analysis thereby producing an environment within which cultural production and reception takes place.

Notes

1. See Todd Gitlin, 'On Media Studies as a Breath of Air Across the Field of Sociology' in Cees J. Hamelink and Olga Linne (eds), *Mass Communication Research: On Problems and Policies: The Art of Asking the Right Questions: In Honor of James D. Halloran* (Norwood, NJ: Ablex Publishing, 1994), pp. 53–59. Gitlin observes a distinction of 'field' from 'discipline'. He further highlights that 'A field, in the sense of high-energy physics, is a territory through which high charges work. It radiates around a set of charged questions...and if things work well, it illuminates' (p. 53). Gitlin refers to the methodological influence of media studies as such an illumination, especially in its attention to 'the workings of media institutions and to the histories of those institutions and the cultural forms they have sheltered and excluded' (p. 54). The approaches to the study of media challenges the social sciences to reflect on the 'totality of society' and pushes us collectively towards questions of 'how...we shall understand a society that routinely, profusely traffics in images; of the part played by technology in transforming human consciousness (and unconsciousness)...of the meaning and limits of the globalization of culture' (p. 57).

2. Hanno Hardt, 'British Cultural Studies and the Return of the Critical in American Mass Communication Research: Accommodation or Radical Change?', *Journal of Communication Inquiry*, vol. 10, 1986 (summer) pp. 117–24. Also see the debates in R. Williams, 'Communications as Cultural Science', *Journal of Communication*, vol. 24, no. 3, 1974 (summer) pp. 17–25; in R. Williams, 'Base and Superstructure in Marxist Cultural Theory', *Problems in Materialism and Culture* (London: Verso, 1980), pp. 31–50; in S. Hall, 'Media Power: The Double Bind', *Journal of Communication*, 24(4), 1974, pp. 19–26; S. Hall, 'The Rediscovery of Ideology: Return of the Repressed in Media Studies', in M. Gurevitch, T. Bennett, J. Curran and J. Woolacott (eds), *Culture, Society and the Media* (London: Methuen, 1982), pp. 56–90.
3. P. C. Joshi, *Culture, Communication and Social Change* (New Delhi: Vikas Publishing House, 1989).
4. G. Murdock, 'Visualizing Violence: Television and the Discourse of Disorder', in Cees J. Hamelink and Olga Linne (eds), *Mass Communication Research: On Problems and Policies. The Art of Asking the Right Questions: In Honor of James D. Halloran*, (Norwood, NJ: Ablex Publishing, 1994), pp. 171–91. Murdock perceives a damaging division in communications studies between the political economists, sociologists and political scientists, whose major interest is in the organization of communications systems and their links to wider social, economic and political formations...and the practitioners of cultural studies, who approach these systems as key sites for the articulation of public discourse and are mainly concerned with the way meaning is organized... (p. 171).
5. Biswajit Das, 'Communication and Power Structure: A Sociological Analysis of an Orissa village', *Doctoral thesis* submitted to Jawaharlal Nehru University, New Delhi, 1991.
6. Denis Mcquail, 'Sociology of Mass Communication', *Annual Review of Sociology*, vol. 11, 1985, pp. 93–111.
7. John B. Thompson, *The Media and Modernity: A Social Theory of the Media* (Stanford: Stanford University Press, 1995).
8. On the press, see M. Israel, *Communication and Power* (Cambridge: Cambridge University Press, 1995); R. Jeffrey, *India's Newspaper Revolution: Capitalism, Politics and the Indian Language Press* (London: Thrust, 2000); and S. Chakravarty, *Press and Media: The Global Dimensions* (New Delhi: Kanishka, 1997). On radio, see P. C. Chatterji, *Broadcasting in India* (New Delhi: Sage, 1987); P. S. Gupta, *Radio and the Raj* (Calcutta: Centre for Studies in Social Sciences, 1995); David Lelyveld, 'Upon the Subdominant: Administering Music on All India Radio', in C. Brekenridge (ed.), *Consuming Modernity* (New Delhi: Oxford University Press, 1996), pp. 49–65; and Kanchan Kumar, 'Mixed Signals: Radio Broadcasting in India', *Economic*

and *Political Weekly*, 31 May 2003, pp. 2173–82. On television, see Gopal Saxena, *Television in India: Changes and Challenges* (Delhi: Vikas, 1996); R. N. Acharya, *Television In India* (New Delhi: Manas Publication, 1987); T. K. Thomas (ed.), *Autonomy for the Electronic Media: A National Debate on the Prasar Bharati Bill, 1989* (New Delhi: Konark Publications, 1990); and S. C. Bhatt, *Satellite Invasion* (New Delhi: Gyan Publication, 1994). On cinema see, E. Barnow and S. Krishnaswamy, *Indian Film* (New Delhi: Oxford University Press, 1980); A. Rajadhyaksha and P. Willeman, Encyclopaedia of Indian Cinema (London: Oxford University Press/British Film Institute, 1994). On communication policy in general, see G. Balagopal, *Usage of Media: A Policy Study on Radio and Television* (New Delhi: Centre for Policy Research, 1992); M. V. Desai, *Communication Policies in India* (Paris: UNESCO, 1977).
9. Peggy Mohan, 'In Between Paradigms: Perspective on Communication Theory for India', *Economic and Political Weekly*, vol. xxvii, nos 15 and 16 (pp. 773–78). Peggy Mohan writes 'communication theory came together as a separate social science back in the 1950's, as a large number of nation states emerged from the colonial experience and grouped around models of national development'. It was born into an atmosphere of certainty and centralized multinational control, where gleaming end products of western development would be advertised to the poor as available lifestyles, with no reflection about the real factors that had started this pattern of development in the West. With certainty, because the message itself was not open to question, and control, because the sources sought not consensus or compromise but conversion, communication theory gave the theoretical foundations to the persuasion front of the western struggle for power, power to channelize the direction of development of the rest of the world in the image of the West (p. 773).
10. Biswajit Das, 'Global Communication and Local Appropri-ation: An Indian Experience' in Z. H. Zaidi and Vanita Ray (eds), *Mass Media in Third World* (New Delhi: Kanishka Publications, 2002): Also see Biswajit Das 'Beyond Boundary?: Globalisation of Indian Communication'. Paper presented at Interdisciplinary Seminar on Globalisation, Language, Culture and Media at Indian Institute of Technology Kanpur, 30–31 January and 1 February 2001, organized by Aligarh Muslim University and Indian Institute of Advanced Studies, Shimla.
11. Biswajit Das, 'Theories of Communication: Logical and Normative Groundings'. Paper presented in the Workshop on Communication, Anthropology and Sociology, 15–17 December 2003, organized by Indian Council of Philosophical Research at India International Centre, New Delhi.

12. See Gurevitch et. al., *Culture, Society and the Media;* also see J. D. Slack and Martin Allor, 'The Political and Epistemological Constituents of Critical Communication Research', in *Journal of Communication,* vol. 33, no. 3, pp. 208–18.
13. Scholars like P. F. Lazarsfeld (1941) and J. Blumler (1980) label it as 'critical'/'administrative'. Gurevitch et. al., *Culture, Society and the Media,* classify it as 'Marxist'/'liberal pluralist', William Carey, 'Mass Communication Research and Cultural Studies', in James Curran, M. Gurevitch and J. Woolacott (eds), *Mass Communication and Society* (London: Arnold, 1979), pp. 315–48, categorizes it as 'interpretative'/'positivistic' and R. K. Merton, *Social Theory and Social Structure* (Glencoe: Free Press, 1957), while discussing sociology of knowledge, proposes a two-fold typology on the role of ideas in society. He identifies corresponding tendencies to embrace different methodological strategies in two different continents. Thus, he equates American communication research to 'positivist empiricist epistemology' and European communication research as 'dialectical philosophical approach.' The empirical tradition is as much European as American and stemmed much from broad social, political and intellectual interests in the West.
14. S. Hall, 'The Rediscovery of Ideology: Return of the Repressed in Media Studies', in Gurevitch et. al., *Cultural Society and Media,* pp. 56–90.
15. The idea of maintenance of 'social order' is derived from the nineteenth century European social thought. This was appropriated in American social science which further threw light on the development of academic disciplines and their social concerns. Further, the influence of pragmatism on the social reform movement of the 1920s, backed by 1940s' and 1950s' social research had a considerable influence. It changed the climate of the 1960s and guided the expressions of social sciences in the 1970s. For a detailed analysis, see Hardt, 'The British Cultural Studies'.
16. J. G. Blumler, 'The Social Purposes of Mass Communication Research: A Transatlantic Perspective', *Journalism Quarterly,* no. 55, 1978, pp. 219–30. Also, see J. G. Blumler, 'The Role of Theory in Uses and Gratifications Studies', *Communication Research,* vol. 6, no. 1, 1978, pp. 9–36.
17. D. McQuail, *Mass Communication Theory* (London: Sage, 1983).
18. See Lee Thayer (ed.), 'Communication: General Semantics Perspectives (New York: Spartan-Macmillan, 1970). David Berlo, *The Process of Communication* (New York: Holt and Rineheart & Winston, 1960); J. Klapper, *The Effects of Mass Communication* (Glencoe: Free Press, 1960); H. Lasswell, 'The Structure and Function of Communication in Society', in Wilbur Schramm and D. Roberts (eds), *The Process and Effects of Communication* (Urbana: University of Illinois Press, 1971), pp. 84–99.

19. See D. C. Whitney and E. Wartella, *Mass Communication Review Year Book*, vol. 3 (Beverley Hills, California: Sage, 1982).
20. Namita Unnikrishnan and Shailaja Bajpai, *The Impact of Television Advertising on Children* (New Delhi: Sage, 1996).
21. Melvin Defleur and Ball Rokeah, *Theories of Mass Communication*, 4th edition (New York: Longman, 1982); Lasswell, 'Structure and Function of Communication'.
22. McQuail, *Mass Communication Theory*.
23. W. Goode, *Explorations in Social Theory* (New York: Oxford University Press, 1973).
24. Armand Mattelart, 'For a Class Analysis of Communication', in Armand Mattelart and Seth Siegelaub (eds), *Communication and Class Struggle*, vol. 1 (New York: International General, 1979), pp. 23–73.
25. S. Thomas, 'Some Problems on the Paradigm in Communication Theory', in D. C. Whitney and E. Wartella (eds), *Mass Communication Review Year Book*, vol. 3 (Beverley Hills, California: Sage, 1982).
26. Philip Eliott, 'Uses and Gratifications Research: A Critique and a Sociological Alternative', in J. G. Blumler and E. Katz (eds), *The Uses of Mass Communication: Current Perspectives in Gratifications Research* (Beverely Hills, California: Sage, 1974).
27. Paul Hartman, B. R. Patil and A. Dighe, *The Mass Media and Village Life* (New Delhi: Sage, 1989); Kirk Johnson, *Television and Social Change in Rural India* (New Delhi: Sage, 2000).
28. Todd Gitlin, 'Media Sociology: The Dominant Paradigm', in Denis McQuail (ed.), *McQuail's Reader in Mass Communication* (London: Sage, 2002), pp. 25–35. Gitlin outlines five assumptions. The first one refers to (*a*) commensurability of the modes of influence, (*b*) power as distinct occasions, (*c*) the commensurability of buying and politics, (*d*) attitude change as the dependent variables, and (*e*) the fifth assumption: followers as 'opinion leaders.'
29. Gitlin,…, discusses that because of intellectual, ideological and institutional commitments, sociologists have put forward critical questions. The idea behind the relative unimportance of mass media lies a skewed, faulty concept of importance, similar to the faulty concept of power as maintained by political sociologists, specially those of the pluralist persuasion. Like pluralism, the dominant sociology of 'mass' defines it as a fundamental feature of its subject.
30. Dallas W. Smythe, 'The Political Character of Science (Including Communication Science), or Science is not ecumenical', in Armand Mattelart and Seth Siegelaub (eds), *Communication and Class Struggle* (New York: International General, 1971), pp. 171–76.
31. See Gitlin,…, as a detailed critique of the dominant paradigm of limited effects.

32. For detailed reviews see Binod C. Agarwal, 'Culture, Communication and Development: An Indian Perspective' in *Third Survey of Research in Sociology and Social Anthropology*, vol. 1 (New Delhi: ICSSR and Manak Publications Pvt. Ltd, 2000), pp. 296–325; Surendra K. Gupta, 'Sociology of Communication', in *Survey of Research in Sociology and Social Anthropology* (New Delhi: ICSSR and Satvahana Publications, 1985), vol. II, pp. 151–67; Samirendra Ray, *Communication in Rural Development: A Public Policy Perspective* (Shimla: Institute of Advanced Studies, 1995); G. N. S. Raghavan, *Development and Communication in India* (New Delhi: Gyan Books, 1992); P. Patankar and Lillian De, *Social Communication in Family Planning: A Case Book* (New Delhi: Orient Longman, 1973).
33. For a detailed discussion see Srinivas R. Melkote, *Communication for Development in the Third World: Theory and Practice* (New Delhi: Sage, 1991).
34. P. Roy, F. B. Waisenen and E. M. Rogers, *Impact of Communication on Rural Development: An Investigation in Costa Rica and India* (Hyderabad: National Institute of Community Development, 1969); Y. V. L. Rao, *Communication and Development: A Study of Indian Villages* (Minneapolis: University of Minneapolis Press, 1966); S. C. Dube, 'Development Change and Communication in India', in W. Schramm and D. Lerner (eds), *Communication and Change, The Last Ten Years and the Next* (Honolulu: The University of Hawaii Press, 1976), pp. 98–118; K. E. Eapen, 'Development Communication: A Country Cousin Syndrome', *ICCTR Journal*, vol. 1, no. 1, pp. 67–74.
35. E. Rogers, *Communication and Development: Critical Perspectives* (Beverley Hills, California: Sage, 1976); also see E. Rogers, *Diffusion of Innovations* (New York: Free Press, 1962); E. Rogers, *Modernisation among Peasants: The Impact of Communication* (New York: Holt, Rine Hart and Winston, 1969); E. Rogers and Lawrence D. Kinkaid, *Communication Networks: A New Paradigm for Research* (New York: Free Press, 1983).
36. Armand Mattelart, 'For a Class Analysis of Communication' in Armand Mattelart and Seth Siegelaub (eds), *Communication and Class Struggle*, vol. 1 (New York: International General, 1979), pp. 23–73.
37. Vibodh Parthasarathi, 'The Problem', *Seminar* 455 (*Alternatives in Communication*), 1997 (July).
38. Binod C. Agarwal, *Media Anthropology and Rural Development: Some Observations on SITE* (Ahmedabad: ISRO, 1976); also see by the same author, *Social Impact of SITE on Adults* (Ahmedabad: ISRO, 1977); *SITE Social Evaluation: Results, Experiences and Implications* (Ahmedabad: ISRO, 1981); *Communication Revolution: A Study of Video Penetration in India* (Ahmedabad: ISRO, 1989) and Binod C. Agarwal and Arbind K. Sinha (eds), *SITE to INSAT: Challenges of Production and Research for Women and Children* (New Delhi: Concept, 1986).

39. Vinod Pavarala, 'Breaking Free: Battle Over the Airwaves', *Economic and Political Weekly*, 31 May 2003, pp. 2166–67. Also see Vinod Pavarala, 'Building Solidarities: A Case of Community Radio in Jharkhand', *Economic and Political Weekly*, 31 May 2003, pp. 2188–97; Fredrick Norohna, 'Community Radio: Singing New Tunes in South Asia', *Economic and Political Weekly*, 31 May 2003, pp. 2168–72.
40. Mattelart, 'For a Class and Group Analysis'.
41. K. Sadanandan Nair and Shirley A. White (eds), *Perspectives on Development Communication* (New Delhi: Sage, 1996); Jan Servaes, Thomas L. Jacobson and Shirley A. White, *Participatory Communication for Social Change* (New Delhi: Sage, 1996); Shirley A. White (ed.), *Participatory Communication: Working for Change and Development* (New Delhi: Sage, 1996); Shirley A. White, (ed.), *The Art of Facilitating Participation: Releasing the Power of Grassroots Communication*, (Ithaca: Cornell University, 1999).
42. Armand Mattelart, 'For a Class Analysis of Communication' in Mattelart and Siegelaub, 1979 (see footnote 36).
43. Arvind Singhal and Everett Rogers, *India's Information Revolution* (New Delhi: Sage, 1989).
44. J. Halloran, 'The Context of Mass Communication Research', in E. Mcanny, J. Schnitman and N. Janus (eds), *Communication and Social Structure* (New York: Praeger, 1981), pp. 21–57. Halloran observes that the 'critical' umbrella covers a variety of approaches and in fact, there are those who would suggest that some of the more extreme ideological positions should not really be classified as social scientific research.
45. Alan Swingwood, *The Myth of Mass Culture* (London: Macmillan, 1977). Swingwood points out that a sense of 'economic determinism' and 'historical fatalism' were unable to grasp the capitalist culture. Neither did capitalism decline and collapse as 'historical necessity' nor did the capitalist economy degenerate to a point of 'barbaric meaninglessness.' Instead the capitalist economy reached a point of dizzy height and made a greater impact in society through its mediating influence. The various institutions and complex forces brought a delicate balance in the civil society.
46. Karl Marx and F. Engels, *The German Ideology* (London: Lawrence and Wishart, 1970).
47. Nicholas Garnham, 'Contribution to a Political Economy of Mass Communication', *Media Culture and Society*, vol. 1, no. 2, 1979, pp. 123–46; Graham Murdock and Peter Golding, Capitalism, Communication and Class Relations', in James Curran, Michael Gurevitch and Janet Woolacott (eds), *Mass Communication and Society* (London: Edward Arnold, 1997), pp. 12–43.
48. Peter Golding and Graham Murdock, in G. Cleveland Wilhoit and Harold de Bock (eds), *Mass Communication Review Year Book*, vol. 1 (London: Sage, 1980), p. 72.

49. Dallas Smythe, 'Communications: Blind Spot of Western Marxism', *Canadian Journal of Political and Social Theory*, vol. 1, 1977, pp. 1–27.
50. T. Adorno, 'On Popular Music', *Studies in Philosophy and Social Science*, 9, pp. 17–48.
51. Graham Murdock, 'Misrepresenting Media Sociology', *Sociology*, 14, 1980, pp. 457–68.
52. A. Dorfman and A. Mattelart, *How to Read Donald Duck: Imperialist Ideology in the Disney Comic* (New York: International General, 1975) and T. Gitlin, *The Whole World is Watching* (Berkeley: University of California Press, 1975).
53. Garnham, 'Contribution to a Political Economy'. Also see by the same author, 'Toward a Theory of Cultural Materialism', *Journal Of Communication*, 1984, pp. 314–20.
54. Quintin Hoare and Geoffrey N. Smith (eds and trans.), *Selections from the Prison Note Books of Antonio Gramsci* (London: Lawrence Wishart, 1971).
55. Louis Althusser, *For Marx* (London: Allen Lane, 1969).
56. S. Hall, 'The Rediscovery of Ideology: Return of the Repressed in Media Studies', in Michael Gurevitch, Tony Bennett, James Curran and Janet Woolacott (eds), *Culture, Society and Media* (London: Methuen, 1982), pp. 56–90.
57. Per Stahlberg, *Lucknow Daily: How a Hindi Newspaper Constructs Society* (Stockholm: Jannes Snabbtryck, 2002); Milton Israel, *Communication and Power* (Cambridge: Cambridge University Press, 1994).
58. P. C. Chatterji, *Broadcasting in India* (New Delhi: Sage, 1987).
59. Ananda Mitra, *Television and Popular Culture in India: A study of the Mahabharata* (New Delhi: Sage, 1993); Prabha Krishnan and Anita Dighe, *Affirmation and Denial: Construction of Femininity of Indian Television* (New Delhi: Sage, 1990); Nandini Prasad, *A Vision Unveiled: Women on Television* (New Delhi: Har Anand Publication, 1994); Nilanjana Gupta, *Switching Channels: Ideologies of Television in India* (New Delhi: Oxford University Press, 1998); Ammu Joseph and Kalpana Sharma (eds), *Whose News? The Media and Women's Issues* (New Delhi: Sage, 1994); Sevati Ninan, *Through the Magic Window: Television and Change in India* (New Delhi: Penguin Books, 1995); Amrita Shah, *Hype, Hypocrisy and Television in Urban India* (Delhi: Vikas, 1997); A. Rajagopal, 'The Rise of National Programming: The Case of Indian Television', *Media, Culture and Society*, vol. 15, no. 1, 1993, pp. 91–111; A. Rajagopal, *Politics after Television: Hindu Nationalism and the Reshaping of the Public in India* (Cambridge: Cambridge University Press, 2001).
60. Ashish Nandy, *The Secret Politics of our Desires: Innocence, Culpability and Indian Popular Cinema* (New Delhi: Oxford University Press, 1998); Madhava M. Prasad, *Ideology of the Hindi Film: A Historical Construction* (New Delhi: Oxford University

Press, 1998); M. S. S. Pandian, *The Image Trap: M. G. Ramachandran in Film and Politics* (New Delhi: Sage, 1992); Sumita Chakravarty, *National Identity in Indian Popular Cinema 1947–87* (Austin: University of Texas Press, 1993).

61. Peter Manuel, *Cassette Culture, Popular Music and Technology in North India* (Chicago: University of Chicago Press, 1993); Theodore S. Bhaskaran, *The Message Bearers: The Nationalistic Politics and the Entertainment Media in South India* (New Delhi: Sage, 1981); C. Brosius and M. Butcher (eds), *Image Journeys: Audio Visual Media and Cultural Change in India* (New Delhi: Sage, 1999).

62. It is significant to draw attention to a special issue on media-culture in one of the leading left academic journals. When the media, and its media-culture, is yet to be rigorously debated in Indian left politics, this issue either reflects that the left academia have completely taken a cultural turn, or they are being taken for a ride by the cultural studies tradition in the US. For details see the issue of *Social Scientist*, Vol. 28, No. 3 and 4, (July) 2000, Tulika Print Communication Services Pvt. Ltd.

63. See Lawrence Grossberg, 'Cultural Interpretation and Mass Communication', *Communication Research*, 4, 1977, pp. 339–54. Also see 'Interpreting the Crisis of Culture in Communication Theory', *Journal of Communication*, 29(1), 1979 (winter), pp. 56–69; 'Cultural Studies Revisited and Revised', in M. Mandr (ed.), *Communications in Transition* (New York: Praeger, 1983), pp. 39–70; 'Strategies of Marxist Cultural Interpretation', *Critical Studies in Mass Communication*, 1, 1984, pp. 392–421.

64. G. Murdock and Peter Golding, 'Capitalism, Communication and Class Relations' in James Curran, Michael Gurevitch and Janet Woolacott (eds), *Mass Communication and Society* (London: Edward Arnold, 1977).

2

INVESTIGATING COMMUNICATION:
Remooring the Contours of Research

BISWAJIT DAS, VIBODH PARTHASARATHI, GUY POITEVIN

The Overture and the previous essay amply illustrated the great chasm in the disciplinary trends of communication studies in India. This essay will unfold the state and status of communication research in India. The modalities for the present discussion are threefold: in the first section, a thumbnail sketch has been provided to unearth the politics in and behind communication research in India. In the second section, existing debates in the area of communication research are unravelled; it also reopens elements of these debates and explores the emerging trends to understand the linkages. Finally, we offer preliminary thoughts on apprehending 'communication' along these lines and the research underway.

Political Contexts of Research

It is apparent that communication research in India owes its genesis and growth to our encounter with the West—an encounter in which the latter's academic and public policy fulcrums often acted out in a seamless manner. While in the social sciences in India, there were fruitful debates and discussions on the epistemological and ontological implications of specific fields of inquiry, rarely has communication research had the privilege of such inquiries. From the initial stages, communication research continued with the tradition of logical positivism as borrowed from the West, that has continued till date. This tradition became the edifice for communication researchers as it suited policy makers and developmentalists engaged in the national reconstruction project. Communication was viewed more as an applied discipline to be used for communicating 'Development' across the country.[1]

Accordingly, professionals were required and institutions to train such professionals emerged. Research was correspondingly prioritized and the questions asked were suited to the requirements for the growth of professionals, programmes and the importance of 'mass' communication media. Communication as a conceptual category was understood as an external input in the development process. The externality of communication caused much confusion; in fact, it enabled the technocrats to use and abuse it the way they wanted. All through, technocrats imposed the indispensability of technologies for communicating development programmes; the task of social scientists was to carry out their instructions, locate appropriate 'labs' for these initiatives, and assess their immediate impacts. Communication policy followed more a logic of the market since it explored the capacity to deliver goods, and the acceptance of such goods in society. Wherever it failed to secure its credential as a supplier of goods, it criticized the receiver or user of goods as not worthy, and needing attitudinal changes. Research also explored the various dimensions of motivations, efficacy, effectiveness that could lead to better communication between policy and beneficiaries. New vocabularies were added to communication research such as effects studies, diffusion studies, impact programmatic studies and so on.[2] These were then the prime weaknesses that marked nearly three decades of the diffusionist approach to the planning and study of communication. While the diffusionist tradition suited the needs and requirements of various policy making and administrative department of the government, very often being co-sponsored by international and bilateral add agencies, it only helped the government in sharpening its statecraft in mustering and managing the art of communication. The statecraft's fascination for diffusionist tradition underlined the nature and meaning of communication in Indian society. Such an ahistorical sense of communication drifted the discipline away from being a social science constituency and developed it more as a technical enterprise. It is quite a pity that even today in universities, communication is viewed at par with vocational courses, being related more with the production of images and news rather than, to say the least, ideas behind such production.

Throughout these endeavours, communication research conducted its enquiry by isolating specific elements of the society as independent variables. As a result, it was unable to grasp the complexities of cultural and social processes; it ended up with assumptions on the stability of individuals in their social relations, the compatibility of cultural world views, the resilience of traditional sociocultural systems and so on. Communication research avoided addressing issues such as structures of social formation, location of authority and distribution of power, the very elements which built up systemic configurations. The simplistic nature of the unduly media-centred concerns of much research was a methodological and ideological shortcut for media determinism. Equally, it was always superficial to seek the effect of one institution on another rather than the conditions—economic, social, symbolic or political—under which certain media practices appeared to be curtailed or promoted.

The enumerations above also show the extent to which research and policy under the influence of modernization was governed by a 'transmission' view of the communication—one which focussed on distribution rather than exchange of ideas.[3] The earliest behavioural tradition emphasized, and led to, a simplistic unidirectional relationship between sender, message and receiver and consequently a naïve conception of media effects.[4] This was refined, to the extent of a relatively more active conception of media audiences, with influences from the 'user and gratification' approach of Blumler; nevertheless, the matter of linear chain of causality remained essentially unrefined. The overemphasis on media technology was part and parcel of this obsession with diffusion and the measuring of 'impact'. This led scholars to view media technology out of any social or economic context—both of its making and its deployment. In fact, at the very core of the diffusionist approach was the desire to appropriate context to communication technology.

We also notice that the crests of such discourses closely followed the transfer, adoption or import of media technologies into India[5]—as encapsulated in the previous essay. Remarkably enough, this was as true of the 1960s as of the 1990s. It was through a set of cognitive, political and economic contacts that communication research grew not only in positivistic (fact and data) and normative (ideological and metatheoretical) terms in various phases, but came to be 'conditioned' as it were within India. Instead of realizing and overcoming such a dynamics of 'knowledge flows', these have attenuated in the last decade.

A significant feature of the 1990s increase in writings on communication has been their origins—the great majority emanating from outside India, especially by Indians studying, researching and/or teaching in US universities. While these have contributed in rethinking the role of communication in the social sciences, somewhere amidst all this we seem to have lost the ground, or desire, for our treatment of a unique historicity and contextuality. This deems it important to engage with the 'politics of location' if we are to evaluate, let alone evolve, the contours of a truly independent and indigenously grounded research agenda. As with revitalizing other older disciplines imported from the West, sociology and anthropology, in the sphere of communication too substantive structures and social formations of the region under investigation must be brought into view.[6]

While official research persisted with the objective empirical mode, quite a few who did not continue with the empirical tradition resorted to investigating the subjective dimensions in communication research. It is here that we see the 'qualitative turn' in communication research, and therein the advent of ethnographic, interpretative and most recently historical research in communication. The latter two developments will be elaborated in the next section; for now, a few aspects of ethnographic communication research may be put forward.

First, not all research conducted within the rubric of qualitative research subscribed to similar arguments; in fact there were variations within this.[7] A large number of studies were based on personal experiences of people associated in different capacities in various sectors of mass media.[8] The other genre of writings were illustrative, making them simply, and wholly, descriptive studies.[9] All these studies lacked analytical ability and explanatory powers. Studies during and after the 1990s no doubt tried to transcend the diffusionist approach underpinning audience research by seeking to explore the diversity of television reception, searching for and understanding 'meaning', given the plurality of identities that actually constitute 'couch potatoes'.[10] Although ideologically one can differ with these studies, one cannot undermine their scholarly contributions. Nevertheless, in thinking about the possible contours of research of television audience, we have been reminded that

> Some of the questions we need to ask in such research will reflect the distinctively Indian conditions of the medium and its reception, and there will be other questions which have been pursued in other societal contexts which we might raise as well. If it is exclusively the latter, we will only be replicating, both theoretically and methodologically, the enormous work done in the West about television audiences.[11]

Second, however much the social science paradigm offers an integrative frame of reference, we find that the contours of contemporary communication research in India cannot be deduced merely from the state of academic and official research.[12] For these quarters have not, do not and often cannot, reflect the full spectrum of questions sought by various social actors. For one, the class character separates most visibly 'thinkers' and 'workers' in the sphere of communication, especially evident when commenting on 'interventionist' practices. More unfortunately, it indicates a division of labour, wherein media scholars and researchers simply 'feed' on the labour—cognitive and experiential—of media practitioners, social animators and cultural workers. These experiences have further caused division within communication scholarship; while researchers are engaged in questions of the generation of knowledge, practitioners are concerned directly with aspects of social change and/or reform. Furthermore, not all practices in communication research can be ascribed for social transformation as they have reformist as well as radical tendencies. Of late, 'participation' has become the buzzword for social transformation; it is being appropriated by officials and practitioners alike. Although this term potentially has an explanatory power, the way this method and research has been ardently 'deployed' with regard to 'communication' in development concepts and strategies is suspect, as explained in the previous chapter.[13] There is a shared realization that this approach is agentive, that is, it depicts a state of affairs, usually in the countryside, which morally requires and thus legitimizes in their own eyes an active involvement of modern secular missionaries—armed with their media tools to 'inform' and 'change'. Equally, there is an agreement that participatory method/action/research is weighed down by the same internal contradictions as the former academic discourse on 'participant observation'.[14] There is no point in reopening the old theoretical debate on issues of research methodology here; nevertheless, those concerned with issues of overt or covert social power cannot avoid being also concerned with research strategies—whether engaged in pure research, applied research or action research, within and beyond the social sciences.[15] Without a broader vision in which to locate the concerns of the communication researcher, we are bound perennially to lament the inconclusiveness of research and of 'intervention'. However, it is not our intention here to revisit the site of either this general argument, or that of institutional versus independent research in particular. Through initiatives engaged in a combined perspective of research and action, we seek to raise some fundamental queries about the contours of the subject matter of 'communication' itself. Hence, a critical take on the sociology of knowledge pertaining to our field of inquiry becomes essential in the treatment of the conceptual and substantive categories in communication research.

Third, we have observed that a certain ahistorical and decontextualised idea of communication is a crucial ideological support for those working to see, by all means and at any cost, the triumph of new information-communication technologies. The ideology of the communication revolution is prompting utopian hopes of a new era in both industrial and industrializing societies. However, the significantly new dimension of the modern electronic church, and its various congregational orders, is that it commits itself to transform both levels of reality—material and symbolic. We suggest an urgency to strike at the bottom of this by apprehending those substantive social and cultural developments for which the term 'mass communication' has become an anachronism, and 'new media' a grossly ahistorical misnomer. We must not be blinded or seduced by the promises of our own era's new media because they are not new at all. We ought to realize that such 'newness' is constructed, in fact variedly constructed in and across different eras—as in the past, the present.[16]

Elements of a Critical Turn

As the malaise of past research in communication in India is being recognized, it appeared differently to researchers of different persuasions and belonging to different intellectual concerns. While some continue to congratulate themselves on their geotechnological alignments, others realized more concretely the myopia in dominant trends; while still others see themselves struggling against the impasse. The latter indicate that fresh and exciting work is being carried out at a variety of levels on a host of substantive themes. The convergences of perspective these demonstrate are sufficiently striking to justify the makings of an altered—more grounded and responsive—research agenda. Pursuing these demand means, foremost, being receptive to a kind of intellectual pluralism that traverses inherited modes of inquiry.

Such a fusion should start from the methodological underpinnings in the field of communication itself.

At a time when the field of communication is still steeped in its impassionate functionalist origins,[17] qualitative studies emerged as a conscious initiative to impart the critical function of historical investigation and sociological understanding of communication. The central concern in this shift was due to a realization within academia on whether communication research was meant for the legitimation of state policy, or for critical reflection towards the growth of knowledge. This resulted in more and more scholars from social sciences addressing issues and questions pertaining to communication studies.

There are two dimensions to the 'qualitative turn' in the field of communication—that pertaining to its objectives and its substance. While it was assumed that 'the quantitative' enabled highlighting patterns, the significance and richness of qualitative studies lay in its capacity to reveal, and detail, associated social processes, that is, processes wherein society produces and maintains forms of interaction and structures of meaning. As a corollary, examinations sought to take into account that we, as constituent groups and individuals of society, neither solely 'react' to new economic contexts of communication, nor merely 'consume' its technological and cultural artefacts. Rather, we live by interpreting experiences and incessantly acting upon them, albeit in varying kinds and degrees of success. Such 'activity' is as true for a conversation between a group of people, as the inception of telegraphic exchanges or that grounded by computer mediated communication. It is from a perspective equally emphasizing the overlapping socio-economic process associated with the advent of communication technology, the creation of administrative and/or industrial subsystems of the media and the interventions of human agency therein, that its historical novelty must be approached and demonstrated.

Inspite of recognizing the raison d'etre of the qualitative approach, there persisted in some circles a belief that qualitative studies signify another name for historical research. This misconception led communication scholarship to be divided into the domains of history and theory—alleged to be mutually exclusive—such that history writing was assumed to impede contributions to theory. This has hindered harnessing the synergy between history writing and theory building in communication. As this is central to the scope of ideas in this essay, one will briefly recall the potential of their integration. Communication research is, and needs to be, historical in two ways. First, because it is grounded in the knowledge of communication processes of the past and how they have come to acquire their present form. Second, it is designed to account for historical and comparative variation, thereby refraining from crude generalizations based on the presumed universality of, or a dominant mode among, communication processes. On its part, communication history needs to be theoretical such that it goes beyond an explanatory collection of facts from, and about, the past.[18] Influenced by the general rationale guiding the qualitative approach, communication history must necessarily hint at the 'deeper' roots of what appear to be contemporary and dazzling phenomenon—whether they concern the specificities of the media industry or the trajectory of mediated cultural practices.

Interpretative Tradition

The critical turn also saw to the adoption of the interpretative traditions from the social sciences in communication research. One of the best advocates of a radical shift in analytical perception from a passive consumption of products to an anonymous creativity of users through focusing on the rift that inaugurates the use of the product comes in the work of de Certeau.[19] For now, we would like to refer to the concepts of 'use', 'usage' and 'user' elaborated by some others.[20] We generally speak of users with reference to buyers of private and public goods and services—'use' is related to consumption. The institutional idea of 'usage' is directed to improving the commercial and administrative relationship of a consumer with a commercial firm, a service agency or a state department; this relationship should be more human, more rewarding, more profitable to the user! Clearly, in this semantics, the user is understood to fit as a client or customer into the two categories—of economics and administration. They are not intended to break away from them but to better partake of their facilities; on the other side of the transaction, commercial firms, private and public service agencies aim to meet expectations to better attend to the user's need and wish. If we refer to the services that the media offer, a small amount of autonomy conceded to the user is useful for a quantitative understanding of his behaviour, as attested to by the many viewer, reader and user-functionality surveys. In the overabundance at offer, the user figures as the one who gives the proposed innovation its meaning and relevance— 'customization' is within the prescribed and standardized definition of the possible uses of the goods or services under consideration. The supply of commercial or administrative goods initiates the process and accounts for the particular attention of which the user is the object. The prerogatives of the user are therefore doubly limited and circumscribed.

An anthropological or sociological insight into the social relation of usage may reveal a different picture of the user. The latter's behaviour has been studied at length, especially with regard to the new media and communication tools. The user often appropriates, misappropriates, pirates, resists and even rejects. The development of new forms of social uses takes time and does not always correspond to the original plan designed by the system promoters. In a more subtle and hidden way, everyday practices reveal an array of individual methods, uses, stratagems and pilfering.[21] The user may not remain a passive consumer or repository of information, only browsing through the material that he is fed with. In the end, the user's tactics—which can be silent, disobedient, ironic, or poetic—can get away with and even avenge the dominating power of the productive forces. Eventually, the user may remain the controlling agent and have the final word in the marketplace. They elude the imposed codes, turn them upside down, appropriate the very means of their subjugation and instead of participating and playing the same games, diverts them towards different targets.

This is a step forward in the right direction; it has generated a number of microlevel insights and lines of inquiry that may enrich a comprehensive research agenda in critical communication theory.[22] Nevertheless, a few observations are worth merit.

Much of what has been said in this context stems from the utopia of a public and free, reciprocal self-learning; it is assumed that the mutual cooperation of all in a worldwide synergy of competences, imagination and exchange of ideas would mediate a reconstruction of the social link between human beings by subverting the boundaries of all territorial powers.[23] But looking around us, we see quite the reverse. Contrary to initial expectations, the so called 'new media' did not increase community links nor set up an information agora with a wide range of diverse voices striving towards harmony.[24] The 'new media' appears to have increased individualization, mediation[25] and simulation.[26] This was the case with the 'old media' as well. Studies have shown that people who spend the most amount of time in front of the television tend to accept whatever televised scene is broadcast daily as the real world; they therefore display the greatest possible social conformity in their attitudes and judgement.[27]

Therefore this euphoria over 'new technology, first, carries the danger of seamlessly meshing with a media industry that incessantly excludes a range of (other) voices and standpoints—those that may be referred to as non-dominant communication.[28] For long we have known that the media serve 'to reinforce a consensual viewpoint by using public idioms and by claiming to voice public opinion'.[29] Thinking otherwise conveniently ignores the ways in which needs, desires and identities are shaped by what is on offer—that the market gives us the freedom and the options to become what we buy. Specifically in response to current euphoria, however, we must point out that simply because our media–culture offers a variety of pleasures to be 'read' in different ways, we must not assume that attempts to maximize the diversity of ideas and representation within the system are redundant.[30] Doing so would become yet another rendition of the media conglomerates' claims that ultimate power lies with the consumer. Some contributors in this volume[31] have demonstrated how media products and services have been sculpted into a variety of simulated, fictional and realist settings of daily life that offer a definite order of commercial rationales and cultural references.

Second, and very often consequently, in their euphoria of stressing these creativity and subversion, proponents of the new ethnography tend to underplay or even bypass questions of power.[32] This is particularly difficult to analyse, as questions of power are not clearly revealed by mere insights and descriptions of particular products or ways of using them. Consequently, the dynamics of the audience's or user's relationship with media enterprises remains unrevealed, as do wider inquiries on how these relations are, in turn, arbitrated by the unequal, the material and symbolic resources of the 'mass media'. Thus, the question arises, are we not overestimating the power of individual receivers/users? In pondering over this, we wonder whether research attributing so much autonomy to the consumer is not merely a reaction against earlier research which stressed the determinant pressure of social structures and technologies!

Ways with Structure

There is a strong desire and necessity among critical researchers to give due weight to the contexts within which institutions of communication unfold. Consequently, there is significant weight on the way available research materials are contextualized theoretically in the first place.[33] This gained not just intellectual but political significance in recent years, when the belief in communication revolution ushering the world community into a new civilization has unleashed tremendous hopes and aspirations among people in various societies. But assessing the sociability, uses and benefits of such technologies in communication research must never blur or ignore the context in which these technologies are to be situated.

Although there is considerable agreement that the best way to study communication technologies is in their context, however, to study technology in context is really 'to take a particular position on what constitutes that context and thus to enter a terrain where there is little agreement'.[34] What has held promise is a realization that the study of communications technology is not only an opportunity to bridge the gap between various disciplines, but it also allows the complex problem of the general effects of technology to be discussed in more manageable terms.[35] This is precisely because of the opportunity to examine how the interplay of technology, industry and the larger social fabric act upon coexisting conditions. Nevertheless, it is yet to be agreed which conditions require consideration, how these conditions are interrelated and in what way technologies exist in relationship to those conditions.

> The concept of context is, in other words, a substantial theoretical problem, however most studies of communication technologies assume that they already understand its solution. More often than not, context is invoked as a sort of magical term, as if by claiming to take context into consideration, one could banish the theoretical problems of its specificity.[36]

The techno-industrial regimes in our times may mediate human interaction to such an extent that they may even determine new socio-economic, cultural and theoretical orders for sections of society who are able to partake of those mediatic experiences. But the blinkers of 'political invisibility' (liberalization, deregulation and privatization) hide the joint plays of market and state power strategies. Studies within different paradigms have come up with varying conceptions of what constitutes context and, consequently, on the ways in which technologies emerge and exist in such a context.

Similar to the way the term 'context' stares at us as a problematic category is the case with the term 'structure' which thus needs elaboration. One needs to explore mechanisms whereby structure is viewed as constraining and enabling; equally, it needs to be looked at as being not external to action but reproduced through the concrete activities of daily life.[37] This is because the media are at the heart of this interplay and structuration on count of their dual dynamics in our times. On the one hand, they are central to the economic order; they have played a role in organizing consumption and leisure since the early twentieth century, as one contributor in the volume shows,[38] and are today assuming a central role in orchestrating production and distribution in all spheres of knowledge, as another contributor has argued.[39]

On the other hand, the media are symbolic activities through which people make sense of the world, of each other and of their own place within this. Consequently a 'deeper' take must explore how the situated interpretations and activities of users are linked to the workings of the media industry itself, and of the general economic and symbolic formations that shape its production and people's relation to them. This is where Williams' emphasis on the materiality of culture and communication is directly relevant.[40] To restore this missing context we need to explore how cultural production and consumption are structured by wider economic and symbolic formations.[41]

Critical research in communication in India must also pay attention to the ways the pleasures of the text are structured by the producer's strategies for maximising their returns. To understand the use value we need to contextualize its relation to exchange value. In doing so, it would be not only naïve to believe that exchange value subordinates use value, but it would also undermine the importance of the third dimension of media commodities, their symbolic values.[42] Thus, in evaluating the rationality of the frameworks governing media production, one ought to remember that media texts are not a purely physical commodity; they concern symbolic, primarily disembodied, artefacts as well. Thus, at stake here is the complex interplay between exchange value, use value and symbolic value—something deserving much more investigation than has been done.

In this scenario, to view commodification as a descriptive trait of media texts alone would be a methodological error. Commodification concerns those developments by which the interrelationships between constituents of the productive base of communication processes underwent a change. Thus, integral to this transformation is the commodity status of cultural producers, the commodification of the relations of cultural consumption—listening, viewing, reading, surfing—and the commodity status of cultural consumers, that is viewers, listeners. Looking more closely at and around these phenomenon, one is bound to witness transformations in symbolic forms itself—a shaping that is in addition to the way technology more explicitly shapes changes in disembodied symbolic forms. Thus, commodification is a much deeper and overarching process affecting the entire productive base of contemporary media configurations. It is in these interrelated instances that one witnesses the emergence of what is now known as the production of consumption.

Driven by the sensibilities demonstrated above, critical researchers have the potential to play a more influential role in our understanding of media users as well, both in opening fresh lines of investigations and revisiting well-established research questions. Before we jump at questioning the obvious, it must be reiterated that this is not to suggest that critical research does not support their claims empirically; on the contrary, it draws material from a diverse set of studies and methodologies to generate its own 'data'.[43] Furthermore, the objectives of enlarging the base of data is not simply towards applying specific social sciences theories to data to substantiate general laws.[44] In diametrical opposition to how conventional communication research tends to view empirical findings as an end product—thus remaining a pure datum, devoid of meaning[45]—critical researchers see these as questions that need to be answered in other ways.

> They go beyond the abstracted empiricism of much mainstream work and the 'thick description' characteristic of many interpretative studies. Equally, they reject the abstract theorizing of someone like Jean Baudrillard, where grand speculations float conveniently free of sustained empirical reference. But the key characteristic of critical research is its approach to explanation...[it] moves beyond immediate acts of consumption and response to analyze the underlying structures that provide the contexts and resources for audience activity and go on to demonstrate how they organize the making and taking of meaning in everyday life.[46]

While recognizing that the space and time of one's restricted territory of daily life is the privileged milieu of construction of social links, we most emphasize that investigating communication constitutes, on the one hand, investigating the grounding of a social order, and on the other hand, scrutinizing the creation of social meaning. As a corollary, instead of the '"thick description" characteristic of many interpretative studies', critical interpretation operates at two levels: it involves not only a full account of users' own interpretation of their consumption activity, but also a sustained attempt to show how situated experiences and meaning systems are connected to and shaped by the wider symbolic and social formations.[47] In other words, critical researchers are driven by the desire to illustrate the complex and overlapping process whereby individuals engage with, and come to realize the meaning of, social relations.

Apprehending 'Communication'

We need to expand the horizons of research questions so as to cover and measure up to, the whole system of social relations that a particular form of communication incorporates or reveals. To study that form would also mean to analyse the particular aspects of the relations of communication that commercial and/or politico-jural interventions, first, project by themselves on account of its own internal structuring and, second, tend to inaugurate at the level of society at large. As a consequence, investigating communication as a process forces one to recognize and explore its multiple dimensions. Although unfolding themselves as an overlapping aggregate, such a complex of dimensions could be separated for conceptual clarity and analytical scrutiny. In doing so, the way in which these dimensions have been epistemologically viewed, methodologically prioritized and their interrelationships approached, has given rise to a number of 'standpoints' on communication. Situating oneself in any one of these standpoints, quite obviously, influences the entry point of an academic investigation or policy dialogue, as also the questions raised and methods employed therein.

We see communication not as a substance with attributes but an ensemble of activities, more like constellations of varying, and often seemingly distant, social processes. In other words, we assume that communication processes are transitive activities directed towards how we think about, see and hear the world, and through that, how we come to relate with each other. Here we distinguish three kinds of activities at work: (*a*) information as the circulation of ideas and knowledge; (*b*) relation as a social rapport underlying and acting upon such circulation; and (*c*) intention as aspirations to exchange, share or control. Stemming from this, we can construct different sets of dynamics, based upon which a number of systemic figures are actually possible, that is, depending upon the way these dynamics overlap with one another.

Any communication process is a social action, a rapport between people. Whatever its form, medium and techniques, when information is circulated, news broadcast, knowledge imparted, commodities advertised, etc., the important feature is that a relational process takes place between social entities. The implication is that communication should not be understood as a mere transfer of information or a cognitive happening. This is a secondary aspect and we miss the point when we consider it as mere information process. Instead of focusing on the means of information, their techniques and their degree of effectiveness in conveying a message,[48] let us view the whole process as a medium of social action. As a matter of fact, information itself is subject in its content, form and use to purposes which are not cognitively informative but socially performative. Any use of a medium is itself instrumental and subservient to objectives which have nothing to do with information but with social control, cultural leadership and possibly overall hegemony. Information is a modality of a power relation.

Communication processes, by the very relational pattern that it inaugurates, is performative of a particular type of human behaviour, social relation and structuration, depending upon the conditions in which symbolic goods are distributed and appropriated. Contrary to production relations, very little attention has been focused on usage relations. A newspaper, a video film, a public speech, a poster with an image, a poster with a slogan, a slogan at a demonstration, an email message, a photo, web sites, etc. call for different types of intellectual reactions and modes of human relations. Information means are not neutral carriers of information; each of them—written, visual, audio, informatic—conditions in its own way its contents and shapes a particular social rapport through the form of its usage. Images for instance have a strength of their own as much as written words induce specific mental logical attitudes.[49] With writing techniques appear bureaucratic states and pyramidal hierarchies, centralized economies, universal religions with normative scriptures, written laws, etc. With printing presses appear newspapers and public opinion, techno-scientific progress with industrialization. With audio-visual and informatic mass media emerge a civilization of simulacrum, decentralized and transversal societies which challenge the hierarchical authoritarian power of territory bound regimes.

Moreover, society in the main is a system of rapports, a pattern of interdependency. Communication processes operate as a subsystem of a wider web of social linking. Whatever the form and media of the processes, the latter are imbedded into those networks or systems of social relations of which they represent a subsystem. Let us therefore focus on the social relations of communication in the same way as we analyse the social relations of production. Let us study the production of communication practices—including our own practices—as a particular social asset and stake within the whole context of society as a system of action and interaction with many actors competing for control and domination.

A critical research agenda suggests, fundamentally, that communication processes should necessarily be approached within the whole context of the social fabric and the structures of cognition in which they take place. That communication processes cannot refer only to the tools and forms, reiterates the legitimacy and relevance of communication as a social science concept being congenitally grounded in its multidisciplinary dimensions. As long as communication research addresses only isolated segments of existence, it is not able to articulate a comprehensive discourse on such overlapping fields and it will not serve the purpose of a scientific enterprise.

Apprehending the interaction of communication and society is seen as being decisive for us. The tendency to insist on any one as being the determinant has been as much the cause of controversy as the reason for their relationship being misconstrued. Although it is usual to begin with the influence of communication on society, such a standpoint indicates little concern with the ways in which communication processes—their technological basis, industrial contours and emanating cultural forms—came to have a particular form in the first place. On the other hand, society could be said to influence communication in two ways: first, by the prevailing social relations which shape the productive base of the latter; and second, by the prevailing values in the former which govern the direction and dynamics of the latter. That the first instance, in turn, affects the internal structure of communication processes itself, forces us to appreciate the dialectical relationship between communication and society. Thus, *we deem it* more prudent to look at communication processes in terms of successively changing, and overlapping, sets of economic, symbolic and technological fields.

If the poststructuralist insight that subjects should not be essentialized but are always in a process of social formation is valid, then it is incumbent upon us to examine the overall 'ecology' within which such subjects are constructed. However, if subjects' experience of themselves and the world is always a social process, then the forms of our connections to the world are also part of that construction.[50] However, despite its overt poststructuralist influence, cultural studies in India has been mostly focused around issues of meaning—primarily of symbolic, mediatic forms but also technological fonts. In fact, cultural studies as a whole has not addressed in any useful, or empirically grounded, manner the relations of cultural production and consumption. At the same time, the understandable rejection by critical thinkers of McLuhan's thesis has resulted in ignoring the complex endeavour of theorizing mediums. While McLuhan's rather isolated stress on the means of communication led him to ignore the relations of production and, importantly in our era those of consumption, reducing 'the medium is the message' to a buzzword has driven into oblivion its analytical value.[51] This is where Williams' 'deeper' political economy continues to retain its most significant permanence.

As a corollary, methodologically, we refrain from either viewing communication processes as being autonomous from socio-economic activity, or posing either media technology or the emanating cultural forms as being determinant. Recognizing that communication processes are 'co-determined'[52] by various instances namely, material (availability of raw materials), economic (demand-supply equations of commodities and labour), technological (levels and distribution of means of communication as also those of accompanying skills), symbolic (information, knowledge or ideology) and institutional (the nature of social organization in conjunction with all this takes place), one seeks to explore them as an interplay between these instances.

We realize that the essential character of communication processes does not reside merely in the advent of a technology or the creation of textual, sonic or visual phenomenon alone. Rather, it concerns the varied set of altered, both redefined and fresh, social activities incorporating such processes. More specifically, it concerns different ways in which knowledge—as information, cultural forms, ideologies or commodities—came to be socially, and indeed industrially, produced and circulated; the manners in which these processes further shaped how individuals relate with forms of knowledge and through that, to each other and to society as a whole. In short, it concerns the character of a specific ecology of communication, an overlapping complex that cannot be analytically reduced to 'texts' or 'technologies', let alone epistemologically grasped as so. This then is the methodological core binding the diverse essays in this anthology—a shift away from viewing forms of media to apprehending an ecology of communication.

Notes

1. Although in the 1970s itself some scholars reflected on the limitation of their past work (such as Rogers (1976) on the whole this approach, with minor modifications, continued into the 1990s; see for instance Melkote (1991). For an incisive review of these developments, see Das (2003).

2. For a detailed review of these works see, Agarwal (2000) and Gupta (1985).
3. Carey (1989).
4. For instance see Patankar and De (1973).
5. Sinha (2000); Gill (2004); Singhal and Rogers (1989).
6. Singh (2003).
7. For an early anthropological work, see Agarwal (1976).
8. Such as Awasthy (1976), Baruah (1983), Duggal (1980), Kumar and Chandiram (1967) and Masani (1975).
9. Namely Bannerjee (1964), Mukherjee (1954), Natarajan (1962) and Shukla (1944).
10. Krishnan and Dighe (1990). Some have considered aspects demonstrative of 'resistance' by television viewers, albeit in a prudent way (Mankekar [1999]).
11. Pavarala (1999: 103).
12. Agarwal (2000).
13. A spectrum of works are mentioned in the previous essay. For a short, critical review of these, see Poitevin (1983).
14. Wright and Nelson (1995).
15. See 'Communication for Socio-Cultural Action' by Jitendra Maid, Pandit Padalgare and Guy Poitevin in this volume.
16. See the collection of essays in Gitelman and Pingree (2003).
17. For example Roy et al. (1969) and Rao (1966).
18. Christians and Carey (1981).
19. de Certeau (1990: vi–vii, xlv–xlviii, 50–68). Also, de Certeau (1980).
20. For instance see Andre Vitalis in His (1996: 185–86) and Dard (1992) for a set of concepts centering on the usage of domestic electronic objects.
21. Among the earliest and most vociferous proponents of 'resistance' by viewers is found in Fiske (1987).
22. Prime works include Mitra (1993) and Rajagopal (2001).
23. One of the challenges here is of electronic literacy to facilitate a dialogue in as many voices as possible. For this diversity of voices to be possible, in many countries, governments, citizens and media interests have collectively defined a number of principles, in particular competition and diversity, moral standards and access for all, support for innovation, creation and production. The same principles have not been transferred to the international arena despite increasing globalization of information. See for instance the 'Commission of the European Communities White Paper' in His (1996: 90–97).
24. One of the most articulate philosophical advocacy of the political utopia of a worldwide 'virtual agora'—a computer based direct democracy in real time now possible through modern communication technology—is made by Lévy (1997: 26–29, 65–94).

Investigating Communication 87

25. We understand the concept after the formula of McLuhan 'Medium is the Message', the full implications of which are still to be articulated. Nevertheless this marks the end of the classical definition of power, as power also 'circulates', its origin can no more be located.
26. On the concept of 'simulacra' and 'simulation', see Baudrillard (1981b: 12–17, 26).
27. See Vitalis (1996: 189). The suggestion that the receiver can always correct the received messages using the filter of his/her own opinions and experience can be of a very limited effect; the receiver cannot have enough experience in so many fields to judge the symbolic experiences brought to him. Besides, the media industry has already determined the priorities and choice of subjects to be shown as relevant.
28. Parthasarathi (1997).
29. Woollacott (1982: 109).
30. Murdock (1989).
31. 'A Question of Choice', by Maitrayee Chaudhuri, and 'State, Market and Freedom of Expression' by Uma Chakravarti.
32. Poitevin (1997). This point has been made by many others, including Tomaselli and Prinsloo (1990) and Garnham (1990). The absence of looking at power relations in the Indian scenario is prominent in the set of otherwise very insightful essays in Brosius and Butcher (1999).
33. Murdock (1989: 226–49).
34. Slack (1989: 329).
35. Goody (1977: 46).
36. Slack (1989: 329).
37. Giddens (1984: 25) and (1986: 533).
38. 'Construing a "New Media" Market' by Vibodh Parthasarathi.
39. 'That Persistent "Other"' by Pradip N Thomas.
40. Williams (1977).
41. For instance, it has been pointed out that India, which is a producer of cultural commodities in its own right, has been forced to open its doors to the US film industry not only as a result of GATS, but also as a result of Section 301 measures taken by the USTR. See Thomas (2003). Possible policy-measures to stem the wider corporatisation of our media environments are a rare sight in India; for one such creative, albeit now forgotten, document on public broadcasting, see FIFV (1997).
42. Murdock (1989).
43. Murdock (1989).
44. Wallerstein et al. (1997).
45. Bourdieu (1984: 18).
46. Murdock (1989: 227).
47. Ibid.

48. Our distinction is close though not similar, to that of Régis Debray opposing 'communicate' to 'transmit' as two antithetic semantic fields; see Debray (1997: 15–23).
49. Goody (1993).
50. Jhally (1993).
51. Baudrillard (1981a: 172).
52. Mosco (1996).

Bibliography

Agarwal, B.C., *Media Anthropology and Rural Development: Some Observations on SITE* (Ahmedabad: ISRO, 1976).

———, 'Culture, Communication and Development: An Indian Perspective', in *Third Survey of Research in Sociology and Social Anthropology*, vol. 1 (New Delhi: ICSSR and Manak Publications, 2000), pp. 296–325.

Baruah, U.L., *This is All India Radio* (New Delhi: Publications Division, Ministry of Information and Broadcasting, 1983).

Baudrillard, J., *For a Critique of the Political Economy of the Sign* (St Louis: Telos Press, 1981a).

———, *Simulacres et simulation* (Paris: Galil•e, 1981b).

Benjamin, W., 'The Work of Art in an Age of Mechanical Reproduction', in *Illuminations*, translated by Harry Zohn (New York: Shocken, 1968).

Bourdieu, P., *Distinction: A Social Critique of the Judgement of Taste* (London: Routledge and Kegan Paul, 1984).

Brosius, C. and M. Butcher (eds), *Image Journeys: Audio Visual Media and Cultural Change in India* (New Delhi: Sage, 1999).

Carey, J., 'A Cultural Approach to Communication', *Communication as Culture* (Boston: Unwin Hyman, 1989), pp. 13–36.

de Certeau, M., *La Culture au pluriel* (Paris: Christian Bourgois, 1980).

———, *L'invention du quotidien, 1. Arts de faire* (Paris: Gallimard, 1990).

Chambat, P. (ed.), *Communication et lien social* (Paris: Editions Descartes, 1992).

Chanan, M., *The Dream That Kicks: The Prehistory and Early Years of Cinema in Britain* (London: Routledge, 1995).

Christians, C. and J. Carey, 'The Logic and Aims of Qualitative Research', in G. Stempel III and B. Westley (eds), *Research Methods in Mass Communication* (New Jersey: Prentice-Hall, 1981).

Dard, P., 'Le Fantôme du Cybernanthrope' in Pierre Chambat (ed.), *Communication et lien social* (Paris: Editions Descartes, 1992), pp. 139–58.

Das, Biswajit, 'Theories of Communication: Logical and Normative groundings'. Paper presented in the *Workshop on 'Communication, Anthropology and Sociology'*, 15–17 December 2003 organized by

Indian Council of Philosophical Research at India International Centre, New Delhi.

Debray, R., *Transmettre* (Paris: Odile Jacob, 1997).

Duggal, K.S., *What Ails Indian Broadcasting* (New Delhi: Manohar, 1980).

Fernandes, W. and R. Tandon, (eds), *Participatory Research and Evaluation: Experiments in Research as a Process of Liberation* (Delhi: Indian Social Institute, 1981).

FIFV, 'A Vision for Television', *Seminar* (Alternatives in Communication), 455, 1997 (July).

Fiske, J., *Television Culture* (London: Methuen, 1987).

Garnham, N., 'The Myths of Video: A Disciplinary Reminder', in *Capitalism and Communication: Global Culture and the Economics of Information* (New Delhi: Sage, 1990), pp. 20–55.

Giddens, A., *The Constitution of Society: Outline of Theory of Structuration* (Cambridge: Polity, 1984).

———, 'Action, Subjectivity and the Constitution of Meaning', *Social Research*, no. 53, 1986, pp. 529–45.

Gill, S. S., *Information Revolution in India: A Critique* (Delhi: Rupa, 2004).

Gitelman, L and G. Pingree, (eds), *New Media, 1740–1915* (Cambridge: The MIT Press, 2003).

Goody, J., *The Domestication of the Savage Mind* (Cambridge: Cambridge University Press, 1977).

———, *The Interface Between the Written and the Oral* (Cambridge: Cambridge University Press, 1993).

Gupta, S. K., 'Sociology of Communication', in *Survey of Research in Sociology and Social Anthropology, Vol. II* (New Delhi: ICSSR and Satvahana Publications, 1985), pp. 151–67.

Hall, A. G. and R. Tandon (eds), *Creating Knowledge: A Monopoly? Participatory Research in Development* (New Delhi: Society for Participatory Research in Asia, 1982).

Hartman, P., B. R. Patil and A. Dighe, *The Mass Media and Village Life* (New Delhi: Sage, 1989).

Heyer, P., 'Empire, History, and Communications Viewed from the Margins: The Legacies of Gordon Childe and Harold Innis', *Continuum: The Australian Journal of Media & Culture*, vol. 7, no. 1, 1993.

His, A. (ed.), *Communication and Multimedia for People: Moving into Social Empowerment over the Information Highway* (Paris: Fondation Leopold Mayer pour le Progres de l'Homme, 1996).

Innis, H., *Empire and Communication* (Toronto: University of Toronto Press, 1972).

Jhally, S., 'Communications and the Materialist Conception of History: Marx, Innis and Technology', *Continuum: The Australian Journal of Media & Culture*, vol. 7, no. 1, 1993.

Johnson, Kirk., *Television and Social Change in Rural India* (New Delhi: Sage, 2000).

Krishnan, Prabha and Anita Dighe, *Affirmation and Denial: Construction of Femininity of Indian Television* (New Delhi: Sage, 1990).

Lévy, P., *L'intelligence collective—Pour une anthropologie du cyberspace* (Paris: La Decouverte, 1997, first published 1981).
Mankekar, P., *Screening Culture, Viewing Politics: An Ethnography of Television, Womanhood, and Nation in Postcolonial India* (Duke University Press, 1999).
McLuhan, M., *Understanding Media* (New York: McGraw-Hill, 1964).
Melkote, S. R., *Communication for Development in the Third World: Theory and Practice* (New Delhi: Sage, 1991).
Mitra, Ananda, *Television and Popular Culture in India: A Study of the Mahabharata* (New Delhi: Sage, 1993).
Monteiro, A. and K. P. Jayashankar, 'The Spectator-Indian: An Exploratory Study of the Reception of News', *Cultural Studies*, 8 (1), 1993.
Mosco, V., *Political Economy of Communication* (Sage, 1996).
Murdock, G., 'Critical Inquiry and Audience Activity', in Brenda Dervin, Lawrence Grossberg, Barbara J. O'Keefe and Ellen Wartella (eds), *Rethinking Communication* (Newbury Park: Sage, 1989), pp. 226–49.
Nair, S. K. and S. A. White (eds), *Perspectives on Development Communication* (New Delhi: Sage, 1996).
Parthasarathi, V., 'The Problem', *Seminar* (Alternatives in Communication), no. 455, 1997 (July).
Patankar, P. and Lillian De, *Social Communication in Family Planning: A Case Book* (New Delhi: Orient Longman, 1973).
Pavarala, V., 'Studying Television Audiences: Problems and Possibilities', *Journal of Arts and Ideas*, nos. 32–33, 1999 (April), pp. 95–106.
Poitevin, G., Review of *Creating Knowledge: A Monopoly? Participatory Research in Development* by A. G. Hall and R. Tandon (eds), *Sociological Bulletin*, vol. 32, no. 2, 1982 (September), pp. 220–24.
———, 'Subaltern Participation or Democratic Cooperation'. Paper presented at seminar on 'Culture, Communication and Power' organized by CSH and CCRSS, February 1997.
Raghavan, G. N. S., *Development and Communication in India* (New Delhi: Gyan Books, 1992).
Rajagopal, A., *Politics after Television: Hindu Nationalism and the Reshaping of the Public in India* (Cambridge: Cambridge University Press, 2001).
Rao, Y. V. L., *Communication and Development: A Study of Indian Villages* (Minneapolis: University of Minneapolis Press, 1966).
Rogers, E., *Communication and Development: Critical Perspectives* (Beverley Hills: Sage, 1976).
Roy, P., F. B. Waisanen and E. M. Rogers, *Impact of Communication on Rural Development: An Investigation in Costa Rica and India* (Hyderabad: National Institute of Community Development, 1969).
Singh, Y., Background paper towards workshop on 'Social Sciences: Communication, Anthropology and Sociology', organized by the Centre for Studies in Civilizations, New Delhi and the Indian Council of Philosophical Research, New Delhi, 2003.

Singhal, A. and E. M. Rogers, *India's Information Revolution* (New Delhi: Sage, 1989).
Sinha, D., 'Info-Age and Indian Intellectuals: An Unfashionable Poser', *Economic and Political Weekly*, 25 November 2000.
Slack, J. D., 'Contextualising Technology' in Brenda Dervin, Lawrence Grossberg, Barbara J. O'Keefe and Ellen Wartella (eds), *Rethinking Communication* (Newbury Park: Sage, 1989), pp. 329–45.
Thomas, P., 'GATS and Trade in Audio-Visuals: Culture, Politics and Empire', *Economic and Political Weekly*, 16 August 2003.
Tomaselli, K. G. and J. Prinsloo, 'Video, Realism and Class Struggle: Theoretical Lacunae and the Problem of Power', *Continuum: The Australian Journal of Media & Culture*, 3 (2), 1990.
UNESCO, *Our Creative Diversity. Report of the World Commission on Culture and Development* (Paris: UNESCO, 1995).
Vitalis, Andre, 'ARTICLE' in A. His (ed.), *Communication and Multimedia for People: Moving into Social Empowerment over the Information Highway* (Paris: Fondation Leopold Mayer pour le Progres de l'Homme, 1996).
Wallerstein, I. et al., *Open the Social Sciences* (New Delhi: Vistaar, 1997).
Williams, R., 'Base and Superstructure in Marxist Cultural Theory', *New Left Review*, no. 82, 1977 (November–December).
Woollacott, J., 'Messages and Meanings' in Michael Gurevitch, Tony Bennett, James Curran and Janet Woollacott (eds), *Culture, Society and the Media* (London: Methuen, 1982).
Wright, Susan and N. Nelson, 'Participatory Research and Participant Observation: Two Incompatible Approaches', in Susan Wright and Nici Nelson (eds), *Power and Participatory Development: Theory and Practice* (London: ITP 1995), pp. 43–60.

PART 1

CONSTRUCTIONS AND CONFIGURATIONS

EDITORS

Introduction

As knowledge accumulates, we turn to the past to test established interpretations. For instance, with the growth of scholarship in communication theory in recent years, not only does the history of media appear to have greater significance but it also provides wider possibilities for disciplined investigation. This section is thus driven by an interest to, first, analyse the interplay of communication and society, in a manner that historicizes configurations of the former. This will contribute to knowledge in those streams of research that attempt to demonstrate how our present media culture has emerged from the past. Towards this, we are aided by the fact that the sphere of cultural production is such that with the passage of time one is not only able to draw greater lessons from the past, but accumulate wider material and, significantly, intellectual resources to do so.

Second, this historical turn also prevents us from dissociating communication from those dimensions of an aggressive modernity, namely, the faith in progress and the will to transform an old world of obsolete traditions. While post modern enthusiasts are celebrating and pleased to side with the flow of the present moment, critical analysis has to look behind and beneath it. For, an understanding of the history of these terms deepens our appreciation of their multiple meanings, empirical utility and normative potential. The dynamics at the centre of modernity's institutional nexus establish the basic parameters for everyday experience, but they do not, in themselves, provide the discursive and representational resources that render it meaningful.[1] Thus, to understand how human relationships and societal norms become the playing field for mediatic practices, we need to examine modernity's cultural formations by revisiting questions on configurations of the media, ideology and governmentality, itself a discursively complex exercise.

This is the twin context in which something can be said about the first section, wherein essays represent the ways of thinking that are enmeshed in the problems of a history of the present. These paradoxes make possible and lie behind the discussion in much of this volume, but are engaged with in a more direct and exhaustive manner here by looking at three arenas—public policy concerning communication technologies, the administration of broadcasting and the domain of the media industry. This section is aimed in part at enlarging the compendium of knowledge of various institutions of the media, but more at enriching it by cross examining individual inferences. The objective is to present the relationships between historical variables shaping specific configurations of the media within an era, as also a continuum of certain dynamics across eras, across techno-industrial configurations. Thus, starting from the telegraph, through the gramophone, radio, television, newspapers and computer mediated communication, we seek the elements of a more general approach to the dynamics of the media—from colonial, through late colonial to postcolonial times. Influenced by currents in 'historical sociology',[2] the objective of the coupling of essays in this first section is at once empirical and theoretical, their implications methodological and epistemological, be it media history or communication theory.

We begin by looking at the most significant 'new media' of the nineteenth century, the telegraph. 'Beyond the reach of monkeys and men'? raises significant insights on the relationship between state, private enterprise and intellectual property rights within nineteenth century colonial India. As Deep Kanta Lahiri Choudhury puts it, the right of patent which guaranteed the preservation of intellectual property rights was solely restricted to registration, that is recognition by the Crown, of inventions made only on British soil. This patent was no simple ordering of ideational activity; it was embodied in the physical design of the device under patent. This embodiment and physicality crucially distinguished between what was recognized by the metropolitan state and what was palmed off in the colony. Moreover, the discursive formation of the early nineteenth century colonial state directly intervened in information flows to the colonized society, a restrictive flow that also implied the political maintenance of certain institutionalized silences and absences. Ultimately, this strategic manipulation of knowledge meant the disruption of rational information feedback systems arguably essential to the partly consensual narrativizing of the nation.

The veiled political import of this has been never more crucial over the last 150 years than in todays transition into informatization. From the 1960s, the state had initiated a series of informatization programmes in successive waves, food crops, hygiene, birth control being the primary objects of such mega-missions. It is in these efforts at outreach that we witness the earliest incorporation of systemic media technologies—be it SITE in the 1970s or NICNET in the 1980s. By structuring techno-information systems in a particular way, attempts were made to forge alliances at four distinct levels— with the population, the family, the community and the nation, something visible in health campaigns today.[3] 'Information Society as if Communication Mattered', argues that although India shows signs of the onset of an 'information society', there is a need to ensure that human interaction has centrality in it. Differentiating between information and communication, and tracing the roots of 'information society' as a techno-utopia in which technology is accorded greater agency than people, the essay explains why and how in the world's largest democracy an information society with a communicative foundation is to be constructed. The essay identifies the Indian state—at a time when it is witnessing, the ascendance of market-led forces not always at its own terms—as the key medium-cum-mediator in founding the proposed information society. Criticising the government's past performance for being insufficiently communicative vis-à-vis its citizens, Dipanker Sinha contends that in the postliberalization era a number of cues should induce the Indian state to shed its defensive role in the mechanical installation of 'information society'.

This chapter, when read after the previous one, also reflects the fragile character of the decolonisation project in post-British India. We may argue that information and regulation in a particular policy domain is at one a colonising project in itself and a vehicle for more general surveillance and intervention. Viewing colonialism as a project of modernity, 'Mediating Modernity' looks at 'colonialism' as a project of modernity in the sense that the societies the colonialists possessed, administered and reformed elsewhere, were understood as objects to be surveyed, regulated and sanitised. Colonial projects were culturally and strategically complex. They entailed a whole worldview that imagined economic, political and cultural representations. The dynamics at the centre of colonial modernity's institutional nexus establish the basic parameters for everyday experience, but they do not, in themselves, provide the discursive and representational resources that render it meaningful. The practice of governing can conversely be understood as a discursively complex exercise. This complexity can be assessed through various dimensions that the colonial modernity has articulated and attempted to establish through a 'colonial order' in the alien society. The Indian example to Radio Broadcasting reveals one of these instances where information and regulation in a particular policy domain—is at once a colonising project in itself and at the same time contradictory in formulation and implementation. Besides, whether the official campaign of radio propaganda was ever able to deliver that management of public opinion? To put it simply, did official radio propaganda make any impact on the wartime public opinion of the native? These are some of the questions, which still haunt the scholarship.

Although radio is no longer a government monopoly, it would be wrong to assume that this in itself is a sign of democratization.[4] Such an assumption would successfully hide two phenomena. First, that privatization and deregulation of broadcasting does not mean much if it fails to play a vital role in our lives, reflect our anxieties and aspirations as a society. Second, the degovernmentalization of broadcasting itself has a long and meandering past in India, which poses many issues in writing its history.[5] Interestingly, a cursory look at this points out that since the late 1980s, proponents of democracy and laisez faire equally started to speak in the language of individual freedom and choice. 'In Search of Autonomy' takes us through such debates, constantly emphasizing that the dialectics of autonomy and privatization, which contrary to popular perception are not necessarily complementary, be considered in the context of the global processes of the retreat of the state and the demand for 'free flow of information'. We may recall that the idea of 'free flow of information', originating in the 1970s, arose out of the concern for making information free from governmental control and censorship. But in the same breath it must be mentioned that a major boost to these ideas was given by the media conglomerates claiming to have the sole capability of providing objective news. The first part of Shanti Kumar's essay discusses how the nationalist agenda of public broadcasting defined the question of 'autonomy' in Indian television from the early 1950s to the late 1980s; especially how, during this period, the concept of 'national programming' served as the guiding framework for broadcasting policies in India, thus culminating in the drive to rapidly expand the Doordarshan network during the early 1980s. The second part of the chapter examines how the rise of corporate television since the 1990s has posed a serious threat to Doordarshan's hegemony over national programming.

This influences us to share another observation on standing research in communication: viz., almost all writings venturing into the past of our media focus on the state—colonial or post-colonial. Undoubtedly this has brought forward significant scholarship concerning aspects of the early media configurations in the colonial era.[6] However, this state-centredness, together with the culturalist emphasis in media studies as a whole, has led to minimal investigations on the industrial and commercial foundations of the incipient media industries, especially that of the business of early recorded music.[7] This is where 'Construing a "New Media" Market' bring in a fresh perspective by excavating the varied commercial mechanisms that together went into the making of the incipient records industry. The essay scrutinizes aspects concerning the emergence of the domestic market for prerecorded music in a peripheral economy like British India during the first decade of the twentieth century. By grasping the interplay between the dynamics that propelled the manufacture of recorded music, the mechanisms of merchandising the 'Talking Machine' and the grammar of advertising for machines and music, Vibodh Parthasarathi shows us how 'music on record' was 'delivered' in and within India. Herein, explicit is an emphasis on the fact that integral to the economic order of the incipient records industry was the creation of value systems conditioning its nascent market. Because our current perception of 'canned' music has so deeply been shaped by the nature of consumer products subsequent to the gramophone, and the image systems around these products, we tend to ignore how their relationship came to be grounded in the first place.[8] It is unmasking this historical construction that forms the locus of the author's investigation into the commercial representation of the Talking Machine as a 'new media' during the formative decade of the records industry in India.

The successive integration of radio and television into the commercial framework added new possibilities to the world of creating value systems, and through that to selling goods and services. That advertising agencies, along with proprietors of the print and electronic media, not merely position advertisements but mediate the manifest content—and the 'flow' of television content[9]—is evident to all. But today it would insufficient to say that content has been commodified; that was a phenomenon which began with the commercialization of the mass media. The shift we notice everyday in the media from 'content' to 'product' is not merely indicative of a new commercial semantics; it is demonstrative of a new epistemology of 'information'. Its exponents unabashedly argue that advertisements create the necessary conditions for 'free choice', and thus constitute a prerequisite for the successful functioning of democracy in the market. It could, however, well be argued that the media's financial dependence on corporate advertisements logically erodes its autonomy, and thereby its role as the fourth estate of democracy. Keeping alive this debate, 'A Question of Choice' explores the contradiction between the visible surfeit of choices the consumer is offered today and the invisible constraints that commercial forces wield over the media— constraints deciding not only the range and limit of choices but operating in a manner that render such forces towards further invisibility. Maitrayee Chaudhuri argues that advertisements in the media have functioned as rhetorics of India's project of economic liberalization to alter the central motifs of Indian public discourse. This reiterates the author's proposition that the relationship between the apparent freedom of the individual and that of the press in a market dominated media environment needs careful analysis. This is in line with her intent to explore the contradiction between the freedom of the consumer/reader/viewer to excercise options, and the controls on the media eroding the very freedom of the fourth estate of our liberal democracy. It is within this space that the consumption of commodities and services globally come to imply, the author infers, not just the satisfaction of material aspirations but imbibing a new identity, both economic and cultural.

This is the reality of our virtuality or, if you like, vice versa! But all this takes place in a less dramatic manner than how it may appear here; hence, we tend to gloss over it in our daily lives, or insufficiently investigate it in our analytical pursuits. Realizing that a history of the media ought to be not merely idiographic, the section illustrates a theoretical and methodological pluralism, which traverses conventional disciplinary boundaries. In doing so, authors have recognized advances in fields of inquiry seemingly distant—from history of technology to business history, from social theory to policy studies. This, we believe, is central to remooring the field of communication in India. The 'interdisciplinary' character to this volume is not to convince readers that the terrain being covered here is multi, or even transdisciplinary. Rather, we wish to stress the importance of political economy as a mode of inquiry facilitating such an interplay—an interplay evident, additionally, as much within as between these writings. Congenital to such interdisciplinarity is the risk of not fully satisfying sociologists, anthropologists, historians and cultural theorists; but like any other risk, this has been exciting to compile and will be worthwhile to pursue further.

Notes

1. G. Murdock, 'Communication and the Constitution of Modernity', *Media, Culture and Society*, 15, 1993, pp. 521–39.
2. I. Wallerstein, *Open the Social Sciences* (New Delhi: Vistaar, 1997).
3. The coming of a new set of information products and services during the 1990s facilitated the expansion of the domestic communication industry and the corporate sector joined in; these very four levels became the playing field to expound their brands, products and services. Be it statist or corporate interests, we notice the creation of a new visuality of the human body, the family, the community, the nation and that of progress in general, based on values that variedly appear to be historically alien, analytically contradictory and ideologically conservative. Mani Shekhar Singh and Aditya Bharadwaj, 'Communicating Immunisation: The Mass Media Strategies', *Economic and Political Weekly*, 19–26 February 2000.
4. Frederick Noronha, 'Who's Afraid of Radio in India?', *Economic and Political Weekly*, 16 September 2000.
5. S. Poduval, 'The Possible Histories of Indian Television', *Journal of Arts and Ideas*, 32–33, 1999 (April), pp. 107–18.
6. On early cinema, see P. Woods, 'Film Propaganda in India, 1914–1923', *Historical Journal of Film, Radio and Television*, 15, 1995, pp. 543–53; S. Hughes, 'Policing Silent Film Exhibition in Colonial South India', in Ravi S. Vasudevan (ed.), *Making Meaning in Indian Cinema* (New Delhi: Oxford University Press, 2000). On early radio, besides the contribution by Biswajit Das in this volume, see D. Lelyveld, 'Transmitters and Culture: The Colonial Roots of Indian Broadcasting', *South Asia Research*, 10 (1), 1990.
7. An exception being Kinnear's writings which, however, are limited to tracing the trajectory of individual firms; see his *The Gramophone Company's First Indian Recordings—1899–1908*

(Bombay: Popular Prakashan, 1994); and *The Gramophone Company's Indian Recordings—1908 to 1910* (Australia: Hidelberg, 2000).

8. For instance, so used to we are today to recorded music as our primary mode of musical entertainment, and our homes as the primary site for its consumption, that we assume a congenital relationship between them. So much so that in research in ethno-musicology and cultural studies in India, a focus on live music—be it performative or ritual—is implicitly associated with the study of forms and sites of music pertaining to agrarian, rural societies.

9. The idea of looking at television programming in terms of 'flows' has been theorized and explained at length in R. Williams, *Television: Technology and Cultural Form* (London: Routledge, 1990).

1.1
Fulcrums of Administration

3

'BEYOND THE REACH OF MONKEYS AND MEN'?
O'Shaughnessy and the Telegraph in India, c.1836–1856[*]

DEEP KANTA LAHIRI CHOUDHURY

The invention of the post produced politics...
We do not politick with the Mogol.
—Montesquieu, *Mes Pensèes*, no. 1,760 [1]

This is a study of the early history of the telegraph in India. The East India Company's government in India introduced a number of important technologies like the steamboat, the railway, gaslights and the telegraph during the first half of the

---

[*]This chapter is based on a section of my M. Phil. dissertation 'Communication and Empire: The Telegraph in India, c.1830–1856', supervised by Professor S. Bhattacharya, Jawaharlal Nehru University, Delhi. I also thank Professor C.A. Bayly, University of Cambridge, for his kind help. All errors and opinions are mine. According to the editors' requirements I have edited this essay originally published in the *Indian Economic and Social History Review*, 37 (3), 2000. Almost five years later there are many things I could add, qualify, and clarify. However, I have not added to or materially altered the original argument. For a more extended argument about the colonial state, the Asiatic Society, and 'traditional' versus 'modern' routes of communication, please see the article.

nineteenth century. This essay focuses on the early experiments in telegraph carried out by Dr William Brook O'Shaughnessy between 1836 and 1839, and the system he established by 1856. Dr O'Shaughnessy came out to India as a medical officer in 1834 and was soon a prominent member of the Asiatic Society and the European scientific community in India. He experimented with the telegraph within a year of Samuel Finley Breese Morse's experiments in the United States. Morse is recognized as the inventor of the telegraph and the author of the Morse Code. An analysis of O'Shaughnessy's life and times is impɔrtant in understanding the system of telegraphs he established in India. It also focuses on questions regarding original invention and intellectual property rights in India in the first half of the nineteenth century.

Under O'Shaughnessy's direction, miles of overhead telegraph lines cut across the sky to link Peshawar, Agra, Bombay, Madras and Calcutta to the military cantonments and important European settlements in the 'interior'. The great gulf between the bustling hubs of colonial and mercantile commerce like Calcutta and Bombay and the interior or hinterland was physically and visually illustrated by the telegraph and its high poles that transected the countryside. Most of the basic structure was built with rapidity after 1852, and by 1856 the first telegraph network of over 4,000 miles was in place. The telegraph, railways, steamboats and the centralized postal system were the pride of the administration under the Governor General Lord Dalhousie when he left India in 1856. A few months after his departure, the uprisings of 1857 broke out. The British government in India was never to be the same again. The transformation of the state in India, and in part the uprisings of 1857, have to be viewed in the context of the technologies that the East India Company introduced during the period 1830–56. These technologies, in turn, need to be examined in terms of policies of the centralizing state in this period. O'Shaughnessy's activities are placed against the backdrop of the period 1830–56 to understand both his career and the system he helped build. His career in India exemplifies the transition from 'orientalist' governance to state initiative in science and technology. This is also a study of an early government monopoly and its ideology. State policy was crucial in determining the contours of research and development. Colonial technology, like the legal or the commercial system, was a fait accompli that was to subsequently become a bitter site of subversion and repression, negotiation and appropriation. As an early commentator observed on the cause of lack of progress in 'Indian science and research', '... Surely not a want of genius: undoubtedly not a want of funds; but want of encouragement from that source which can alone make the task effectual; the Government.'[2]

O'Shaughnessy was very much a part of the change in the 1830s: centralization of government, institutionalization of scientific enterprise and the hardening of imperial attitude. The imperial state was defining its role as well as the roles of its personnel during the 1830s, especially the role and activities of Europeans in the public arena. There was a rigid and restrictive definition of the space for individual enterprise. Given his presence at the senior levels of the Asiatic society and his official position at the mint, O' Shaughnessy was at the centre of these happenings. When Dr Saroj Ghose argues that '...liberal and firm government support induced him [O' Shaughnessy] to come out of the laboratory and launch a grand technological enterprise',[3] the historical context and the imperatives within which O'Shaughnessy worked does not emerge. The shift from an innovator to an administrator while O'Shaughnessy implemented the telegraph was not necessarily a natural process for an original mind. It was a period that saw the transition from original scientific enquiry and individual research to state-controlled technological enterprise.

The First Proposal for a Telegraph in India

The first proposal to build a telegraph system in India came in 1838 when Adolphe Bazin offered an elaborate if impractical proposal. Bazin proposed to build an 'Electro-hydraulic telegraph for effecting correspondence between Calcutta, London and the rest of the world'. A subcommittee was constituted with O'Shaughnessy to consider the proposal. The committee was requested to submit a report on the proposal by August 1839. It rejected Bazin's proposals. O'Shaughnessy argued for a more simple system than the one proposed. He pointed out the problems of humidity and moisture confronting any plan that proposed to use non-insulated 'common-electricity' in the climatic condition of India. The notion of an efficient and economical single wire and code system was unacceptable to Bazin and this was the ultimate ground of O'Shaughnessy's rejection of the proposals. O'Shaughnessy commented, 'M. Bazin's plans, although very ingenious, were altogether impracticable, and demanded the use of thirty conductors where only one is actually requisite.'[4]

O'Shaughnessy's interest in electrochemical conductivity is evident from as early as 1835. Given his experiments in 1835–36 with batteries and electrical conductors and his own statements, it would appear that he was well into the telegraph experiments by 1837. In 1835–36, he built an electromagnetic motor and was involved in the construction of a 1,000 cell Mullins battery. In a letter to the Secretary to the Government Bengal, O'Shaughnessy described himself as the man 'who in 1837 declared an electric telegraph to be a practicable thing....[and] proved it to be so in 1838'. He went to record that the 'reward' for his early efforts was 'universal ridicule for the advancement of such visionary and impracticable ideas.'[5] It would appear that his breakthrough in electromagnetic communication came in 1838. His first successful experiment with the telegraph was conducted in May 1839 and he described his experiment in September in *The Journal of the Asiatic Society*. In this essay, he mentions at least one previous occasion where he had fallen into the 'error of indulging prematurely in dreams of useful results, and of reasoning unguardedly from the model to the machine.'[6]

The history of the practical implementation of the telegraph project is entangled with the history of electricity and electrochemical conductors. The process recorded a crowded history with several successful improvements in design. Volta created the battery, Oersted noted the connection between electric current and magnetism, and Joseph Henry built the electromagnet. Schilling and Henry offered models that Sir William Fothergill Cooke and Sir Charles Wheatstone adapted in building a complicated five-needle telegraph instrument around late 1837. Steinheil of Munich announced his success, again with a relatively complicated system, in September 1838. S.F.B. Morse, the man who is acknowledged to be the first to successfully install the telegraph, would later claim that he had worked it all out in his mind as early as 1835. The period, then, was clearly one of intense competition over the successful patenting of a telegraph system. Morse's first successful demonstrations were held in front of friends only in late 1837. Morse built a circuit of 1,700 feet of copper wire on the premises of the University of New York. A commercial organization of iron and brass workers from New Jersey, Messrs Vale, was interested and agreed to finance Morse who applied for patent rights. Government support came in 1844 and he built the line from Baltimore to Washington. Between 1837 and 1839, it was a question of patenting the most efficient device, code and system. This question of originality and authorship raised the stakes considerably in a politically charged context in which nations were increasingly accorded their status in a civilizational hierarchy based on technological achievement.[7]

O'Shaughnessy's 1839 experiment laid down the characteristic pattern of his contribution. Iron rods half an inch in diameter, supported by bamboo poles covered a circuit of 450 feet multiplied by 240 feet at the Botanical Gardens in Calcutta. O'Shaughnessy discovered for himself that the 'igniting distance increased in an arithmetical ratio with the mass of the conducting wire', that is, it was the optimum balance between the diameter of the wire and its length which determined its resistance to conductivity. He designed a battery of 12 to 20 pieces of platinum wire with zinc plates. He designed the signalling instrument with the help of skilled watchmakers and mechanics in Calcutta. The experimental part of the system used the resources of the two leading mechanics at Calcutta and Grindle's watchmaking workshop.[8] His original design incorporated important elements of indigenous metallurgical skills as well as the urban skills concentrated in Calcutta. These skilled and trained workers as well as the workforce involved in the village forge are easily ignored in the accounts of indigenous participation, as is the daily labour of entire families on the construction site. From curious crowds and farseeing businessmen to metal workers and *mistris*, a broad spectrum of the indigenous population was a part of the success of O'Shaughnessy's telegraph project. Iron rods were easily available and cheap. Bamboo was abundant in Bengal. These measures were not just economical at this juncture but were original in doing away with insulators, non-conductors and winding apparatus needed in a wire system. He also came up with another unique invention; he used a two-and-a-half mile stretch of the Hooghly river, in place of wire, to complete the circuit. He was one of the earliest to experiment with a system for using water as a conducting medium for electricity.

A study of the early experiments of O'Shaughnessy reveals several significant features. First, he pursued original research to implement his scientific projects. This made him a pioneer in many areas of translation of science into technology. Second, O'Shaughnessy used material and resources available to him in India to build his instruments and conduct his projects. This allowed him to link up with different skills and traditions. Third, his contributions were made more original by their simplicity of design. It has been argued that O'Shaughnessy's activities represent a 'downward adaptation' of technology from the core to the periphery.[9] But this was not necessarily a more crude system or design. O'Shaughnessy's originality lay in his ability to replace and substitute technology. Throughout the period 1835–50, he exhibited his interest in a wide variety of scientific and academic subjects. As early as 1837–38, he experimented with photographic equipment.[10] This was, again, when photograph technology was in its infancy and his camera was original in that he manufactured it in Calcutta. Yet, locating his exact place in a narrative of telegraphic invention proves to be difficult because of the time that elapsed between his 1839 experiments and the final system sanctioned by the government in 1852. It would appear that the Irish innovator missed the mark chronologically in the short period of the telegraph patenting race between 1835 and 1837. But since this was a phase in the history of the technology of the telegraph when the claim was to make not just the first but also the most efficient instrument, the question becomes more complex. The question of how original his inventions were in the history of technology needs to be put differently. What needs to be asked is; what was the level of support and opportunity he received to record his inventions and what was the intellectual milieu within which he operated? This would serve to indicate what O'Shaughnessy himself thought he could claim to have achieved and what the state or the metropolis to which he looked for support was willing to recognize.

Intellectual Property Rights in the Colony

Patents have been discussed as indices of technological progress. Scholars have pointed out that the number of patents are inadequate indices of the quality of technological progress. Patenting is the key to the technological hierarchy between technology-generating and technology-duplicating countries. As Basalla pointed out, 'every industrialized nation in the West has made patenting a national institution.'[11] Their numbers and description have provided a base upon which to investigate further scientific and technological activity.[12] This is not to argue that patents caused technological change but to point to the continued use of patents in most industrialized nations, both as an integral part of nationalist ideology as well as a centralized record of invention. The patent was not restricted to the field of ideas but, in this period, was manifest in the physicality of the object under patent. The artefact was both a statement of individual innovation as well as a public declaration of monopoly for profit. The artefact was an object to be seen, a subject of public knowledge and a challenge for further innovation and improvement. Sir William Blackstone noted, 'The King's Grants are a matter of public record....Open letters...so called because they are not sealed up but exposed to open view. And therein they differ from certain other letters of the King, which not being proper for public inspection, are closed up.'[13] Patents were valuable means of diffusion of scientific and technological knowledge and of promoting competition between innovators.

There were no patent rights available in the colony. Only those inventions that were made on British soil could be registered in the Patent Office. The patent system was introduced in India as late as 1856 and then only notionally. A properly manned office with an extensive archival facility emerged almost a decade later.[14] Patents were crucial not only as records of innovations but also as standards for measuring technological superiority. Nationalism was therefore enmeshed with the question of intellectual property rights. The ideology of technological superiority was promoted through a 'heroic' narrative of competing European, British and American national inventors, and patents were the overt manifestations of this increasingly powerful ideology. The absence of this legal safeguard and support structure distinguished between what was recognized by the metropolitan state and what was given recognition in the colony.

The telegraph was the result of a long process of theoretical and practical innovation. By the 1830s the telegraph needed to be implemented on a tangible plane. It was a question of time and the most efficient model. In this competition to be the first and the best, O'Shaughnessy did not stand a chance. India was separated from European metropolitan areas by a considerable period of sailing time. The Suez Canal had not been built and steamships were still in their infancy. It was still an India where the Anglo-Indian received the 'packet from Home' after long intervals. The average time taken in the 1830s was anything between four to six months sailing time. Faced with a large time lag and the lack of a standardized record, O'Shaughnessy was doomed to remain a 'colonial inventor', a special case for India. No device that he designed had a chance of recognition outside the patent system. The crowded nature of the development of the telegraph in this period combined with the lack of an adequate measure of comparison and record meant that the question of O'Shaughnessy's originality became an impossible question to answer.

Patent Companies versus Enterprise in India

The Court of Directors forwarded the next proposal for an electric telegraph in India in 1849. Governor General Lord

Dalhousie, faced with the start of The Afghan wars and the demands of a newly annexed Burma, readily endorsed the idea. Whishaw, an employee of the British patent-holding Gutta Percha Company, offered to build a telegraph for India. The technological know-how would come from Britain; the labour and finance from India. The plan proposed a wholly subterranean telegraph network. This also meant a calculation of enormous profit from the use of *gutta percha* as an insulator. The Court asked about the 'suitability' of the electric telegraph for India, that is, how viable was the telegraph technology in the context of India; the Government's opinion about the type of system to be adopted for India, that is, overground versus underground lines; the suitability of *gutta percha* as an insulator; the strategic and commercial potential and need for the telegraph in India; finally, the suitability of Whishaw's proposals for India.[15]

Dalhousie and his Council referred the matter to the Military Board to report after consultation with their telegraph 'experts'. The two most qualified authorities in India were Dr O'Shaughnessy, and his superior officer at the Calcutta Mint, Lieutenant Colonel William Nairn Forbes. Lieutenant Colonel Forbes was the architect of the Mint and St Paul's Cathedral in Calcutta. He was not only one of the most senior scientific officers in British India but also an 'expert' on the telegraph because he had recently visited England and physically 'seen' the 'inside' of a telegraph office.[16] This expertise with its emphasis on visual observation needs to be placed against the fact that when the system was completed in India, the Telegraphs Act forbade all 'public' from seeing the inside of a telegraph office without permission of the authorities. One of the reasons behind the prohibition might have been the fear of duplication and uncontrolled diffusion of the early instruments and system.

O'Shaughnessy and Forbes both rejected Whishaw's proposal. The *gutta percha* recommended as a coating to protect the lines was found to not last very long, especially in the saline conditions that were common in southern Bengal. The two experts concluded that the suggestions of the patent-holding Gutta Percha Company were not suitable for implementation in India. However, in their reports the two of them took opposite positions. They differed over the question of overhead lines versus underground lines. The lines in Britain were overhead lines while in parts of the continent, especially Prussia, the underground cable system was followed. O'Shaughnessy suggested the use of underground lines. His main criticism of the proposal was the projected costs and the profit margin for the Gutta Percha Company. He argued that the *gutta percha* needed to be much improved before it could be used as an insulating coating. O'Shaughnessy thought that the underground network offered greater security against interruption by not being visible and vulnerable to human and elemental damage. After rejecting Whishaw's proposal, O'Shaughnessy offered to build the system for Rs 250 per mile in contrast to Whishaw who put the basic cost at Rs 750 a mile. He went on to make it very clear that he was not interested in being asked to conduct experiments over a small distance. He offered, 'I would be happy to undertake the work for the whole of the line or any part above 100 miles at the terms proposed.'[17]

Lieutenant Colonel Forbes recommended the overground telegraph line. To further confirm this point, Forbes suggested that since O'Shaughnessy had experimented with the electric telegraph earlier, he should be instructed to construct experiments over a few miles to sort out the question of overhead versus underground telegraph lines. Once the system to be adopted had been decided upon, the whole project should be given to a British patent-holding company. It was on Forbes' recommendation that the government had given the monopoly for steam navigation to a British patent-holding company in 1828. The railways already followed a similar scheme. Forbes was a trained engineer, one of the most senior authorities on issues of science and technology and official advisor to the government. He emphasized the efficiency of metropolitan expertise and the utility of turnkey projects for India by British patent-holding companies.[18]

When the Military Board forwarded the reports to the government, they gave answers to the issues raised in the Court's despatch. They concluded about Whishaw's proposal that 'his preparations of gutta percha for insulating the wires...may not prove successful in their present state for either the overhead or the underground system.' While they stressed the relevance and necessity of the telegraphs for India, the Board advised that the introduction of the electric telegraph and the choice between the overhead and the underground lines 'would be most judiciously attempted by carrying out two experimental lines for a short distance, one on each of the systems advocated.'[19] The government entrusted O'Shaughnessy with the building of the initial line. The following comment was scribbled in pencil on the back of the report with enclosures sent by the Military Board to the Governor-General-in-Council: 'O'Shaughnessy's (report) is the more practical, Forbes' the more facetious. O'Shaughnessy to begin at once.'[20] However, the official decision concurred with the Board's recommendation, which required O'Shaughnessy to 'consult Colonel Forbes on all points connected with experiment above ground.'[21]

Previous research has glossed over this difference of opinion at the elite scientific level of British India. O'Shaughnessy complained in a letter to the Secretary to the Government of Bengal that he was:

> opposed in limene by the Chief Scientific Authority in Bengal, Lieutenant Colonel Forbes, who publicly and privately declared me to be unfit for such employment, further then concerned with 'preliminary experiments instituted on the scale of a few yards' to smooth the way for the English Engineers and Patentees: ...I defy the most unfriendly judge to find evidence of an atom of neglect or carelessness; nevertheless, it is quite clear that I have given dissatisfaction to the Mint Committee (of which Colonel Forbes is a member) who manifestly consider that I should not have undertaken any employment but under their control....Under all these circumstances...I have successfully carried into effect all that I had promised to perform...I have saved Government from the rapacity of the patentees to whom Colonel Forbes officially advised that the introduction of the electric telegraph in India should be committed.[22]

The Military Board did not accept Colonel Forbes' 'strong objections' against 'any measure that would compromise the honour or good faith of the Government by infringing legally or morally the rights of Patentees in England'. Another member of the Board, Lieutenant Colonel Hawkins, supported Forbes. Hawkins argued that since Whishaw's proposal and O'Shaughnessy's interest lay in building an underground telegraph, the overground system should not be 'subjected to inexperienced and impractical experimenters in India...suggestions should be submitted to the considerations of the Projectors in England in preference to their being tested under the present circumstances in this country'.[23]

These conflicts of interest are important both because of the issues and the men involved. Forbes was trained as an engineer. His institutional and military background may have led to an instinctive dislike of civilian experimenters and individual initiative. O'Shaughnessy was a varied innovator who experimented widely beyond the discipline of medicine in which he was originally trained. Furthermore, O'Shaughnessy was his junior at the mint. Forbes might have felt increasingly threatened by O'Shaughnessy's rise to favour. The matter at stake was whether the government in India was capable of undertaking successfully an enterprise that was not directly constructed from and by Britain. In the case of the steamships and the railways, little chance had been taken. In the case of the telegraphs, the government in India was prepared to conduct its own technological enterprise independent of British 'Engineers and Patentees'. This illusion of independence was to be lost rapidly, especially after 1857, but for time being the man in the field had won.

The First Telegraph System

The total distance covered by O'Shaughnessy's telegraph line from Calcutta to Kedgeree was 82 miles.[24] His problem was the difficulty involved in avoiding the payment of patent fees or infringing upon registered patent rights. His system, though being built much after successful networks in Europe and North America, had to be 'original' to avoid encroaching on patent rights. By the 1850s, O'Shaughnessy knew enough about the English and American telegraph systems to avoid patent problems. O'Shaughnessy used iron rods that weighed a ton to the mile. This followed up on his first experiments and was noticeably different from the systems used in America and Europe. His use of locally abundant iron and bamboo was substitutive. He used bamboo for the telegraph poles. Bamboo was easily replaced, flexible against strong winds and less expensive economically and ecologically than timber posts. Iron rods were relatively immune from 'gusts of wind or ordinary mechanical violence'. They could not be tampered with and their mass allowed a free passage to electrical current that atmospheric turbulence did little to inhibit. This innovation made redundant the entire baggage of wires, expensive winding instruments required to get the tension in the wires, insulators and glass or ceramic non-conductors. Iron was easily available in India and local forges were common in villages that could be used for repairs. Even if transport costs were added, and transport was not a problem as long as there were elephants, iron rods were cheaper than the wire system. He recorded that the 'overground system on the plan I have followed presents the great advantages of rapidity of construction, exceeding cheapness, and immunity from storms, lightning and wanton injury.'[25]

O'Shaughnessy designed a battery of 12 to 20 pieces of platinum wire with zinc plates. He redesigned the telegraph instrument so that it could be worked 'in all weathers without danger of interruption'. He was assisted in the construction of the instruments by the workshop run by G. Grindle in Calcutta. O'Shaughnessy stated that he could provide 'all stations with complete sets of instruments of every kind of battery, reverser, telegraph and alarm, with dozen reserve telegraph instruments, less than a hundred rupees'. In 1853 the signalling instrument 'was reduced to such a condition of simplicity that when deranged they could be set right by mere boys' without which he thought 'regular and sustained correspondence would be totally impracticable'.

Accordingly, because of the rapid polarisation of the magnetic needles, he successively tried and rejected the English Vertical Needle[26] Instrument and the American Dotter.[27] The magnet in the needles became permanently polarized because of the electricity in the air during thunderstorms and stopped activating the markers. He recorded that under the special climatic conditions in India, 'these [American and European] deceitful and complicated instruments are certain to become disordered....I therefore dismiss all considerations of the elaborate toys to which I allude, which however creditable to the skill of the constructor, are practically but of insignificant value.'[28]

He designed in place of these instruments a Single Needle Horizontal Telegraph in 1853. He recorded that it was 'now in use in all our stations and with which we work all weathers without danger of interruption'. He also simplified the electric current reverser in 'solidity and strength, until it now totally differs from any instrument of the kind used elsewhere'. O'Shaughnessy records how he was driven 'step by step to discard every screw, lever, pivot and foot of wire, and framework and dial, without which it was practicable to work'. He used the technological skill and materials available locally. His telegraph instrument was simple enough to be built by the signallers at the cost of 3 *sicca* rupees including profit on the construction.[29]

He invented his own signal transmitter, iron lines, reverser, battery, and telegraph code. He claimed to have simplified and modified all aspects of the telegraph so that it 'totally differed from all telegraph systems in use anywhere in the world.'[30] Metropolitan experts like C.S. Wollaston and C.V. Walker wrote testimonials congratulating O'Shaughnessy. The Superintendent of the South Eastern Telegraph Lines in Britain wrote to him in 1853, 'I have 80 telegraph stations, and 211 needles, and have but four stations with assistance competent to magnetise the needles...with the use of such simple arrangements such as yours (*I do not know why it has been hitherto overlooked*) we could get over this difficulty [emphasis mine].'[31]

The simplicity of the instrument was matched by its signalling speed. The average signalling speed on the continent and in Britain was around 20 words per minute in the 1850s. This was often less the result of efficient instruments and more because of skilled and experienced operators who could guess correctly at the word before it was completed. This was called 'cutting in' and was practised widely by the more experienced signallers comfortable with the language. O'Shaughnessy's instrument matched this average easily and without the benefit of any 'cutting in' by signallers. The Gutta Percha Company certified that tests on 130 miles of telegraph line showed that by means of instruments of the construction adopted by Dr O'Shaughnessy... [one could] without difficulty communicate and read at the rate of 20 words per minute.'[32] His code devised for use in the telegraph department approached the English alphabet rationally and used the least number of signals for the ones used most often. In this statistically consistent approach, his code was perhaps second only to Morse's.

Large-scale construction began on 1 November 1853 at 20 different places and in three rapid phases. A temporary or 'flying' line of iron rod and bamboo was set up for immediate communication and mainly for military use. This was quickly replaced by permanent posts, etc. On 24 March 1854, the Superintendent of the Electric Telegraphs in India, O'Shaughnessy, wired to the Governor General conveying his respects from Agra. Dalhousie telegraphed his congratulations in reply. Five months after start of construction, 800 miles of telegraph were operational. O'Shaughnessy won over the question of amalgamation with the railways. While admitting to the advantages to be had from following the railroad he foresaw difficulties between the interests. The telegraph was not to be built solely as a complementary system to the rails. In 1856, over 4,000 miles of telegraph were functioning. Dalhousie had gone on to annex Pegu, the Carnatic and the rest of central India. By the end of 1855, the entire line from Sagar Island, on the coast near Calcutta, connecting the key military cantonments in upper and central India until Peshawar, was complete.

The Routes Followed by the First Telegraph System

Controversy dogged the direction of the first line to be built. O'Shaughnessy suggested that a line west to Chinsurah be built. This could then be extended to Agra and Peshawar. He described the strategic and commercial advantages of such a line. He assessed commercial needs in terms of indigenous demand. According to him:

> A very large return would, in the opinion of the mercantile gentlemen consulted, be made from Mirzapore and mercantile and banking establishments of Muttra, and the Marwaree shroffs. The newspapers of Upper India would also contribute....I would consider it highly probable that these items with the amount above specified (Rs. 8 for 480 words for Calcutta and Bombay) would pay a large sum beyond the yearly expenditure and leave the telegraph eighteen hours available in the day for the use of the government without charge.[33]

J.E.D. Bethune recorded a dissenting note on the direction of the first line. He argued that until the whole line from Calcutta up to Agra was built there would be no information and commercial feedback. He suggested instead a line to Diamond Harbour or Kedgeree: 'it will be very important to have in what degree the merchants will show themselves disposed to use the opportunity offered them for having instantaneous intelligence...my own belief is that a line to the Harbour would pay but nobody wishes to correspond between Calcutta and Chinsurah, and nothing could be learned on this head in that direction until a much greater distance has been reached.'[34] The government agreed with him. The first line then was to service colonial commerce. Its lifeline was the harbour. The final solution saw all the differences reconciled. Forbes' recommendation for an overhead system was adopted. O'Shaughnessy was given the responsibility of building the system. Bethune's suggestion of servicing colonial commerce was followed. As an agent of the colonial state, O'Shaughnessy was permitted a limited and particular kind of entrepreneurial freedom. When Dalhousie called the establishment of the telegraph in India a 'national experiment',[35] he did not mean India as a nation. It was a national experiment for Britain, an investment in empire. The telegraph as it was founded had little to do with indigenous demand and supply. Adley proposed that the Calcutta-Peshawar-Agra-Bombay connection be joined with an inner loop connecting Agra-Bombay-Madras-Calcutta. While the main line to Peshawar was complete by 1856, the inner loop connecting the three colonial metropolises with Awadh and Agra was not complete. A line from Calcutta to Peshawar was built, Agra was joined to Bombay, and Bombay linked to Madras. In 1856 the line connecting Calcutta and Madras was yet to be built. In all cases Dalhousie chose the shortest and quickest route to 'meet the immediate necessities of the time.'[36] This presented a problem in 1857 as Calcutta was starved of official information and Agra, the headquarters of the North West Frontier Provinces, was isolated because of the breakdown of the Company's communication networks in central India.

The 'rationalization' of the space of India was not just restricted to survey maps and ideologies[37] but effected through the tangibility of telegraph and railway lines. They were the symbols; visual manifestations of imperial power. As the system was built, it incorporated hierarchies of access and scale, of town and country. The difference and distance between the bustling port cities of Calcutta and Bombay and the villages in the interior were made tangible by the skyline broken up with tall poles carrying the humming telegraph wires. This disciplining of space was evident in the telegraph network inaugurated in 1856. It was a linear, rational and mathematical network that linked the commercial and military nodes of the colonial state. Dalhousie explained the two principles behind the system: 'uniformity of management and unity of authority.'[38] These echoes of Benthamite ideas found visible expression in the telegraph system. O'Shaughnessy was very much a part of this ideological context. In his own perception of his achievements and in the systematic elaboration of the network, he reveals the context within which he worked.

O'Shaughnessy's Perception of his Achievements

O'Shaughnessy's own assessment of his achievements changed over the period 1835–56. In the 1830s, O'Shaughnessy's eagerness to join in the debates of his contemporaries in the

West was clear, as was his need for metropolitan recognition. He ranked his name among the pioneers of the telegraph: Henry, Cooke, Wheatstone, Steinheil and Morse. He was clearly aware of the work of these contemporaries and perhaps lacked the confidence to realize how close a contemporary in time he was to these pioneers. He acknowledged 'many eminent philosophers, such as Brande, Faraday, Wheatstone and Fox' and also that he was 'induced to institute the experiments...by the statements' he had read in 'several periodicals regarding similar attempts in England, Europe and America...and by the actual patenting adoption by the directors of the London and Birmingham railways of a plan by Professor Wheatstone'. O'Shaughnessy referred to Steinheil's article which was translated in the May issue of *Sturgeon's Annals of Electricity* and articles on the subject in *The Philosophical Magazine*, *The Transactions of the Royal Philosophical Society* and *The Arcana of Science*.[39] He published the correspondence he had with the government on the attaching of lightning conductors to powder magazines. In this debate, Faraday, James Prinsep, Roberts and Sturgeon were cited as taking the same side as O'Shaughnessy on the issue. Clearly perceiving himself to be making an original contribution to the question, O'Shaughnessy wrote, 'Our opponents are Messrs. Daniell and Harris, and both these gentlemen, I know not why, have lost their temper in the controversy'.[40] He later claimed that he was the first to cover the longest telegraphic distance. This was, he argued, because he used iron wires instead of the copper wires used by Morse for his experiment. Compared to copper, the much higher resistance of iron as an electrical conductor meant that the actual distance of 13 miles he had covered would be the equivalent of at least 21 miles of copper wire. This was an interventionist and scientific role in 1839; by the 1850s, his attitude had changed.

O'Shaughnessy valued his contribution in 1852 at a sum of Rs 20,000. In an assessment of his contribution, he cited Dr Locke of Cincinnati, who was awarded the equivalent of Rs 20,000 for the single-needle telegraph in 1851. He gave the example of James Prinsep being rewarded with Rs 5,000 for his survey of the Salt Lakes. He also mentioned case of Dr

McClelland and the reward he received for his unremunerated services as Secretary to the Coal Board. He requested for a grant of Rs 20,000. However, the cases he cites are so diverse that they serve to illustrate O'Shaughnessy's changing perception of his contributions. He had shifted from his earlier attempt to engage in debate with frontline scientific achievements and experts in the West. In 1852, O'Shaughnessy was citing examples of survey and enterprise, and throwing in his lot with the surveying enterprise that came to be important after the 1830s when the Survey Department and the Great Trigonometric Survey was institutionalized.[41] What O'Shaughnessy perceived to be his task and his achievement was the successful establishment of a telegraph system in India along models already established in the West. The movement from an inventor who intervened in leading scientific and technological debates to duplicator and administrator-entrepreneur reflects the limits of individual scientific enterprise in the colony in the first half of the nineteenth century.

The institutionalizing of scientific research and the state's monopoly over information networks intersected in the life of the Irish inventor. O'Shaughnessy was constantly aware of his distance from the metropolitan centres. Aware of the work of his contemporaries on the continent, and in England and America, he defensively stressed the difference between his system and those in use abroad. His instruments were the best for India, he claimed. What can already be sifted out are the two main motifs that O'Shaughnessy would later use to assess his own work and ask for recognition of others. First, his special knowledge as a scientist living and working in India. His expertise and contribution was the adaptation of science and technology to the special geographical and climatic conditions in India. Second, he claimed to have designed what was most efficient and economic in the Indian context. Thus, economy, efficiency and suitability in the Indian context were the main elements. O'Shaughnessy was seeing himself as an innovator whose main achievement was the adaptation of science and technology to the Indian condition. These then were, perhaps, the limits within which the innovator could achieve in the first half of the nineteenth century.

The Culture of Science

The colonial state in India underwent fundamental changes over the first half of the nineteenth century. Strong trends towards centralization of the imperial state combined with increasing regulation of the initiative permitted to its employees and its non-official sections. In 1828, the government formally forbade any official involvement with the media. In 1830, it prohibited the use of clothes worn in the Indian fashion during hours of duty and in public. The gaslights, steamships and the railways all went to metropolitan bidders. The initiative for these enterprises had originally come from private individuals and Eurasian and European businessmen but the government increasingly tightened its lines of control over enterprise in the colony. If the government rejected the proposal to award the telegraph to patentees, what it allowed was a rigidly controlled department of state to run the enterprise.

Institutionalization of previously dispersed activities was combined with stringent control over the public sphere partly exercised through the manipulation of postal rates. Between 1830 and 1850, the state was perfecting the exercise of invisible controls: manipulation through subsidy; moral and legal persuasion; and fiscal control. As Stokes put it, possibly paraphrasing Clive's famous statement regarding an imminent 'revolution' in Indian society on the eve of the Battle of Plassey in 1757, 'the revolution of Indian society was to be silently and unobtrusively effected', after the 1830s.[42] Historians have contested this view of the early nineteenth century as one of revolutionary change. The argument is that the period was more one of consolidation and control rather than change. The Company's government was constrained in India by financial difficulties while in the West, Britain was recovering and consolidating her position after the Napoleonic Wars. The period 1830–50 is described as the 'age of hiatus' in India and an age of 'constructive conservatism' in Britain.[43] This essay argues that the period was important in fashioning certain basic policies and attitudes.

O'Shaughnessy studied medicine at the University of Edinburgh. He also needs to be placed in the particular context of the Scottish enlightenment. The influence of 'common-sense philosophy' in the science curriculum in Scottish educational institutions was combined with an education in all aspects of philosophical debate.[44] An important element in the Scottish school was its emphasis on the process of hypotheses following from experiments rather than the implementation of general principles into practice. The Military Board congratulated him on his 'devotion to the cause of inductive science.'[45] Late seventeenth century chemists saw matter as made up of three elements, or 'earths', as they were called: vitreous earth gave solidity to matter; fluid earth gave it liquidity; and fatty earth, which was later called phlogiston gave it combustibility. These were the old Aristotelian elements of earth, water and fire but without air. Air was thought to be inert and not a part of other materials. All the while, a more analytical science was being built on these ideas. Working within these traditions, O'Shaughnessy saw electricity as a means of translating between the physical and the animate world, using basic elements such as air, water and fire. This research laid the basis for studies in conductivity and conductors.

His experiments were a search for the unity between the vital or living and electrical forces. In his search for the unity between the living or the vital forces and electrical currents, O'Shaughnessy followed Salva in locating in the human body the fact of such correspondence. In his diagrams he used circles and circuits, centres and peripherals and in his textual description he used Roman images such as the 'fasces',[46] the staff of state and citizenship. He experimented with electrical correspondence via the human body: 'sympathetic flesh telegraphy'. O'Shaughnessy wrote that the 'delicacy of the impressions of touch transcends the sensitivity of all other senses. The eye and ear are liable to distraction by casual sounds or phenomena, while the attentive touch knows no interruption'. He concluded that the 'most perfect sympathy is practicable between the signalists, and that as fast as the signal can be felt. In short, with but little less velocity than the articulations of language or writing of stenographic characters, this silent but thoroughly intelligible, and *still most secret of all correspondence* can take place [emphasis added]'.[47]

Emphasizing the mechanical aspect of inventions, he could link up with the artisan skills in India. However, O'Shaughnessy was also a member of the new order being brought in. As the installer of the telegraphs in India, his role was that of an administrator. This was a model that derived much of its impetus from the state seen as a machine. This was a part of the same discursive formation that led Thomas Watt to 'think' of the 'sun-and-planet' system for the wheel-pistons of the steam engine.[48] In the case of O'Shaughnessy, it was the 'fasces' and the notion of central control. By the 1850s, the emergence of anthropology and geology increasingly combined with the trend towards the wide influence of the biological model.

As early as 1839, O'Shaughnessy was preoccupied with secrecy and exclusion. Secrecy was implicit in the constitution and the elaboration of the telegraph system. The ethic of reform and amelioration that characterized many of the administrative decisions in this period was also conservative. O'Shaughnessy's main claim in the 1850s was that 'what the Government had proposed as a mere preliminary experiment has been brought into the condition of a Public Department.'[49] In 1853, he commented on the telegraph codes in circulation saying that, 'the alphabet is entirely an arbitrary one, and gives no clue to its recollection'.[50] He drew up several codes for use by the government and the military. As he recommended, 'it would be highly desirable for each public department: Political, Judicial, Financial, Military, etc., to prepare codes of numbered signals, orders, ciphers.'[51] He concluded, 'secret codes of this kind will ensure the transmission of despatches without their meaning being intelligible to the signalers.'[52] By September 1857, a recently knighted O'Shaughnessy had completed a 'Secret Cipher Code', which was 'forwarded to the Commissioner of Scinde and the Chief Commissioners in the Punjab.'[53]

The 'Legacy' of O'Shaughnessy

The history of communications under British rule has conventionally been written as the history of these institutions as public utilities. Officials writing from within the service revealed postal and telegraphic expansion under their administration as an expanding process servicing increasing numbers of people, symbolic of the benevolence of British rule.[54] Often written by retired officials in the employ of the administration or commissioned to celebrate significant anniversaries of communication systems in India, they see them in terms of a smooth naturalistic expansion and an equally smooth transition from imperial control to Indian nationhood.[55] Previous writing on the telegraph has stressed the pioneering role of O'Shaughnessy in the establishment of the telegraph in British India, and the utility of the system for the future of an independent nation. In the preface to the centenary history of the telegraph, Prime Minister Jawaharlal Nehru described the telegraph as 'one of the oldest public utilities' in the world.[56] Vijai Govind wrote in conclusion to his discussion of the contributions of O'Shaughnessy that 'he was a practical pioneer conferring a great boon on India.'[57] Studies of O'Shaughnessy and the first phase of the telegraph have continued within this tradition of writing. In an essay that summarizes in part the detailed findings of his thesis, which dealt with the scientific and engineering aspects of the telegraph, Ghose concludes:

> The history of the telegraph illustrates how rapidly, given special conditions, a western technology can be diffused .... Steamships and cannons facilitated colonial conquest, while the printing press, the telegraph and the railways established communication and transportation links necessary for efficient government. The experience of India suggests just how effective those links could be, creating *a technological legacy* that was later to serve the interests of an independent nation [emphasis mine].[58]

It is this notion of technological 'legacy' that this essay investigates. It argues for a study of different phases in the history of institutions and systems, and the need to know why a system developed in the way it did. This essay studies O'Shaughnessy as an inventor and an administrator, tries to show the hybrid character of his activities, and examine why it is so difficult to place him within a category. Recently,

Baber has stressed that the historical record would seem to suggest that a view that holds technology transfers under colonialism as inherently colonial is as simplistic as a view that would argue that colonialism was a relatively civilizing process, unconditionally facilitating the spread of science and technology from the core to the periphery.[59] The controversy between Forbes and O'Shaughnessy was a debate conducted at various levels. Both O'Shaughnessy and Forbes employed similar images and metaphors. One of O'Shaughnessy's major criticisms of the overground system was its vulnerability. They agreed that the lines must be protected by special police from 'birds, monkeys and thieves'. In his proposal, O'Shaughnessy wrote, 'our tracks will often run through *a howling wilderness* tenanted only by wild beasts, or mere savages in human form [emphasis added]'.[60]

The 'howling wilderness' of India was a reality. But it was not the only one. The telegraph, in its first phase, illustrated the differential nature of commercial and technological access; the indigene had to pay more, travel more and study physics, chemistry and electronics before the knowledge and technology of the telegraph became accessible. Lines of communication, perhaps for the first time in history, would not follow human habitation. It was a geographical reorganization of the nerves of communication within the subcontinent. Rational links were forged between the colonial centres and port cities; the rest was seen as an empty space or a 'howling wilderness'. William Forbes echoed O'Shaughnessy's phrase describing the telegraph as the 'still most secret of all correspondence', when he recommended that the lines must be raised 'beyond the reaches of monkeys and men.'[61]

The indigenous user was not the primary political or economic concern. Until 1835, indigenous letters had to pay a double rate for transmission of letters through the post office. This was to penalize these correspondents for using cheap light Indian paper.[62] This double charge was abolished and the Post Office Act 1837 tried to regularize the different rates charged by the provincial governments. In the budget and annual statements of the telegraph department, indigenous messages were classed as 'native' messages separate from private messages. What is even more interesting is that their returns were not included in the totals of profit and loss till as late as 1859.[63] A mutineer being executed is said to have exclaimed, pointing at the telegraph: 'It is that accursed wire that strangles us'. This is important in the context of the first telegraph establishment and the indigenous reaction to it. The telegraph system discouraged indigenous users. Private telegrams were delivered free of cost within a certain radius of the telegraph station, beyond which the rates increased proportionally with distance. Since the telegraph station was usually situated in the heart of the European settlements, the indigenous user had not only to pay more but also to travel greater distances to avail of these facilities.

Conclusion

In his life O'Shaughnessy played out some of the elements at work in a colonized country. The possibility of an autonomous scientific project in the colony in the 1830s that went beyond the colonial status and entered into competition with the metropolis was lost during the 1850s. O'Shaughnessy was reduced by the inexorable logic of colonialism into a blind imitator and was knighted by the metropolitan state for his excellence at mimicry and duplication of the metropolitan models. He began to fall out of favour with the government after the 1860s. He was the creator of telegraphs in India and exercised his control with what was likened at times to despotic whimsy. Younger men and different work disciplines made him an anachronism in the minutely bureaucratized structure after 1857. The telegraph after 1857 had much more to do with administration and management than with experiments. This study of the first phase of the telegraph in India sets it within the historical context of the early nineteenth century. It shows the limits, both external and internal, within which inventor and invention could exist in this period. The direction and nature of state support for technological innovation was very important in this period and was changing from a more elastic to a relatively rigid institutionalization of research. The Telegraphs Act XXXIV of 1854 was the first to lay down much of what has continued in acts regulating communication. The Act of 1885 and others since adhere to its basic template.

There were two forces clearly at work subverting scientific enterprise in the colony. At the level of structure the colonial state steadily enforced bureaucratization as is repeatedly illustrated by O'Shaughnessy's life. Secrecy dominated the moral economy of scientific enterprise while the bureaucratic principle dominated its structure. At the level of ideas, the state enforced the exclusion of the indigene from the continuing electrical innovations connected with the telegraphs by circumscribing science with secrecy. The exclusion of the indigene does not mean that his knowledge systems were excluded; rather he was physically discouraged and local artisanal skills used during the first system of the telegraphs in India were not any more a part of the project. Thus, knowledge regarding the science and technology of the telegraphs did not permeate indigenous society, as did the knowledge of printing technology. The use of a technology has to be crucially distinguished from the diffusion of a technology.[64] That the telegraphs came to be very widely used in India does not in any way imply knowledge about their principles of operation. O'Shaughnessy was very much a part of this system of secrecy and established the telegraph as the 'most secret of all correspondence'. Not surprisingly, his major interest after becoming the Superintendent was the formulation of secret cipher codes. Secrecy became a project in itself. This explains why O'Shaughnessy left innovation and became an administrator, not advancing knowledge but shrouding it in secrecy. The logic of colonialism thus subverted the logic of science by embalming it in secrecy, and this desire to control and circumscribe reduced scientific enterprise in the colony into empty mimicry. That is the main reason why O'Shaughnessy appears as a tragic figure—as much a propagator of colonialism as its victim.

Notes

1. The epigraph is from Geoffrey Bennington, 'Postal Politics and Institution of Nation', in Homi K. Bhabha (ed.), *Nation and*

Narration (London/New York: Routledge and Kegan Paul, 1990), pp. 121–37.
2. James Silk Buckingham, 'Editorial', *The Calcutta Journal*, no. 146 (Calcutta: The National Library [henceforth NL], 28 July 1819).
3. Saroj Ghose, 'The Introduction and Advancement of the Electric Telegraph in India', Ph.D. dissertation, Jadavpur University, Calcutta, 1974, p. 247.
4. W.B. O'Shaughnessy, 'Memorandum Relative to Experiments on the Communication of Telegraph Signals by Induced Electricity', *The Journal of the Asiatic Society* (henceforth JASB), vol. JLVIII, 1839 (September), pp. 714–31.
5. Home Department, Public Proceedings, 23 April 1852, No. 13: From W.B. O'Shaughnessy, Superintendent of the Electric Telegraph, to J.P. Grant, Secretary to the Government of Bengal, letter dt. 10 February 1852, National Archives of India (henceforth NAI), Delhi.
6. O'Shaughnessy, 'Memorandum'.
7. G. Basalla, *The Evolution of Technology* (Cambridge: Cambridge University Press, 1990), pp. 60–61.
8. Home Department, Public Proceedings, 21 June 1850, No. 28: From the Military Board to Major General Sir John Hunter Littler, with enclosures, dt. 4 June 1850, NAI.
9. M. Gorman, 'Sir William O'Shaughnessy, Lord Dalhousie, and the Establishment of the Telegraph System in India'. *Technology and Culture*, vol. 12, no. 4, 1971, pp. 581–601.
10. *Proceedings of the Asiatic Society*, August 1839, Asiatic Society Library, Calcutta (henceforth ASL); John Falconer, 'Photography in Nineteenth Century India', in C.A. Bayly (ed.), *The Raj: India and the British 1600–1947* (London: Antique Collectors Club Ltd, 1991), p. 267.
11. Basalla, *The Evolution*, pp. 120–24; H.I. Dutton, *The Patent System and Inventive Activity during the Industrial Revolution: 1750–1852*, (Manchester: Manchester University Press, 1984); C.T. Taylor and Z.A. Silbertson, *The Economic Impact of the Patent System: A Study of the British Experience* (Cambridge: Cambridge University Press, 1973).
12. Jacob Schmookler, *Invention and Economic Growth* (Cambridge: Cambridge University Press, 1966).
13. W. Blackstone, 'On the Rights of Things' *Commentaries*, Vol. 11, 18th edition (London, 1825), p. 316.
14. Charles Osmond, *The Law of Patents in India* (Calcutta, 1836), p. 17. I thank Mr Arijit Chaudhury for lending me a copy of this book.
15. Home Department, Public Proceedings, 26 September 1849, No. 13: Dispatch from the Court of Directors, NAI.
16. Home Department, Military Board, 14 December 1849, No. 8479: To the Secretary, Government of Bengal, NAI.

17. Home Department, Public Proceedings, 4 April 1850, No. 48: Report from Dr W.B. O'Shaughnessy, to Captain Scott, Secretary to the Military Board, dt. 24 December 1849 (henceforth 'Report I'), NAI.
18. Home Department, Public Proceedings, 4 April 1850, No. 49: From Lt. Col. W.N. Forbes, Mint Master and Superintendent of Government Machinery, to Capt. Scott, Secretary to the Military Board, dt. 19 February 1850 (henceforth 'Report II'), NAI.
19. Home Department, Public Proceedings, 4 April 1850, No. 47: From the Military Board to Sir Henry Elliott, Secretary to the Government of India, with enclosures, NAI.
20. Ibid.
21. Home Department, Public Proceedings, 4–11 April 1850, No. 429: From Sir Henry Elliott. Secretary to the Government of India, endorsing the Board's recommendations, NAI.
22. Home Department, Public Proceedings, 23 April 1852, No. 13: Letter from W.B. O'Shaughnessy, Superintendent of the Electric Telegraph, to J.P. Grant, Secretary to the Government of Bengal, dt. 10 February 1852 (henceforth 'Letter'), NAI.
23. Home Department, Public Proceedings, 21 June 1850, No. 28: From the Military Board No. 1061, to Major General Sir John Hunter Littler, dt. 4 June 1850, NAI.
24. Home Department, Public Proceedings, 23 April 1852, No. 12: From the Secretary, Government of Bengal, to the Secretary, Government of India, with enclosures including O'Shaughnessy's 'Abstract' and a Minute by the Governor of Bengal, dt. 15 April 1852, No. 258, NAI.
25. Home Department, Public Proceedings, 23 April 1852, No. 13: From W.B. O'Shaughnessy, Superintendent of the Electric Telegraph: Abstract account of construction of the experimental electric telegraph line from Calcutta to Kedgeree etc., to J.P. Grant, Secretary to the Government of Bengal, dt. 3 March 1852 (henceforth 'Abstract'), NAI.
26. Also called the Single Needle galvanoscope. It was used together with Cooke and Wheatstone's 'ABC' instruments. It was worked by a battery and a reversing handle, or two tapper keys, the motions to the right and left end of the index corresponding to the dashes and dots of the Morse alphabet. The needle was of soft iron and kept magnetized by the action of two permanent magnets. It was widely used in England in the 1850s.
27. The important innovation in this instrument was its ability to clearly record the intervals during which current was applied to the line. It used Morse's dot and dash method until Royal Engineering House, Vermont, USA, introduced an alphabet printing telegraph widely used until the 1860s.
28. Home Department, Public Proceedings, 23 April 1852, No. 13: 'Abstract'.
29. Ibid.

30. Ibid.
31. W. B. O'Shaughnessy, *Instructions Relative to Instruments and Offices for the Indian Telegraph Lines* (London, 1853). Letters, dt. 18 August 1853, published as appendices, Victoria Memorial Museum and Library, Calcutta (henceforth VMML).
32. Ibid.
33. Home Department, Public Proceedings, 4 April 1850, No. 48, Report I.
34. Home Department, Public Proceedings, 4 April 1850, No. 50, Minutes by the Governor General and J.E.D. Bethune, dt. 26 and 28 March 1850, NAI.
35. Home Department, Public Proceedings, 23 April 1852, No. 14: Minute by Dalhousie, Governor General, dt. 14 April 1852, NAI.
36. Home Department, Public Proceedings, 20 May 1853, No. 16: Minute by the Governor General, dt. 7 May 1853, NAI.
37. Matthew H. Edney, *Mapping an Empire: The Geographical Construction of British India 1765–1843* (Chicago: Chicago University Press, 1997), pp. 333–35.
38. Eric Stokes, *The English Utilitarians and India* (Delhi: Oxford Universtiy Press, 1982, first edition, Oxford, 1959), p. 251.
39. O'Shaughnessy, 'Memorandum'.
40. W.B. O'Shaughnessy, 'Official Correspondence on attaching of lightening conductors to powder Magazines', *JASB*, vol. IX, 1840, pp. 277–310; *JASB*, vol. X, 1841, pp. 6–10.
41. Edney comments on the drive to centralize and institutionalize the Great Trigonometric Survey after 1830: '(T)he GTS lost its character as a personal institution...and was transformed into a proper institution [emphasis added]'. Edney, *Mapping an Empire*, p. 262.
42. Stokes, *The English Utilitarians*, p. 235.
43. C.A. Bayly, *Imperial Meridian: The British Empire and the World 1780–1830* (London: Longmans, 1989).
44. See C.M. Shepard, 'Philosophy and Science in the Arts Curriculum of the Scottish Universities in the Seventeenth Century', Ph.D. dissertation, University of Edinburgh, 1975.
45. Home Department, Public Proceedings, 4 April 1850, No. 47: From the Military Board to Sir Henry Elliott, Secretary to the Government of India, with enclosures, NAI.
46. Home Department, Public Proceedings, 4 April 1830, No. 48: Report 1.
47. O'Shaughnessy, 'Memorandum', pp. 714–31.
48. Egon Larsen, *A History of Invention*, reprint (Faridabad, 1975), p. 39.
49. Home Department, Public Proceedings, 23 April 1852, No. 13. Letter.
50. O'Shaughnessy, *Instructions*, VMML, p. 34.
51. Home Department, Public Proceedings, 4 April 1850, No. 48. Report I.

52. O'Shaughnessy, *Instructions*, VMML, p. 45.
53. Home Department, Public Proceedings, 9 October 1857, No. 1: From H.L. Anderson, Secretary to the Government of Bombay, to C. Beadon, forwarding no. 397, dt. 26 September 1857, NAI.
54. I.G.J. Hamilton, *An Outline of Postal History and Practice* (Calcutta: Thacker & Co., 1910); E. Bennet, *The Post Office and its Story* (London, 1912); G.R. Clarke, *The Story of the Indian Post* (London: John Lane the Bodley Head, 1921); E. Murray, *The Post Office* (London, 1927).
55. Kishanlal Shridharani, *The Story of the Indian Telegraph* (Delhi: Manger, Government of India Press, 1953); M.R. Anand, *The Story of the Indian Post Office* (Delhi: Manger, Government of India Press, 1955); *The General Post Office Centenary Volume* (Delhi: General Post Office, 1954), including articles by I.K. Gujral, Suniti Kumar Chatterjee and R.C. Majumdar. I thank Dr Basudeb Chatterjee, Calcutta University, for letting me access this volume.
56. Shridharani, *Indian Telegraph*, preface.
57. Vijai Govind, 'The Origin of Electric Telegraphy in India with Special Reference to O'Shaughnessy's Contributions', *Proceedings of the Seminar on Science and Technology in the 18th and 19th Centuries*, Session 11, Delhi, 1980, p. 297.
58. Saroj Ghose, 'Commercial Needs and Military Necessities: The Telegraph in India', in Roy MacLeod and Deepak Kumar, (eds), *Technology and the Raj: Western Technologies and Technical Transfers to India 1700–1947* (New Delhi: Sage, 1995), p. 172.
59. Zaheer Baber, *The Science of Empire* (New York: State University of New York Press, 1996), p. 10.
60. Home Department, Public Proceedings, 4 April 1850, No. 48, Report I.
61. Ibid. No. 49, Report II.
62. Home Department, Public Proceedings, Post Office, 26 January 1835, No. 17: Observations and Instructions of Government on the subject of the surcharge on native letters with copies sent to the Committee of the Customs and Post Office, NAI.
63. Home Department, Public Proceedings, Electric, 4 February 1859, Nos 1–3, from the Superintendent, Electric Telegraphs Containing returns of messages; 3 March 1859, No. 8 from the Superintendent, Electric Telegraphs, containing returns of messages, NAI.
64. For the difference between cultural diffusion and geographical relocation, see Donald R. Headrick, *Tentacles of Progress* (New York/London: Oxford University Press, 1992).

4

INFORMATION SOCIETY AS IF COMMUNICATION MATTERED: The Indian State Revisited

DIPANKAR SINHA

In this era, information is often transformed into a neutral commodity, and communication is reduced to acts of transmission. The human problems communication scholars must address today are not easily resolved through additional information, rather, they arise from providing people with the means for productively managing conflicts and making choices together (Deetz and Putnam 2001).

The very title of this essay reflects a kind of spirit and tenor that would contest the commonsensical, popular and even mainstream scholarly assumptions, ideas and formulations about the ideological foundation and practice of the information society. The mainstream theory building on the theme, which has directly or indirectly as its point of departure Daniel Bell's classic *The Coming of Post-Industrial Society* (1973), rests on the premise that information society is the best available springboard for communication; so much so that the information and communication have been used synonymously in numerous studies which I would not even attempt to list here. The point I would seek to put forth is rather methodological in nature. To the mainstream variety of scholars, information being the central input of communication and communication being essentially 'transmission of information', there was hardly any reason to imagine one without the other. As a result, there was little attempt to investigate a paradoxical scenario in which the growth of information society would take place without much regard for communicative practices. If the academics think like this, the policy makers could not be far behind. No wonder that, in policy discourse on/of information society, marked by much hype and rhetoric, communication (to be explained subsequently) and related matters find little space, if at all. In the process, information society becomes an apolitical and mechanistic construction.

In this backdrop, this essay is an attempt to understand the ways in which a specific kind of ideology of the information society is being constructed and propagated within the framework of governance, which in turn leads and gives credence to a specific kind of discourse on/of information society. The essay seeks to situate the idea and implementation of information society within the broader political economic process to address the *methodological knot* that snaps its ties with communication. For this purpose, the essay resorts to an unconventional route, by seeking to combine the background and the current context of the process under consideration. We focus on the twists and turns in the statecraft, including its relations with the market, in order to ultimately highlight the area of convergence between the two hitherto contending entities, namely, the state and the market. Judging by present day trends, we argue that insofar as laying the communicative foundation of the information society is concerned, both the state and the market are riding each other's back to show remarkable indifference to it. The two major premises that guide the analysis here are:

- That the difference between *mechanistic installation* of the information society and its *organic integration* to the soil in which it is supposed to emerge and exist lies respectively in it not having or having a communicative foundation. In the section on 'Information Society:

Technotopia?' we shall elaborate the distinction between *installation* and *integration*.
- That the state in India, despite being under severe strain vis-à-vis the growing might of the market, still remains the most powerful medium-cum-mediator, not only in the sense of being the repository of information—its storage, retrieval and dissemination—but also in the sense of being an extremely powerful actor/channel of mediation of meanings in the life of Indians, through which such organic integration of the information society could possibly take place.

Communication Matters

Before we deal directly with the Indian scenario it is necessary to justify the proposition that information society must be rooted in communication. It is our basic contention that in any society, particularly those which boast of a democratic polity, the construction of information society cannot be limited to its technological and economic dimensions. In terms of its technological dimension, the information society is supposed to promote information technology (IT) as the 'key enabling' force. The diffusion of IT in this case rests on the idea that technology deployment is an essential precondition to social transformation. As far as the economic dimension of the information society is concerned, information is regarded as the most powerful factor of production, most vital input to economic transformation vis-à-vis the transition from the industrial economy to information economy. The roots of such an idea can be traced to economist Fritz Machlup (1962)—the man who coined the term 'knowledge worker'—whose initial observations continued to be refined by his paradigmatic successors (Porat and Rubin 1977). Information is thus hailed as the central resource, service and commodity. No one contests the view that the technological and economic dimensions are very important. However, the problem arises when these dimensions overshadow the cultural and political dimensions, which are as vital to the construction of information society.

The constricted, technocratic vision of the information society finds its condensed expression in concepts like 'Automated State' in which the idea is that the state, being guided, managed and empowered by all-powerful IT, would do everything 'automatically', to the extent of being reduced to a form of technology itself. One can dismiss such concepts as absurd, but the fact remains that they are part of the growing discourse which looks up to IT as a *wunderkind* that eradicates all social ills without much strain. This is precisely the root of the technocratic conceptualization of the information society in which cultural and political dimensions are undermined. By the cultural dimension of the information society we refer to the *awareness* of the importance of information for individual and collective development, with the idea that there is more to information than mere data and mechanical transmission of messages. Information in this case is not an end in itself but a means to facilitate communication which we define as a process articulation of social relations through making, unmaking and neutralization of meanings. Communication, to go a step further, is a process of negotiation, a struggle and contestation over meanings. Grossberg et al. (1998: 15) remind us that the complexity of the notion of communication, especially in relation to mediation, intensifies in view of the fact that it embodies all four senses of the term mediation: (*a*) reconciliation, (*b*) the difference between reality and an image of interpretation of reality, (*c*) the space of interpretation between the subject and reality, and (*d*) the connection that creates the circuit of the communication of meanings.

Communication, thus perceived, becomes essential for constructing the political dimension of the information society, which calls for direct and active popular participation in its construction, through ideas and actions. In a way, the Free Flow of Information, Freedom of Information, Right to Information (to be referred subsequently), Right to Communicate are resonance of the information society's political dimension, or lack of it. One does not need to devote much space to state a obvious point: that rulers around the world, especially in the developing states, are not quite attracted to these political propositions, most of which are at best accorded lip service. The cultural and political dimensions are sought to be undermined by the powers that be because these dimensions give rise to an organic form of information society, rooted in various communicative channels—not just the most prevalent government-to-people (G2P) channel, but also people-to-government (P2G) and the most vital people-to-people (P2P) channels. The visualization of information society by the policy makers associates the latter two channels with 'friction' which comes in the way of 'universalizing' the wonder technology through replication. It also obfuscates, as we shall argue subsequently, the locus and trajectory of power in a democracy.

Indian Rulers: Daniel Bells' Shadow Disciples?

'Information society is knocking at India's door'. It may be a dramatic expression but not an exaggerated and infrequent one. Yet questions ought to arise about its kind and the way it is sought to be implemented. To reiterate, a specific kind of information society cannot be replicated; nor can there be an information society of a singular kind. There can be multiple information societies, but no information society with a unilinear, unilateral and universal form. Thus, the best way to learn a lesson from Daniel Bell, whose pioneering study. mentioned earlier, brought information society within the orbit of mainstream social theory, is to look into his parameters as clues, but not to make any effort to replicate his version in our soil. Bell, after all, had his specific focus on the American economy when he announced the coming of the postindustrial society. His identification of the year 1956 as the passing of the industrial society was based on the statistical observation that in that year the number of workers in the service sector had surpassed that of the industrial sector, thus ushering in a revolutionary transformation of the American economy, in the liberal sense of the term. While Bell's prime concern was not the replication of the newly incarnated 'society' he, in elaborating its main attributes, had noted certain developments which the later day theorists and policy makers found quite appropriate for mechanical transplantation in other societies, including the non-western variety, to suit their political interests.

Among the attributes identified by Bell, the first one—change from the goods producing to service society—caught the imagination of the policy makers bent on using information society as an instrument of politics. At a time when greater stress on human and professional services acquires a global character, this attribute comes to be regarded as the 'surest sign' of the coming of the information society by policy makers who would hardly think beyond. The second and the third attributes facilitate the construction of a friction free information society even further, with greater intensity. Let us elaborate the point. In explaining the second major feature—the centrality of theoretical knowledge—of the information society, Bell mentions a point which would go on to serve the purpose of policy makers to the greater extent possible. He would argue that the fusion of science and technology in the new society would change the character of technology, so much so that a high degree of predictability would be the order of the day. Going even a step further, he would mention that it would lead to the end of the 'trial-and error' empiricism. Designating intellectual technology as the third main feature of the new society, Bell would elaborate how the technology of the postindustrial society acts as the instrumental mode of rational action to replace social reality with 'techno-social reality'. It would, by ensuring perfect information, also replace in the economic realm, imperfect competition with perfect competition. Even if one cannot vouch for their reading of his works, Bells' shadow is writ large on the IT-savvy policy makers in India.

To refer back to the coming of the information society in India, there is no doubt that IT hardware, IT software and IT enabled-services have witnessed rapid and spectacular growth, leading to a far-reaching and substantial change in the economic scene. The growth of the information sector has been particularly evident since the mid-1990s (Kelkar et al. 1991). There has been a substantial increase in available volumes of information, which is both the cause and consequence of a significant leap forward in terms of information processing and of the fact that information technology has fast acquired the status of a 'basic infrastructure'. In this context, an economist (Chandrasekhar 2004: 21–22) analysing the situation in India visualizes a three-dimensional change in the economic scenario. First, it is expected to result in the growth and diversification of the IT sector itself, leading to expansion of the output and employment in the production of both currently available and new IT products. Second, the use of IT in agricultural, non-IT manufacturing and service sectors is to transform the nature of production in these sectors with major implications in terms of labour productivity, growth and employment. Third, the penetration of IT into activities outside of production is expected to reshape the way work, markets and leisure would be organized and the way individuals and communities can trade and access improvements in the quality of life, deepening of democracy and major advances in human development indicators.

All these are fine, but a democratic polity at the same time has to show a marked tendency towards continuous exchange of ideas, opinions and experiences concerning these changes and their impact. But the question is how far the Indian rulers are ready to go through the necessary rigour that invariably accompanies such communicative endeavour. The Indian policy makers seem to be more interested in presenting the information society as a 'readymade solution' to development, maintaining silence on the more important questions of diffusion and access to IT, the necessary preconditions to development. The problem becomes all the more grave when the discourse, celebrating the coming of the information society in India, contains proclamations, slogans and rhetoric prioritizing technology deployment while providing lip service to the more fundamental question of human development. Focus on the transformatory potential of IT, without addressing the question of greater access of common people to expanded opportunities, gives rise to a top-down information 'system' which precludes facilitation of learning (to be distinguished from e-learning)—through a trial and error method—from the society to the policy level. IT thus becomes a problem solver 'from above' without being integrated to the everyday life of the people and their problems. In addition, in such a mechanistic and elitist approach any kind of feedback is treated as 'unnecessary' and dissent or critique as 'illegitimate'.

India has many instances of such approaches. Typical examples would include District Information System of National Informatics Centre (DISNIC) and Computerised Rural Information Systems Project (CRISP), two prominent programmes of the Government of India, introduced with much hype in the late 1980s. DISNIC was introduced to computerize all district offices in the country while CRISP was meant to provide software for planning and monitoring Integrated Rural Development Programme (IRDP). The very objectives of the schemes would lead one to think that these programmes would be implemented in a decentralized framework. But the reality was far from it. The programmes, conceived and controlled from capital New Delhi, remained 'central schemes' meant to initiate people 'down below' to the IT-led 'information system'. As the following comment on the programmes goes: 'What is noteworthy is that the approach [of the DISNIC]...was completely centralized. The conception of the idea, spelling out of objectives and choice of applications were all done by NIC [National Informatics Centre]....The information needs were assessed by a group located in New Delhi and [sic] have been treated as standard for all the districts in India. The software design and specification of databases were also standardized and originated in New Delhi. The initial recruitment of personnel and their placement in districts was [sic] also centrally done' (Bhatnagar and Schware 2000: 23, brackets mine). The commentators further add that as far as the CRISP was concerned it was slightly more decentralized in terms of the states having the initiative in the purchase of hardware and training of district level functionaries. But at the end of the day it remained under the iron grip of centralization because the design of software and the reporting system were centrally controlled. If the two instances cited here are from the fag end of the state dominated era, let us see what the scenario has to offer us in the days of liberalization.

Liberalization: Communication as Blind spot

India is currently undergoing a critical process of transition whose depth and spread can only be compared to the days when it emerged as an independent state in 1947. The state which had entrusted itself with the enormous task of development in the then newly-independent country is now rolling back its responsibilities. A detailed discussion of the reasons of the retreat of the state is beyond the purview of this essay. However, as a 'logical' outcome of the introduction of the Open Door policy in 1991, the state has paved the ascendance of the market. The market, on the other hand, after playing the role of an appendage to the state for almost five decades, is entering every conceivable sphere of the Indian economy, even in areas such as defence which had long been the exclusive preserve of the state.

Any discussion on the construction of information society in India cannot but refer to the fact that the process coincides with the advent of the market era in development. With the onset of the current mode of globalization which acts as a foundation to both the spectacular growth and reach of IT, and liberal economic reforms, India—not only a vast geographical space but also a market with vast human resource— also came to be recognized as a potential base for the information society. It is true that 'informatization of the Indian economy' and the 'emergence of strong service sector' were part of the state guided discourse of development. But the process of informatization, despite its growing importance, remained an out and out economic process. With the advent of the market era, the growing status and importance of information led to its 'colonization' by technology, which has had its bearing on the conceptualization and construction of the information society in India. This kind of information society remains short on communication, at least the way it is being conceptualized here.

This was perhaps fated to be so if one considers the way the liberalization process was implanted on Indian soil. The decision to adopt liberal economic reforms was passed in the world's largest democracy by a 'minority' government, without any worthwhile debate in the Lok Sabha, the lower house of the parliament composed of elected representatives of the people. Thus, a momentous step in postcolonial India's life was taken by keeping it beyond the *contested terrain*. When the then Prime Minister Narasimha Rao referred to the 'broad consensus' prevailing in India, he identified the industry and business circles and the media as the repository of such consensus, having made no reference to citizens and civil society organizations. Interestingly, while Rao also mentioned parliament as yet another platform for 'consensus' he expressed his opposition to any kind of debate on the issue by the representatives of the people. Reacting to expressions of dissent of some members of the parliament, he is quoted having made a classic observation: 'I had not expected this....At a time when the reforms package was hailed everywhere...*this debate has brought a setback or is likely to bring a setback*' (Sinha 1998: 33 [italics mine]). Ironically, the state's tactical move to stall discussions and debates on the liberal economic reforms in India did not serve its purpose. As Atul Kohli observes, various forces—left-leaning intellectuals, not-so-convinced Congress activists and hostile rural groups—stunted the venture, leading only to a 'halfhearted liberalization'(Kohli 1990: 305–38). It is interesting to recall here that the Indian state had met with the same kind of situation when it had tried to push through land reforms without caring to addressing the local forces (Frankel 1978).

The case cited here is only one among many. It is also symptomatic of the deeper process at work, which can be considered as the hidden transcript of Indian politics—the recalcitrant attitude of the political class to communicate with the ruled. The underlying idea in the case cited above is that 'information'—in the form of policy decision to adopt the market path of development—has been given and there is no further need for feedback from the people. Critiquing what we have described as the bubble of consensus (to be explained further in the section on 'Information Society as Technotopia') Deepak Nayyar (1998) notes:

> ...there was no consensus. [T]he old consensus has broken down while a new consensus has not emerged. The oft-stated view that there is a political consensus...is not correct because such a consensus exists only among the rich, the literati and the influential...it does not have an acceptance at the level of people, most of whom are poor or silent and thus unheard.

One must, however, guard against the general tendency to identify the market as the sole actor precipitating this kind of process. The most novel feature of the process being described here is the changing role of the state which seeks to keep citizens in detention incommunicado in order to give way to the market, which was under its tutelage in postcolonial India. This new found bonhomie between the two and its implications cannot be underestimated.

The Paternalistic State and its Citizens

It is also important to point out that the communicative mode of the once-dominant Indian state was nothing to be proud of. The postcolonial Indian state followed the colonial state in enforcing, as Sudipta Kaviraj contends (1997: 232–33), the 'problem of intelligibility'. 'Democratic institutions in India', Kaviraj goes on to add, 'did not have a historical preparation through a political discourse which debated, in the vernaculars and in terms which reached the ordinary Indian citizen'. To a great extent Kaviraj's observation is true. Only that it needs to be further qualified. Before we do that let us deal with the recent history of the communicative mode of the Indian state vis-à-vis its citizens.

The Indian state need not be put in the same scale with that of the Nazi and the Fascist state in Western Europe or even the Chinese state vis-à-vis the Tianenmen Square massacre in terms of its hostility to the 'civil society'. However, when it comes to encroaching the space earmarked for 'civil society' the state tried to do a good out of it—in seeking to retain the leverage of communication in its own hands. The primary reason could be found in the paternalistic nature of the postcolonial developmental state. It was a state which was more a guardian of the citizens rather than their representative. The paternalistic instinct also gave rise to a dangerous trend. The successive rulers of the Indian state acted in a manner which revealed their inclination to regard the power of the state and the power of the people as binary opposites. Still, the fact remains that the state had to resort to a communicative mode which would exploit, rather than exclude, ordinary citizens. The dynamics of the Indian political process would continue to produce, at the other end of the spectrum, protests and resistance—targeted against the state and its way of governance—and the rulers could not but address them. On occasions the insecurity of the rulers would reach its limits, as it happened when the emergency was declared in the mid-1970s. It was the crudest and the farthest manifestation of aggressiveness of the Indian state which decided to make public communication its first and foremost 'victim'. But even during the emergency the state had been playing the role of a medium-cum-mediator in seeking to justify its actions through political pronouncements and state controlled media. This had to be so because the power holders knew that one day or the other they would have to seek people's mandate. The mechanics of representative democracy and its relations with the state is a vital point that needs some more elaboration. In this context, Partha Chatterjee (1997: 97–103) observes that the postcolonial Indian state, in its pursuit of 'self-definition' suffered from a tension. It is in the sense that while the state was always trying to project the process of economic development, the planning to be more precise, as a 'rational' process embodying the 'single universal consciousness of the social whole', at the same time it had to negotiate with the process of representative democracy as far as politics was concerned.

To explain further, the state in a representative democracy, by virtue of the very methodology of its governance, needs to negotiate through a frictional path. This remains true despite the fact that the Indian state in its earlier incarnation did not care enough to make its institutions intelligible to the people. Whether it likes it or not the state has to mediate its policies through society with its disruptions, ruptures, tensions, turbulence and the structure of inequality. Like the grand patriarch of a typical Indian joint family the state would try to convince, by mixing various tactics, the dissenting members that it is on the 'right track'. This is the reason why one would find instances of the state celebrating its achievements and providing explanations, and even excuses, of its failures. In some cases, the state would seek to coopt the oppositional discourse by means of what has been called the 'tactics of illusion' (Krishna 1996: 238–57). On occasions such cooptation tactics would run beside an aggressive gesture. As Jayal has shown (1999: 164), in the case of the Narmada dispute, on the one hand, the official discourse would describe Narmada as 'liquid gold', not only to highlight its potential for energy and irrigation, but also to project the dam as intrinsic to the cultural identity of Gujarat; on the other hand, the state would turn aggressive in describing those opposing the construction of the dam as 'enemies of Gujarat'.

Further, the explanations and/or excuses provided by the state would not only compel it to create conciliatory gestures at times, it would also leave space for articulation of displeasure, disbelief and dissent. Thus, for instance, while the state would falsely boast of 'people's participation' in the Community Development Programme (1952) the 'fictional claim' would be contested in various quarters, even in the Balwant Rai Mehta Committee, which was constituted by the state itself to study the failure of the programme and suggest reformist measures. The same story could be found in a different context at a much later stage in the case of the dreadful famine in Kalahandi and the suppression of facts by the state. In this case, as a response to public interest litigations before it, the Orissa High Court pronounced a very adverse judgement which, by implication, indicted the Indian state for gross violation of citizens' rights (Jayal 1999: 94). The question is, is it possible to indict the market forces in the same way, that too so directly, for providing misinformation? In general, the market forces prefer to remain 'invisible', being involved in mediation by proxy—as distinct from the statist mode of mediation in which the state, even in its most detached mood, was visible. If that is not enough the market mode of mediation is misleading because, in order to rule by proxy, it leaves the state at the forefront to face all the potshots.

To reiterate, when it came to the making, unmaking and neutralization of meanings of development, the state in its days of supremacy acted as the 'medium', perhaps a reluctant and awkward one, but a medium nevertheless. But in the same breath we would argue that in the face of the market dominance, the Indian state is slowly but steadily altering this practice along with its abdication of the 'direct role' in development. It is acting as a 'facilitator' to the market to promote and publicize a 'friction-free' path of governance-cum-development discourse, with IT as the buzzword. However, the state, specifically those who control the state power, would do well to realize that this would not help them in the long run; on the contrary, it would create a lot more friction than they ever imagined.

Information Society as Technotopia

The following paragraph, written in the Indian context, reveals how the technotopian construction of the information society takes place:

> Imagine, hundreds of queue-weary citizens flocking to Internet kiosks for everything....Imagine, a farmer accessing the net to find out crop prices! Imagine, citizens' groups web-tracking public expenditure...thus creating ideal, real democracy. If they are imaginary scenarios today, they are very soon going to be ground reality....Andhra Pradesh is on the highway to 'governing the e-way....Gujarat is leveraging IT....IT is at the helm of affairs in Karanataka....Orissa's use of IT in urban development has done away with middlemen entirely....Rajasthan has started a little late but now has taken a swift path to 'E'... (Dey 2000: 302).

How far off from ground reality is this kind of text? It is this sort of high-tech euphoria that needs to be 'mediated'. The question of mediation comes in because, as mentioned at the outset, we make a distinction between *installation* and *integration* of information society. The former is a process that one fits or puts somewhere so that it is ready to be used and the latter a process in which the concerned things become closely linked to form the part of the whole. To repeat, installation is a mechanistic-technocratic and (illusively) predictable process; integration is an organic one with lot of unpredictable consequences. Why the distinction is so crucial to the discussion here can be further explained by Scot Lash's ideas about information society itself. To quote Lash (2002), who finds the successive conceptualizations of Bell, Touraine (1974) and Castells (1996) inadequate for understanding the complexities and finesse of information society:

> I think one should understand the information society ...in contrast to other analyses of it....I would understand the information society somewhat differently than it usually has been understood....First and perhaps foremost is to look at the paradox of the information society. This is, how can such highly rational production result in the incredible irrationality of information overloads, misinformation, disinformation and out-of-control information....This is a theory of unintended consequences (p. 2).

From here Lash goes on to illustrate how information society is simultaneously a *Disinformation Society*, in which the greatest rationality of production has consequences in the irrationality of consumer culture. Lash makes yet another observation which is of seminal importance in our discussion. He observes that informationalization on a world scale leads to a 'massive surplus of exclusion'. He explains: '...the previously exploited, semi-skilled and ethnic accumulation... now takes place not on their backs but behind their backs. A self-excluding overclass leads to a forcibly excluded underclass. Such is the way of the global information order' (p. 5). This is precisely the point that is relegated to the silent zone by the Indian state enjoying the new found bonhomie with the market. The product of such bonhomie-turned-conjugality is the hype that in the IT-led information society, technology would define the needs and aspirations of the people. Such hype completely ignores the fact that much of the IT affair—the research and development linked to it, the specific kind of technology that is to be marketed in a country like India and its nature of deployment—is guided by a severely inequitable Global Information Order.

In a way the steady advent of the market and its growing publicity of a technocratic development process, as evident in the technotopian construction of the information society, has been a boon in disguise for the retreating Indian state. The latter, which was often indicted for being exploitative, now finds a new and more convenient route of survival—by conforming to the market-backed scenario of exclusion. Strange as it may sound, in this case at least the state seems to be riding the back of the market. It also leaves the state with the opportunity to diminish its key role as the medium-cum-mediator. As a result, the Indian state is referring more and more to the market forces and less to itself in the development discourse. Simply put, the Indian state is now relying more on exclusionary communication, rather than exploitative communication.

The technotopian construction of the information society has apparently saved those who control the Indian state from a lot of explaining. While the rulers still have to seek the people's formal and periodic mandate, the publicized presentation of information society as 'rational' and 'technical', to a much greater degree than that of planning, has made it possible. The fact that the information society is sourced from technology has only helped the matter because technology is traditionally and 'naturally' considered a more professionalized and specialized subject in which non-specialists are supposed to have little say, if at all. One can go as far as to argue that the state-market cohabitation in India, as displayed in the case of technotopian construction of information society, rests on two foundations: first, the practices (Foucault 1984) of 'rarefaction' and 'prohibition'; and the second, the attempted construction of the bubble of consensus.

Foucault mentions a number of procedures by which the production of discourse is at once controlled, selected, organized and redistributed. Of them prohibition, 'the most obvious and familiar practice', according to Foucault, imposes a direct restriction on what a discourse can say or do, thus resulting in a complex discursive grid. Another set of procedures is also mentioned by him, which does not prohibit discourses but regulates them internally by keeping them within a limit. This comes to effect, as Foucault explains, by determining the condition of their application, by imposing a certain number of rules on the individuals who hold them. On this practice of rarefaction Foucault writes: 'none shall enter the order of discourse if he does not satisfy certain requirements or if he is not, from the outset, qualified to do so'. IT and information society are perfect constitutive elements for the 'order of discourse', for eventual cleansing of public policies of 'irrational' politics based on inputs from a non-specialized public. They are to remain out of the contested terrain. This is what intensifies the growth of the bubble of consensus, which we have mentioned earlier. It can be described as a preconceived, deliberate and motivated attempt to create an impression that the interests of all strata of people are the same and undivided and people acknowledge it by subscribing to a common set of beliefs, despite the fact that reality is different. The bubble of consensus, which is also promoted by the mainstream print and electronic media is considered a very useful tool by which the electorate is sought to be influenced. IT thus is a fashionable political slogan, even if the idea is to depoliticize the masses. For the state it implies lesser mediation.

Perhaps the most pertinent instance till date of the technotopian construction of the information society by the Indian state is the Report on *India as Knowledge Superpower: Strategies for Transformation* (Report II 2001). The Report is also testimony to how the Indian state, at a time when its development mode is being increasingly guided by the market-led forces, could relegate communication as a 'tool' or 'appendage' of governance. The Task Force, constituted by the Planning Commission which authored the Report, visualized the creation of the 'knowledge society' in India with a view to 'empower and enrich its people' (p. 1). The Report views knowledge as a 'powerful tool to drive social transformation' and accordingly advocates the generation, absorption, dissemination and use of knowledge to create 'economic wealth and social good for all' and a 'just and equitable society'.

However, in the Report the whole process of transformation is predicated upon the '*broadbased and diversified* scientific and technological infrastructure' (italics mine). Apparently it is a welcome proposition which can go entirely wrong if the state prefers to have the infrastructure created, managed and controlled by a handful of conglomerates. For the latter, profit, rather than public welfare, is the primary if not the only objective. The probability of this kind of scenario cannot be undermined in view of the fact that the Report ambitiously mentions that India, after having failed to reap the benefits of the industrial revolution, needs 'leapfrogging' (p. 8) to the 'knowledge society'. In such a scheme of things, IT has the obvious status of the primary change agent which interweaves the so called technology drive (marked in the Report as bio-technology, communications technology, space technology and so forth) and the so called service drive (such as, disaster mitigation, telemedicine, wealth generation and so forth) towards the 'knowledge society'.

No less important in the context of our discussion, the section 5.7 of the Report has the heading 'communications' which is defined in terms of microprocessors, bandwidth, optic fibre and so forth. The major means of the futuristic projection of the IT-led transformation is identified (p. 18) as 'connectivity' with two interrelated parts; physical (such as highways, waterways) and electronic. Notwithstanding the occasional (and superficial) references to the importance of 'native knowledge' and human capital, the whole thrust is on the construction and codification of a technocratic information society in which one kind of knowledge, briefly depicted here, would reign supreme (that too with only lip service to human agency). The whole Report, including the important section on *Knowledge Society: Approach and Action Plan* (pp. 57–70) reflects that the central idea is that there could be only one kind of knowledge as an organizing principle of a potential 'knowledge society' and the multiple kinds of knowledge which reside at the opposite pole are by themselves incapable of giving rise to a knowledge society *proper*. It follows therefore that because of their inherent 'deficiency' the other kinds of knowledge would at best enjoy a secondary and complementary status, trying to fit in to the IT-led 'knowledge society'.

Being Organic, Being Local

If communication is the blindspot of the much-publicized technotopia of information society, the common people are its missing link. The question therefore is: how should one do away with the blindspot and bring back the missing link? The most effective way is to lend local character to the information society as an alternative, in tune with the local setting and milieu. It also implies bringing in a specific kind of IT to a specific kind of locality, keeping in mind the available quantity and quality of local knowledge, skill and resources of the communities. It is more a question of giving people access to the new technology to facilitate the development of their own knowledge and skill and better utilization of their resources. In the broader sense, it also calls for creating and mediating new meanings and modes of expression and negotiating the existing ones through such a process.

In the globalization-friendly policy discourse of the Indian rulers, the local and/or localization acquire the status of endangered concepts. It is because the Indian policy makers seemed to be guided by an ahistorical, aspatial and misleading perception that there is necessarily an antagonistic relationship between the global and the local. They remain oblivious of the fact that since the 1990s in particular there is both growing literature (Appadurai 1995; Friedman 1995; Kearney 1995; Strassoldo 1992) and field-level consciousness on the cohabitation and interface of the global and the local (often described as 'glocal'). As a result, there is a realization that when it comes to creating new meanings and negotiating the existing ones at the local level, the global flows do not necessarily act as a constraint. In the context of our discussion it is worthwhile to note that one of the by-products of the increasing awareness and stress on the global-local has been a more realistic and tolerant attitude towards the state. This point, if taken into cognizance, might give some food for thought to the Indian policy makers when it comes to the general policy of rejuvenating the state, and in the more specific context of carving out a state with communicative foundation as far as establishment of the information society is concerned.

If such an endeavour is regarded by the Indian political class as 'retrogressive', they should be better informed that there are voices among the information society specialists who argue vociferously in favour of a state which accepts that it has come a long way from its old-type paternalistic territorial form and consequently takes care to create information distribution channels. These channels are distinct from the 'commercial' information distribution channels created mainly by the market forces, which remain out of bounds for the disadvantaged and the disempowered sections of society. Thus, even in the days of liberalization there are calls for rejuvenation of the state in the interest of democratization of IT. The following observation, made by a scholar who expresses the apprehension that the retreat by the state would lead to worse obstacles to the 'free flow of information', is illustrative enough: 'In spite of the setbacks...it is too hasty to say that the state is no longer a capable entity to act for the public goods and is doomed to demise....It is expected that...[the] state is still to be relied upon as an actor to undertake public policies and resolve social disorder coming with the new technology' (Wang, website 2004: 7).

Observations and comments like this remind us that the state still has a key role in governance—in developing regulatory frameworks, maintaining law and order, developing infrastructure and promoting human development, all of which are, beyond any doubt, the essential preconditions to an organically rooted and meaningful information society. The foremost requirement for the state is to acquire a human face. Khandwalla (1999), in a vein that is quite similar to that of Wang, argues that the Indian state despite having some 'dark spots' has shown an 'above average performance'. Noting that the state provides a continuity with the past Khandwalla, who is otherwise quite favourably disposed towards liberalization, has this to say: 'The solution may not lie in wholesale repudiation of the Indian state in a sort of epoch-ending *tandava* destruction'(p. 232). His so called 'menu of options' earmarked for the reformed Indian state includes promotion of self-regulation, associative and direct democracy and civil rights along with better political management through cooperation with the non-governmental organizations, competence, probity and accountability. One hardly needs to explain that the options mentioned are both a cause and consequence of a more communicative state willing to mediate in a people-friendly manner.

To reiterate, we are arguing in favour of a rejuvenated and more communicative Indian state, notwithstanding its not-so-glorious past record. We do it because of the single most important factor that in comparison to the market the state, by its very constitutive (political) logic, is supposed to pay greater regard to the greater number of people under its jurisdiction. This leaves the state as a facilitator with great potential when it comes to the construction of an organically-rooted, locally-rooted information society, our prime concern. Obviously, the term local in this case goes much beyond its geographical connotation; it is as much political, social and cultural as anything else. When it comes to the Indian state it is a positive sign that after showing unduly long reluctance to democratic decentralization—since the days of the Constituent Assembly—it has passed the Seventy-Third and the Seventy-Fourth Amendment Acts to the Indian Constitution in 1992. The amendments accord constitutional importance to the panchayats and municipalities—the institutions of rural and urban local governance respectively—thus ensuring the constitutional-political validity to democratic decentralization. True, the journey from the days of Lord Ripon (who had pioneered the conceptualization of 'local self-government' in India) to these amendments 'took more than a century' (Report I 1995: 12). However, as the platitudinous statement goes, it is better late than never. Gauging the possible impact of the Seventy-Third Amendment Act, an analyst approvingly writes: '...the amendment provides an important opening to resurgent social forces and its impact is likely to be strengthening of grassroots democracy and a reshaping the alignment of social forces' (Srivastava 1999: 76). We would add that since India has a predominantly rural face, the panchayats in particular are of utmost importance for democratizing development.

The panchayats and the municipalities can be utilized as channels for bringing IT to the grassroots level. It can be done, for instance, though imparting training to elected representatives of the people in both rural and urban/semiurban areas with a view to ensure citizen awareness and participation in IT-enabled services. In rural India, for instance, the Gram Sabha, which has been given constitutional validity by the Seventy-Third Amendment Act, could be mobilized for this purpose, harnessing its potential as a local grassroots level agency of the state. Gram Sabha, which invites attendance of all families living within the jurisdiction of the Gram Panchayat, has been conceived as a platform for exchange of ideas and opinions among the common people about local developmental issues. The issues that find prominence in Gram Sabha meets are discussed at the block and district levels before they are supposed to be taken up by the State Planning Board.

Ultimately of course, insofar as the organic information society is concerned, it is a question of combining what we may term as *localization of politics* with *localization of technology*. The preceding paragraphs reveal that giving effect to such a combination is an exceedingly complex task. The complexity is compounded not only by general political issues; it is made so by technological issues as well. As Kenneth Kenister points out (1997), technological localization involves more complex issues than routine localization of software in terms of both content and language. In highlighting its 'cultural dimension' Kenister refers to 'the adaptation of programs...in such a way that they seem fully consistent with the assumptions, values, and outlooks' of the culture in the recipient society. If we add to it the assertion that it has to be done, as in the case of India, within a space marked by inequalities in both material and symbolic terms, surely the market, driven primarily by profit motive, is not going to keep itself preoccupied in this task. Neither is it feasible that the market should be left alone to decide the matter. The following remark, made in the specific context of the Internet in India, is also relevant in the general context of the information society as such: '...if market forces alone are allowed to drive the Internet's diffusion and use, India's experience with this exciting new medium may be stunted. A strategic vision and a creative regulatory framework...are needed so that its potential can be harnessed not only commercially but also...in the areas of development and governance' (Kudaisya 2001: 1768–69). Thus, one cannot but think of the state to act as a medium-cum-mediator to encounter and negotiate with this complex process.

In this context, we can refer to one of the most discussed and debated issues of contemporary times, the Right to Information (RTI). There is hardly any doubt that this right can be an effective check on both the state and the market, by making them a little more conscious of the ordinary people's right to transparency and accountability. This is also the reason why the RTI has gained recognition far and wide as one of the inalienable features of democratic polity and administration. A detailed discussion on the evolution and nature of the right is beyond the scope of this essay. However, it should be mentioned that in India six states—Delhi, Goa, Tamil Nadu, Karanataka, Rajasthan and Maharashtra—have passed the RTI Act. Though there is no uniform standard as far as the formulation of the right in these respective states are concerned (arguably, the most reform minded states are Delhi, Goa and Maharashtra), the fact remains that they are the fruits of long and sustained struggle of the civil society. In this context mention can be made of organizations, such as, the National Campaign on the People's Right to Information, and especially in the case of Rajasthan, of the 'people's struggle' waged by Mazdoor Kisan Shakti Sangathan (MKSS). What is particularly noteworthy here is that in a country which still carries forward the colonial legacy in the information and communication sector—in the form of the Official Secrets Act, the Indian Evidence Act, the All India Services Conduct Rules (especially its Rule 9 which prevents information being given to ordinary citizens) and so forth—the state has taken the initiative, though in a limited manner, of formulating a right that has been the long standing demand of the citizenry. Incidentally, the impact of the struggle over the RTI has also reached the precincts of Lal Bahadur Shastri National Academy of Administration, Mussourie, the training centre for officers of the Indian Administrative Service. The Academy, in terms of a letter written and circulated by its then director who specifically mentions MKSS contribution to the growing awareness of the RTI, motivates the government servants to recognize the RTI 'to dramatically increase the strength of the citizen to understand and challenge...the arbitrary exercise of state power' (Document I 1996: 70). To remind us of an obvious point, the Academy which is subjecting itself to such a reorientation, is a state institution.

This brings us again to the point that the Indian state, so to say, remains not only the organization which exercises authority in the life of its citizens in one way or other (Khilnani 1997), it also remains, despite all odds, the only organization—with a vast array of agencies and agents—which is still looked up to by the people as something that exists for them. If the Indians are critical of the state (or more specifically, perhaps government) in many cases, it is also because they expect it to do something for them and chastize it for not doing enough. The influence of the state on people is still extraordinary, which has manifested itself both through the over-dependence of the citizens on the state and through the state's belief in its omnipotence, with dangerous implications for the democratic polity. But a balanced approach is needed, not through a diffident state increasingly unsure of its power and potential, but through a combination of political will and skill meant for promoting humane governance. Such a state can initiate measures to ensure greater transparency and accountability, contribute to building social and technological infrastructures with a view to provide greater access and sharing among people, give fillip to opportunities to promote ideas, arguments and positions and so forth. While the market forces themselves would not and cannot do it alone, the state can enter into a sort of partnership with these forces by convincing them that they should also strive to contribute to human development, if not for anything else but at least on the ground that such contributions would also help them in the long run—in having a greater base of 'potential consumers' and greater market.

Concluding Remarks

Keeping in mind one of our major premises—that the Indian state itself still remains the most effective mediator vis-à-vis the people—one can conclude that by trying to conform to the market-led exclusionary communicative mode, rather than seeking to reform it to the extent it is feasible at the moment, it is only endangering its own survival. To what extent such a self-denying and self-negating trend is due to compulsion and to what degree it is part of the 'survival strategy' in the current political economy scenario is a matter that needs separate discussion. It is true that the Indians, like others elsewhere in the world, now live in an era in which there is a global, fundamental, multidimensional grid and engagement to turn 'citizens' of the state into 'consumers' and 'clients' of the market. But the process of transition would not be as smooth as it seems in the first instance. This might be the reason why, as mentioned in the preceding section, the exponents of the neoliberal mode of development are backing out from their earlier euphoric call of the 'end of the state' and seeking to 'bring the state back in' (even as facilitator and protector of the market forces). One has to give credit to their foresight, based on the revised understanding of the reality, which underlines the survival and justification of the state at a global level. As for the Indian state, if its strength, amidst many drawbacks, lies in its potential to mediate meanings in the life of the people, it should be harnessed by all means. In this endeavour the Indian state must also work with the non-state forces which are supposed to have direct contact with the local people and microknowledge of the locality. Those who manage the Indian state must on their part realize, irrespective of their political affiliations, that there is always a midway between the two extremes, (*a*) being up in arms against the market forces, an option which is impractical and unrealistic in the globalized world today; and (*b*) being totally subservient to the market, an option which is self-defeating and self-destructive to the core. Could not the information society, by way of its construction and legitimation in India, be a point of turn around for the Indian state as a better, efficient and more effective medium-cum-mediator?

References

Appadurai, Arjun, 'Disjuncture and Difference in the Global Cultural Economy', in Mike Featherstone (ed.), *Global Culture: Nationalism, Globalization, and Modernity* (London: Sage, 1995), pp. 295–310.

Bell, Daniel, *The Coming of Post-Industrial Society: A Venture in Social Forecasting* (Cambridge, MA: MIT Press, 1973).

Bhatnagar, Subhash and Robert Schware (eds), *Information and Communication Technology in Development: Cases from India* (New Delhi: Sage, 2000).

Castells, Manuel, *The Rise of the Network Society. The Information Age: Economy, Society and Culture*, Volume 1 (Oxford: Blackwell, 1996).

Chandrasekhar, C.P., 'Revisiting the Digital Promise', *Resurgence*, nos. 159–160, 2004 (January), pp. 21–25.

Chatterjee, Partha, 'Development Planning and the Indian State', in Terrance J. Byres (ed.), *The State, Development and Liberalization in India* (New Delhi: Oxford University Press, 1997), pp. 82–103.

Deetz, Stanley A. and Linda L. Putnam, 'Thinking About the Future of Communication Studies', in William B. Gudykunst (ed.), *Communication Yearbook 24* (Thousand Oaks: International Communication Association and Sage, 2001).

Dey, Bata K., 'E-governance in India: Problems, Challenges and Opportunities—A Futures Vision', *Indian Journal of Public Administration*, vol. XLVI, 2000 (July–September), pp. 300–13.

Document I: Letter from N.C. Saxena, Director, National Academy of Administration, 'On the Right to Information', *Lokayan Bulletin*, vol. 12, no. 5, 1996 (March–April), pp. 69–75.

Foucault, Michel, 'Order of Discourse', in Michael Schapiro (ed.), *Language and Politics* (Oxford: Basil Blackwell, 1984).

Frankel, Francine, *India's Political Economy, 1947–1977: The Gradual Revolution* (Princeton: Princeton University Press, 1978).

Friedman, Jonathan, 'Being in the World: Globalization and Localization', in Mike Featherstone (ed.), *Global Culture: Nationalism, Globalization and Modernity* (London: Sage, 1995), pp. 311–28.

Grossberg, Lawrence, Ellen Wartella and D. Charles Whitney, *Media Making: Mass Media in a Popular Culture* (Thousand Oaks: Sage, 1998).

Jayal, Niraja Gopal, *Democracy and the State: Welfare, Secularism and Development in Contemporary India* (New Delhi: Oxford University Press, 1999).

Kaviraj, Sudipta, 'The Modern State in India', in Martin Doornbos and Sudipta Kaviraj, *Dynamics of State Formation: Indian and Europe Compared* (New Delhi: Sage, 1997), pp. 225–50.

Kearney, Michael, 'The Local and the Global: The Anthropology of Globalization and Transnationalism', *Annual Review of Anthropology*, vol. 24, 1995, pp. 547–65.

Kelkar, Vijay, Devendra Chaturvedi and Madhav K. Dar, 'India's Information Economy: Role, Size and Scope', *Economic and Political Weekly*, vol. XXVI, no. 37, 1991 (14 September), pp. 2153–66.
Kenister, Kenneth, *Software Localization: Notes on Technology and Culture*, Working Paper no. 26 (Cambridge MA: Massachusetts Institute of Technology, 1997). Quoted with the permission of the author.
Khandwalla, Pradip N., *Revitalizing the State: A Menu of Options* (New Delhi: Sage, 1999).
Khilnani, Sunil, *The Idea of India* (London: Penguin, 1997).
Kohli, Atul, *Democracy and Discontent: India's Growing Crisis of Governability* (Cambridge: Cambridge University Press, 1990).
Krishna, Sumi, 'The Appropriation of Dissent: The State vis a vis People's Movement' in T.V. Sathyamurthy (ed.), *Class Formation and Political Transformation in Post-colonial India* (New Delhi: Oxford University Press, 1996).
Kudaisya, Gyanesh, 'India's New Mantra: The Internet', *Current History*, 2001 (April), pp. 162–69.
Lash, Scott, *Critique of Information*, (London: Sage, 2002).
Machlup, Fritz, *The Production and Distribution of Knowledge in the United States* (New Jersey: Princeton University Press, 1962).
Nayyar, Deepak, 'Economic Development and Political Democracy: Interaction of Economic and Politics in Independent India', *Economic and Political Weekly*, 1998 (5 December), p. 3129.
Porat, M.U. and M.R. Rubin, *The Information Economy*, Volume 1 (Washington, DC: Office of Telecommunications, US Department of Commerce, 1977).
Report I: *Status of Panchayati Raj in the States of India* (New Delhi: Indian Institute of Social Sciences, 1995).
Report II: *India as Knowledge Superpower: Strategy for Transformation* (New Delhi: Planning Commission, Government of India, 2001).
Sinha, Dipankar, 'Communication for Liberalization in India: The Take-off Stage', *Asian Studies*, vol. XVI, no. 2, 1998 (July–December), pp. 18–40.
Srivastava, Ravi, 'Two Steps Forward, One Step Back', *Seminar*, 473, 1999 (January), pp. 71–76.
Strassoldo, Raimondo, 'Globalism and Localism: Theoretical Reflections and Some Evidence', in Zdravko Mlinar (ed.), *Globalization and Territorial Identities* (Avebury: Aldershot, 1992).
Touraine, Alain, *The Post-Industrial Society* (New York: Wildwood Press, 1974).
Wang, Ching-ning, 'Communication Technology and the Retreat of the State', http://is.gseis.ucla.edu/impact/f99/Papers/wang.html. Accessed on 26 April 2004.

1.2
Landscapes of Commerce

5

CONSTRUING A 'NEW MEDIA' MARKET:
Merchandising the Talking Machine, c.1900–1911*

VIBODH PARTHASARATHI

The formative years of the business of recorded music, approximating the years 1900–1911, mark a watershed in the industrialization of cultural production in India. Much of what distinguished early recorded music stemmed from the industrial articulation of musical activity it brought into being. As the first 'new media' of twentieth century India, its implications for human knowledge—for the production and circulation of such knowledge—were profound.

It is pertinent to recognize that the business of recorded music germinated under free market conditions in colonial India. This gains significance amidst the current euphoria on

---

*This essay has emerged from my ongoing research on the Records Industry and Music Culture in early twentieth century India. I thank the India Foundation for the Arts, Bangalore, and the Charles Wallace India Trust, London for supporting my research at crucial junctures. This essay has benefited tremendously from readings by, amongst others, Biswajit Das and Dunu Roy. I am in gratitude to Parna Das for aggregating advertisements from some of the newspapers I have referred to, and Narendra Shrimali, for sharing his fantastic stories about, and collection of, early 78 rpm records.

the 'free market', the contending standpoints of which invariably bypass historicizing private entrepreneurship in the media industry. We recall that the business of recorded music had evolved as a private enterprise in the last decades of nineteenth century America, Britain and Germany. And it was private, predominantly foreign capital—and not state patronage and concessions—that sculpted the incipient records industry into, and within, India during the first decade of the twentieth century. The colonial state was not a 'player' in this sector, as it was during the formative years of the other two media of the early twentieth century, viz. radio and cinema.[1] Nor was it a significant 'regulator' during the formative years of the records business, as it was in other emergent markets of the colonial and free worlds.[2] All this impresses us to view the business of recorded music as the first metaphor for those phenomenon that ushered the modern media industry in India.

Integral to the economic order of the incipient records industry was the creation of value systems conditioning its nascent market. Because our current perception of 'canned' music has so deeply been shaped by the nature of consumer products subsequent to the gramophone and the image systems around these products, we tend to ignore how their relationship—that between a product line and its image system—came to be grounded in the first place. For instance, so used to are we today to recorded music as our primary mode of musical entertainment, and our homes as the primary site for its consumption, that we assume a congenital relationship between them.[3] What gets ignored is the historical construction of this relationship, a formulation so complex and deep that it appears as a 'natural' state of being.

In the earliest years of the gramophone era, we can imagine a number of sites which became the playing field for shaping the perception and representation of recorded music as a 'new media'. Amongst these, advertisements in newspapers are of historical significance and analytical relevance. In the formative years of the business, advertising formed a crucial fulcrum for not just selling Talking Machines but discoursing upon 'music on record' in more wider terms. In appreciating the overwhelmingly elite character of recorded music as a form of entertainment during these years, advertisements in English newspapers provide an apt terrain to understand the sensibilities that fuelled the merchandizing of both machines and music.

Reflecting upon all this, it may seem natural to begin by asking, when was 'music on record' born in India. Intuitive as this may be, such a question would indicate a false start. What is casually understood as the 'birth' or 'advent' of recorded music is a complex phenomenon; it concerned far more than the import of the technology of audiography, the commercialization of music recording, or the creation of disembodied sonic artefacts. Towards a more rounded understanding of early recorded music, we must recognize its multiple dimensions, viz. not only its technical and material making but equally the nature of cognitive and cultural encounters it announced. In doing so, we realize that we can never really pinpoint when recorded music—as a form of enterprise and entertainment—was born in India; it was something that grew, like Vishnu in his incarnation as Vāman.

What we can grasp, as this essay will reveal, are the conditions within which 'music on record' grew, both as an entrepreneurial activity and a cultural form. Revisiting a complex totality of historical processes, this paper will lay out the social conditions propelling this business at the dawn of the twentieth century. Scrutinizing the various instances and sites that facilitated the germination of early recorded music, I will demonstrate how the retail trade constructed a market for 'Talking Machines'—in particular, the ways in which advertisements in newspapers contributed to this process. While this opens up wider issues concerning cultural production and reproduction, this paper will primarily weigh the extent to which the changing discourse in advertising reflected the changing conditions in the nascent music industry. By grasping the interplay between the manufacture of machines and music, the mechanisms of merchandising and the grammar of advertising, I shall explain how 'music on record' was, not really born but, 'delivered' in and within India.

In the first two sections, I focus on merchandising during the mercantile and manufacturing phases of the early business of recorded music. In the first section, I begin by enumerating the circumstances which led to the grounding of the business in British India; thereafter, I analyse these years to identify the emergent landscape of advertising in this period. Similarly in the second section, once I chart out the years in which the mass manufacture of recorded music developed, I revisit these years to see how its dynamics also influenced the propagation of machines. In the third section, I address the changing nature of actors and acts involved in propagating 'music on record'. Since most of its consumer–listeners were located in three, urban sales hubs of recorded music—Calcutta, Bombay and Madras—our primary, although not exclusive, focal point are the leading English newspapers of these cities. I conclude with a set of methodological reflections and analytical inferences on this journey into our past, a past which holds many a clue about the germination of our present media culture.

Part 1: The Formative Contours

The innocuous Talking Machine made its initial inroads as a technological curio in the India of the 1890s.[4] Evidently, the only note of indigenization during these years was its nomenclature.[5] Both the principal formats were sold here: the cylinder based phonograph, originally an Edison creation which offered the possibility to record and replay music on the same machine, and the disc-based gramophone, invented by Berliner, which only replayed pre-recorded music.[6] However, for the earliest European and American exporting firms, the singular objective was to sell machines in India; recording music for Indian listeners was not their prime objective. Firms remained content with replicating a uniform set of recordings, with the advantage of scale this brings, for sales all over the world including India.

Two factors amended these primordial conditions.

Hitherto, the element of novelty was the prime factor for the Talking Machine's popularity in India. With improvements in equipment and recording quality, the perception of recorded music in India started changing from curiosity to avid attraction. But most of the discs and cylinders sold in the

Indian market were 'English airs'—snatches of comic shows, acts of mimicry, songs and dance melodies, etc.[7] Sensing a growing demand for 'Indian' music by the turn of the century, domestic traders began emphasizing the need for local content to their overseas suppliers.

On their part, for the Euro-American firms the necessity to sell local music was provoked from another condition that characterized the increasingly distinct transnational market for recorded music. In the early years of the twentieth century, international trade in recorded music unfolded in a situation which was not only non-monopolistic but saw varying formats. Consequently, competition between leading Euro-American equipment makers signified a race between rivalling recording technologies—and therefore between consumer formats of the Talking Machine.[8]

All in all, at a time when the character of recorded music was becoming the locus of distinction for the growing Indian consumer-listener, the content of 'music on record' became of central relevance to entrepreneurs. In short, an interlinked set of influences on the supply side overlapped with the emergent demand for country-specific music.

The Building of a Business: The Expedition Years

The first years of the twentieth century saw entrepreneurial moves on two overlapping fronts: to capture emerging markets for recorded music and, in the process, to ensure one format prevailed over the other. This brought an urgency among firms, hitherto competing to sell machines, to aggregate a repertoire of recordings from outside Western Europe and North America, in local languages and styles. In their race to record 'native' music, the Euro-American firms resorted to a modus operandi that history had witnessed before. They organized 'Recording Expeditions' to countries in the old and new worlds. While the latter, especially in South America, were the focus of American firms, their European contenders were looking at their frontline countries and eastwards. In the spring of 1902, the Gramophone and Typewriter Limited (GTL) from London sent Fred Gaisberg to record music in Italy, Armenia, Georgia, Ukraine and elsewhere in the Russian empire. This tour by GTL's principal recording engineer was clearly motivated by a sense of competition perceived by the firm in the early years of the century. And his recordings from these tours proved to be immensely profitable for his company.[9]

Gaisberg's Far Eastern expedition in the winter of 1902, in which India was the first and most important sojourn, was a continuation of such mercantalist forays. Although the Orient was a different, if not difficult territory for this American-born engineer, he was full of missionary zeal. Leaving Britain to gain vital footholds in India he wrote: 'As we steamed down the Channel into the unknown I felt like Marco Polo starting out on his journeys'.[10] Soon after arriving in Calcutta, Gaisberg found that the Englishmen he was to liaise with had no clue about Indian melodies, either musically or commercially. So he resorted to experience first hand the kinds of songs and singers that were popular—and gauge the tastes of connoisseurs and patrons from among whom, he thought, might emerge the consumers of GTL's records. Attending music performances at theatres, private parties and fêtes in different parts of Calcutta, he began zooming in on probable singers. Among the many he recorded, the most prominent were Goharjan and Jankibai, the latter charging Rs 3,000 for her recording. All recordings by Gaisberg were sent to GTL's records pressing factory at Hanover in Germany. The finished 7 and 10 inch discs—with recordings only on one side of the disc, as was the norm in those years—were imported into India during the spring of 1903, and sold exceedingly well.

The significance of this expedition should not be misconstrued by viewing it as the first venture in the business of recording music in India.[11] The trajectory of indigenous commercial ventures in recorded music in India indicates that this honour goes to Hemendra Mohan Bose.[12] The historical weight of Gaisberg's visit lies in it creating a fresh set of conditions for the business of recorded music—the opening up of British India as a market for pre-recorded local music by foreign firms. Learning from this, GTL undertook recording expeditions to India almost annually: in 1904–05 led by William Sinkler Darby, in 1906–07 by William Gaisberg, Fred's younger brother,[13] and in 1908 by George Dillnutt, Fred's assistant during his maiden visit. Moreover, recognizing that business with British India was more extended and profitable than with most Asian countries, rival firms were not to be left behind. Nicole Freres from London sent an expedition in 1904; from across the Atlantic, The American Talking Machine Co. sent a recordist to India, after touring China, in 1905.[14] The race was on for who had canned more 'native' music. By 1906, the International Talking Machine Gmbh, known by its 'Odeon' label, had established itself in India as the principal rival to GTL—they being the only two among the big firms operating in India to make both machines and discs. In 1907, it sent its first recording expedition to India. Not to be undone by its national rival, Beka from Berlin promptly dispatched an expedition in 1907–08. By 1907, India was next only to Britain and France in importing discs from Germany.[15]

We thus see the circumstances and logic driving the spate of recording expeditions from 1902 onwards. All these recordings were taken back for pressing at the factories of the respective concerns, the final products being shipped all the way back to India. Importantly, as the amount spent on recording music increased during the expedition era, the price of records was maintained for the fear of consumers being induced to buy a rival firm's repertoire of 'native' records.

In the competition for India, expeditionary firms overlapped and vied with the efforts by the much smaller Indian firms. While the latter's entrepreneurial trajectories have been documented in detail,[16] what is significant here is their diverse character. The social basis of domestic entrepreneurship was different from that of the foreign firms; they were venture capitalists—often from unrelated fields—for whom the incipient business offered investment opportunities, unrestricted by government regulation and monopoly interests. We may add that the more significant amongst these earliest domestic ventures were born largely through collaborations between an indigenous entrepreneur and foreign records manufacturer, such as between Bose and Pathe of France.

Positioning the 'New Media': Arbitrating the Technology

Having enumerated the formative conditions of the business of recorded music in India, let us review this period to see how these dynamics impregnated the merchandising Talking Machines.

By the late 1890s, shops in India which combined the sale of domestically manufactured consumer products with that of select imported goods, began selling Talking Machines, as observed by social historians in Bengal.[17] In their earliest commercial announcements in newspapers, Talking Machines were simply listed along with harmoniums, organs, music boxes et al. in advertisements by leading importers of musical instruments.[18] By 1899, we see advertisements exclusively for phonographs and gramophones appearing very occasionally with visuals of these machines; some vendors offered both formats, cylinders and discs.[19] Their advertisements carried rudimentary pronouncements on the virtues of the 'new media':

> These Machines TALK, SING, RECITE
> PLAY BANDS, ORCHESTRAS &c, &c
> They Permanently RECORD HUMAN VOICES and reproduce them naturally.[20] (original caps)

That the records themselves constituted a lesser proportion of the business of foreign firms at the beginning of the twentieth century, is evident by the space and emphasis on machines in these advertisements. What also strikes us is that records were sold at uniform prices—i.e., without much distinction on the quality of recordings, the popularity of 'artists' or the subject matter of aural forms. The price of a cylinder or disc was determined by its physical attributes—viz., the cost of its constituent raw materials, and the size of records. Most conspicuous, however, was the variety of formats being advertised, a clear reflection of the competitive character of the business, elaborated upon earlier. The challenge was how to sell a product line which itself existed in rivalling formats, the principal two being the disc and cylinder.

Firms chose a varying set of semantics to drive home the superiority of their format, prices ranging from Rs 37 to Rs 800. From 1903–04 onwards, GTL advertisements for their machines repeatedly stressed: 'there are several talking machines—there is only one gramophone'.[21] On the other hand, firms like Nicole which was known more for its discs that machines, repeatedly mentioned in their advertisements that their discs could be 'used on any disc machine'.[22] Adding to this semantic jugglery was the presence of various models of the 'Graphophone', the trade-marked name for disc machines made by Columbia.[23]

Agents of foreign firms and local vendors alike sought to emphasize in their advertisements the quality and external finesse of the machines, its tone arms—a vital component—and its brass horns—vital to the gadget's visual appeal. Retailers like Mullick Brothers in Calcutta spelt out in their advertisements the technical quality of products in more general terms, viz., 'no metallic sound', 'new patented tapered arm' and 'improved records'.[24] Others sought to expand the market by festive offers, for the *pooja* season in Calcutta and Christmas in Madras. This was as much an indication of the existing competition, as a recognition of the spending patterns of the trendy upper middle classes which formed the bulk of the consumers of this 'new media'. Soon foreign firms like GTL too realized the importance of advertising aggressively and intensively during local festivals, like the *pooja* season in Bengal, as they were used to in Britain during Christmas.

Amidst all this, fascinating is the changing pronouncements in the advertisements of the Talking Machine Hall, which sold the cylinder format by Hemendra Bose. In the earliest years, the firm sought to capitalize upon the familiarity and popularity of the names behind the music—its advertisements, thus, prominently mentioning the names of Rabindranath Tagore, Dwijendra Lall Roy, Lall Chand Bural et al. This was part of the modus operandi of the time. Much before Bose, in 1903 GTL was the first to come up with its first 'vernacular' record catalogue offering music in over a dozen Indian languages on discs of 7 inch and 10 inch; and much after Bose, in 1907 Beka's advertisement of their 10 inch 'Indian' or 'native' records in Madras newspapers by local retailers Stanley Oakes & Co. and A.H. Guznavi & Co. prominently listed the name of all singers.

But tempered by the rising swadeshi wave of the first decade of the twentieth century, we spot a gradual repositioning by the Talking Machine Hall. From mid-1906, its typical advertisements carried in their copy jingoist punch lines: 'Records made in your own country', 'much superior to records made by foreign artists' or simply 'Swadeshi records'.[25] In fact, the swadeshi movement provided fresh business opportunities for many firms, nearly all of which recorded and sold popular songs like *Vandemataram*.[26] But Bose also seem to perceive a threat to his cylinder format by the activities of the expeditionary firms, all of whom were using the disc format. Rather cleverly, he pushed his cylinder models by highlighting their ability to record and replay music; thus providing potential buyers a product on which they could both listen to pre-recorded cylinders and make their own recordings—as he had done at the beginning of his career. The copy of these new series of advertisements in mid-1907 began by asking bluntly: 'Can you make records with your talking machine?'.[27]

Part 2: Consolidating the Business

What is noteworthy in the expedition era is not so much the rising quantum and competing outputs in this incipient business.[28] Rather, it is the consequences of the totality of the production of and trade in recorded music on the 'war of formats'—and thereby on the merchandising of Talking Machines—in India.

Imperatives of Mass Manufacture: An Expeditionary Settles Down

As things stood during the middle of the first decade of the twentieth century, the cylinder format seemed to have been better than the disc: its inherent advantage of offering both recording and play back capabilities on the same machine, and the fact that the grooves on discs wore out sooner than those on cylinders. Moreover, for discs that played from the circumference towards the centre, that is 'inward movement' discs—the tone of the reproduced sound had a tendency to grow weaker as the circle contracted.

But the expedition years resulted in a glut of the inward-moving disc machines—since this was the format adopted by the overwhelming majority of foreign recording firms. This lead to the gradual marginalization of rival formats, be they cylinder or the outward-moving disc formats. Cylinder firms had to fall in line. For instance, Pathe reissued Bose's earlier cylinder recordings on discs and by the second half of the decade, it began focusing on records sales more concertedly in East Asia. In India, Pathe concentrated on the other, 'newer' media it was commercially involved in: cinematography.

In this light, the historical consequences of the expedition era lies in it establishing a product that best encapsulated what the disc machine represented at that juncture, viz. a particular way in which pre-recorded music came to be manufactured, both technologically and commercially, and consumed. In other words, the mid-1900s announced the proliferation of the disc-based Talking Machine as a product that was at once a technological and a cultural form.

Thus, from a condition of varying possibilities of formats—and thus for the technological form of recorded music, we see how its economic organization succeeded in narrowing down one alternative. The entrepreneurial forces behind Berliner's product had marginalized those holding out for Edison's machine. Although cylinder records remained in India until 1910, the market rapidly grew around single and double sided discs. Mediated by a cross current of interests that characterized the entrepreneurial forces at play, the disc had become *the* format for disembodied music in India. The ascendancy of the disc over the cylinder format was harnessed even by the vendors of disc-based dictaphones, a far smaller market in India, in the following decade. For instance, in 1913, in response to a letter of interest for purchasing a dictating machine by the office of the Diwan of Mysore, the supplier, Roneophone Ltd of London, stressed that 'the recording and reproduction on flat surfaces is superior to cylinders', besides touching upon the 'portable and easy storage' qualities of their dictating machines.[29]

As the new dynamic reached an equilibrium during the expedition years, the cost of records—of a particular type, for a specific market like India—became the crucial variable for the competing firms. Consequently, their first attempt was to harness the advantages of scale and the second, to reduce the cost of raw materials. Although the original expeditionary, GTL, was witnessing a rise in its turnover of sales in machines and records in British India, the cumulative and complex environment of competition forced GTL to start thinking of ways to minimize costs in this rapidly expanding market.

At its Annual General Meeting in December 1907, two landmark decisions were taken. First, to drop the word 'Typewriter' from the firm's name, henceforth to be known as 'The Gramophone Company' (GC). Second, GTL decided to build a records factory in Calcutta, larger than the one simultaneously proposed at Barcelona and 'equivalent to that in Paris'. The choice of Calcutta as the location for GTL's records factory was evoked by two factors. First, it facilitated a ready and cheap access to the biggest global source for shellac, the principal ingredient for making discs.[30] Second, Calcutta being an eastern port, it would be easier and less expensive for GTL to ship discs to East Asia which hitherto, like India, was serviced by its Hanover factory.

As with all turning points in history, the first truly mass manufacturing facility in India emanated from a gestating sets of constraints and interests. In fact, The Gramophone Company's factory at Sealdah in Calcutta, which included units for assembling machines, cabinet making and record pressing, was the largest facility outside Europe and America. Here, GC began turning out 1,000 records a day; by 1909 out of a stock of 150,000, around 100,000 were 'native' records.[31] Staffed by British-trained Indian recording technicians, by 1911 it employed over 100 people a day, besides select individuals looking after its studios in Delhi, Lahore and Bombay.

Locating all this in the wider economic terrain of pre-World War I British India steers us to three observations. First, the general conditions in the formative years were characterized by the recorded music industry being dominated by foreign, especially British capital, the negligible development of an indigenous factory industry here being in accordance with the wider economic dynamics of British India as a whole.[32] Second, and more particularly, it was from their role as comprador traders—a la Vallabhdas Lakhimdas, Beka's biggest agent in Bombay—or as an appendage to foreign capital—as indicative from Bose's commercial expansion—that the first domestic manufacturers of recorded music originated, albeit at a scale resembling a cottage industry. Last, GTL's Sealdah plant, despite being the biggest in the colonial world, was also a case where a factory system was transplanted to India. As was with the smaller, domestic facilities, except for all the machinery, spare parts and technical know-how—GC's 'Indian' facility were dependent on the foreign mother firms.

Fashioning Disembodied Music: The Sculpting of Entertainment

If the first decade of the twentieth century defined the contours of the making of recorded music, they were equally significant in shaping the mechanics of its merchandising. From around 1908 we notice not only an intensification in advertising but, importantly, a substantive shift in advertising discourse. This is most amplified in the case of machines; in fact, Talking Machines were the object around which such a shift was instrumentalized. This change concerns a move away from highlighting the technical qualities and aesthetic traits of machines, to focusing upon the character of the social encounter the machine could facilitate. This was reflected in an attenuation in advertisements on the musical instrument per se, and through this a stress on recorded music as a cultural practice. These values expressed themselves in various forms in a host of advertisements.

First, it took the most obvious form of a direct and active projection of recorded music as a new and distinct form of entertainment. What was conspicuous in advertisements were the reasons given for buying Talking Machines—viz., 'you need not travel....The only perfect reproduction of the human voice', 'the entertainer...laugh for you, play for you'.[33] We may recall that before the gramophone, the quintessential symbol of a 'techno-cultural' music practice was the pianola. As a product of ninetieth century inventions in the mechanical reproduction of music, the pianola's attraction lay in its automated musicality, quite unlike the piano, which required skill, knowledge and labour. Consider the following copy for 'The Auto Piano' which had a lithograph of men dressed in business suits standing around an upright, with another man seated on a Cheshire chair.

> After the desk is closed
> Nothing relaxes the tension of business like music
> Nothing else is so completely satisfying and restful.
> Music is perfect recreation in the fullest meaning of the word.
> The Piano that every one can play without the knowledge of a note of music.[34]

While weighing this text together with its visual imagery, we ought to realize that the nature of musical practice in the piano was different in nature from that in the pianola. Whereas the piano stood for an active and informed musical practice, listening to the melodies on a pianola was portrayed as recreation, especially for those not skilled in music. The gramophone was a step further in this direction; it could not just 'play' musical notes like the pianola, but it could 'playback' the human voice itself.

The numerous advertisements for the Pianola and Music Boxes, from before the turn of the century, reveal that the sociocultural conditions for the commercial propagation of 'mechanised music' existed in India well before the advent of the Gramophone as a commodity. The incipient records industry in colonial India built upon this fertile material and commercial terrain of mechanized music and musical entertainment in two ways. First, by projecting 'music on record' as a commodity form that could satisfy the desire to listen to singers and musicians from distant cities and aspired cultures within the comfort of the home. Second, by pitching the 'automation' signified by the gramophone as being advantageous in both learning and listening to music. Here is an extended copy that perfectly illustrates these discursive details:

Reasons why people buy Gramophones and Gramophone Records
<u>A desire</u> to hear songs or musical selections that are familiar
<u>To hear</u> some song or pieces of music that you know well, but wish to listen to some particular performer's manner of rendering
<u>A wish</u> to study cultured music, excerpts and numbers from the great opera and composers, sung by the world's most famous artists or played by the master orchestras and bands of the principal music centres
<u>To enjoy</u> the best options in your own homes
Every Gramophone Record is a Work of Art.[35] (original underline)

What we see emerging rather rapidly is a whole new character of human interaction being added to advertisements. The technomusical personality of the gramophone was now being integrated with the social contexts within which recorded music was being consumed. In its merchandizing, the Talking Machine was asked to speak its own story. This is indicative of what can be called a prehistoric anthromorphizing[36] of commodities, a phenomenon which decades later got qualitatively amplified with the advent of television advertisements.

Second, advertisements began swaying more harmoniously to the tune of this music machine. One expression of this was the suggestion that recorded music could accompany, and even enhance, existing forms of entertainment. The most common illustration of this was records of melodies that accompanied dances like the waltz, what were called 'Dance Records'. The advantage of these lay, as one advertisement proclaimed, in enabling the 'general public in out stations where a Good Band is often unprocurable, to enjoy a Dance to music played by the finest Bands'.[37] This ad goes on to specify that on purchasing the listed set of 'Dance Programme Records', 100 Ball Programmes will be made available free. What we must also realize is that it was cheaper to have recorded music for private dance parties than to hire bands, the cost for four performances a month being Rs 150.[38]

Although machines were a significant investment, ranging from Rs 200 to 1,600, the recurrent costs of purchasing records was comparable with the price of one ticket to a concert or a ball. But records were a commodity whose value could be extracted collectively and continuously—it could be listened to by more than one person, again and again. Thus, commercial representations by the records industry sought to create a synergy between existing modes of musical entertainment and the economic rationality of recorded music.

The third construction of the personality of recorded music surfaced with the introduction of cabinet machines in the last years of the first decade of the twentieth century. In these models, the speaker-horn, once fetishised for its brass finish, was either detachable, or enclosed within wooden Victorian cabinets. Not surprisingly, attention and attraction returned to the physical aesthetics of the furniture-looking Machines; advertisements harping upon the quality of the cabinets' wood—'Mahogany',[39] 'Fumed Oak' or 'Satin Walnut'.[40] This is strikingly similar to the emphasis on the ornately carved cabinets of the organ marketed in India over 10 years ago.[41] The appearance of the cabinet machines was not just a rationale to buy the latest and improved models; the corporeal traits of this consumer gadget were sought to be integrated with the aesthetics of the upper class Indian home, viz.,

> Pygmy Grand model, hornless for a Boudoir or Private Sanctum (no horn to carry).[42]

The renewed emphasis on the non-musical aspects of tastes led to an all encompassing sales pitch, some advertisements beginning with a bold poser—

> In all seriousness, is your home complete without a Gramophone?[43]

This particular advertisement goes on to clarify that these machines are 'self contained in magnificent cabinets, with no visible sign of its purpose'.

Clearly, the Gramophone had moved on from being either solely a gadget for musical entertainment, or an object for display. It was presented as a commodity seamlessly in tune with prevailing tastes of furniture in the homes of the aristocracy, professionals, civil servants and business classes, the prime pleasure-seekers of recorded music. That by the end of the first decade the Gramophone was being sold in furniture shops and 'lifestyle' stores, like P. Orr & Sons in Madras, is overtly symptomatic of this—a marketing strategy which reiterated the upwardly social status attached to this 'new media'.

Part 3: Construing the Market

The alternating narratives so far demonstrate the co-emergence of two 'historical moments' in the formative years of recorded music. The 'first moment' illustrates the overlapping circumstances of entrepreneurial interests and economic contexts that unfurled the business in recorded music; the 'second moment' reveals a set of social and cognitive encounters involved in the commercial construction of 'music on record' as a merchandize. We could view the two moments as the anatomy and morphology associated with the growth of early recorded music in India, as long as each moment is recognized to impel the other. This section looks at their key impelling instances in detail.

The 'first moment', the circumstances shaping the manufacture of and trade in recorded music, indicates its character being influenced by an interplay of interests and contexts that were at once local and international. Let us briefly recall the conditions shaping the growth of this business. For the earliest players in the Indian market, recording and producing music constituted a very minor proportion of their business. Concurrently, to maximize profits, they sought to minimize expenditure on recording music, content only with replicating a uniform set of recordings, with the advantage of scale this brought. But this dynamics unfolded in conditions which were not only non-monopolistic but saw varying formats. Players who competed to sell machines along similar business models, constantly strove to provide something new and more relevant. This provided the logic for and culminated in the spate of recording expeditions from 1902 onwards. Although the amount spent on recording music increased (during expedition era) the price of records was kept at a minimum, otherwise consumers would buy a rival firm's repertoire of records. As the new dynamics reached an equilibrium, the cost of records produced for the Indian market became the crucial variable. A manufacturing facility within a colony having a large domestic market and closer to other emerging markets would put British firms at a big advantage in India. Thus, the first truly mass manufacturing facility emerged in India amidst a milieu where rival firms sought to maximize gains and minimize costs.

Retailing 'Music on Record': Distribution and Propagation

Developments in the trade in and manufacture of recorded music also impacted its distribution in India. Very much like the telephone just before it, and the radio much after it, the gramophone entered the market at the apex and very slowly seeped down.[44] That the market for recorded music in the first decade of twentieth century India was an elite market was not solely due to the price of machines. We believe, additionally, that precisely because recorded music was marketed as entertainment in the private sphere, was its social and commercial penetration limited compared to, say, early cinema which was commercially portrayed as a 'public' medium. In the formative years, even within this niche market, the proliferation of machines and music was geographically uneven in the subcontinent. In Madras Presidency, its proliferation was late, and initially slow; in the cities of Calcutta and Bombay it was the fastest and widest, while in the Northern cities, it was somewhere in between.

As mentioned at the outset of this writing, small shops importing musical instruments were the first to retail the Talking Machine. By the late 1890s, a wider set of traders were importing Talking Machines, along with other European luxury products targeted at the rich, such as sewing machines, bicycles and umbrellas. Interestingly, while in India cycle shops were an ideal springboard for selling Talking

Machines and other imported products—as the bicycle was amongst the earliest symbols of European technomodernity for the Indian consumer—in England things were looked at differently; only when the sale of Machines moved away from cycle shops, around 1909, that the Gramophone found itself rising in status.

Just before the turn of the twentieth century, Talking Machines started being sold in places which in retrospect seem more plausible—shops selling pianos, music boxes, harmoniums and other 'western' musical instruments. As the imports picked up, the leading music instrument retailers joined in, such as Harold & Co. of Calcutta and S. Rose & Co. of Bombay.

With the opening up of the Indian market after the first few expeditions, local vendors were joined by foreign records

Figure 5.1
Profile of Calcutta's Retail Market

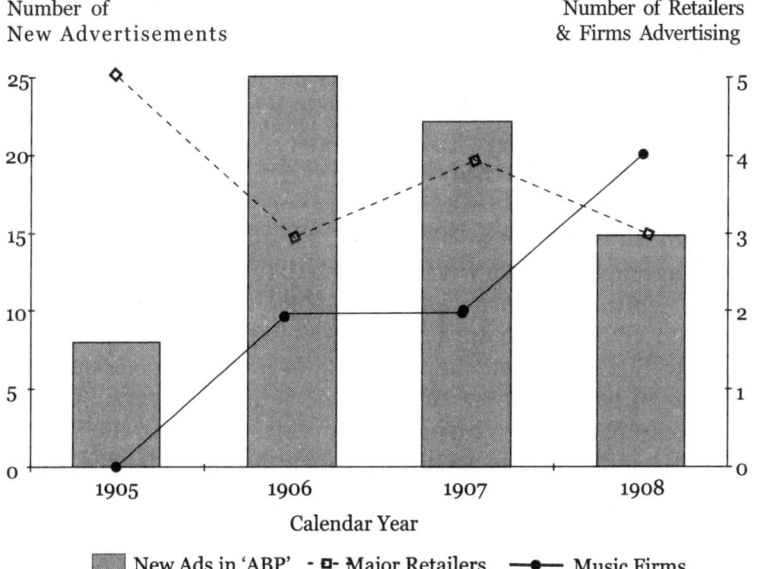

firms and their agents in securing a share of the expanding business. This is not surprising, for, as the sensitivity of foreign records firms to local tastes increased, a wider variety of entrepreneurs sought to cash in on the retail business. Glancing through advertisements in newspapers during the first decade of the twentieth century provides us a mirror of all the hectic activities comprising this, still primarily, mercantile activity.

By the middle of the first decade, we see a rapid increase in the number and frequency of advertisements for machines and records by a plurality of concerns—agents of foreign firms, foreign firms themselves, local manufacturing firms and, of course, local shops and trading houses. Accompanying this, we see three noteworthy developments. First, and most obvious, is the sprouting of vendors who dealt exclusively in machines and records, as much a sign of specialization in retail as an indication of the class status of consumers. Second, some domestic traders were no longer advertising only in their own cities, but across the subcontinent. Their efforts to sell machines and records even outside the three urban hubs,[45] constituted the first signs of an embryonic 'national market' in recorded music. Third, we see the beginnings of consolidation in the retail trade, with foreign companies choosing to have exclusive agents in parts of the country. In 1906, Beka Record from Berlin announced its sole agent in India, Burma and Ceylon,[46] Valabhdas Lakhimdas & Company, Bombay. This firm was a partnership between one of the earliest Talking Machine importers Valabhdas Ranchodas, and a new entrepreneur, Lakhimdas Rowji Taitsee.[47] Despite the increasing number of local retailers and agents, foreign firms also distributed directly, often under-cutting the price of their own dealers, a trait of free market competition in a premonopolistic stage.

And finally, we see shops dealing in lifestyle goods entering the retail market, some of them becoming the agents for foreign companies. For instance, by 1911, Spencer and Co. in Madras announced in its advertisements about it having 'taken over the sole agency' for The Gramophone Company in the province.[48] Despite the prominence of this retail store in the city, its advertisements chose to overwhelmingly highlight,

Figure 5.2
GTL/GC in the Advertisement Markets of Calcutta and Madras

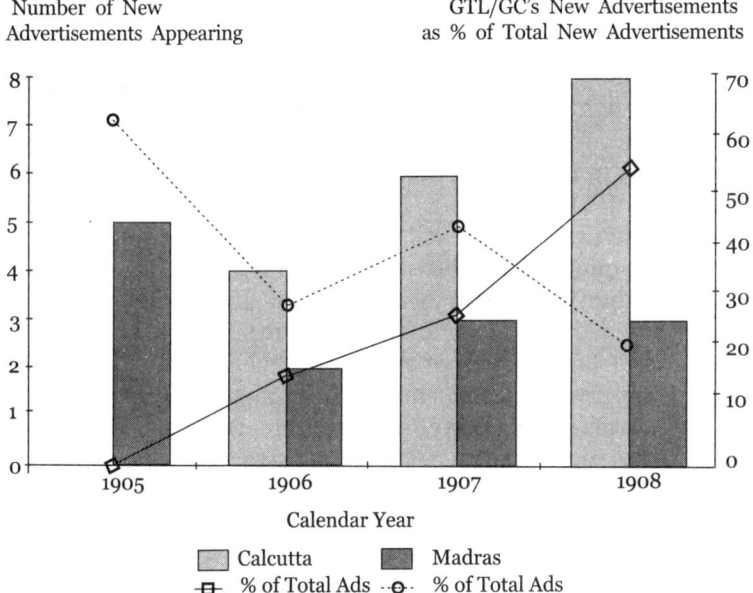

and thereby draw on, the brand identity of the foreign firm. From later that year, the retailer's advertisements provided prominence to the firm's 'His Master's Voice' trademark and different artists belonging to this trademark.[49]

But the retail trade had created other mechanisms for propelling recorded music as well. Hitherto, advertisements carried only a selective list of the singers whose records were being sold, along with the address of the retailer for those seeking complete catalogues. But the introduction of the 'Zonophone' records, a label of the now globalized GC empire, in advertisements in Madras around 1909 changed all this. By 1910, with each new monthly consignment of records, the entire list of singers was provided in the advertisements. GC's thrust on advertising was intensive and extensive, compared to that of any foreign or domestic records manufacturer. Largely focusing on the Calcutta market, their advertisements were not only always on the first page of major English dailies, but were most frequent in niche publications, such as the city's foremost trade magazine, *Capital*. In a September issue of *Capital*, for the first time GCL inserted a leaflet with a list of records of Bands, Western songs, comics, etc., a fresh tool for 'Infotisement'.

Even amongst its small base of consumers, it took almost 10 years for the Talking Machine and recorded music to transcend their status from that of a curio. This was also the time it took the retailers to understand the limitations and possibilities in the local market. These dynamics were deeply interrelated, each feeding the other: increasing entertainment value of canned music was realized by consumers with the widening of the Indian repertoire of records by firms; conversely, as firms widened the range of Indian songs, music and artists, they found larger sales of machines, the retailers being the first to observe this and emphasize it to the foreign firms.

Not surprisingly, therefore, retailers became central not only to the sales chain but also in constructing a personae for the merchandize. This is evidently discernible in the advertisements, which indicate that retailers were important to both the economic and cultural processes that went into moulding the market of recorded music. But this was a phenomenon not unique to the records industry, although it was more coherently visible here, it being a 'culture' industry.[50] Fortified by their own tradition, retailers strengthened their association with the foreign players first as distributors in the Indian business, gradually joining in to construct recorded music as a new cultural form.

Thus, in evaluating the rationality of the frameworks governing the distribution of records, we must appreciate that machines and records were not like furniture or umbrellas; they concerned a recognisably symbolic artefact. This is illustrated in the 'second moment', in the commercial arbitration of recorded music as a cultural product, particularly in the ways in which advertising came to mediate social encounters concerning this new aural practice. For, in advertisements from 1900 to 1910, we see a gradually growing but concentrated manifestation of the efforts to create a continuum, even a harmonious transition, between the inherited modes of musical practice, and the burgeoning business of recorded music.

An Audience with Music: Producing People for Records

We have made it abundantly clear that as a 'new media', the social grounding of the Talking Machine conveyed a manner in which music came to be produced and circulated—including the material and cognitive forms this entailed—and how these, in turn, shaped the milieu in which people came to relate to disembodied music as a new aurality. As a corollary, apprehending the merchandising of early machines and records must emphasize the redefined and fresh set of discursive practices accompanying it. This is where our focus on advertisements on disembodied music as a kind of meta-media—a symbolic encounter mediating another kind of symbolic encounter—gains renewed credence. For it was by mediating values and information on especially, and through, the Talking Machine that its image system aimed to propel 'music on record' on three counts—as a media technology, a cultural practice and as a knowledge form.

Right from the earliest years, owning a gramophone was as much a sign of wealth as of social status, akin to the more expensive piano, whose price started at Rs 600. Even Fred Gaisberg had observed that the Talking Machine was on par with the umbrella and bicycle as 'a hallmark of affluence'.[51] This is not to deny the absence of cheaper machines, ones that were priced similarly to other technological products imported into India, such as a binoculars and a folding camera—all of which were available for about Rs 100. But the more expensive machines constituted the bulk of the sales in the formative years. An American trade magazine insightfully observed in 1907:

> Cheap outfits are dead-wood, for the simple fact that TM purchasers in that country are either rich rajahs or

English Government employees, the other classes being too poor to buy at all. Naturally, the two classes mentioned want nothing but the best.[52]

This reveals the two, often distinct sociocultural strata which comprised the overwhelming buyers of recorded music; an aggregate scornfully referred to by Coomaraswamy, stridently against recorded music, as the 'bourgeoise public' of the gramophone.[53]

It was to this constituency that recorded music was commercially promoted as a means of private entertainment, in the domestic space of the rapidly urbanizing family units. This included representing recorded music in advertisements as being a superior form of consuming music and in tune with the wider technological modernity of the times, as we have shown. Nevertheless to contend that this mode of listening was perceived as an alternative to live performances,[54] may over-stretch the argument. In the latter half of the first decade, even amongst the gramophone's 'bourgeois public', recorded music was far from considered as being the primary mode of musical entertainment, either as a substitute to a live concert, or even on par with an *in situ* performance. The editor of a local trade journal in his preview of a 'high tea' organized on a ship anchored in Calcutta, judiciously reported in detail: 'The gramophone will discourse during tea. A fine music programme will then be unfolded'.[55]

It is more accurate to infer that advertisements provided a complementing symbolic and ideological microuniverse for recorded music. In doing so, it created a landscape of value system to which, and within which, the gramophone public reacted in varying manners both as consumers and listeners. At a more general level, advertising discourse sought to bridge the rupture between the inherited perceptions of musical entertainment and those emerging from the frameworks governing the production of recorded music. Elaborating this standpoint implies going beyond viewing advertising as a distributive mechanism. Here, the notion of 'cultural frames' becomes significant, as it enables us to pin point the social conditions of the commercial propagation of this 'new media'—a propagation based on experimentation with new, associational relationships between people and things.[56]

Let us illustrate this with a final example.

During the mid-1890s, it was rare for newspaper advertisements to have visuals of Talking Machines, or of a number of models of machines.[57] From 1898, we see a slow but definite growth in the incorporation of visuals of Talking Machines in advertisements—an increase in column space of the photograph/graphic/sketch, a greater detailing of the product and the appearance of such advertisements with visuals at a higher frequency in English language newspapers. This was the case for ads by not only the major foreign firms but those by leading local retailers in a city. But these images were bereft of not only any social or cultural context but of human interaction in general—just the visual of a machine, or at best two: viz., how it looked, say, when its horn was detached and folded in its box and while playing.

As the business proliferated, we see a transformation in newspaper advertisements from being informative, in the strictest sense of the word, to being coherently and visually discursive, in the ideological sense of the term. The pronouncements were not simply on commercial information that enabled sales but sermons on the cultural blueprints of music practice—something necessary to 'deliver' recorded music in India. Such ads began in Calcutta and Bombay, the early hubs of the business. We have been shown how in Madras, where the trade developed half a decade later, the business adopted a discourse expounding the modernity of its products via their advertising.[58] This is explained to rest on three interrelated branches: the technological, musical and cultural 'advantages' of the gramophone over coexisting forms of music practice, as indeed a plethora of evidence in this essay have also demonstrated.

But how did this script disclose itself?

From around 1908, we see graphics and sketches of people in active proximity, if not actually listening, to a gramophone. Furthermore, we observe an overt construction of the social status of the people in these advertisements—through what they wore and the social space where such listening was depicted, viz. in the lounge of a club, 'sitting room' of house, a ballroom or a private parlour. In other words, from 1908 we notice a change in the visual grammar of the commercial portrayal of machines. The juxtaposition of machine with human figures in varying contexts suggested a number of possibilities in which recorded music could be socially positioned. It is this increasingly complex and dense visual interplay of man and machine, together with the ad's copy, that enabled such representations to impart 'cultural frames' about and through recorded music. As a cognitive technology, advertisements for machines mediated a fresh epistemology of music as an aural encounter. Addressing individuals not only as buyers of records but as listeners of recorded music, such cultural frames sought to fashion consumers of records as audiences for music.

Agreed that the image system of mechanical and electrical goods was a new phenomenon at the dawn of the twentieth century—a novelty akin to the image system of the service industry in India during the mid-1990s. But what becomes more striking is the fact that the advertisements of machines as a visual encounter concerned the arbitration of not just a new kind of mechanical good but a new kind of aural, and therefore a social encounter itself.

Its merchandising were deeply aware of this. Ingrained in the mechanisms of the commercial propagation of recorded music was a recognition that 'music on record' did not represent an ordinary product, technology or ideas, but those associated with another, mass produced knowledge form. And it were these sensibilities that got cast in the changing grammar of advertisements in newspapers. In this sense, advertisements on the records industry acted as a meta-media, a form of media that reflected the nature and perception of another form of media. In other words, as a cognitive technology these advertisements sought to construe the cultural being of another cognitive technology, that of disembodied music. It is interesting to note that both these 'technologies' were in their infancy in India, and both were operating in free market conditions. But this was clearly emerging as a global phenomenon, as a study on the records industry in the US between 1910 and 1930 has shown. For it was precisely through an intensive advertising campaign that the Victor Talking Machine Company succeed in convincing consumers that the phonograph was not a toy but a cultural necessity.[59]

Conclusion: The Cultural Economy of a 'New Media'

In conceiving this inquiry, I was well aware that writings within a liberal framework tend to view the media, and communication processes in general, with varying degrees of autonomy from wider socio-economic processes. Opposed to these are approaches that conceptualize the media as part of the larger body of knowledge on social and cultural reproduction, something which unites the diverse nature of critical scholarship in the political economy of communication.[60] It is from such a perspective that this essay aspired to examine the merchandising and marketing of early recorded music.

Taking cognizance of a 'deeper'[61] political economy of communication helped me go beyond the tendency to investigate merely the technological basis and material production in media industries. This influenced me to incorporate an understanding of the cultural and ideological representation of recorded music, equally a part of its pristine making. In fact, the core of my effort occupied the interrelationship between the anatomy of the manufacture of these sonic artefacts and the readily visible morphology of their commercial representation—especially how the construction of the latter is successively influenced by the changing circumstances of the former. With this in mind, my framework emphasized the *dialectics* between the formative structures of the records industry and the emerging discourse of advertising concerned with its products, without the latter being subjected to a 'top-heavy', textual analysis. And having done so, I find that it was the variable and sometimes conditional outcomes of their interrelationship which together 'co-determined'[62] the merchandising of the cultureware of the early records industry.

Juggling with the conjunction of moments which nursed the 'birth' of recorded music, three sets of inferences may be surmised.

First, the import of 'music on record' was commercial and not technological. And the significance of its cultural form was not its autonomous musicality, but the creation of a new set of cultural producers and buyers, products and processes, on the one hand, and the overlapping aspirations of inherited and emerging social interests, on the other. I also discovered that since recorded music instilled a radically distinct mode of musical activity, what was required was not just the creation of new methods of manufacture but the inculcation of new avenues and methods of marketing. Investigating how 'music on record' came to be 'manufactured', in the widest sense of the term—the making of both its economic order and image system—I explained the processes whereby the foremost media culture in the industrial era came to be produced and propagated. In short, an insight was gained into the 'cultural economy'[63] of early recorded music.

Second, and more specifically, we see how the circumstances conditioning the formative business, our 'first moment', actually stipulated a 'second moment'—it demanded a remooring of existing perceptions of music as a socio-sonic experience. Central to the making of this experience were activities constituting the processes of merchandising. This was intricately moulded by two social fulcrums—a new set of commercial agents, the retailers, and a specific mechanism of commercial propagation, advertising. In enumerating both, I identify not only the imprints of the changing economic order of 'music on record', but also how their own shifting contours accompanied, and often emanated from, shifts in this order.

Germane to this process, third, we are able to visualize how advertisements signified a cusp where the interrelated instances of the expansion of the business of recorded music and the construction of an idea of 'entertainment' around pre-recorded music, overlapped to play out almost seamlessly. Advertisements, on the one hand, were an integral part of the process of manufacturing records; costs accrued in advertisements were included in the overall price of the records. On the other hand, they were crucial fulcrums of commerce and culture; besides facilitating the distribution of records as a physical commodity, they desired to shape the sale of 'music on record' by incorporating allusions to a variety of recognisable social situations and settings. This is most evident in the changing discourse in advertisements during the first decade. Thus, advertisements played a doubly important role in construing and constructing the market for the first 'new media' of the twentieth century. Since advertisements do not involve merely acts of a cognitive translation, transliteration or portrayal, my exercise of apprehending them necessitated a scrutiny beneath their textual and visual embodiment. It is this drive that led me to uncover how changes in the structure of the nascent (recorded) music industry found expression in the grammar of advertisements. Furthermore, these advertisements—while vividly reflecting the changing conditions in which recorded music was produced—not only construed it as a cultural form but cogently contributed in constructing a commodity market for 'music on record'. Thus, we find that the processes of the creation and proliferation of value systems that support and complement the economic order in which recorded music germinated, were as important as the order itself. In fact, I am in a position to assertively infer that they were part and parcel of the social organization of that order.

Notes

1. Woods (1995) has portrayed the colonial state's deployment of cinema in propaganda during the film industry's formative years, 1914–23, in India; regarding radio, see Lelyveld (1990).
2. Although this is evident in the absence of a policy on copyright in recorded sound, it is more marked in the case of tariffs. For instance in Spain and Australia, import duties during the first decade were specifically geared to protect local/national markets. In India, while tariffs on the import of machines and records began during World War I, this was shaped by the demands of a war-time economy rather than the desire of the colonial state to regulate and/or profit from the records business.
3. So much so that in research in ethno-musicology and cultural studies in India, a focus on live music—be it performative or ritual—is implicitly associated with the study of forms and sites of music pertaining to agrarian, rural societies.
4. A cursory look at the history of audiography indicates that it was a by-product of the efforts to expand the permissible boundaries of transporting sound. For Edison the invention of sound recording was precipitated by the need for an autographic telegraph: a kind of an audio fax. Of the numerous potential uses Edison envisaged of the phonograph, two contrasting identities of the nascent technology can be deduced. The first, as a machine to aide

office administration, as was Edison's priority, akin to a dictaphone—principally to record the spoken word. The second, as an instrument to mechanically reproduce music, the 'musical phonograph'—to replay pre-recorded songs, melodies, mimicry and other aural amusements (Laing 1991: 4; Middleton 1990: 84).

5. When in 1895 Maharaja Lal & Sons became the first dealer of phonographs in Delhi, the cylinders were known as '*Churi*' and the machine, '*Churi-ka-Baja*'. De (1990).

6. The story of the genesis of these 'formats' can be encapsulated as follows. In the early 1890s in the US, coin operated musical phonographs were installed in neighbourhood drug stores, cafes and gradually 'phonograph parlors' (Gelatt 1977; Read and Welch 1976). But for these entrepreneurs, the entertainment value of pre-recorded music hinged around distributing not only a wide variety of recordings but multiple copies of a specific recording. With an eye on this growing market, Berliner realized it would be easier to replicate numerous copies of a flat surfaced disc from a masterdisc, via a metal 'stamper'—akin to a negative in photography. In 1893 he began selling his cheap gramophone player and seven-inch disc records made of hard rubber. And in 1895, his engineer-colleague Fred Gaisberg, found shellac better than hard rubber for these mass produced discs. It is these interrelated developments in the US of the mid-1890s that resulted in the pre-history of sound recording giving way to the inaugural phase of the business in recorded music (Laing 1991; Martland 1997).

7. Parodies by Bert Sheppard, such as 'The Laughing Song', were particularly popular. Gaisberg (1942: 57).

8. Martland (1997).

9. Gaisberg's recordings of the Italian tenor Enrico Caruso in Milan proved to be the biggest contribution to GTL's immediate profits and eventual success in the formative years. Martland (1997).

10. Gaisberg (1942: 52).

11. Joshi (1988) and Manual (1988).

12. Kinnear (1994). Although Bose undertook recordings on cylinders before the turn of the century, these were aimed at preserving the voices of his friends, and thus for non-commercial, private use. But within a couple of years, and with the assistance of the French firm Pathe, Bose transformed his interest into a commercial venture, marketed as H. Bose Records.

13. William Gaisberg's expedition was two-staged—in the summer of 1906 and winter of 1907—as he found it hard to tackle the heat during the first run and went back to London.

14. 'Trade Topics' *Talking Machine News* (hereafter, *TMN*), vol. 3, no. 28, August 1905, p. 151.

15. *TMN*, vol. 5/67, Dec 1st 1907, p. 534.

16. Kinnear (1994). For an overview, see Kinnear (1992).

17. Sarkar (1973).

18. *Indian Mirror*, 1 November 1898, p. 1, advertisement by Harold & Co.
19. *Indian Mirror*, 12 July 1899, p. 1, 'The Phonograph' advertisement by Paul & Sons; *Indian Mirror*, 2 August 1899, p. 1, 'Phonograph and Graphophone' advertisement by Dwarkin & Son.
20. Such as the second advertisement, above.
21. Madras Mail, 12 October 1903, p. 7, advertisement by GTL.
22. *Pioneer*, 28 February 1906, p. 23, advertisement by Nicole Records.
23. Ibid., p. 24, advertisement for three models of Columbia Graphophone.
24. *Amrit Bazar Patrika* (hereafter *ABP*), 2 January 1905, p. 11, advertisement by Mullick Bros. 'Agents: The GTL', *ABP*, 19 September 1905, p. 8, advertisement by Mullick Bros.
25. Advertisements by The Talking Machine Hall in *ABP* of 30 April 1906, p. 8, of 21 May 1906 and of 3 January 1907.
26. Chandvankar 2002.
27. *ABP*, 27 May 1907, p. 9, advertisement for the New model Phonograph by The Talking Machine Hall.
28. By 1907 one estimate computes the total Indian imports to be around 600,000 records. Gronow (1983: 60).
29. Karnataka State Archives: GM File Part VI; 1912–15 (311 of 1912), pp. 1–20.
30. The chemical composition of Shellac made it ideal for such a use: it was hard when dry (therefore not easily perishable) but could be softened and moulded like clay for stamping the engravings from the master-disc.
31. 'Gramophone Company's New Factory at Calcutta', *TMN*, 6/86 February 1907, p. 504.
32. Mehta (1955).
33. Two new series of advertisements by The Gramophone Company in *ABP*, 21 July 1908, p. 1 and *ABP*, 3 September 1908, p. 1.
34. *Capital*, 13 August 1908, p. 329, advertisement by T.E. Bevan & Co. of Calcutta.
35. 'Music for the love of it', *Capital*, 5 November 1908, p. 929, advertisements by The Gramophone Company.
36. Jhally (1993).
37. 'Gramophone and Band Music', *Capital*, 3 December 1908, p. 1143, advertisement by The Gramophone Company.
38. Report: 'Band for Bandra', *Bombay Chronicle*, 26 March 1913, p. 6.
39. 'From Rs 200 to Rs 1600', *ABP*, 2 May 1908, p. 1, advertisement by GTL.
40. 'The Phonogrand', *Madras Mail*, 3 December 1910, p. 1 advertisement.
41. In the late 1890s, pictorial advertisements for the organ, invariably covering one-third column space on page one, categorically mention that the 'music desk are elaborately carved'. For in-

stance *Indian Mirror*, 5 November 1898, p. 1, advertisement by Harold & Co.
42. (Original brackets) *Capital*, 26 May 1910, p. 1151, advertisement by The Gramophone Company.
43. *Capital*, 3 December 1908, p. 1143, advertisement by The Gramophone Company.
44. It has been argued, with varying empirical evidence, that the substantive push to the popularization of recorded music in Bombay Presidency during the early 1920s was due to the increase in records of 'stage music' (Joshi 1988), while that in Madras Presidency during the 1930s was in conjunction with the 'talkies' (Hughes 2002).
45. Such as in Lahore, *The Tribune*, 14 November 1907, p. 7, advertisement by Sada Nand and Dewan Chand of The Central Gramophone Depot.
46. 'Trade Topics', *TMN*, vol. 4/40, May 1906, p. 153.
47. 'Trade Topics', *TMN*, vol. 3/27, July 1905, p. 111.
48. *Madras Mail*, 13 January 1911, p. 8.
49. *Madras Mail*, 31 October 1911, p. 7.
50. Well before the business of recorded music emerged in India, Jamshedji Tata land opined something similar on the character of local retailers-traders: 'Our small community is, to my thinking, peculiarly suited as interpreters and intermediaries between the ruler and the ruled in this country'. Statement in the *Times of India*, 12 April 1894, quoted in Ghosh (1985: 173). Although the context of his statement was the relationship between Parsi businessmen towards foreign firms, its import reflects the attitude of the Indian bourgeoisie as a whole during late colonial India.
51. Gaisberg (1942: 57).
52. 'Foreign Trade Expansion', *Talking Machine World*, vol. 3, no.3, March 1907, p. 3.
53. Coomaraswamy (1981: 190).
54. Hughes (2002).
55. *Capital*, 17 December 1908, p. 1235.
56. Leiss, Kline and Jhally (1990).
57. This must not be misunderstood as being due to the incipient state of print-advertising technology, and/or that of advertising practice in general in India. For, during these years the same newspapers carried many visually rich ads for other products—be they three-column photographs (prominently ads for organs) or detailed pencil sketches (like in ads for Dewars whisky which showed men in a 'drawing room' socialising with glasses in their hands).
58. Hughes (2002).
59. Kenney (1999).
60. Among these, the three classics are Mattelart (1979), Garnham (1990) and Murdoch and Golding (1977).
61. Williams (1977).

62. Mosco (1996).
63. Dimaggio (1977).

Bibliography

Chandvankar, S., 'Vande Mataram: A Most Popular and Evergreen Indian Song', 2002. http://www.mustrad.org.uk/articles/mataram.htm

Coomaraswamy, A.K., *Essays in National Idealism* (first published in Colombo, 1909) (New Delhi: Munshiram Manoharlal, 1981).

———, *Essays in Nationalism* (New Delhi: Sundeep Prakashan, 1981).

De, S.K., *Gramophone in India: A Brief History* (Calcutta: Uttisthata Press, 1990).

Dimaggio, P.J., 'Market Structure, the Creative Process, and Popular Culture', *Journal of Popular Culture*, vol. 11, no. 2, 1977, pp. 436–52.

Gaisberg, F., *Music Goes Round* (New York: Arno Press, 1942).

Garnham, N., 'Contribution to a Political Economy of Mass Communication', in *Capitalism & Communication: Global Culture and the Economics of Information* (London: Sage, 1990), pp. 20–55.

Gelatt, R., *The Fabulous Phonograph, 1877–1977* (New York: Macmillan, 1977).

Ghosh, S.K., *Indian Big Bourgeoisie* (Calcutta: Subarnarekha, 1985).

Gronow, P., 'The Record Industry: The Growth of a Mass Medium', in Richard Middleton and David Horn (eds), *Popular Music 3* (Cambridge: Cambridge University Press, 1983).

———, 'The Record Industry Comes to the Orient', *Ethnomusicology*, vol. 52, no. 2, 1981, pp. 251–84.

Hughes, S., 'The "music boom" in Tamil South India: Gramophone, Radio and the Making of Mass Culture', *Historical Journal of Film, Radio and Television*, 2002 (October).

Jhally, S. 'Communications and the Materialist Conception of History: Marx, Innis and Technology', *Continuum: The Australian Journal of Media & Culture*, vol. 7, no. 1, 1993.

Joshi, G.N., 'A Concise History of the Phonograph in India', *Popular Music*, vol. 7, no. 2, 1988, pp. 147–56.

Kenney, W.H., *Recorded Music in American Life: The Phonograph and Popular Memory, 1890–1945* (New York: Oxford University Press, 1999).

Kinnear, M., 'The First Indian Disc Record Manufacturers', *The Record News*, vol. 5, 1992 (January).

———, *The Gramophone Company's First Indian Recordings—1899–1908* (Bombay: Popular Prakashan, 1994).

———, *The Gramophone Company's Indian Recordings—1908 to 1910* (Victoria: Author, Heidelberg, 2000).

Laing, D., 'A Voice Without a Face: Popular music & the Phonograph in the 1890s', *Popular Music*, vol. 10, no. 1, 1991, pp. 1–9.

Leiss, W., S. Kline and S. Jhally, *Social Communication in Advertising* (New York: Routledge, 1990).

Lelyveld, D., 'Transmitters and Culture: The Colonial Roots of India Broadcasting', *South Asia Research*, vol. 10, no. 1, 1990.

Manual, P., 'Popular Music in India 1901–86', *Popular Music*, vol. 7, no. 2, 1988, pp. 157–77.

Martland, P., *Since Records Began: EMI the first 100 years* (London: Batsford, 1997).

Mattelart, A., 'For a Class Analysis of Communication', in A. Mattelart and S. Siegelaub (eds), *Communication and Class Struggle: 1. Capitalism, Imperialism* (New York/Bagnolet: IG/IMMRC, or International General/International Mass Media Research Centre, 1979), pp. 23–70.

Mehta, M.M., *Structure of Indian Industry* (Bombay: Popular Book Depot, 1955).

Middleton, R., *Studying Popular Music* (Open University Press, Milton Keynes, 1990).

Mosco, V., *The Political Economy of Communication* (London: Sage, 1996).

Murdock, G. and P. Golding, 'Capitalism, Communication and Class Relations', in J. Curran, M. Gurevitch and J. Woollacott (eds), *Mass Communication and Society* (Edward Arnold in association with The Open University Press, 1977), pp. 12–43.

Read, O. and W.L. Welch, *From Tinfoil to Stereo: Evolution of the Phonograph* (Indianapolis: Howard W. Sams & Co., 1976).

Sarkar, S., *The Swadeshi Movement in Bengal, 1903–1908* (New Delhi: Peoples Publishing House, 1973).

Williams, R., 'Base and Superstructure in Marxist Cultural Theory', *New Left Review*, no. 82, 1977 (November–December).

Woods, P., 'Film Propaganda in India, 1914–1923', *Historical Journal of Film, Radio and Television*, vol. 15, 1995, pp. 543–53.

6

A QUESTION OF CHOICE:
Advertisements, Media and Democracy

MAITRAYEE CHAUDHURI

India is widely seen as the world's largest democracy and increasingly also as a major economic player, a role which is attributed to India's new economic policy of liberalization initiated in the late 1980s. Proponents of both democracy and free market economy speak in the language of individual freedom and choice. A principal tenet of liberal democracy is that of a free media. Exponents of modern market economies argue that advertisements create the necessary conditions for 'free choice', a pre-requisite for a successful functioning of democracy. It could, however, well be argued that the media's financial dependence on corporate advertisements logically erodes its autonomy and thereby its role as the fourth estate of democracy. This is an old debate but one that has acquired significance in India more recently with the onset of liberalization.

The Context

Indeed this essay has to be read in the specific context of liberalization, the rapid growth of the advertisement industry and its impact on the media. Central to the rhetoric of advertisements in this period have been the concepts of choice and freedom that I seek to interrogate in this essay. We have seen major and dramatic changes in both the print and electronic media in the last decade. The most evident of these changes has been the number of channels on television, the additional supplements of newspapers and the increasing presence of new and glossy magazines. The more obvious of the changes has been the apparent proliferation of 'choices' that an individual has. The less obvious of the changes has been the control of corporations on the media through ownership and indirectly through advertisements. I seek to explore in this essay the contradiction between the very visible surfeit of choices that the media consumer has today and the much less visible constraint that the market wields over the media. This constraint decides both the range and limits of choices but operates in a manner that renders this control invisible. This it does with the closed circle of ideas with which advertisements operate. These ideas suffuse the media, blurring the boundaries between what is recognizable as an advert and that which may well pass off as a feature, news, or even an editorial (Inglis 1972: 101).

I argue here that advertisements in media have functioned as rhetorics of India's project of economic liberalization to alter the central motifs of Indian public discourse. The new Indian state in 1947 had stressed on growth with equity, not only as a model of development but also as critical slogan that defined independent India's public discourse. Development was projected as an important goal of the state for growth alone was seen as an answer to feed, clothe and provide shelter to India's poor. The poor, the peasant and the worker were imagined as the significant people that the nation constituted itself of and for whom the state had to address itself to. Gandhi's choice of apparel dramatized the social concerns of the national movement. Socialist reservations of the fallout of a free market for India expressed itself in the formations of the National Planning Committee by the Indian National Congress way back in 1938, an early precursor of India's path to a state plan oriented development.[1] This is not the place to talk about India's experience of a mixed economic development. Many would be sceptical of the nature of state licensing it spawned. But few would perhaps deny that the state had to keep in its rhetoric a commitment to an expressed concern for social security of the poor. The state itself now speaks of equity with efficiency.[2] The earlier slogan was growth with equity. While the state therefore finds it difficult to shift its rhetoric entirely, the actual contents of its policies speak the language of the market. Advertisements are more free to speak an unabashed language of individual consumption, freedom, choice, leisure and privileged pleasure.[3]

My questioning of the concept of 'choice' is therefore linked to the concept of the 'individual' and 'individual freedom', increasingly evident in the context of today's ascending ideology of market liberalism. Furthermore, the relationship between the apparent freedom of the individual and the freedom of the press in a market dominated context is fraught with the contradictions between the freedom of the consumer/reader to choose and the market control on the media which erodes the 'freedom of the media'. This addresses the thorny question between representative democracy and capitalism. As Therbon (1977) points out, capitalism as an economic system implies a society in which the imperatives of capital accumulation are dominant. This 'rule of capital' as he calls it runs counter to the 'rise of democracy', which implies a form of state in which electoral power has been equally distributed on the democratic principle of 'one person, one vote' and where the basis of representation is not wealth and influence, but universal suffrage and the 'sovereign will of the people'. Can these two principles coexist? Are they compatible or will they always be in conflict? And if they are in conflict, which will win? These are questions that have been intrinsic to the debate of liberal democracy.[4]

To extend Therbon's argument one could contend that since the end of the Cold War, the dismantling of the Soviet Union and the Eastern block, there has been a euphoric sense of the inevitability of capitalism and its supposedly necessary corollary, democracy. In India itself, an adequate appreciation of the sense of 'collective relief' of the middle class to the opening up of the market has to be understood not only by the sheer logic of availability of a large range of consumer items previously unseen, but also by the belief that the state had monopolized the media, particularly the state owned television and radio. I write 'collective' in quotes for it is the articulated opinion that emerges in the media that 'voices' and 'frames' this collective. Internationally, the collapse of the existing socialist states, the criticism of centralized state systems were for real. And a legitimate wariness existed about centralized control of information.

The Argument

A significant point of departure for us here in India is the fact that while the media opens up, while corporations actively recast the media, the state prerogative and primary importance to issues of 'national security'—itself a highly potent and possibly contested concept—continue. It is therefore even more pertinent to explore what exactly 'choice' means. And pose the question: are we overemphasizing the power of advertisements if the state does exercise almost absolute powers in some spheres? This in turn leads us to the question of spheres itself and the kind of ranking and prioritizing that the state accords to different issues like 'national security', 'development', 'freedom of expression' and different sections of India's populace—the poor, the middle class, the rich. Such an exercise may help clarify the concept of choice itself.

I would argue that as the state's agenda shifts away from a professed commitment to the real 'mass' of people—workers, peasants, tribals, students, women, the lesser mobile middle class—the rhetoric of abstract 'national security' gains ascendance. It is an abstract commitment to 'national security' rather than a tangible accountability to its people that the state spouts forth. One of the seamier sides of globalization that we stand witness to is the coupling of aggressive market liberalism with revanchist cultural nationalism.[5] Finding the enemy of the state becomes the prerogative of the nation. Alongside this obsessive concern with the security of the state (also read as the free way of life), manifest most grossly in the United States of America's policy of war against terrorism, runs the debate between market liberals and their critics.

India in the last few years has seen the opening up of the media to the private sector. Market liberals such as Murdoch have forcefully tried to put forward their argument that 'market competition is the key condition of press and broadcasting freedom, understood as freedom from state interference, as the right of individuals to communicate their opinions without external restrictions. Market-led media ensure competition. Competition lets individual consumers decide what they want to buy' (Keene 1991: 52). State protected media are also criticized for ignoring the interests of advertising. It is argued that the media should simultaneously provide two services, supplying programmes to audiences and audiences to advertisers. Other criticisms levelled by market liberals are about the paternalism of state protected media and that it squeezes, confines and reduces choice (ibid.: 53–56).

Critics of market liberalism on the other hand have been appalled by the systematic envelopment of human consciousness by corporate speech:

> Following Adorno and Horkheimer, they condemn advertising for universalising false images of abundance, novelty and freedom of choice. In reality, says its critics corporate advertising encourages individuals to fling themselves onto the treadmill of commodity consumption....*Advertising deadens the nerves of civil society*. It seduces citizens into using and discarding somethings and into disregarding others. Private desires stifle public spirit: nobody cares a nickel about anybody but themselves. Profanity, mindlessness, glitz and waste triumph (ibid.: 84, emphasis mine).

The point in question is that a sociological understanding of advertisements ought to stay clear of assessing the impact of an advert by its immediate fallout in terms of increase of the sale of the object advertised. What is of far greater significance is that as a whole, advertisements create a culture of entitlements that make a notion of good life marked by ideas of a just and free medical system, common and equal education, a wholesome and lovely environment both dull and silly.[6] Or worse still create an atmosphere which forecloses such questions from being asked. It thereby 'manufactures a product of its own: the consumer, perpetually unsatisfied, restless, anxious, and bored. Advertising serves not so much to advertise products as to promote consumption as a way of life' (Lasch 1978: 72). This is what is meant by 'the closed circle of ideas' or 'the magic system'. Once these ideas suffuse public discourse, the possibility of dissent itself is threatened.

My study is based on my almost regular perusal of some English newspapers and magazines namely *The Times of India* (TOI), *The Hindustan Times* (HT), *The Hindu, Women's Era, Femina, India Today, The Week* and *The Outlook*. The scope of such an exercise is limited to the English medium and the metropolitan cities. The English readership in India, though insignificant in terms of percentage, wields an influence which cannot be accounted by numbers. Their self proclaimed exclusiveness and their simultaneous claim to have an all-India reach are an essential part of a pattern of development, intrinsic to globalization, which is integrally a top-down and exclusivist process. The logic of such a process is a development which is uneven and fragmented, at the international, national and the local levels. In this entire process advertisements play a critical role, making one world of people and things more visible and rendering another world out of vision. As we thumb through the glossy pages of these magazines, pages of advertisements beckon us to a world of the rich, the famous, the successful; their work and their leisure, their public and private images.

I do not deal here only with the images which these advertisements beckon us with. I have dealt with this aspect exclusively elsewhere (Chaudhuri 1998, 2001). I address here the broader question of the relationship between advertisements and the media on the one hand, and between an advertisement driven media and democracy on the other. Critical to this discussion is the question of how does one identify an advertisement. It has been suggested that recognizing an advertisement is an easy business, something which audiences 'routinely accomplish'. The implicit intention to sell seems the deciding core which differentiates advertisements from other kinds of messages conveyed by the media (Pateman 1983). In fact, advertisements differ from each other in significant ways which can lead to three distinct kinds of advertising: direct advertising, shared advertising and indirect advertising. Direct advertising refers to advertisements commissioned by manufacturing companies and produced by agencies. It is what we most commonly understand as adverts. Shared advertisements is where the expense of an advertisement may be shared by two or more interested companies, or, in the case of 'advertorials', by the magazine and manufacturer. Indirect advertising refers to the support which successful promotion or marketing can provide upon which all forms of advertising depend. My own study of the English print media suggests that this is a form that has acquired salience.

> Manufacturing companies or hired agencies and public relation services work to provide magazines with up-to-date product information. This kind of promotion aims to encourage journalistic attention in the hope that it will reap favourable 'free' advertising benefits. The scale and significance of indirect advertising is hard to detect, as it may be incorporated into a magazine article or consumer advice page at the discretion of journalists and editors (Myers 1983: 481).

I attempt therefore to peruse the more indirect manner that commerce makes its presence felt in the pages of the media. I, however, confine myself to the text of the media with the intention of recording: (a) the debate within the media world for the need for and impact of advertisements; (b) the case that the advertisement industry itself makes for its own increasing role on the media; and (c) the imprint of the language of the sponsors in the advertisements themselves. The last is a methodological point for too often do we discuss advertisements in such a way as to almost empty them of sponsorship. This trend has acquired greater salience with studies that have demonstrated that the consumer is not a passive entity but a creative agent who can both subvert and transform the meaning that sponsors inscribed on the adverts. This may well be the case for one or the other advert, of one object or another. Advertisements companies know that. The effectiveness of a particular campaign is not our concern here. It is the generalized impact of advertisements as a whole that alter public discourse. Subversion as we all know operates within the paradigms laid down by the dominant section.

In the next section therefore I attempt two things: (a) draw upon writings by people who are in the business of selling, of promoting advertisements and of media managers; (b) draw attention to the increasing volume of features which are about advertisements in the media. Both processes reflect a proactive role by the advertisement industry to argue out their case in the media. Central to their discourse are the core ideas of choice and freedom, individual liberty and free market economy.

Advertisers and the Language of Market Liberalism

This essay, as would be evident by now, rests on the assumption that advertisements are a vital component in the organization and reproduction of capital. I have argued that the ideological role of advertising in society extends far beyond this limited commercial extent. The significance of advertising cannot be gauged only by looking at how effective a particular advertisement is in terms of selling the intended object while that may well be the yardstick of the copywriter. But the sheer power of the advertisement industry ought to be gauged by the simple fact that no newspaper or magazine can really be commercially viable without advertisements. An analysis of advertisements in the print media therefore has to be located in the context of the overall transformation of the media, where advertisements you booked and paid for were really old stuff; the real thing was what you got through ordinary news (Williams 1980).

Public discourse ceases to talk about issues of social justice.[7] Instead the media regales us with the 'happening' places and people. The page three phenomenon is now also part of the electronic media. These are not advertisements as we commonly understand them for no product is being promoted. Instead what gets reported and talked about in the media tends to encourage a condition of unbroken purchase and prodigality. It redefines 'good life'. A typical instance I quote from a leading newspaper. The 'news' item titled 'Bhang, Booze and Bonhomie: Holi Menace Sweeps City' reports among other happenings a party planned at the home of a journalist: ' "We're having a Holi bash for the consecutive year," informs Shukla, who has ensured that his "family-and-friends affair" turns out to be the talk of the town. "I'm expecting my politician and bureaucrat friends, besides those from the TV industry and the fashion fraternity"'(Arora 2001).

My survey of the English print media since 1993 has shown that it is not only the presence of advertisements that was witnessing dramatic growth but features on advertisements, sales, market strategies. Accompanying this were frequent write ups on child rearing, housekeeping, professional attire and demeanour that were actually presented as news items or researched pieces apparently having nothing to do with sponsors. Papers and magazines often carried lifestyle articles of the rich and famous, interviews of models and fashion icons until the reader really never knew which item in the magazine or paper was sponsored and which was not.

What to me seems significant is that proponents of this change in India, while arguing for the decisive role of the market, move beyond a defence couched only in the language of sale. They also articulate a world view. They state that the long years of independent India's tryst with planned development is passe. And today India is a society which has become 'plural'. 'And in a plural society, if you try to impose one opinion, a difference of opinion starts' (Das 1999: 58). Plurality here does not refer to India's fabled diversities—ethnic, religious, economic. What it does refer to are individual differences in taste and choice. This change of meaning accompanies many others, the concept of social commitment for one which itself is posited against individual choice. 'You can't be an isolated island thinking that you have a responsibility of changing society's heart. People are aware of things….We are not a homogenous lot….Every individual is unique....' And 'there may be violence in the front pages of newspapers but the reader may not be interested in it any more. He may go for sunny side journalism only.' The tale which hangs thereby is: 'If you manage to help your reader in becoming successful, then he will stay with you. Also, when he's successful he celebrates, and when he celebrates he consumes more. And when he consumes the advertiser is satisfied. That is the cycle' (Das 1999: 60).

What we have is a simultaneous focus on 'selling' and a construction of an ideology of consumption, individualism, free choice and the good life. We therefore are not only flooded with advertisements telling us to buy but messages that rearticulate how the Indian middle class ought to think.

As mentioned earlier the media has been witnessing not just advertisements but proliferating features on advertisements and the good life. The American public relations magazine in India, *Span* carried special features on advertisements. The gist of the articles is that, 'Advertising can drive down prices in a competitive market. It offers us a variety of choices. It can also help us to vicariously fulfil our fantasies of freedom and adventure without having to play basketball like Michael Jordan' (Hood 1998: 8). Most significantly advertisements are part of a discourse on the free market and democracy. It is denied to those who live in other kinds of societies. The post 1989 public discourse has increasingly veered to a position that unbridled capitalism alone can ensure democracy.

> Advertising represents the triumph of the consumer over the power of producers and vested interests. *Commercial advertising, at least, is found only in societies where individuals have the right to choose their own goods and services* from competing suppliers. Ads convey critical information about price, quality and availability. Furthermore, in many cases ads are indistinguishable from the product; to consume is to express yourself through the symbols that ads have invoked (the thrill of driving a new car down a highway is a good example of this phenomena)....As in other areas of our lives—such as *family or faith—free enterprise is a means by which*

we seek meaning and enjoyment. The extent to which advertising contributes to that function is greater than is usually perceived (Hood 1998: 8–9, emphasis mine).

This conjoining of family and faith with free enterprise is immensely significant in suggesting both the naturalness and sanctity of a market economy. What else could be more sacred, more important to a person than family and faith. For our purposes how much more evident can the ideological role of advertisements be. Images are powerful in advertisements. And John Hood, who is the president of the John Locke Foundation, a think tank based in North Carolina, referring to the power of these images writes:

> Whatever the source, it is obvious that in these cases the advertising becomes, in a way part of the good being purchased. To some extent, the buyer of a new mustang convertible is buying the feeling that the advertisements for the convertible have expressed, a sense of freedom or adventure.
> Some may view this side of advertising as a vice, but I see it as a virtue. It doesn't mean that advertising actually creates a demand for a product. It's not that powerful. The desire for goods and services to make our lives safer, cleaner, easier and more enjoyable is already implanted deep within us. What advertising does is merely to bring that desire out into the open, and give it a distinct form (ibid.: 10, emphasis mine).

The thrust of the argument is that both the desire goods and services that advertisements offer are 'natural', implanted deep within us. Hood approvingly cites James Twitch who observed;

> Advertising is simply one of a number of attempts to load objects with meaning. It is not a mirror, a lamp, a magnifying glass, a distorted prism, a window, a trompel'oeil, or a subliminal embedment much as it is an ongoing conversation within a culture about the meanings of objects. It does not follow or lead so much as it

interacts. Advertising is neither chicken nor egg. Let's split the difference: it's both. *It is language not just about objects to be consumed but about the consumers of objects* (Hood 1998: 100, emphasis mine).

Readers would notice that my sources are from the popular media in India. I did not have to do a search to find out articles on advertisements. Indeed my study started with a concern for the images in the 'real' adverts but found out soon that something else was happening here. A self conscious attempt seemed underway to build a discourse on advertisements in the popular print media. The 1990s had euphoric articles on advertising for it is 'the life-blood of modern business'.

> Liberalization hasn't catered to any other sector as it has done to the Indian advertising Industry. The pace of its growth kept scaling up since then and attained propositions for the market watchers the world around. With near stampede of products in the market it was inevitable. Gone are the days when you had the choice of selecting products from the limited national brands. Today the multinationals seem to have penetrated into almost every consumer product range (Badal 1997: 110).

The ideological role not only celebrates the burgeoning growth of the market but reminds the Indian middle class of the long years of denial under Nehruvian socialism. Men and women depicted in the advertisements speak for the entire upper and aspirant upper middle classes' desire to break from a past where public discourse spoke of thrift and of obligations to society—now perceived as obstruction of the individual's desires and potentials. Along with the dismantling of red tapism, licences and restrictions, Indian men and women have also been 'freed'. I present below a very typical reminiscing to the 1980s.

> If a style guru ensconced in some temperate clime deemed tight (Guess!) jeans in...I had to be seen in a pair ....That meant, in those pre-liberalization days a visit to

the friendly neighbourhood smuggler's. Since I was a student and my father wasn't Dhirubhai or...who ran the petrol pump down the road, that meant also parting sorrowfully with the grimy notes saved from a meagre allowance. All for that pre-washed, light blue work of art. Or beseeching letters were sent off to American cousins (*Saturday Times* 12 December 1998).

My central contention has been that an analysis of adverts alone is not enough. One has to bring to notice the proactive manner in which the corporate sectors and the advertisement industry themselves make their presence felt in the media. Integral to this are the increasing number of opinion polls and surveys conducted by the corporate sector on the readers/customers/audience. The distinctions between these necessarily blurs. The 'reader' you would recall is really the 'customer' and today the advertisement industry is brain storming about who the customer is. I draw just one or two of such reports of surveys conducted. These surveys make explicit the rationale with which advertisers operate but which disappear from the text of the advertisement itself.

'What drives Sybil?' a lead article in *Brand Equity* (a supplementary of the *Economic Times*) debates on possible Indian customer profiles. 'The AP Lintas universe prefers to slice Indian consumers into survivors, savers, enhancers and splurgers....The urban and rural poor are survivors and savers are the middle classes. Enhancers are the urban upper class, and splurgers the rich' (*Brand Equity* 16–22 June 1999). It is widely known that product advertisement has generally given way to lifestyle advertisements. Hence the language of advertisements are more about the consumer than the object to be consumed. The advertisements themselves therefore give overt profiles of the new generation. Advertisements demand that the media seek an audience who is 'hedonists', who likes to 'experiment' and has an attitude to spend.

There are two points that I wish to make. One, that the image of the Indian drawn up has customer in mind and no analysis can escape this commercial context. Two, that the 'splurger' is of defining significance. Not all can afford the wonders that advertisements project. But they can desire and aspire to be like them. A new normative Indian has slowly come into being. I find David Chaney's observation of interest where he tries to show how 'the new social form of lifestyles was coloured by some of the broader narratives of the cultural forms of consumerism', summarized under the headings of 'fantasy, excess, spectacle and citizenship'. The first three are reasonably self-evident. The last is not. Chaney's reason for using it is that he found no better way of putting the idea that mass marketing, as with other forms of mass democracy, offers the illusion of equal participation and indeed even the glory of 'national culture' without much of its substantive powers (Chaney 1994). This I think is a very useful way of understanding advertisements and the images they extend. Everybody can look and hear the advertisements. (many in India still do not have access to TV sets, radios) Few can read advertisements. Fewer still can read English advertisements. The numbers that can actually possess the goods advertised would be smaller still. But theoretically everyone has access to advertisements, to the pleasure of looking, to desiring.

While the advertisement industry has its own research apparatus to explore changes in the new Indian (customer) there are other sponsored surveys also conducted on different segments of society. One such survey of college students conducted in the major cities affirm that this new generation of students are unapologetic about its competitive attitude to life, their unabashed self-interest (Pathak 1994: 73–87). Such attitudes, the survey moreover suggests were markers of the 'maturity' of the New Generation as opposed to their 'honest but immature' predecessors swearing by Che Guevara and looking for 'causes' to uphold. While 'this generation is probably the most lonely, calculating, overstressed generation of youngsters that India has ever seen', it is optimistically concluded that that this singular emphasis on 'individualism' might well lead to collective good. 'The New Generation might well be the harbinger of a social revolution.' With the collapse of the socialist world, 'social revolution' takes on new meanings. And the advertising world has been quick to seize the lexicon of an earlier era of movements and radicalism towards their own ends. The women's movement has been no exception to this process (Chaudhuri 2000).

Scholars have pointed out the distinction between the functional and emotive function of words. In the former one applies what is called a 'linguistic rule', the role of which is to stabilize responses to a word. Definitions hold good for the functional or cognitive function of words. But for the emotive, the suggestive there is no linguistic rule to stabilize meanings. In Stevenson's system therefore, '...emotive "meaning" is something non correlative to and independent of descriptive (or cognitive) meaning. Thus, emotive "meaning" is said to survive sharp changes in descriptive meaning. And words with the same descriptive meaning are said to have quite different emotive "meanings". "License" or "liberty" for e.g.' (Lodge 1978). Bakhtin had stressed that contexts are already textualized. The new generation Indian steps into a world rich in meanings and allusions. Words have histories embodied in them. And words common in pubic discourse need to be redefined with the shift in state policy. Advertisements are important for this purpose.

Is this an Ad? The Blurring of News, Interviews and Adverts

Features and write ups on the advertisement industry and reports on various commissioned surveys are not the only ways that the new ethos of commerce makes its presence felt in the media. My survey of newspapers and magazines since 1993 indicate that while *The Times of India* moved in the direction of commercializing early (with its price cut, dismissal of tenured editorial staff, its range of supplements, city editions dealing almost exclusively with lifestyle articles), it was really a forerunner of a practice that has felt its presence in almost all publications. A number of national newspapers now regularly publish business supplements which report on the progress of important industries be it fabrics, tourism, telecommunications, steel, information technology, advertising. The spread and success of such supplements are themselves a measure of the deep penetration of the communication system by the corporations.

Newspapers and magazines are increasingly awash with columns on changing lifestyles, the social circuit of industrialists, diplomats and socialites. In all an entire ethos and structure of beliefs are created which compose the ideology of advertising and of its sponsoring system. A typical feature in the *Saturday Times* (supplement of TOI) titled 'Take A Break This Sunday' reads:

> Today we find ourselves in the midst of a cataclysmic change. The work place is metamorphosing into an intensely competitive, consumerist, sometimes savagely professional environment, where every yuppie is competing for a foothold on the career ladder for fat pay cheques, fatter perks and fancy titles. It was bound to happen when the economy opened up. Undeniably, the multinational way of life is here to stay (*Saturday Times* 17 December 1994).

The reader gets to know what people do to have a break. Yoga, music, the 'Once a month I fly down with my family to our farmhouse in Bangalore' all in a sense tell us the kind of things we can all do or dream. Advertisements build on this, telling us further what to do with our workplace, our leisure, our family and privacy. There is a feeling of boundless new possibilities to be explored through the boundless new products that arise everyday. The articles, the focus, the advertisements form a continuum. The reader in a very real sense can move from an article like the one above on 'weekend breaks' to an advertisement without any sense of rupture. An important way this functions is the manner in which the line dividing news from advertisements, advertisements from features is the proliferation of interviews with 'celebrities', itself a proliferating tribe and a term which has entered currency in India only postliberalization.

The print media also carries a large number of features on the changing lifestyle of the new generation Indian. While articles on the new emerging norms of families, marriages, career choices, gender relations are common, there are explicitly sponsored features which also deal with profiles of 'the new Indian.' For instance *The Economic Times* describes in a feature titled 'Outsourcing comes home' the new needs of 'specialized providers' for 'Indian metro professionals who are as time-poor as their American counterparts' (19 October 1999). A 'Response Feature' entitled 'White Goods and Woman: Consumer Durables and Finance' (TOI 16 June 1995) writes on 'catering to her changing needs'. Starting with Sushmita Sen's words, that 'the essence of a woman is motherhood and she teaches a man to love and care', the feature goes on to say how while 'motherhood is associated with the word "housewife", and 'evokes the traditional concepts of feminity which holds good even today', cognizance has to be given to the fact that 'women have confidently assumed a new role, that of a professional'. The demands for consumer goods is placed in this context.

Since homes become central sites of consumption in capitalism we not only have many adverts on kitchen designs but also have the researched piece on kitchens themselves. *Saturday Times* thus carries an article on workable designs for homes: 'A good kitchen has to be well designed with comfortable work areas. All research about fatigue and inefficiency on account of work areas not being close together in offices, applies to kitchens as well. Added to it is the concern for safety....Good storage space is essential to any kitchen' (17 December 1994).

Significantly the print media itself has to advertise itself. An image has to be cultivated and a segment of reader/consumer/audience has to be identified. *The Times of India* and *India Today* in particular use their image as publications with a high profile readership to attract advertisements. *The Times* thus carried an advertisement in the front page with a big black blurb written 'Last 3 days' with the following write up:

> The front page of *The Times of India* carries an air of distinction about it. In fact, it can make sure that there are no last three days.
> As advertising professionals will agree, the front page solus ad gets pride of place. It is the first ad in the reader's day, and has the best chance of making a sale. The solus ad is the only display ad on the page, with very little to distract (25 February 1995).

Newspapers and magazines thus have a profile which is carefully cultivated. There has been a remarkable increase in the exclusiveness and specialization of newspapers and magazines in the last few years, facilitating the catering of advertisements to the likely purchasers. For example, a cursory comparison of advertisements in *India Today* and *Women's Era* suggest different target groups. A comparision of the nature of advertisements in different publications is not our concern here. I refer to this aspect only to emphasize the concerted effort of the advertising industry to reach every potential reader who is also a potential customer.

A central attempt of this essay has been to understand the relationship between advertisement and media. I have understood advertising as a commercial activity that is firmly locked into a total structure of communication system. My central intent here has been to understand the ideological transformation that an advertisement driven media can bring about in public discourse. I have argued that key to this ideological transformation are ideas of choice and freedom that market liberalism promotes. In the above two sections I have attempted to demonstrate that advertisements alter media not by the 'real' adverts alone but by a range of methods. Important to my core argument has been the understanding that mass communications groups interweave a national structure of values and attitudes. The significance of advertisements lies therefore not in one advert or another, but in the closed circle of ideas that it creates where even a suggestion that adverts are constraining would be laughed at. What I am arguing therefore is that it is not the loss of this or that advertising client to a newspaper or magazine that would be important. These things would happen in the normal competitive run of things. What cannot happen is a wholesale movement away caused by management and editorial styles. The harmonious interaction of advertising and editorial styles which consistently reproduce and endorse the consumer's way of life necessarily persists.

The Print Media on its Redefined Relationship with the Market

It is widely accepted today that:

> ...*publications are almost mortally dependent on advertising revenue*. The cover price of publication brands move within a narrow band. While the material cost and news gathering cost of newspapers have gone up (several have folded up in the last few years) the cover price has remained stagnant. So the bottom line of any publication business can be pushed up only in advertising revenue (Ansari 1999, emphasis mine).

A market-driven media has 'to capture the advertiser', for which 'the media must attract the right reader....If you have to get advertisements, you have to get the audience to stay in your publication. And if you want him to stay it has to be for him, because today's is the "I" generation. So, if your offering doesn't help him become successful, if it doesn't entertain him, he's not interested' (Das 1999: 57). This matter of fact tone, the recourse to pragmatic market sense all effectively constitute the new rhetoric.

> The trouble with print media is the high gestation period for returns and the high cost of production. The newspaper's or magazine's cover price alone doesn't cover these costs. As such the reader has got used to getting his newspapers at highly subsidised rates. If the cost of producing the paper is Rs 5 and if you are selling it at Rs 2 then you are selling it at a higher subsidy. Naturally, you have to depend on advertising cost to cover your cost. On the other hand, if you try to sell the paper at Rs 5 today, how many readers will buy it? But the fact is that the cover price has to go up, because as more of the advertising revenue gets divided between television, direct marketing, the Internet etc., more value migrations will take place, and advertising may not cover the print media's costs. *For the moment, print media*

> *cannot do without advertising as it accounts for 80 per cent of your revenue* (Das 1999: 58, emphasis mine).

From the perspective of the media manager who wants to be commercially viable the options seemed to be closing down. As Das goes on to elaborate:

> The advertiser, thus, becomes the primary customer of the print media, and he uses the print media as a vehicle to reach his customer who happens to be that medium's reader. So, *I, the print media, am not trying to get readers for my product, but I get customers, who happen to be my readers, for my advertisers.* My target audience becomes those whom the advertiser wants to reach out to, and the advertiser wants to reach people who are young at heart—15 to 35. People who have the disposable income, who have the attitude to buy and to spend....This is my psychographics. This is not in money terms only. That way, even a paanwalla might read my paper, but he won't spend. *Advertisers like to reach readers who are successful, who celebrate life, who consume, who are early adopters, who believe in experimentation, who are hedonists. In this respect, youth is a strong reference point, representing what's modern and trendy.* Those who are older will also read what excites the youth because it's aspirational for them and don't want to fall behind. For those who are younger this youth is the role model (ibid., emphasis mine).

Such commercial imperatives of liberalization made its presence felt most dramatically in the changes that TOI underwent until the whole paper took on the appearance of a tabloid. Of course the circulation figures soared. An insertion in the *Brand Equity* supplementary of *The Economic Times* (a sister publication of TOI) reads:

> We hate to admit it, but there's hardly any difference between The Hindustan Times and The Times of India, Delhi. We then have a graph of comparative circulation figures and the text reads: 'Not editorially, of course.

What we are talking about are the numbers. 546, 212 copies in circulation. Just 3.6 per cent less than the No. 1. Too close for comfort. The Times of India. The No. 2 daily in Delhi?' In 1993, the TOI figures were 171079 as compared to HT at 343763 (16–22 June 1999).

The alleged 'reader friendly' approach of TOI was most evident during an interview with the then editor of the TOI, Dileep Padgaokar that appeared in the Metro Channel broadcasted on 26 June 1999. The programme was discussing the inadequate coverage of the Northeast in the media. His response was that perhaps the reader may not be interested. This perhaps captures what Bhaskar Das describes as the sunny side of journalism. This is perhaps also what Inglis sought to put across about an instance of a business supplement which argued that 'the fundamental challenge of democracy' is that people 'don't always want what is good for them'. The unexamined assumption is that the sales curve is the measure of the rational choice and the unsolicited desire of consumers in a free market economy (Inglis 1972: 55).

Journalists of an earlier generation in India saw their role quite differently. The print media in India had a historical role to play in the anti-imperialist national movement, and in independent India saw for itself a role in the establishment and running of a fledgling democracy and a poverty stricken country. Ajit Bhattacharjee, the then Director of the Press Institute of India writes:

> For several weeks I have been going through mainline English-language newspapers looking specifically for field reports and feature articles on happenings in the rural parts of our country, small towns and growing slum colonies. Some 70 per cent of our people live in these areas which, to my mind, comprise the 'real India'...the national press, presumed to provide the information that moulds the opinions of senior policy makers, politicians, academics and journalists themselves. They are expected to serve as watchdog over the system of governance, a role traditionally described as that of the 'Fourth Estate' (1999: 47).

And again Bhattacharjee emphasizes:

> The responsibility of the media in a democratic developing country is not the same as in affluent, advanced countries, where there is less of a gap between the privileged few and the under privileged many, and society has stabilised. Until the few, who include the policy makers and executors, are made aware constantly of the condition of the rest the gap will widen until the system breaks down (1999: 48).

Bhattacharjee's views are clearly not in sync with the 'sunny' journalism advocated by Das. A shift of accountability is clearly taking place. The moot question being: is the media accountable to the corporations by providing eventual consumers? Or is the media responsible to make policy makers aware of the conditions of the dispossessed?[8] Our study of an advertisement-suffused media shows that the concerns of the poor, the low middle class are either rendered invisible or framed in a manner that makes them look responsible for their own plight. For the mantra of market liberalism is that were they of any mettle, the market would have rewarded them. For the market is both fair and free.

Conclusion

I had proposed at the start that the relationship between the apparent freedom of the individual and the freedom of the press rests on a basic contradiction between the freedom of the consumer/reader to choose and the imperatives of market control on the media. I have sought to explicate this by analysing: (*a*) how the text of the advertisements and features within the print media speak the language of sponsors; (*b*) how the advertisement industry itself makes a case for its own increasing role on the media; and (*c*) how the media itself understands the change. While contextualizing the essay within the broader debate of democracy, media and capitalism I locate it in the particular context of India's new economic policy. A central contention has been that advertisements in the print media have sought to make a break in the public discourse in India during this period.

Another point that I have stressed upon is that the role of advertisements cannot be gauged by looking at 'real' adverts alone or by the prospects for a single product:

> The institution must also generate a moral as well as an economic climate which controls attitudes towards consumption, modes of perception, linguistic conventions and changes. To sustain real inquiry into this process we must also notice how powerfully the ethics of advertising suffuse the whole system of communication (Inglis 1972: 9).

Even a cursory look at the English print media in India would show that the attitudes, the ethics of advertising promoted are that of an idea of good living characterized by an aspiration at once wistful and familiar towards the lifestyle of the very rich; the ostentatious display of wealth and worldly success; the acquisition of objects (including beautiful women) in order to secure one's social identity. Apart from this generation of a moral as well as an economic climate that advertisements produce, it is critical to appreciate the fact that advertising is locked firmly into a total structure of communications system. This is the point that this essay has sought to make. We have gathered from the stated position of the media barons and management that the first intention of a newspaper or of a commercial television is to gain advertising revenue. A newspaper's relation to its advertising backers therefore varies according to its circulation and its reader's social habits. We have also seen how newspapers and magazines carefully cultivate its image in consonance with the image of the reader/customer (Chaudhuri 1998). This dependence on sponsors, however, does not imply that a particular organization will necessarily dictate its editorial policy on some line or other (though it may), but rather the much more elusive result will be that the topic and tone of a publication will be deeply coloured by its place within the commercial structure. What we have found is that there is a harmonious interaction of advertising and editorial styles, styles which consistently reproduce and endorse the consumers' way of life. As I have argued in the course of the essay, one can barely discern the line between fact and fiction, news and advertisements. The style which blend editorials with advertisements and advertisements with news has an easy presumption about the style of telling, for the manner never really admits of contraversion. For the style is also a code of manners and, it follows, a structure of values.

Simply put, the central values are extreme wealth, sexual attractiveness and rapacity and competitive success. Attainment of the values is signalled by acquiring the appropriate objects, using them, throwing them away and acquiring replacements. At the same time the circle of advertising information is tightly closed to the intervention of such questions as 'Who goes short while you produce more?', 'Do we need what you produce?', 'Who pays for you anyway?', 'How do advertisements constrain the freedom of the media?', 'How can an individual be "free" to "choose" when the information available is entirely suffused with corporate speech?' Such questions cannot of course be asked, because it is the nature of the total systems that they close the circle against alternatives. For:

> The whole concept of democracy is bound up with this concept of rational argument, and the democratic concept of equality partly to be elucidated with reference to the fact that rational argument appeals to criteria which entail a verdict that is irrespective of persons. If, however, I change your views by giving you injections, or by causal manipulation of any other kind, then I destroy this equality, for I see you as manipulated, myself as manipulator (MacIntyre 1962: 68).

What advertising must therefore do is to close the circle against reason (which is impossible) and embody the non-rational way of life as normal on the one hand and argue that the rationality of the corporate world is the rational on the other. The first it does by talking about prodigal consumption as an intrinsic way of being and of freedom of choice without perceiving what alternatives remain neglected or suppressed and without naming actual suffering and scarcity. These are critical freedoms for any society but for India where the majority are poor and dispossessed, the freedom to choose too often simply does not exist. The choices we make are thus limited in number and largely empty of social significance. The second it does often by overtly defending advertisements as instruments of democracy. We have seen how the media has over the last few years in India had features in defence of advertisements.

Views on the relationship between democracy and private aggrandizement are intensely contested. They also rest on alternative understandings of both the content and motor of democracy. I have attempted to show how an increasing control of the market of Indian media has been accompanied by a vigorous campaign that the market alone ensures freedom, democracy and happiness. I have also sought to show how the meanings of key words like freedom, democracy, choice, collective responsibility are getting redefined. Indeed:

> ... there is a structural contradiction between freedom of communication and unlimited freedom of the market, and that the market liberal ideology of freedom of individual choices in the marketplace of opinions is in fact a justification of the privileging of corporate speech and giving more choice to investors than to citizens. It is an apology for the power of king-sized business to organise and determine and therefore to censor individual's choice concerning what they listen to or read and watch (Keene 1991: 87).

Notes

1. I am not suggesting that the Nehruvian model was socialist. Indeed I have elsewhere analysed the First Plan Document on Women to argue precisely the contrary. See Chaudhuri 1996. But an attempt to mitigate the harsh impact of corporate capitalism and protect the Indian economy from the vagaries of international capital was certainly there. Significant for our concern

in this essay, the media was entrusted with a social responsibility for India's less privileged section.
2. Yashwant Sinha, the Finance Minister of the National Democratic Alliance (NDA) government, presented the annual budget on the slogan of equity with efficiency. *The Hindu,* 1 March 2002.
3. Its in a sense ironic that between the writing of this essay and its publication, the United Progressive Alliance (UPA) has come to power while the National Democratic Alliance (NDA) led by the BJP which had conducted a blitzkrieg campaign of 'India Shining' advertisements has been defeated. The present Prime Minister Manmohan Singh, widely seen as the architect of India's liberalization policy remarked that 'We are not going to pursue privatisation as an ideology'. And the Congress led UPA has been addressing the concerns of the peasants, a category that had been virtually eclipsed in the media in the last decade.
4. A recent article by Harish Khare in *The Hindu* addresses this in the context of the entry of extremely rich members in the Rajya Sabha which political parties have felt obliged to accommodate. Khare terms it as the 'Silvio Berlusconi phenomenon' (2004: 10).
5. This is an issue that seems to be occupying space in the public discourse after the defeat of the NDA.
6. This point is important in the background of an increasing tendency within sociological literature to argue that the consumer is no passive entity and responds autonomously to adverts.
7. Once again after the 2004 elections which was seen as evidence of the disenchantment of the poor and marginalized with liberalization, the English print media has been carrying pieces that reflect this.
8. This is a point that has resurfaced in a big way after the 2004 national elections. The many opinion and exit polls simply failed to gauge the resentment of the marginalized against the NDA. The media was not able to identify the issues that were of central concern of those who are now being termed even within the media as belonging to a 'non-shining' India.

Bibliography

Ansari, Tariq, 'Is publishing a sunset industry', 1999. Cited in Bhaskar Das, 'The Paper Chase', *Gentleman*, June 1999, pp. 57–61.
Arora, Akash, 'Bhang, Booze and Bonhomie: Holi Mania Sweeps City', *The Hindustan Times*, 10 March 2001.
Badal, Kumar, 'Advertising Glory', *Rashtriya Sahara*, July 1997, pp. 110–12.
Bhattacharjee, Ajit, 'Fourth Estate no More', *Gentleman*, June 1999, pp. 46–50.

Calfee, John E., 'How Advertising Informs to Our Benefit', *Span*, December 1998, pp. 10–15, 58–60.
Chakrabarty, Gargi, 'Rubbing people the right way', *Business Standard*, New Delhi, 7 January 1998.
Chaney, David, *The Cultural Turn* (London and New York: Routledge, 1994).
Chaudhuri, Maitrayee, 'Citizens, Workers and Cultural Emblems: An Analysis of the First Planned Document In India', in Patricia Uberoi (ed.), *Social Reform, Sexuality and the State* (New Delhi: Sage, 1996) pp. 211–35.
———, 'Advertisements, Print Media and the New Indian Woman', *Social Action* (July) 1998, pp. 239–52.
———,'"Feminism" in Print Media', *The Indian Journal of Gender Studies*, vol. 7, no. 2, 2000, pp. 263–88.
———, 'Gender and Advertisements: The Rhetorics of Liberalisation', *Women's Studies International Forum*, vol. 24, no. 3/4, 2001, pp. 373–85.
Das, Bhaskar, 'The Paper Chase', *Gentleman*, June 1999, pp. 57–61.
Ewen, S., *Captains of Consciousness: Advertising and the Social Roots of the Consumer Culture* (New York: McGraw Hill, 1976).
Friedan, Betty, *The Feminine Mystique* (New York: Laurel, 1983).
Hood, John, 'In Praise of Advertising', *Span*, December 1998, pp. 8–10.
Inglis, Fred, *The Imagery of Power: A critique of Advertising* (London: Heinemann, 1972).
Keene, John, *The Media and Democracy* (Cambridge: Polity, 1991).
Khare, Harish, 'The *Dhanatantra* age begins', *The Hindu*, 7 July 2004.
Lasch, Christopher, *The Culture of Narcissm* (New York: Warner Books, 1978).
Lee, Martyn J., *Consumer Culture Reborn: The Cultural Politics of Consumption* (London: Routledge 1993).
Lodge, David (ed.), *Modern Criticism and Theory: A Reader* (London: Longman, 1978).
MacIntyre, A.C., 'A Mistake about Causality in Social Sciences', in P. Laslet and W.G. Runciman (eds), *Politics, Philosophy and Society*, 2nd series (Oxford: Blackwell, 1962).
Mike, F., *Consumer Culture and Postmodernism* (London: Sage, 1991).
Myers, Kathy, 'Understanding Advertisers', in H. Davis and P. Walton (eds), *Language, Image, Media* (Oxford: Blackwell, 1983), pp. 205–23.
Neimark, Jill, 'Why we Need Miss America', *Femina*, 1 February 1999, pp. 50–52.
Pateman, T., 'How is Understanding an Advertisement possible?', in H. Davis and P. Walton (eds), *Language, Image, Media* (Oxford: Blackwell, 1983), pp. 187–204.
Pathak, Rahul, 'The New Generation', *The Week*, 30 May 1994, pp. 73–87.

Therbon, Goran, 'The Rule of Capital and the Rise of Democracy', *New Left Review*, 1977, no. 103, pp. 3–42.
Thompson, John B., *Ideology and Modern Culture* (Cambridge: Polity Press, 1990).
Williams, Raymond, 'Advertising; The Magic System', *Problems in Materialism and Culture* (London: Verso, 1980), pp. 184–91.

1.3
Arenas of Assimilation

7

MEDIATING MODERNITY:
Colonial Discourse and Radio
Broadcasting, c.1924–1947

BISWAJIT DAS

This essay centres around a contradiction: 'colonial modernity' is something that needs to be critiqued, theorized and discussed.[1] It views 'colonialism' as a project of modernity in the sense that the societies the colonialists possessed and administered, were understood as objects to be surveyed, regulated and sanitized. Colonial projects were culturally and strategically complex. They entailed a world view that imagined economic, political and cultural representations. The natives appropriated these representations in distinctive and conflicting ways.

The dynamics at the centre of colonial modernity's institutional nexus establish the basic parameters for everyday experience, but they do not, in themselves, provide the discursive and representational resources that render it meaningful. The practice of governing can conversely be understood as a discursively complex exercise.[2] This complexity can be assessed through various dimensions that colonial modernity has articulated and attempted to establish through a 'colonial order' in the alien society. The present essay attempts to examine colonial modernity's cultural formations.

Historical accounts of radio broadcasting in India have invariably highlighted the institutional accounts without much concern with radio's wider social, cultural and political implications.[3] Although many would contest that claim, it may be that historians have not always made their understanding of the wider historical context as clear and explicit as they think they have. The Indian example of radio broadcasting reveals one of these instances where information and regulation in a particular policy domain is at once a colonizing project in itself and at the same time contradictory in formulation and implementation. Besides, was the official campaign of radio propaganda ever able to deliver that management of public opinion? To put it simply, did official radio propaganda make any impact on the wartime public opinion of the native? These are some questions which still haunt scholars. For instance, the consensus about the power of radio propaganda proved remarkably durable. For last eight decades or so, it has never been challenged; rather, with passage of time, politicians and scholars alike seem to have become only more convinced that the mass media in general and radio in particular provided a weapon uniquely capable of effectively moulding the ideology of the masses. Certainly a remarkable degree of unanimity characterized the findings of those who set out to investigate the power of the medium. Almost all interwar studies stressed their enormous power, using metaphors like 'hypodermic needle' or 'magic bullet' to characterize that power in contrast to the weakness of the mass of people who, whether they liked it or not, received the message which the medium generated. But the question remains unanswered: did the weapon work? Did it reach its target and did it then make the desired impact on that target? In seeking to find answers to these questions and the earlier ones, this essay sets out to reexamine the history of radio broadcasting in India within the first three decades of the twentieth century.

Policing the Radio

The development and growth of radio broadcasting in colonial India can be situated within three competing institutional identities. These identities were incompatible to one another. While the emerging young Indian entrepreneurs attempted to exploit the potential of the medium for a fortune, the British Broadcasting Corporation (BBC), on the other hand tried to experiment its own model by developing a medium for the nation. The colonial state rejected both these proposals and monopolized the medium amidst the fear of uncertainties and possible anxieties.

Although the colonialists had keen interest in radio broadcasting, especially after its usefulness to the government during the general strike and as a potential instrument for communication and publicity, however, there was slow progress in the development of radio broadcasting in India.[4] As Lord Reading was involved in a scandal in England, there was no concerted effort during his tenure in India. However, the private entrepreneurs were given the go ahead with their ventures.[5]

Two Parsee entrepreneurs, R. M. Chinoy and Sultan Chinoy floated a company in 1923 and registered in July 1924 called the Indian Radio Telegraph Co. This company with the help and support of the Marconi Company had started constructing transmitters at Poona in 1925.[6] But a scandal the Marconi Company was involved in sealed the future prospect of this company. However, radio broadcasting was kept alive in India by amateur radio clubs in Calcutta, Bombay, Madras and Lahore. Due to financial constraints, some of these clubs could not afford to continue. A regular broadcasting service went on the air from 1927, when the Indian Broadcasting Company Ltd, a private concern came into being. As Lionel Fielden wrote in his autobiography: 'A group of Indian businessmen fired by the financial successes of European broadcasting, had floated a company in 1927, with a too-meagre capital, built two weak little stations at Calcutta and Bombay. In the following three years they had gathered some 7,000 listeners and lost a great deal of money. The Government of India, which then and later with considerable wisdom thought broadcasting a curse was thereupon bullied by the vested interests of radio dealers to buy the transmitters....'[7] Why the commercial venture could not succeed to establish an independent broadcasting service was another question, but the various forces that helped in initiating an effort need to be analysed, so that the history of radio broadcasting can be understood and situated in its context. There were various forces: for instance, the Marconi Company had control over two-thirds of the total assets of the Indian Broadcasting Company and another individual, Raja Saheb Dhanrajgiriji Narsingirji had control over holdings almost equal to Radio Telegraph Company.[8] The Chinoy brothers were not only agents of Marconi's technology but went one step ahead by setting up a company with several distinguished people on the board.[9] This company was constantly in touch with a former employee of BBC named Eric Dunstan. By the time Dunstan arrived in India, the British company was taken over by the Indian government and made into a corporation. Although the Indian Broadcasting Company mobilized resources for the infrastructure, it lacked capital to run the company. The colonial government according to its agreement dated 13 September 1926, asserted for a genuine Indian company over which the colonial government had sole monopoly for five years.[10]

It was intriguing that on the one hand the colonial government encouraged private entrepreneurship, especially when it had no clear cut policy on radio broadcasting. Once it realized the importance of the medium and its possible role, it hesitantly took over but without any vision for future expansion as it required investment, which the state did not want to commit to.

Private initiative did make an effort in the urban areas, but the early outcome was disastrous. Due to an inadequate startup fund and a five-year monopoly from the government of India, the early entrepreneurs invested the funds in building infrastructural support but were unable to raise sufficient operating revenues through its share of licence fees. The fate of broadcasting was resigned to the hands of the colonial state, which hesitantly kept the two stations in operations. The colonial government tried to close down the service twice in two successive years but both times it succumbed to the pressure from legislators, licence holders and the private sector (particularly radio dealers burdened with inventory). In order to meet the expenses, the bureaucratic machinery levied a 50 per cent import duty on radio equipment, putting broadcasting even farther out of the reach of most Indian audiences.¹¹ The number of listening licences increased only after the BBC inaugurated its Empire service in late 1933. This service was aimed primarily at resident Europeans and conducted entirely in English. No doubt the Empire service heightened the expectations of the Anglophiles, but it hardly received attention from the Indian listeners.

While the young Indian entrepreneurs failed in their mission, the BBC had keen interest in Indian broadcasting. In fact, BBC officials were astonished by the indifferent attitude of the colonial government to the new medium. The BBC's manager John Reith approached the India office with offers of help, but was told to write to the government of India directly. Reith's letter to the India office had advocated the advantages of centralized broadcasting in India, following the pattern that was developing in Britain: '[T]he erection of broadcasting stations would provide a connecting link between all parts of the Indian empire, bringing even the most outlying districts into close touch with the principal cities.'¹²

Reith considered the need and importance for Indian broadcasting and he contemplated setting it up himself.¹³ For BBC officials, it was an excellent opportunity to display their Victorian ideal of a public service. The BBC planners adjudged India as the right place for experimentation as it could provide enormous opportunities for social and material improvement.¹⁴

In numerous memoranda Reith and his colleagues tried to impress upon India's highest officials not simply the value of programming to and for the natives, but the urgency of nationalizing broadcasting in the public interest, including protecting it from purportedly less civic minded usurpers.¹⁵ On the contrary, radio broadcasting was strictly kept under the centre as it apprehended that it could be used as a political weapon by the provinces for anti-imperial purposes as highlighted by a former head of Information in India.¹⁶ Further, a note by the viceroy determined the status of radio broadcasting in India as the viceroy wrote that 'the unscrupulous politician or too parochial local government will not find the small uplift stations suitable instruments for their purposes'. Reith penciled in the margin, why not, if there are lots of them?¹⁷

Reith's concerted efforts to establish a BBC model in India was unsuited for a more fundamental reason. In the BBC ethos, government sponsorship ceded to an autonomous public corporate trust which ensured that British broadcasting reflected the progressive charge to educate for democracy with the guided development of a respectable national culture transcending class and regional divisions. But the cultivation of what would be in essence a nationalist institution, especially under an agency paid for but not directed by officials, was certainly not an ambition of the British colonial government in India.

While Reith had wishful thinking about the future pattern of broadcasting and its modalities, the colonial state hardly showed any interest. Coincidentally, about the same time as Reith was lobbying for an India office, R.W. Nicholson, Director of Wireless, and the Government of India, put up a memorandum for departmental discussion on what should be government policy when broadcasting developed under private enterprise. The outcome of this discussion was a letter to the provincial governments embodying the central government's provisional conclusion. It was clearly in the opposite direction of centralized control and government ownership. The operative sentences were:

> It might be possible perhaps for Government themselves ...to rate in the monopoly of providing broadcasting services in India. But...any such solution is undesirable and that it is clearly best that the development of broadcasting services on the country should be entrusted to private enterprise under suitable regulation and control.[18]

It delegated the power to grant licenses to set up broadcasting stations—'only one license for each specified area'—to the provincial governments. In that context it commented:

> The government of India have considered an alternative proposal that only one company should be licensed for the whole of India, with a monopoly of establishing stations in any area desired. Such a solution...would follow the practice in the U.K. The Government of India

however, are provisionally of the opinion that in such a vast country as India, and on the existing state of development of the science and practice of broadcasting in this country the grant of such an extensive monopoly would be unnecessary and unduly restrictive.[19]

It was not that the colonial officials entirely failed to consider the potential benefits of radio broadcasting. The secretary of state for India argued in 1926 that '[I]f broadcasting can be made to reach the villager in his own language, the assistance which would be afforded to Government...in spreading accurate information and combating dangerous unfounded rumors and agitation's would be very great'. The villager was the man most liable to be misled and at the same time he was the man on whom a good influence would have the greatest result.[20]

However, village broadcasting was promoted not by the colonial government but by the romantic champions of Indian tradition. The advocates of this tradition were the former army officers and civilians who were back in England after long years of service. For them India always meant the villages as these officials had travelled across villages. The urgency to do something for the village life always haunted these Indophiles. Incidentally, it also coincided with the Gandhian project of nationalism. For both, the village became the epicentre of real India.[21]

After considering the possibility of sponsoring a community listening scheme at the time the Indian Broadcasting Company (IBC) was chartered, the central government departments decided such schemes were impractical and costly experiments. Delhi officials were hardly enthused about the prospect of independent systems dotting the countryside, especially with the IBC in such a tenuous position. Since the rural systems fell under the rubric of education, it was transferred to the quasi-representative provincial ministries under the Government of India Act of 1919. The central Government could not legally disallow them. Ultimately the Government of India made a virtue of necessity. Since no revenue would be derived from village uplift, provincial governments would be prepared to put their hands in their pockets, the secretary for Industries and Labour concluded smugly in 1934.[22]

Village broadcasting or community listening was initiated by its proponents, for whom India lived in villages. The new mass medium—the great boon of modern science as one enthusiast put it—was to be employed to keep the Indian peasant content in his natural habitat. Instead of families gathering hearthside around radios in the privacy of their own homes, Indian listeners would congregate in the village square or headman's courtyard to hear official uplift programming in the local vernacular blaring from a community receiver that carried no other frequencies. Instead of flooding the rural airwaves with metropolitan influences, the radio was to offer a utopian image of the village brought to its potential with clean water, fat cattle, sturdy crops and vaccinated children.[23]

Since broadcasting in India was an expensive and risky undertaking for any agency, organizers of the Indian National Congress and other political movements—even if they had exhibited strong interest in the new medium in the 1930s, which they did not—could not introduce broadcasting simply because they lacked the resources to do so. India's technological limitations were daunting especially outside the cities. The questions of how radio would be powered, and how to pay for expensive facilities and expertise, all of which would have to be imported, were sufficient discouragement to most.[24] Besides, technicalities of radio broadcasting shrouded an aura of uncertainty as to who would be its audience and who would pay for it. These questions were linked.

It was not mere a technocratic solution that was significant but the division it created in terms of urban, elite India from the countryside; the real India was of outmost importance. An imported radio set cost Rs 400 or more, a sum which put their purchase outside the range of all but the most affluent Indian families and resident Europeans. Clustered in the bigger cities, only this audience—English speaking, endowed with electricity and a shared taste for high western culture—presented a clearly defined market. To meet costs the government levied a 50 per cent import duty on radio equipment, putting broadcasting even farther out of the reach of most Indian audiences.[25]

While broadcasting languished in the Delhi departments, its proponents pushed on with their ambitions to implant the radio in village soil. Lending the campaign influence and financial assistance in London was the Indian Village Welfare Association, whose prominent membership included Lady Irwin, wife of the former viceroy, the Marquess of Lothian, a Scot aristocrats and Bhupendra Mitra, the Indian High Commissioner amongst other dignitaries.[26] Besides, officials like Hardinge and Strickland impressed upon the British audience through newspaper articles and lectures in various institutions such as the East India Association the lack of interest by the colonial state to implement the project.[27]

At the outset, the logistical problem created much tension. For instance, the very design of the loudspeaker and the upkeep of the battery, its supervision and maintenance caused much anxiety for creating a common space in the rural area. The romanticists' construction of the 'common space' was purely from a pragmatic and technical reason as it amounted to continuous monitoring and responsibility. Since there were limited government field staff at the village, the village patriarch was the obvious choice. The Romanticists failed to understand the power dynamics in the countryside and instead constructed the notion of self-imposed public space in the rural India. Although the authorities in Delhi had suggested early on that the supervisory role should go to the most obvious representatives of the state, the police, but by the 1930s this affiliation was clearly prudent.[28] In 1935 private stations were set up in Peshawar in the North West Frontier Province and in Allahabad in the united provinces which started broadcasting programmes for rural audiences.

The Romanticists' healthy respect for peasant audiences and their venerated elders made broadcasting appear to be an unproblematic exercise of paternalistic good will. But by nature broadcasting was a unidirectional mode of communication; what the villager heard was a determined from a distant, unseen location, the transmitting station. Advocates of rural broadcasting conceived of this matter as benign, their role as programmers being straightforwardly in the best interest of their audience and their knowledge of what peasants needed and wanted complete.[29]

However, the structural design of the receiver clearly demarcated the nature of control and relationship the villagers would have with broadcasting. It clearly indicated that they would be a passive and perhaps not even an assenting audience. As one of the designers, Hardinge boasted of its impenetrability, of the locking of the set at the time of its installation so that all working parts are entirely inaccessible. Outwardly the set was supremely simple, only a key hole and a switch marring its exterior. Internally, it was a masterpiece of construction, with controls to fix the volume and the wavelength reception, the latter a clear recognition that other broadcasts—distant Russian programmes for instance—were potentially available to Indian listeners. The machine was intended to contribute to a healthy mystification of broadcasting suited to the hamlet mentality, or as Hardinge put it, the village was simply provided with a box which speaks when the headman turns a key. In essence, the Report on broadcasting admitted, broadcasting was forced upon the villager.[30]

Hardinge's account of the Peshawar experiment gave evidence of the scepticism with which even presumably loyalist communities greeted the new medium. At least some villagers associated the new technology with the surveillance operations of the state. At some places considerable suspicion was shown as to the intentions. Hardinge admitted people wondered whether the government proposed installing the village receivers in order that it could listen to what the villagers were saying, or whether the intention was to enable it to communicate with aeroplanes.[31] Broadcasting was perceived to be yet another means by which the government would milk the rural cultivator. It had been anticipated that villagers would eagerly subscribe to the service through contributions toward the costs of the set and renewable licence. But Punjabi peasants, burdened by the expense of rural uplift, expressed relief that at least they were not required to purchase community loudspeakers.[32] Even when broadcasting become commonplace in India, few were still scared that it was a scheme to raise taxes.[33] Neither were the moral sensitivities of the broadcasting agents fully trusted: '[W]hen we wanted to climb roofs in order to erect an aerial, we were suspected of wishing to peer into the houses of neighbours and so violate the purdah of their women folk'.[34]

Ironically, considering the general unease with which imperialists greeted any politicized vision for broadcasting, the existent model of community listening came from an unlikely source, the Soviet Union. The Soviet planners had inaugurated a scheme to broadcast state ideology and instructions via public receivers to peasants and urban workers undergoing the transition to a collectivist organization. In functional terms the analogy was not inept. As in India, the Russian landscape was dominated by illiterate villages supported by primitive technologies. Like India's colonial regime, the Soviet counterpart was faced with the challenge of disseminating messages of state to populations previously outside the elite range of their reception. More remarkable was the fact that sponsors of Indian rural broadcasting enthusiastically held up the Soviet example without any apparent discomfort about the propaganda project it embodied.[35]

The BBC, in its quest for a workable national model for India, had concluded that the only notable difference between Russian and Indian conditions was that in the latter the hand of the government must not be obvious. But though the BBC offered some assistance to the village broadcasting schemes, promising Frank Brayne a second hand transmitter if he got his Delhi system off the ground, such experiments could only be an elementary stage in the evolution of what London broadcasters decreed must be a national service on the BBC model.[36]

The government run broadcasting set up was called the Indian State Broadcasting Service (ISBS). The ISBS was changed into All India Radio (AIR) in June 1936. As Fielden wrote:

> I had never looked the title ISBS which to me seemed not only inworldly but also tainted with officialdom. After a good deal of cognition which may seem ridiculous, now, but there apparently simple and obvious things do not always appear easily. I had concluded that All India Radio would give me not only protection from the clause which I most feared in the 1935 Act, but would also have

the suitable initials AIR. I worked out a monogram which placed there letters over the map of India...But, when I mooted this point, I found that there was immense opposition in the secretariat to any such change. They wanted ISBS and they thought it fine. I realised that I must employ a little unnatural tact. I cornered Lord Linlithgow after a viceregal banquet and said plaintively that I was in a great difficulty and needed his advice. I said I was sure that he agreed with me that perhaps it was a pity to use the word broadcasting at all, since all Indians had to say broadcasting—broad was for them an unpronounced cable word. But I could not, I said, think of another title; could he help me? 'Indian state', I said was a term which, as he well knows, hardly fitted into the 1935 Act. It should be some thing general. He rose beautifully to the bait. 'All India'? I expressed my astonishment and admiration. The very thing, but surely not 'broadcasting'? Splendid I said and what beautiful initials. The viceroy concluded that he had invented it, and there was no more trouble. His set name must be adopted. Thus, All India Radio was born.[37]

Not only had Fielden masterminded a national broadcasting system but also trained a generation of people to address larger issues in colonial India. From the beginning the technologies and machinery for broadcasting had been imported into India; once conceding the demand for a national system, even Delhi conservatives recognized that professional expertise would have to be imported as well. It came in the person of the BBC's Lionel Fielden, who arrived in 1935 to take the position of AIR controller. The BBC model that Fielden championed was highly centralized; the regional stations were allowed limited local programming. But though this paradigm excluded makeshift and Indianized local services like Brayne's, it was founded on a premise of significant autonomy of official interference.[38]

By late 1936 the newly renamed All India Radio had taken over the Peshawar and Delhi services, citing inadequate management, persistent problems with batteries and equipment, and financial failure along with the uplist programming's lack of quality and appeal. Provincial governments were still expected to raise the funds for village receivers, presumably from taxes, but it was decided that AIR should take the responsibility for all the programmes. In place of a multitude of linguistically specialized stations operating close to the ground, the centre was now held capable of accommodating India's cultural and linguistic diversity. News bulletins and other programmes were henceforth translated into the major provincial languages at Delhi and transmitted from there to closely supervised regional stations. Under the guise of improvement, appropriation by the expanding state apparatus in actuality signalled the end of independent broadcasting in India.[39]

The government of India demonstrated a newfound enthusiasm for radio with the construction of 12 high-powered stations over the next three years. With Congress party administrations about to take office in eight of the 11 provinces, officials anxiously discussed strategies for how broadcasting might be secured at the centre without constitutional entitlement. The operative strategy was to establish a powerful enough network of stations so that provincial bodies would be discouraged from contesting central control and setting up their own.[40]

The government of India had inaugurated a national broadcasting system, yet for all the debates about whether and how radio would be employed in India, the nationalization of broadcasting was almost inevitable in the broader context of state building in the late 1930s. Like interventionist regimes everywhere, the British government defensively cobbled together a complex of centralized agencies to regulate and infiltrate India's burgeoning sphere of public culture.[41]

The critical difference between the BBC and AIR was that the former had been turned over to a putatively independent trust while the latter was in the tenacious grip of a declining imperial state. Fielden's antipathy towards the establishment that sustained this, combined with his own nationalist sympathies, finally drove him from India. But by then he had trained a generation of radio experts in the BBC style and not again would the national model for Indian radio be seriously challenged.

The postwar development of radio came out with a subsequent plan which envisaged that every person in India, wherever he was situated, would be provided with a broadcast programme in his own language, which he could pick up even with an inexpensive receiver.[42] The intention was very clear as it was aptly captured by the speech delivered by Sir Mohammad Usman on the need for improving post and telegraph services in the Post Masters General conference 'We have won the War. We have now to win the peace'.[43] It corresponded well with the ruling agenda of the Indian elites who filled the professional and technical ranks, and who were poised to appropriate the mantle of government administration and public life in the new nation state. Any worthwhile broadcasting which seeks to serve the mass of the people is inherently nationwide in its scope and national in character, declared one academic critique of the village broadcasting schemes. These could be nothing more than a standing invitation for the perpetuation and aggravation of the baneful spirit of provincialism and of the numerous sectional interests other than which there were no more serious obstacles to national progress.[44]

The colonial state apparatus continuously engaged itself in a dialogue between imperialism and nationalism. As the

> national movement expertly employed its press, its touring leaders and mass spectacles to reconfigure—at least rhetorically—the body of the Indian public that counted, the British had to respond in kind, with its own messages and own propaganda machinery. Hence the irony of a near extinct colonial regime building a highly articulated state apparatus to counter nationalism lock step with the political nation its opponent was constructing. But by this time, of course, the colonial government feared enemies from states and political movements to the left and right of liberal Britain, outsiders seeking converts among the disgruntled Indian Public. The radio was held the most dangerous vehicle for foreign propaganda, and in anticipation of 'ether wars' all states regimes attempted, in futile fashion, to barricade the airwaves.[45]

Managing Public Opinion

The history of public opinion during the colonial period was quite complex as people were often capable of holding a number of different, even contradictory attitudes at the same time. The colonial state on the eve of the early twentieth century had substantially widened the base of liberal public sphere to circulate public opinion and new knowledges in order to ensure the efficacy of colonial power itself.[46] The management of public opinion by the colonialists was extremely difficult as it not only influenced the government but also threatened it. The colonial state's effort to create a public opinion could not be reduced to mere propaganda. Propaganda was as important as counter propaganda to consciously provide information. Instead, we would like to view propaganda as a combination of fact, fiction, argument or suggestion that would culminate in an effective public opinion.[47] The colonial state became a site where there was a continuous struggle to claim and reclaim the public sphere and legitimacy of public opinion by the Indians as sovereign subjects. While colonial power aimed to improve the moral conditions of the colonial subjects, colonial governmentality with its political rationalities and instrumentalities of rule made the idea of progress a desirable goal for the colonial subjects.[48] In the formative years of radio broadcasting, the colonial state had no clear cut policy neither did the colonialists discourage political discussions on the radio:

> It would be undesirable to prohibit the broadcasting of political matter, such as speeches by leading politicians, which may indeed, be of great educative value and the banning of political matter broadcast by others would reduce the value of political and propaganda matter broadcast by Government. At the same time there is obviously some danger of the use of broadcasting for the propagation of matter which is either of a seditious character....[49]

It was well realized by the colonialists that radio broadcasting could be used as a means of spreading education and as an aid to propagate the government's point of view among the rural population. But the financial implication restrained further effort by the colonial state. Except for censorship of political information, the colonialists had no systematic strategy of propaganda in the initial years of radio broadcasting in India. Neither did the issue of censorship remain uncontested among the officials.[50] The colonialists' attitude of liberalism was well reflected in a note sent by Haig: 'It is necessary to see that there is no undue bias in favour of any particular point of view, and that the government gets its due share of publicity. The object should be to keep the balance even'.[51]

The colonial state's participation in the manipulation of public opinion through radio was minimal. There were other institutions through which the state seemingly presided over, not the government. The colonial state almost followed the line of argument of the British government that propaganda should as much as possible be left to unofficial actors. It accorded with Britain's long standing liberal tradition which encouraged the view that the government should do for the people only what they could not do for themselves.[52] It had left the responsibility of selecting a censoring officer to the provincial government who was instructed to work in consultation with the company. Overall the colonial state kept the general control and vigilance over wireless censorship and provided delegated power to the provincial governments.[53] Most of the official propagandists continued to rely upon older, liberal categories of thought to reconcile themselves to what had been disclosed. The liberal tradition encouraged the continuity of a centuries old respect for discourse.

But the latter half of the 1930s was uncomfortable for the colonial government as there was stiff opposition both from the home front as well as the foreign powers. In both these cases, the image of the empire was at stake.[54] While making an inquiry about the foreign and anti-British propaganda, one of the civil servants commented that the gradual extension of good Indian programmes as a counter attraction would eliminate whatever danger there was from foreign broadcasts being picked up.[55] To a large extent, the colonial officials retained their English political tradition which did not subscribe to the idea that political behaviour could be controlled by those who manipulate primitive, biologically-based instincts of people. All that the colonial state provided between the wars was sporadic, grudging support for enlightened, dedicated civil servants who worked with the colonial government to develop systematic approaches for the coordination of government policy and governmental publicity.

The repeated successes of Germany by May 1940 made the government concerned about how, without resorting to jamming, it could prevent Indians from listening to Nazi broadcasts. The Maharaja of Jodhpur reported, '[A]t 8 p.m. everyday practically every owner of a wireless receiving set in the city tuned into the broadcast from Berlin...there was a marked tendency to believe, the German rather than the British news'.[56]

The central government suggested a policy of penalizing private licence holders if they allowed people in the neighbourhood to listen to German broadcasts, while they were free in the privacy of their homes to listen to what they liked. The Madras government's view, as endorsed by the governor, is reflected in the following note: 'A complete prohibition on listening would be a good thing if it could be enforced completely. But without a huge Gestapo Organisation that would be impossible'.[57]

From 1 June 1940, the central government prohibited holders of commercial receiver licences from publicly disseminating broadcast by the axis powers.[58] The question of jamming enemy broadcasts was considered but given up. An officer of the Southern command had asked the provincial government of Madras to propose jamming enemy broadcasts as a general policy to the central government. The chief engineer pointed out the practical difficulties—'with our communications and interests strung out all over the world, we stand to lose more than we gain by creating chaos in the air'.[59]

Lionel Fielden wrote letters to F.W. Ogilvie, who had succeeded Reith as the Director-General of the BBC. Towards the end of 1939, he called a conference of all station Directors and asked them to carry out a certain amount of elementary mass observation in order to try and discover what rumors were current.' On the basis of reports he wrote:

> The general feeling is that in every strata of society and throughout India, there is what one might call a mild

anti-British feeling which at present amounts to not much more than a certain amusement at British embarrassments and a tendency to regard British news and British newspapers as suspect.

The Hindustani news bulletin from Berlin was widely listened to and regarded as more truthful than the English version. One of the handicaps in launching a counter-propaganda was the crippling legacy of the Indian government's earlier financial policy. AIR in 1939 started broadcasting to foreign audiences. The first such broadcast was in Pusthu and was addressed to listeners in Afghanistan. External broadcasts expanded rapidly under the impact of World War II, when many of these services were the joint responsibility of AIR and the Far Eastern Bureau of the British Ministry of Information. The external services of AIR now broadcasting 57 hours a day in some 25 languages, including six Indian languages and English.

Subsequently, AIR's external services developed and were initially part of the central news organizations. External broadcasts, as already mentioned, started in October 1939 with a broadcast in Pusthu directed at Afghanistan. With the advance of the axis powers in West Asia and Southeast Asia and their propaganda offensives in these parts, the British government thought it necessary to take counter measures. This was done by coordination of foreign broadcasts through the Far Eastern Bureau of the British Ministry of Information and AIR. The foreign broadcasts were organized under two different categories. There were broadcasts which were directed to Indians overseas in a number of Indian languages. By 1945 AIR was putting out 74 daily broadcasts in 22 languages. By 31 March 1947 the number of daily external broadcasts had come down to 31.

The loss of listeners for colonial radio caused much concern for the officials. A report submitted by Brander to BBC shows that the credibility of the BBC overseas broadcasts of war news was low, because these often showed:

> ignorance of small points of sensibility to Indians. Again and again little things slipped in, e.g., in a recent reference

in a talk to Australia to the Black hole of Calcutta, which has now disappeared from the history books here... as a discredited atrocity story. Had we no one going through all our scripts to point out where the toes were we treading on?

The Radio talks aired in countries like Australia and New Zealand had severely affected credibility of the medium, as a result the Indians preferred to listen to other transmissions. As one of the Indian brigadiers mentioned 'to insult "Asiatic people"' and instanced Curtin's recruiting speech '"we are fighting to obtain a White Australia"'.... It was used by the Japs for field broadcasts and had a direct effect on our Indian troops'.[60]

A counter attraction till the monsoon of 1944 was the broadcasts on behalf of the Indian National Army coming from the Japanese occupied areas in Southeast Asia.[61]

The Indian Director-General of the AIR, A.S. Bokhari, told Brander: 'Don't forget that British prestige in this country has never been lower'.[62]

A couple of months after this remark, the Congress launched the Quit India Movement. Brander's report to his superiors showed the sense of helplessness in the propaganda front which the Raj was feeling:

Congress has an organisation that will cover all India, suiting the lie to the audience everywhere; and we have radio almost completely undeveloped. Nor does radio seemed to be used in a planned way; a speech will be put on, usually without anything like sufficient publicity; or reported, but real propaganda planning is not very evident to the ordinary observer. I am told by the ordinary observer.[63]

The radical elements in the Congress—a group with affiliations to the Congress Socialist Party and led by Ram Manohar Lohia—started their own underground broadcasts on a clandestine transmitter in Bombay from 27 August till they were detected by the police on 12 November 1942. It broadcast regular reports of insurgent activities in different parts of the country from the North West Frontier Province to Bengal and also of police and military brutalities. The themes repeated time and again in these broadcasts were that the villages should adopt a policy of self-sufficiency and refuse to sell to middlemen, stop working on the railways and the factories as these only helped the British military machine.[64]

Even after the success of the colonial state in containing the Quit India Movement by police and military action and even after the allied powers began to register victories, not much enthusiasm was noticed by Brander among the Indian listeners in favour of the Allied victories, because they felt that these would mean a continuation of alien domination. As he put it: 'The crazy state of things is that we now have the Indian audience because we have the victories. They are listening to our bulletins; but these victory bulletins bring many of them no joy, for they see no helpful future for India in our victories'.[65]

Conclusion: Radio and the Constitution of Modernity

The recurrent policy cycle had important implications for our understanding of the relation of policy discourse to institutional practice in radio broadcasting in India. Many would agree that the policy had generally failed and that the discourse did not accurately represent the practice. Most assume, however, that the problems was one of a poor fit between discourse and practice, most solutions were designed to some how make the discourse and the practice more closely resemble each other.

The regularly repeated policy cycle in broadcasting, however, suggested that the principal relation of discourse to practice might not be one of representation at all. In a paradoxical way, policy discourse did 'fit' institutional practice of radio broadcasting in colonial India.

A quick overview of our study shows that during the period under study, the colonial state did not have any interest in developing radio broadcasting in India. The need for investment and expenditure sufficiently discouraged the colonial government. Instead, it encouraged the provinces and business entrepreneurs for the initiative. Once it realized the potential of the medium as well as the outcome of such a venture, it extended the legislative arms and through legal stipulation made the effort out of reach for the private initiative. The colonial state monopolized the medium and its infrastructure. Thus, the colonial government controlled the transmitter and the receiver was left with the people. Such a transmitter–receiver relationship obstructed any healthy development and expansion of radio broadcasting in India.

The weakness of the colonial government was exposed during the war period. The government had to face propaganda through the radio during the war as well clandestine radio networks used by opposition groups at home. It had neither developed infrastructure to counter the foreign powers nor it had sufficient mechanism to curb the clandestine operations. Further, the contradiction within the government regarding tackling propaganda went against it. Thus, the social history of radio broadcasting is not a history of technologies of broadcasting but a history of the way the medium helped to reconfigure systems of power and network of social relations. Our analysis shows that the radio was introduced within particular centres of power and deployed with particular purposes in mind. But once in play, they often had unintended consequences. They are therefore, more usefully viewed not as technologies of control or of freedom, but as the site of continual struggles over interpretation and use.

We need to explore various dimensions that radio broadcasting may have created during this period. No doubt, radio broadcasting's cultural role was shaped by the continual need of the colonial state to assert its political authority and acquire a legitimate power base, and entertainment and news became an important area in the development of national activities that the state seemingly presided over. But the specific characteristics of radio broadcasting, its immediacy and actual quality when allied with the nature of coverage, proved to be a popular substitute with listeners unable to attend the live event. The fostering of national cohesion was not, however, the sole prerogative of the radio.

A crucial point is the mediating role played by radio. Radio is not a neutral agency that simply relays the event to the listening audience. It is an active process that alters the relationship between spectator and event. The listener does not see the event, but is given a verbal image of the event. In other words, a feeling of what the event is, its significance and substance is transmitted via the medium. Unlike the printed medium, radio is immediate and real. Spatial distance from the event is eroded and the listener is transported in imagination to another part of the region, as part of a wider imagined community. In colonial India, such was the case, especially in rural areas, that communal gatherings in wireless households or even in town centres for specific broadcasts were a frequent occurrence. The creation through this communal experience, allied with the nationwide audience construction may have helped to provide a lived, shared experience. Further, selective construction of social knowledge through which we perceive the 'worlds', 'lived realities', their lives and ours into some intelligible 'world of the whole', some lived totality. Radio did not simply relay the events to the audiences, but played a key role in helping to construct and amplify them to a central position within what seemingly constituted a national culture. In so doing, the colonial radio became a truly symbolic national organization in the minds of its listeners. This was achieved through the intrinsic qualities and social groupings, based around the village, town and ultimately the country.

This process involved the developing of a common national memory. Great events and occasions became ingrained in the national psyche. The mediation of events by radio was part of a wider consensus building project which helped facilitate and consolidate the socially conservative strand of nationalism which the state embodied upto the early 1950s. Through radio, a self-image of the colonial empire was held up and it made to believe a 'nation' bound together by a common sense of collective identity. The language used to describe the event, through radio, as the language of totalities, 'we', 'our' and so on all encouraged the individual listener to identify with the event as one member of a wider national community. The regularity of messages through radio, their democratic character and their segmented, yet totalized representation of the colonial state brought listeners into a single time and place, turning listeners into a 'league of anonymous equals', voila, the nation!

Notes

1. Ania Loomba, *Colonialism/Post Colonialism* (London: Routledge, 1998). Also see Nicholas Thomas, *Colonialism's Culture* (UK: Polity Press, 1994).
2. Michel Foucault, *Discipline and Punish* (New York: Viking, 1979). Also see Graham Burchell (ed.), *The Foucault Effect: Studies in Governmentality* (Chicago: University of Chicago Press, 1991).
3. Parthasarathi Gupta, *Radio and the Raj* (Calcutta: Centre for Studies in Social Sciences, 1995). Also see David Lelyveld, 'Upon the Subdominant: Administering Music on All India Radio', in C. Breckenridge (ed.), *Consuming Modernity* (New Delhi: Oxford University Press, 1996), pp. 49–65.
4. Birkenhead to Irwin 15 July 1926, Halifax papers, microfilm, Nehru Memorial Museum and Library, Reel 1.
5. H. Montgomery Hyde, *Lord Reading* (New York, 1967), as cited in Parthasarathi Gupta, *Radio and the Raj* (Calcutta: Centre for Studies in Social Sciences and K.P. Bagchi & Company, 1995).
6. Sultan Chinoy, *Pioneering in Indian Business* (Bombay: Popular Prakashan, 1962).
7. Lionel Fielden, *The Natural Bent* (London: Andre Deutsch, 1960), p. 159.
8. National Archives of India (henceforth NAI)–Industry & Industry–Post and Telegraph–(P.T.) Branch–1927-f.no.60-T(1) and 60-T(3).
9. BBC written Archives, London E1/897/2 1927.
10. See NAI–Industries and Labour–P&T branch–1927 –f.60-T(3) and NAI–Industry & Labour–Telegraph–1927–f.60-T.9.
11. See Government of India, Report on the Progress of Broadcasting in India (Shimla: Government of India Press, 1939).
12. John Reith to Secretary of India, 13 March 1924.
13. J.C.W. Reith, *Into the Wind* (London: Hodder and Stoughton, 1949).
14. BBC EI/923/1.
15. BBC memo on Indian Broadcasting, 26 September 1928 and unsigned memo from BBC, 8 May 1934. IOR L/I/1/445 as cited in Joselyn Zivin, 'The Imagined Reign of the Iron Lecturer: Village Broadcasting in Colonial India', *Modern Asian Studies* vol. 32, no. 3, 1998, pp. 717–38.

16. Note by John Coatman on Broadcasting in India, 28 July 1934, Home (pol) 240/27.
17. Viceroy Lord Willingdon to Reith, 17 September 1934, BBC EI/896/2.
18. A.H. Ley, Secretary, Department of Industries and Labour to all local governments and administrations, No. 153- P.T., 19 May 1924, Para 2 (NAI–Industry and Labour–Telegraph–1924) File 56 (P&T23).
19. Ibid, para 3, section 1 (note).
20. Secretary of State Birkenhead to the Viceroy Lord Irwin, 15 July 1926. Irwin's response, 5 August 1926, India Office Records (IOR) L/PO/3/1.
21. Frank Lugard Brayne, *The Remaking of Village India* (London: Oxford University Press, 1929).
22. Minutes of an informal conference of representatives of departments of Government of India, 8 August 1927, home (POL) 217/27.
23. Zivin, 'The Imagined Reign'.
24. S.N. Roy, Department of Industries and Labour to Public and Judicial Department, India Office, 24 September 1936. India Office Records, public and judicial records, IOR L/P7J/7/754.
25. See Government of India, Report on the Progress of Broadcasting in India, 2–5 (Shimla: Government of India Press, 1939).
26. A.H. Ley, Secretary, Department of Industries and Labour to all local governments and administrations, no. 153-PT, 19 May 1924 (NAI–Industry and Labour–Telegraph–1924, file 56 [PT 23]).
27. Frank Noyce at Department of Industries and Labour to Sir Findlater Stewart at India Office, 27 August 1934, Home(pol) 119/34.
28. Minutes of 8 August 1927. Home(pol)217/27.
29. Zivin, 'The Imagined Reign', p. 732.
30. Report on the Progress of Broadcasting in India, p. 39.
31. H.R. Hardinge, 'Broadcasting and India's Future: The Peshawar Rural Broadcasting Experiment', *The Asiatic Review* 30, no. 108, 1935, p. 768.
32. Malcolm Darling, *Wisdom and Waste in the Punjab Village*, p. 38, as quoted in Joselyn Zivien, 'The Imagined Reign of the Iron Lecturer: Village Broadcasting in Colonial India', *Modern Asian Studies* vol. 32, no. 3, pp. 717–38.
33. India Office note, 1941, IOR L/I/1/445, April.
34. H.R. Hardinge, 1935 'Broadcasting and India's Future: The Peshawar Rural Broadcasting Experiment', *The Asiatic Review*, xxx, 108.
35. Zivin, 'The Imagined Reign', p. 729.

36. BBC note regarding Brayne's project, October 1933, BBC archives, BBC EI/923/1.
37. Fielden, *The Natural Bent*, p. 193.
38. Paddy Scannel and A. Cardiff, *A Social History of Broadcasting: Volume One 1922-1939; Serving the Nation* (London: Basil Blackwell, 1991), Ch. 1.
39. Report on the Progress of Broadcasting in India, pp. 39–45.
40. IOR L/P&J/8/118.
41. Zivin, 'The Imagined Reign', p. 736.
42. NAI, Govt of India, Home Department, Public section, File no. 179/46-Public.
43. Ibid. File no. 101/46-Public, 1946.
44. K. Srinivasan, 'Development of Nationwide Radio Broadcasting in India', *Electro Techniques*, no. 8, April, 1935.
45. Zivin 'The Imagined Reign', p. 736.
46. U. Kalpagam, 'Colonial Governmentality and the Public Sphere in India', *Journal of Historical Sociology*, vol. 15, no. 1, 2002 (March), pp. 35–58.
47. Philip Taylor, *Projection of Britain: British Overseas Publicity and Propaganda*, (Cambridge: Cambridge University Press, 1981), p. 5.
48. U. Kalpagam, 'Temporalities, History and Routines of Rule in Colonial India', *Time and Society*, vol. 8, no. 1, 1999, pp. 141–59.
49. Ley, No. 153-P.T.
50. Coatman's note, 31 May 1927, NAI–Industry & Labour–Telegraph Branch, File 60-T.
51. Haig's note, 2 June 1927, NAI–Industries & Labour–P&T. Branch–1927–no. 60-T(3).
52. Gary S. Messinger, *British Propaganda and the State in the First World War* (Manchester: Manchester University Press, 1992).
53. Clatter's Note, 2 June 1927, NAI–Industry & Labour–Telegraph branch, file 60-T(4).
54. Note by Major M.O. 3.I 26 April, Home-poll-1935-file 52/1/35f, p. 7.
55. Observations of E.M. Jenkins, Home-poll-1935-files 52/1/35f, p. 5.
56. A.C. Lothian to C.G. Herbert, 2 December 1940, NAI–Home-poll (I)–1940 file 60/2(40).
57. Memo, 3 July 1940.
58. Para 5(e) of the document cited in Note 26.
59. D.N. Strathan to Chief Secretary, Madras, 10 June 1940 enclosing Goyder's note, Tamil Nadu Archives SF 123(a), 21 August 1940.
60. J.H. Davenport's summary of Brander's letter of 12 May 1942, BBC Archives E1/880.
61. Brander's report, 11 January 1943, BBC Archives E1/880.

62. Ibid.
63. Davenport to ESD, 31 August 1942, BBC Archives E1/880.
64. S. Sengupta and G. Chatterjee, 'Secret Congress Broadcasts and Storming Railway Tracks', as quoted in Parthasarathi Gupta, *Radio and the Raj 1921–47* (Calcutta: Centre for Studies in Social Sciences, K.P. Bagchi & Company, 1988).
65. Brander's report, 11 January 1943, BBC archives E1/880.

8

IN SEARCH OF AUTONOMY:
The Nationalist Imagination of Public Broadcasting

SHANTI KUMAR

Around 3 P.M. on 12 November 2001, the viewers of Doordarshan and the listeners of All India Radio (AIR) were treated to a rare address that was broadcast to the nation by Mahatma Gandhi on the same day in 1947. The historic event was recreated to commemorate the 54th anniversary of Gandhi's first and last visit to the Broadcasting House in Delhi to record his message to refugees who had been violently displaced from their homes by the partition of India and Pakistan. At the commemoration ceremony, some of Gandhi's favourite *bhajan*s were also played nd a new museum of radio and television was inaugurated at the Broadcasting House by the then Minister of Information and Broadcasting, Sushma Swaraj.

Describing the museum as the first of its kind in the country, Swaraj declared that the historic event was a reminder of the need for 'introspection by the broadcasting agency to contemplate upon its goals as a public service agency.' Anil Baijal, the Chief Executive Officer (CEO) of the Prasar Bharati Corporation which oversees both radio and television broadcasting in India, explained that the goal of this endeavour was 'to preserve our heritage and present it in the shape of a museum for the future generations.' Baijal also reminded the audience that in the previous year, Prasar Bharati had declared 12 November the 'national broadcasting day' in honour of Mahatma Gandhi's historic address to the nation in 1947.[1]

In this essay, I focus on the debates over national broadcasting policies in India by critically evaluating the recommendations of various committees, such as the Chanda Committee (1964), the Verghese Committee (1977), the Joshi Committee (1982) and the Sengupta Committee (1996), which were set up by the national government to provide autonomy for television. In the first part of the essay, I discuss how the nationalist agenda of public broadcasting defined the question of 'autonomy' in Indian television from the early 1950s to the late 1980s. I also demonstrate how, during this period, the concept of 'national programming' served as the guiding framework for broadcasting policies in India, and led to the rapid expansion of Doordarshan as a state-sponsored network. In the second part of the essay, I examine how the rise of satellite and cable television channels since the 1990s has posed a serious threat to Doordarshan's hegemony over national programming in India. I argue that the growing competition between Doordarshan and private television channels has forced the government to rethink its national policies, and create an autonomous corporation called Prasar Bharati to oversee public broadcasting in India. In conclusion, I outline a theoretical framework to address the debates over autonomy by positing a hybrid notion of imagiNation which refers to the ambivalent dissemination of the nationalist ideals of public broadcasting in the rapidly changing world of satellite television in India.

Broadcasting Policies in India

The idea of television broadcasting in India was first suggested in October 1951 by a Scientific Advisory Committee set up by the government to explore the possibility of establishing a pilot station. On 2 February 1953, the Union Minister of Information and Broadcasting, B.V. Keskar, announced the plans to establish an experimental project to examine whether television would be within the economic means of the Indian government. Commenting on the feasibility of such a project, the Minister declared, 'Though television might appear to be a useful thing in the country, the expenses involved in installing it are very high.'[2] India's first Prime Minister Jawaharlal Nehru was very hesitant to commit the government's limited resources for the very high expenses necessary to sustain the electronic medium of television. However, major players in the Indian electronics industry proposed to explore the possibility of commercial operations by organizing public demonstrations of television in major cities like Delhi and Bombay.

In 1959 Philips India Ltd set up a demonstration of closed-circuit television at an Industrial Exhibition in Delhi. At the conclusion of the Industrial Exhibition, Philips sold the broadcasting transmitter and 21 television sets for a fraction of their cost to the government of India. Subsequently, a UNESCO grant of $20,000 enabled the government of India to purchase 55 additional television sets which were set up for community viewing in and around Delhi. A pilot broadcasting centre was set up in the Delhi premises of AIR, and a small team of producers and engineers began experimenting with educational programming and the technical evaluation of broadcasting equipment.[3]

On 15 September 1959, experimental television services were inaugurated in Delhi by the President of India Dr Rajendra Prasad. The experimental service was limited in scope and had specific objectives: to create television programming of educational and cultural value to both urban and rural communities. As part of this pioneering experiment, 66 'Tele-Clubs' were organized in adult education centres in and around Delhi to receive adult education programmes that were broadcast for one hour twice a week on Tuesdays and Fridays. The Tele-Club organizers were trained by AIR researchers to conduct follow up discussions after the programmes, and keep a report the viewers' reactions for later evaluation.[4]

In January 1960, AIR, in collaboration with the Delhi Directorate of Education, began producing one-hour educational programmes for students in higher secondary schools. Since access to television sets was very limited, viewing was organized in Tele-Clubs under the guidance of 'Teacher-Sponsors' who were responsible to present the programming material to the students in ways that were relevant to the prescribed school syllabi. Subjects covered under the educational television programme included, science, history, health and hygiene, language training in Hindi and community affairs. Sometimes student-produced puppet shows and plays were also shown as part of the one hour programme.[5]

To further explore the feasibility of educational television in India, Ford Foundation sent a team of experts from the United States to visit India in January 1960. The Ford Foundation team examined some of the education television programmes made by the AIR staff, visited a number of schools in Delhi and conducted several interviews with school teachers, principals and administrators in the Delhi Directorate of Education. Based on their recommendations, the Ford Foundation granted $564,000 to the Government of India as partial support for a four-year educational project using 250 television sets in nearly 300 higher secondary schools with more than 150,000 students in Delhi.[6]

In December 1964, the government of India appointed a committee headed by Asok K. Chanda to evaluate the performance of, and recommend appropriate changes to, the various media units under the Ministry of Information and Broadcasting. In its report, the Chanda Committee proposed the separation of television from the organizational structure of AIR, and recommended the creation of an autonomous Television Corporation of India to avoid political interference from government officials in the Ministry of Information and Broadcasting.[7] However, on 15 August 1965—the eighteenth anniversary of Indian independence—general television services were launched with daily, one-hour transmissions from the Delhi station of AIR. While entertainment and informational programming were introduced as part of the 'General Service', the proclaimed goal of television broadcasting in India was educational, and programming emphasized issues such as adult literacy and rural development. General Service consisted of a ten-minute 'News Round Up', mostly read by an on-screen presenter in a format developed for audio broadcasts on AIR.[8]

Visual relief was provided by broadcasting the 'Indian News Review', produced by the Films Division of the Government of India, which supplied a number of documentary films for television. In addition, free documentaries were also available from the embassies of foreign governments eager to project a positive image of their country abroad. The film-based programmes were converted into television format using a small 16 mm telecine unit—once again, a gift of the USIS. Since the telecine unit did not have provision for 35 mm films, telecast of film-based materials, including documentaries and feature films, was initially restricted to the 16 mm format. Needless to say, the technical quality of the 16 mm films after conversion into television format left much to be desired. But, given the novelty of the medium neither the producers nor the viewers seemed to complain too much about the blemishes in broadcasts.[9]

On 26 January 1967—Republic Day—Prime Minister Indira Gandhi inaugurated 'Krishi Darshan', a pilot project aimed at evaluating the role of television in the mass dissemination of educational and informational programming for rural development. Cosponsored by the Indian Agricultural Research Institute, the Department of Atomic Energy, the Ministry of Information and Broadcasting, AIR and the Delhi Administration, the programme catered to rural viewers who were provided with community television sets in 80 villages near Delhi. With the active involvement of the government of India and its various agencies to promote broadcasting as a medium for national development, television left its Delhi moorings as transmission centres were set up in cities and towns across India during the early 1970s.

On 2 October 1970, the birth anniversary of Mahatma Gandhi, a television production and transmission centre was set up in Bombay. A cosmopolitan city with a diverse group of viewers in terms of language, religion, class, caste and communities, Bombay represented a challenge for broadcasting, since programming from Delhi was restricted to the national language, Hindi. Although attempts were made to produce programming in Marathi, the major language spoken in the state of Maharashtra, Bombay had a large number of viewers who understood very little of English, Hindi or

Marathi, since they spoke other languages such as Gujarati, Konkani, Urdu and Tamil to name a few.

On 26 January 1973, a television centre was established in the city of Srinagar, as the government felt it necessary to have broadcasting services in the state of Jammu and Kashmir in order to counter programming flowing into India from across the border in Pakistan. Concerns about national security also contributed to the launch of the next television centre in the city of Amritsar on 29 September 1973. With programming in English, Hindi, Punjabi and Urdu, the Amritsar centre catered to viewers in the Indian state of Punjab, but also reached across the border into the city of Lahore in the Pakistani province of Punjab. Indian cinema has always been very popular in Pakistan, and when the Amritsar centre broadcast film-based programming, viewers in and around Lahore flocked to their television sets, much to the consternation of the government of Pakistan. At the same time, television serials produced in Pakistan were very popular among Indian viewers who had very little interest in tuning into the state-sponsored propaganda that was transmitted from the Amritsar centre in the form of news and documentaries.[10]

To counter the popularity of Pakistani television serials, the Government of India mobilized the production centres in Delhi and Amritsar to provide entertainment programming for viewers in the Indian state of Punjab. However, in these early years, the broadcasting centres in Amristar and Delhi did not have the production facilities, personnel or resources to provide a constant flow of entertainment programming to counter Pakistani serials from across the border. Therefore, Indian films and film-based programming in Hindi and Punjabi became a major component of entertainment programming at the Amritsar centre.[11]

In June 1975, when Prime Minister Indira Gandhi declared a state of national emergency in response to the growing opposition to the authoritarian policies of her government, severe restrictions were placed on the freedom of press and political assembly in the country. However, the state-sponsored media of radio and television were for political propaganda about Indira Gandhi's '20 Point Programme' that sought to enlist the nation's support for her government's policies of national development through the emergency. Her son, Sanjay Gandhi, who had no official role in the government, used television to promote his own '5 Point Programme' and mobilized overzealous sycophants in the Congress Party to implement his pet projects of forcible evacuation of slum dwellers in Delhi and compulsory family planning for the poor and the illiterate.[12]

To ensure the mass dissemination of the state-sponsored propaganda during the emergency, the Indian government continued to spread its television network into major cities and towns across India. When the Calcutta television centre was started on 8 August 1975, it presented a peculiar set of challenges to the centralized structure of broadcasting in India. The capital city of West Bengal, Calcutta was—and still is—a stronghold of Marxist and Communist parties which wielded enormous political influence in the state with little or no opposition from the Congress Party which had a stranglehold over the reigns of government at the national level. Needless to say, the political aspirations of the Marxists and Communists in the state were never adequately represented in the national network since it was centralized in its organization and controlled from Delhi by bureaucrats and politicians in Indira Gandhi's government.

When the Madras centre was launched on 15 August 1975, it brought into relief another dimension of the tensions between the states and the central government. The capital city of Tamil Nadu, Madras was—and still is—the epicentre of the DMK and the AIADMK parties which have effectively mobilized the linguistic affinities and cultural identities of the Tamil community in the South Indian state to fight against the centralized authority of the Congress Party at the national level. During the early years of radio broadcasting in postcolonial India, political leaders in Tamil Nadu—even those in Congress Party—had been vociferous in their demands for state-level autonomy, and was often critical of the government of India for marginalizing regional languages and for promoting Hindi as the national language. A major controversy over language erupted in 1957 when the Directorate General of Information and Broadcasting issued a memorandum conveying the government's desire to change the name of AIR to

'Akashvani' (*akash*: meaning sky, and *vani*: meaning voice). Like all stations in the nation, the Tiruchi station of AIR in Tamil Nadu implemented the new policy, but the station director sent the Directorate General a copy of the Tamil newspaper, *Dina Thomthi*, which reported on an agitation against the 'imposition of Hindi.' H.R. Luthra recounts the ensuing controversy in the days following the incident thus:

> The agitation mounted despite clarifications made by AIR that only where the reference was to 'AIR' was the word, Akashvani to be used, but where the reference was to Radio in general local equivalents like 'Vanoli' or 'Nabhovani' may be used. Dr. Keskar, Minister for I & B [Information and Broadcasting] wrote to Mr. Bhaktavatsalam, Home Minister, Madras on August 25, 1958 that AIR had adopted 'Akashvani' as its all-India name in India, and 'it had now become a kind of trademark.' He added that the word Akashvani had been taken from Kannada (where it was the name originally given to the Mysore station from the British days onwards), and it had been adopted because it was easily understood everywhere in the country. While, therefore, there was no objection to 'Vanoli' it was not possible for the Radio to drop Akashvani, which had been adopted as a patent word for the service.[13]

Although the Chief Minister of Tamil Nadu, Kamraj Nadar assured the government of India of the state's cooperation in implementing the new policy on AIR, some Tamil groups continued their agitation into May 1959, with individual agitators threatening to fast unto death if the name change was not withdrawn. At the heart of this contentious struggle over nomenclature is a set of Articles (343–351) in the Indian Constitution which prescribe Hindi in the Devanagari script as 'the official language of the Union' with the continued use of English as 'a subsidiary national language' as long as necessary to facilitate communication among the various agencies of the national and state-level governments in the Union.[14]

Article 351 of the Constitution provides for 'the promotion and development of the Hindi language so that it may serve as a medium of expression for all the elements of the composite culture of India.' To ensure the composite expression of India's diverse linguistic communities, the Constitution directs all Indians to 'secure the enrichment' of Hindi as a national language 'by assimilating without interfering with its genius, the forms, style and expressions used in Hindustani and in other languages of India specified in the Eighth Schedule, and by drawing, wherever necessary and desirable for its vocabulary, primarily on Sanskrit'.[15]

On 1 April 1976, when television was delinked from radio through the official institution of a national network called 'Doordarshan', it was evident that the Constitutional directive to use Hindi by drawing primarily from Sanskrit was still being followed in letter and spirit by the government of India which seemed to have forgotten earlier protests over the Sanskritization of AIR to Akashvani. The prefix *door* meaning tele or distant, and *darshan* meaning vision or sight, the introduction of the term 'doordarshan' to describe television and the corresponding term *'darshak'* to refer to viewers is attributed to J.C. Mathur, who was the Director General of AIR when experimental television services were launched in 1959.[16]

To sustain the state-sponsored agenda of national development, programming on Doordarshan had an almost exclusive focus on issues like agriculture, animal husbandry, poultry farming, education, literacy, health and family welfare. However, there were other programming genres like talk shows, quiz shows, children's programmes, feature-film based music programmes and sports programmes which supplemented the developmental agenda of Doordarshan. Yet, with the goals of national development clearly taking precedence in Indian television, not surprisingly, there was little emphasis on promoting Doordarshan either as a commercial medium for entertainment, or as a public enterprise free from government control.[17]

In the general elections of 1977, when the fledgling Janata Party swept into power by defeating the Congress Party which had suffered its worst electoral losses due to the disastrous policies of the emergency, there was a major shift in the political climate of the nation. The Janata Party, which contested the elections on a slogan of being the people's party, promised to use its sweeping mandate to make several changes to the centralized media policies of the Congress Party, which had been at the helm of national affairs for three decades since the country gained its independence from British rule in 1947.

Among the changes proposed by the Janata Party was the appointment of a former newspaper editor, B.G. Verghese, to head an independent commission to suggest ways to decrease government control over broadcasting in India. Following the recommendations of the Verghese Committee Report, the Janata Party government recommended the creation of an autonomous corporation for public broadcasting called 'Akash Bharati' ('Akash' meaning 'the skies', and 'Bharati' meaning 'of India' in Hindi).[18]

However, the political realities of governance soon caught up with the Janata Party which was being pulled in different directions by the competing interests of its coalition partners. The fall of the Janata Party government and the reemergence of Indira Gandhi's Congress Party in the general elections of 1980, signalled a new phase in the history of Indian television. For one thing, Prime Minster Indira Gandhi's desire to maintain the centralized control over radio and television was well-known, and the Janata Party's much discussed proposal to provide autonomy for the electronic media was immediately shelved by the new government. At the same time, in creating a new ministerial cabinet, Indira Gandhi assigned the influential Ministry of Information and Broadcasting to Vasant Sathe whose enthusiasm for rapidly transforming Indian television was not always shared by the Prime Minister or by the other members of the Congress Party.

When New Delhi was awarded the opportunity to host the Ninth Asian Games in 1982, the Information and Broadcasting Minister found himself at the helm of a major overhaul of Indian television in order to introduce colour transmission services. Officials at Doordarshan, led by Director General Shailendra Shankar, were elated by the opportunity to revamp the technical infrastructure of the national network which had been strapped for funds for over a decade. Shankar, who headed Doordarshan from 1980 to 1985, enthusiastically proclaimed, 'When the history of Indian television is written, Sathe's name should be in colour.'[19]

In December 1982, the Ministry of Information and Broadcasting set up a Working Group under the Chairmanship of P.C. Joshi 'to prepare a software plan for Doordarshan taking into consideration the main objectives of television of assisting in the process of social and economic development of the country and to act as an effective medium for providing information, education and entertainment'.[20] In its two-volume report, the Joshi Committee pointed to the fundamental importance of 'software planning' in the process of creating an 'Indian Personality for Television.'

By mid-1983, potential coverage for Doordarshan grew from 23 per cent to 70 per cent of the population as the number of television transmitters increased from 41 to 180 in less than one year. S.S. Gill, Secretary for the Information and Broadcasting Ministry, proudly announced that the country had created 'the biggest information explosion in the history of communication'.[21] As part of this ambitious plan for the expansion of Indian television, high-power transmitters and low-power relay stations were set up in major cities and small towns across India.

The national network was decentralized only to the extent that large metropolitan cities like Bombay, Bangalore, Calcutta, Madras, Hyderabad and a few other smaller cities had regional language transmission centres. Each of these centres catered to the specific regional interests of their viewers who all shared a common regional language, usually within a single state. Although the languages were different in each of the centres, the programming formats and content remained largely similar across the national network. The political bosses in Delhi managed to sustain their vision of an Indian community of television through a loosely defined yet extremely centralized authority over the administration and programming of the national network. Doordarshan effectively manipulated its monopoly over viewers across the country by strategically scheduling what the network called, 'national programming', during the primetime hours of late evenings and weekends.

During the general elections of 1989, the Congress Party government led by Prime Minister Rajiv Gandhi tried to manipulate Doordarshan's coverage of the various political parties and the major issues and controversies during the election campaigns. Despite the extensive use of state-owned media like Doordarshan to promote Rajiv Gandhi's image, the Congress Party was defeated in the elections as the government was plagued by allegations about bribes paid to the Prime Minister himself by a Swedish company, Bofors, in exchange for a contract to supply guns for the Indian military. After the shocking defeat of the Congress Party in the general elections, a fledgling party called the Janata Dal came into power, and its leader, Vishwanath Pratap Singh, once a close associate of Rajiv Gandhi, became the nation's Prime Minister. V.P. Singh, who had campaigned to rid the government of corruption and bureaucratic mismanagement, also promised to provide autonomy to the state-sponsored media if elected to power. Upon assuming office, the Janata Dal government introduced a new bill for the creation of an autonomous broadcasting corporation called Prasar Bharati (in Hindi, 'Prasar' means 'disseminate', and 'Bharati' means 'Indian').

The Prasar Bharati Bill was a significant milestone in the long-standing quest for 'autonomy' in Indian television. However, the quality of 'autonomy' given to Prasar Bharati was rather diluted in comparison to what had been advocated in 1978 under the rubric of 'Akash Bharati'. The most significant difference was that the Prasar Bharati Bill required the creation of a Parliamentary Committee to oversee the functioning of the Corporation. While critics of this move saw this change as an attempt to curtail the autonomy of Prasar Bharati, the Minister for Information and Broadcasting, P. Upendra, assured Members of Parliament that safeguards were 'built into this Bill with the objective of giving to media the fullest protection from outside interference'.[22]

Shortly after the passage of the Prasar Bharati Act in 1990, the Janata Dal Party suddenly fell out of power before the government could issue the necessary notification to enable the legal creation of an autonomous corporation for broadcasting in India. The party that replaced the Janata Dal government was a minority splinter-group, led by Prime Minister Chandrashekhar, and it depended heavily on the Congress Party's strength in the Parliament to stay in power. Needless to say, the Prasar Bharati Bill was shelved without further action, and broadcasting in India continued to remain under direct state supervision. When the Congress Party withdrew its support for the Chandra Shekhar government and forced new elections in 1990, this time its election manifesto contained a promise for the creation of a commission to study anew the question of autonomy for television in India.

In the general elections of 1990, scarred by the tragic assassination of Rajiv Gandhi during a campaign visit to Tamil Nadu, the Congress Party was voted back into power. As a shell-shocked nation mourned the death of the Congress Party leader, a new government led by Prime Minister P.V. Narasimha Rao was sworn into office. Although the Congress Party government was interested in relaxing several government restrictions on private businesses to operate in the television industry to boost the sagging Indian economy, it paid little attention to the question of providing autonomy to the electronic media.[23]

Waiting for Prasar Bharati

In February 1995, on the eve of the Hero Cup International cricket tournament, the government could no longer avoid dealing with the question of autonomy for Doordarshan after a petition was filed in the Calcutta High Court challenging the authority of Doordarshan's monopoly over television broadcasting in India. The organizers of the Hero Cup, the Cricket Association of Bengal, sold the worldwide rights for telecasting the matches to Transworld Image (TWI) after failing to negotiate a mutually acceptable contract with state-sponsored network, Doordarshan.

Subsequently, the Ministry of Information and Broadcasting asserted that Doordarshan had exclusive rights for broadcasting in India and instructed the government-owned telecommunications provider, Videsh Sanchar Nigam Limited (VSNL), to deny uplinking facilities to TWI. The Cricket Association of Bengal filed a writ petition before the Calcutta High Court challenging the legality of the government's decision to prohibit the use of airwaves by private companies. To facilitate the timely conduct of the cricket tournament, the Calcutta High Court issued an interim order allowing Doordarshan to broadcast the Hero Cup within India, and permitting TWI to telecast the matches to international viewers.[24]

Although the Supreme Court took up the case after the completion of the Hero Cup tournament, the case between the Ministry of Information and Broadcasting, government of India and the Cricket Association of Bengal was extremely significant because of the constitutional issues it raised about the role of the government in regulating the use of the airwaves in India. In its landmark judgement, the Supreme Court held that the airwaves are public property that must be used in ways that ensure the expression of a plurality of views and diversity of opinions in the national community. The Court also ruled that the government of India had a responsibility to use the airwaves to advance the citizens' rights to free speech guaranteed by the Constitution. In its ruling, the Court explained, 'The broadcasting media should be under the control of the public as distinct from Government. This is the command implicit in Article 19(1)(a). It should be operated by a public statutory corporation or corporations.'[25] On the question of broadcasting by private individuals and commercial networks, the Court ruled:

> The question whether to permit private broadcasting or not is a matter of policy for the Parliament to decide. If it decides to permit it, its for the Parliament to decide, subject to what conditions and restrictions should it be permitted. Private broadcasting, even if allowed, should not be left to the market forces in the interest of ensuing that a wide variety of voices enjoy access to it.[26]

In defining the airwaves as a public property free from both state control and commercial forces, the judges pointed to the 'danger flowing from the concentration of the right to broadcast/telecast in the hands of (either) a central agency or of a few private affluent broadcasters'.[27] The Supreme Court's historic judgement ordering the Government of India to 'take immediate steps to establish an autonomous public authority...to control and regulate the use of the airwaves' intensified the demands for reform in Indian television.[28]

The Ministry of Information and Broadcasting set up a Committee headed by Nitish Sengupta to suggest revisions to the Prasar Bharati Act which had been passed by the Indian Parliament in 1990, but shelved by the Congress Party government which came to power in 1991. In its report, published in 1996, the Sengupta Committee, noted the need to rethink broadcasting policies since the rapid proliferation of satellite channels had rapidly transformed the television landscape in India since 1991. Although the Sengupta Committee was created in December 1995 by the Congress Party's government after the Supreme Court issued its order for the creation of a public broadcasting trust, the general elections of 1996 brought a new political formation led by the Bharatiya Janata Party (BJP), called the National Democratic Alliance (NDA), into power. Led by Prime Minster Atal Behari Vajpayee, the BJP set out to fashion a workable majority to form the government. However, unable to sustain its majority in the parliament, the NDA government fell out of power only after a short stint of 12 days at the helm of affairs.

When another political formation called the United Front formed the government, the creation of the Prasar Bharati appeared inevitable, particularly since many of the constituent members of the NDA were parties to the Prasar Bharati Act passed in 1990. On 15 September 1997, the Government of India issued the necessary notification to turn the Prasar Bharati Act of 1990 into law. With the creation of the Prasar Bharati Board on 23 November 1997, the task of ensuring autonomy for television in India now rested with the 15 members of the newly constituted public broadcasting corporation.[29] Now legally enshrined as an autonomous corporation, Prasar Bharati promoted the expansion of Doordarshan by adding more channels to the national network as a strategy to compete with foreign and domestic networks in the realms of entertainment, news and regional language programming.

Doordarshan's impressive plans for expansion were not only supported by the rising advertising revenues, but also by the growing diversity of genres in its programming line up of daytime soap operas, talk shows, top-10 music rotations, and reruns of nationalistic programmes like *Discovery of India*, serials based on traditional folklore like *Chandrakanta*, and religious epics like *Ramayan* and *Mahabharat*.

In a market survey published in 1996, the advertisement agency Lintas reported that commercial revenue in India has been on the upswing since the introduction of satellite television in the early 1990s. The Lintas report notes that within one year (from 1994–95 to 1995–96) the Indian market grew from Rs 7,620 million ($223.5 m) to Rs 10,200 million ($299 m). For the year 1995–96, Lintas estimated, Doordarshan had the lion's share of the commercial revenue, by cornering a whopping $196.5 million (out of a total of $299 million). Zee TV was a distant second with an advertising revenue of $64.5 million and the Tamil language network, Sun TV, gathering a respectable $13 million during this period.[30] From an all time high commercial revenue of Rs 5,727 million in 1997, Doordarshan's share slipped to Rs 4,901 million in 1998 and Rs 3,999 million in 1999 as satellite and cable channels began competing with the state-sponsored network for the viewers' attention.

At the same time, as the Annual Reports (1993–2000) of Doordarshan suggest, from 1991–2001, the national network—the indispensable ideological cohort of the nation state—had grown phenomenally to counter the threat of its transnational and translocal competition in India. In terms of its geographic reach, the network covered 14 per cent of the nation in 1982, 61 per cent in 1992 and 72.9 per cent in 1999. With the launch of the DD-International channel on 14 March 1995, the state-sponsored network extended beyond the political boundaries of the national community and reached viewers across Asia. From 10 programme production centres in 1982 to 20 in 1992, Doordarshan's production facilities grew by over 100 per cent by 1999 to 46 centres. Similarly, the number of broadcasting transmitters in the national network increased from 19 in 1982 to 535 in 1992 and 1,041 in 1999. While Doordarshan reached a mere 26 per cent of the national population in 1982, it reached 81 per cent in 1992 and 87.6 per cent in 1999.

These figures were, however, mere speculations in the rapidly changing Asian markets where unexpected, intervening variables had ruined some of the best of predictions and estimates by media analysts. A case in point is the concept Direct to Home TV (or DTH) which was expected to grow phenomenally after the expansion of the satellite and cable industry in the mid- to late 1990s. In the first half of the 1990s, DTH was embraced by transnational networks such as STAR TV as a strategy to circumvent their dependence on local cable operators across India, who could drop and add channels from their everyday fare to cater to the programming tastes and linguistic preferences of the viewers in their community. However, the DTH phenomenon ran into various problems as the networks recognized that the economics of signal transmission, encryption, distribution, reception, and revenue collection were far too cumbersome in the diverse Asian markets where, despite half-a-decade of intensive probing and surveying, media researchers cannot seem to agree even on the number of television households in any one community.[31]

Shortly after the creation of the Prasar Bharati Corporation, the United Front—which had been most receptive to the ideals of broadcasting autonomy—lost power after a short stint of 12 months in government, when the Congress Party strategically withdrew its support and called for mid-term Elections in 1998. After the elections of 1998, the BJP came back to power, but once again, the government lasted for only 13 months, when one of the regional partners of the NDA, the AIADMK in Tamil Nadu, withdrew its support in parliament. When elections were held in 1999, the NDA alliance gained a comfortable majority to form the government, and it appeared that the third time was a lucky charm for the BJP. However, the future of the Prasar Bharati Bill now appeared more uncertain.

In its election manifesto, the NDA had promised to conduct a thorough review of the Prasar Bharati Act after forming the government. What the 'review' would result in was not clearly spelled out in the document, but some political analysts predicted that the BJP government was 'keen to do away with the half-baked autonomy Prasar Bharati had been provided with.'[32] In the run up to the 1999 elections, the Minister of Information and Broadcasting, Pramod Mahajan, had categorically declared that he was not in favour of granting autonomy to Prasar Bharati as envisioned by the 1990 Act. 'I do not have faith in Prasar Bharati. I want Doordarshan under the control of the government. If we come back to power, we will dissolve Prasar Bharati,' he proclaimed.[33]

Explaining his aversion to the Prasar Bharati Act, Mahajan argued that the question of autonomy may have been relevant in 1990 when there was only one national network in Doordarshan. However, with the growing number of national, transnational and translocal satellite and cable channels competing with the state-sponsored network in the 1990s, Mahajan maintained that there was no longer any need for the government to provide 'autonomy' to Doordarshan. Instead he expressed interest in focusing his attention, and that of his Ministry, toward the development of a Conditional Access System (CAS) to enable the government to better regulate the programming and distribution of satellite and cable television channels in India.[34]

After the 1999 Elections, when the BJP-led NDA alliance returned to power, Mahajan was back at the helm of the Ministry of Information and Broadcasting and he focused his attention on the development of a comprehensive Broadcasting Bill to regulate the activities of the private satellite channels such as STAR TV, ETV, Sun TV and Zee TV, and the commercially-owned cable companies. The goal of the Broadcasting Bill, introduced in 1997, is to create an independent authority known as the Broadcasting Authority of India to oversee a range of broadcasting services in India.[35]

Given the lack of enthusiasm for Prasar Bharati at the highest levels of government, the Board members soon realized that their 'autonomy' would be severely curtailed by political pressures from the government, coupled with the bureaucratic inertia in the various agencies of the Ministry of Information and Broadcasting. As a frustrated member of the Board, Dr Rajendra Yadav once put it, Prasar Bharati is at best a 'fractured autonomy'.

Conclusion

If the adoption of the Prasar Bharati Act by the Indian Parliament in 1990 failed to give concrete shape to the notion of autonomy for television, then the creation of the Prasar Bharati Corporation in 1997 did not put an end to the wrangling over legal definitions, political manipulations and policy confusions in development of public broadcasting. By the end of the 1990s, it became amply clear that the nationalist ambivalence toward granting complete autonomy to broadcasting transcended political ideologies as three successive governments led by the centrist Congress Party, the left-wing Janata Dal, and the right-wing BJP all chose to ignore the core recommendations of the Supreme Court's landmark decision which defined the airwaves as public property. Moreover, as is evident from the policy recommendations of the many government-appointed Committees—from the Chanda Committee in the 1960s to the Sengupta Committee in the 1990s—the goals of creating an autonomous corporation for public broadcasting have always been articulated within the framework of a state-sponsored network which marginalizes alternative imaginations of nationalist autonomy in non-statist terms. In each of these instances, even as the nationalist desire for autonomy in television was being inscribed in the publication of the Committee Reports, it was simultaneously being erased by the policy decisions taken by successive governments regardless of their political ideologies or governing philosophies.

Lest we get alarmed by the ambivalence of the politicians and the policy makers who are drawn to the centralized authority of state-sponsored institutions like Doordarshan and Prasar Bharati in their quest to provide autonomy for television, we must remember that similar concerns have always been raised about the hegemony of the media elite in the discourse of nationalism in colonial and postcolonial India. In his extensive analyses of popular literary texts like newspapers and novels in colonial and postcolonial India, Homi Bhabha finds that the nationalist imaginations of media elites represent the innermost fears and fantasies of the community about its collective sense of identity in relation to the ever changing realities of the outside world.[36] For Bhabha, the narrative fears and fantasies of the literary texts, and the ambivalent imaginations of cultural identity and difference they seek to represent can only be articulated through a 'middle voice' of hybridity. This middle voice, Bhabha argues, is indicated in the double meaning dissemiNation which, in its hybrid formulation, at once conveys a sense of fusion with (the inside/the nation) and diffusion from (outside/the world).[37]

At once playful and powerful, Bhabha's appropriation of Jacques Derrida's theory of dissemination[38] (or difference or deconstruction) enables us to articulate the nation *as it is written* in the narrative ambivalence of imagining an 'Indian' community of television into existence. However, while Bhabha's writings on dissemiNation have extensively focused on print-capitalism and the role of literary narratives of nationalism in the colonial world, they have not examined the televisual narratives of Doordarshan and Prasar Bharati in postcolonial India. In a more recent essay, titled 'Arrivals and Departures', Bhabha finds himself at the 'cusp of an electronic dilemma' as he tries to make sense of the new forms of national and transnational communities that are created by the globalization of television.[39] On the one hand, the electronic communities of television are not 'national' by definition. On the other hand, the rapid flows of electronic media do not lead us to imagine communities that are completely 'detached from national policies of technological innovation, education provision, science policy.'[40]

The hybrid character of communities engendered by the electronic flows of television induces Bhabha to wonder, 'What form of "media"—in the most general and generic sense of the technology of representation, the genre of mediation—would be appropriate' to the 'new rhythms of information and communication' of our time?[41] In what follows, I elaborate on possible answers to the question that Bhabha poses by framing my study of the national community of Indian television in relation to what Jacques Derrida has defined as the 'techno-tele-media apparatuses' of acceleration and dislocation.[42] What is 'accelerated' by the technological apparatuses of television is the ability of users to gain access to a wide range of media and mediated cultures with unimaginable ease. What is dislocated, in this context, 'is therefore, a sense of ontology, of the essentiality or inevitability of being-and-belonging by virtue of the nation, a mode of experience and existence that Derrida calls a *national ontopology*'.[43]

Derrida's deconstruction of the radical dislocation of nationalist imaginations in our time induces us to think of a new mode of autonomy that is now being inscribed and erased—in a flash—by the accelerated flows of televisual technologies and cultures. In this 'moment of exposure,' as Bhabha puts it, a paradoxical 'media temporality' emerges as it shuttles in a double movement to make '*at once* contiguous, and *in that flash*, contingent, the realms of human consciousness and the unconscious.'[44]

To address the 'erasure within exposure' of the 'familiar, domestic, national and homely' through which the autonomy of Indian television is fleetingly revealed, I recast Bhabha's literary notion of dissemiNation into a televisual formulation of imagiNation. As a hybrid articulation of the ambivalent dissemination of nationalist autonomy, imagiNation thus refers to a 'middle vision' of television as it is being exposed and erased by the political and policy debates over the status of electronic media in India. As discussed in the preceding sections, the middle vision of imagiNation is always visible in the policy debates over autonomy in Indian television beginning with the recommendations of the Chanda Committee in the 1960s to the Verghese Committee in the 1970s, and the Joshi Committee in the 1980s to the Sengupta Committee in the 1990s.

For instance, in the early 1960s when television was emerging as a new medium with distinct potential in contrast to AIR, the Chanda Committee Report argued,

> The question still remains whether the new organisation should follow the pattern of AIR and become an attached office of a Ministry or whether it should be made an autonomous corporation, created by a special statute of Parliament. Having carefully considered the question in all its aspects, we have come to the conclusion that to develop on correct lines television must not be

hampered by the limitations of a department; it should have a broader outlook, greater flexibility and freedom of action which the corporate form alone can give.[45]

Although the Chanda Committee Report called for an autonomous corporation for television, when general television services were launched on 15 August 1965 the government of India gave the important task of producing daily, one-hour transmissions to officials at AIR in Delhi. In doing so, the government's broadcasting policy not only subsumed the autonomy of television under the institutional structure of AIR, it also established a central role for the national government in the everyday functioning of the electronic media. Similarly in the 1970s, as television remained under the centralized authority of AIR in Delhi, the Verghese Committee argued for the creation of an autonomous national broadcasting corporation with a highly decentralized structure, and explained its rationale as follows,

> The Working Group are of the view that there should not be autonomous regional corporations or even a federation of State Government corporations. Instead, a single National Broadcast Trust is proposed under which a highly decentralised structure is envisaged. There will be a large measure of power delegated to the regional and local level so that the organisation enjoys the advantages of quick decision-making, sensitivity to local problems, familiarity with local customs and taste, and close linkages with various governments and institutions.[46]

The recommendations of the Verghese Committee represented a promising start on paper, but its concept of a single broadcasting corporation was heavily dependent on the ability of governmental institutions to delegate authority to lower levels in the echelons of power. Therefore, the autonomy of the Akash Bharati Corporation that the Verghese Committee proposed was prone to political interference by officials in the governments at the central and the state levels. While policy debates in the 1960s and 1970s centred around institutional control infrastructure and hardware, the 1980s signalled a new phase in the quest for autonomy in television as the Joshi Committee recommended a shift in emphasis from hardware to software. Invoking the names of nationalist leaders like Mahatma Gandhi, Jawaharlal Nehru and Rabindranath Tagore in support of its proposal to rethink the question of autonomy in terms of software or programming content, the Joshi Committee wrote,

> Software planning is of fundamental importance ... from the point of view of making people aware of the question raised by Tagore, Gandhi and Nehru which has greater relevance to-day [sic] than in the past: *Wither India?* Is India condemned to be merely imitative, ultimately reproducing here an inferior version of the Western culture and civilisation? Or can India be creative, building a new pattern combining the best elements of the modern and traditional cultures?[47]

Although the Joshi Committee Report's recommendations emphasized the need for software planning in the creation of an autonomous 'Indian' personality for television, officials at the Ministry of Information and Broadcasting focused more on hardware development in their quest to rapidly expand the geographic reach of the centralized national network throughout the 1980s. Ironically enough, some of the most creative software planning for the development of an 'Indian' personality for television emerged after 1991 when commercial satellite television channels began experimenting with several programming genres such as music television, soap operas, sitcoms and reality TV shows. As private satellite networks like STAR TV, Sun TV, ETV and Zee TV began competing with the state-sponsored network, Doordarshan, in the 1990s, policy makers and politicians alike were forced to confront the rapidly changing environment of television in India. Explaining the need for reevaluating the Prasar Bharati Act which was passed by the Parliament in 1990, the Sengupta Committee wrote,

> A complete rethinking of the role, organization and functions of Prasar Bharati became necessary in a

multi-channel scenario, mostly driven by market forces, Prasar Bharati needs the requisite degree of flexibility and financial powers to hold its own. There has been a constant debate concerning the quality and purpose of Indian Broadcasting quite for some time now. Some basic questions will have to be addressed to be able to evolve a vibrant and versatile model of a national broadcasting system, including a reinvigorated Prasar Bharati, in a vastly changed and fast-changing scenario.[48]

The question of whether policy makers and politicians are able to evolve a 'vibrant and versatile' model of public broadcasting called for by the Sengupta Committee Report in 1996 remains unanswered yet. But the 'fractured autonomy' that has resulted from the establishment of the Prasar Bharati Corporation in 1997 is yet another instance in the long history of ambivalent policies that shuttle between a nationalist desire to create an autonomous corporation for television and a state-sponsored agenda of maintaining a centralized authority over broadcasting in India. In the process, however, a fleeting vision of autonomy is revealed through the middle vision of imagiNation which is not only visible in policy debates in television, but also reverberates through the structures and hierarchies of broadcasting institutions such as Prasar Bharati and Doordarshan as they seek to compete with transnational networks such as STAR TV and translocal networks such as Eenadu TV and Sun TV. The hybrid articulation of imagiNation of autonomy is also partially visible in a variety of nationalist programming on Indian television: in the passionate erection and annihilation of historical narratives in docudramas like *Bharat Ek Khoj* which are promoted in the name of national integration; in the artificial insemination and dissemination of the seeds of mythic origins in television serials like *Ramayan* and *Mahabharat* which are celebrated in epic imaginations of the nation; in the prodigal production and reproduction of the pedagogical instruments of the national state apparatus through performative roles of everyday characters in innumerable sitcoms, soap operas and dramas.

In each of these instances, what remains most contentious is the question of autonomy in Indian television: Is it an imagined community of cultural production or is it a given product of political-economic institutions? Is it the defined through the terrain of the nation state or is it defied by the transgressions of transnational networks? Is it the residue of archaic traditions or the emergence of a new cosmopolitanism? Is it dominated by the hegemony of nationalist institutions or is it contested by the aspirations of vernacular communities? Perhaps, in each of these questions, both alternatives are at once true and false. Therefore, the question of autonomy in Indian television, I conclude, can be best addressed in a middle vision of nationalism, for which my preferred term is imagiNation.

Notes

1. Quoted in 'Fast Forward to a Slice of History', *The Hindu*, 13 November 2001. See http://web.lexis-nexis.com.
2. UNESCO, Television: *A World Survey* (Paris: UNESCO. Reprint edition, 1972 by Arno Press), p. 105.
3. P.C. Chatterji, *Broadcasting in India* (New Delhi: Sage Publications, 1987).
4. Narendra Kumar and Jai Chandiram, *Educational Television in India* (New Delhi: Arya Book Depot, 1967).
5. Ibid.
6. Ibid.
7. Ministry of Information and Broadcasting, *Radio & Television* (*Report of the Committee on Broadcasting and Information Media*) (New Delhi: Government of India Publications, 1965). Also known as the Chanda Committee Report.
8. V.V. Rao, personal interview. Hyderabad, July 1996.
9. Ibid.
10. Sevanti Ninan, *Through the Magic Window* (New Delhi: Penguin Books, 1995).
11. H.R. Luthra, *Indian Broadcasting* (Delhi: Publications Division, Ministry of Information and Broadcasting, Government of India, 1986), pp. 274–75.
12. For a detailed account of the reasons for, and the consequences of, Indira Gandhi's proclamation of 'emergency', see P.N. Bahl, *Indira Gandhi: The Crucial Years (1973–1984)* (New Delhi: Har-Anand, 1994) and P.N. Dhar, *Indira Gandhi, the 'Emergency', and Indian Democracy* (Delhi: Oxford University Press, 2000).

13. Luthra, *Indian Broadcasting*.
14. Durga Das Basu, *Introduction to the Constitution of India*, 18th Edition (Nagpur: Wadhwa and Company, 1999).
15. Ibid., p. 392.
16. Luthra, *Indian Broadcasting*, p. 434.
17. Ananda Mitra, *Television in India: A Study of the Mahabharata* (Thousand Oaks, CA: Sage, 1993).
18. Verghese Committee Report. Online at http://www.indiantelevision.com/indianbrodcast/legalreso/legalresources.htm#
19. Quoted in Amrita Shah, *Hype, Hypocrisy and Television in Urban India* (Delhi: Vikas Publishing House, 1997), p. 11.
20. Report of the Working Group on Software for Doordarshan, *An Indian Personality for Television* (New Delhi: Government of India Publications, 1982). Also known as the Joshi Committee Report.
21. Quoted in Arthur Unger, 'TV Comes to India: A Talk With its Top Broadcast Official', *Christian Science Monitor*, 22 March 1985, p. 25.
22. 'The Prasar Bharati Bill', in G.S. Bhargava (ed.), *Government Media Autonomy and After* (New Delhi: Concept Publishing Company, 1991), p. 104.
23. For a more detailed discussion of the Narasimha Rao government's liberalization policies in the early 1990s, see Vijay Joshi and I.M.D. Little, *India's Economic Reforms: 1991–2001* (New Delhi: Oxford University Press, 1996).
24. Sharad Varma, 'Air Waves: Public Property', *The Lawyers*, vol. 10, no. 5 (May) 1995, pp. 4–11.
25. Cited in Sevanti Ninan, 'History of Indian Broadcasting Reform', in Monroe E. Price and Stefaan G. Verhulst (eds), *Broadcasting Reform in India: Media Law from a Global Perspective* (New Delhi: Oxford University Press, 1998), p. 13.
26. Cited in Kamal Mitra Chenoy, 'In Depth: The Broadcasting Bill', http://www.ieo.org/broadcast.html.
27. Cited in Praveen Swami, 'Autonomy in Prospect', *Frontline*, vol. 14, no. 19, 1997 (20 September–3 October) www.flonnet.com/fl1419/14191290.htm.
28. Ninan, 'History of Indian Broadcasting Reform', p. 14.
29. The organizational structure of Prasar Bharati, and the current composition of the membership of its Board can be found online at http://www.ddindia.net/dd_prasarbharati.html.
30. Reuters Textline, 'Indian Newcomers Find the Going Tough'. 1 April 1996, web.lexis-nexis.com.
31. For an overview of the DTH and the Pay TV phenomena, see indiantelevision.com, 'The Pay TV Conundrum', http://www.indiantelevision.com/news_analysis/paytv.htm and Connect Magazine, 'Direct to Home Broadcasting Sees Light of Day', http://www.connectmagazine.com/FEBRUARY%201999/Feb99/html/DTH.htm.

32. Vinay Jha, 'Prasar Bharati Fate Hangs in Balance', *The Statesman*, 23 August 1999, web.lexis-nexis.com.
33. Quoted on ipan.com, '"I do not have faith in Prasar Bharati": Minister Declares', 1999, http://www.ipan.com/reviews/archives/0699tv.htm.
34. For an overview of the CAS debate, see Renu Mittal, 'Cable TV is 'CAS'T Away', *Deccan Chronicle*, 15 June 2003, Sunday Edition, p. 1.
35. The structure and functions of the Broadcasting Authority of India, as proposed in the Broadcasting Bill of 1997, can be found online at http://www.nwmindia.org/Law/Bare_acts/broadcastbill.htm.
36. Homi Bhabha, *The Location of Culture* (London: Routledge, 1994).
37. Homi Bhabha, 'DissemiNation: Time, Narrative and the Margins of the Nation', in Homi Bhabha (ed.), *Nation and Narration* (New York: Routledge, 1991), pp. 291–322.
38. See Jacques Derrida, *Dissemination*, translated by Barbara Johnson (Chicago: University of Chicago Press, 1981) and 'Difference', in *Speech and Phenomena* (Evanston: Northwestern University, 1973), pp. 129–60.
39. Homi Bhabha, 'Preface: Arrivals and Departures', in Hamid Naficy (ed.), *Home, Exile Homeland* (London: Routledge, 1999), pp. vii–xii.
40. Ibid., p. viii.
41. Ibid., p. ix.
42. Jacques Derrida, *The Specters of Marx: The State of the Debt, the Work of Mourning, and the New International*, translated by Peggy Kamuf, with an Introduction by Bernd Magnus and Stephen Cullenberg (New York: Routledge, 1994).
43. Ibid.
44. Bhabha, 'Preface: Arrivals and Departures', p. xi.
45. Ibid., p. 210.
46. Ibid.
47. Ibid., p. 18.
48. The Sengupta Committee Report. Online at http: www. indiantelevision.com/indianbrodcast/legalreso/legalresources.htm#

PART 2

ANATOMIES OF ARBITRATION

EDITORS

Introduction

Through successive eras of new and newer media—from the Gutenberg to The short message service (SMS)—we notice the successive transcendence of the sign over the signal. This cumulatively marked the increasing emergence of a man equipped with a greater variety of tools and cognitive structures, both supporting each other. While language was operationalizing its techniques through rhetorics and various mental disciplines, technical innovations were expanding the reach and reproducibility of the disembodied word and speech. Throughout these developments, man's conviction about reality was the substantive referent. As a consequence, cultural or social transformations happened to engineer technical innovations towards enlarging the circulation and exchange of symbolic productions. All media, as signs of social design and interpretation, were carrying man's physical intervention in and symbolic processing of the world so as to create an environment (material and symbolic) corresponding to man's will and vision. They were serving various functions of information, expression and communicative interaction; in the matter of fact, a jungle of signs indefinitely interpreted one another along endless 'chains of interpretors'. In short, these were eras when the relevance and legitimacy of the media was constantly assessed with reference to its subservient function of mediation.

Theoretically, from the point of view of a science of the mind, communication implied a tripartite structural constitution: viz. reality which was facing man as separate/distinct from him; man who tried to apprehend and appropriate it; and media as a set of material and symbolic means which mediate or arbitrate between these different levels. On their part, experts, analysts and critics were essentially concerned with assessing the mutual relations of these three instances: reality, man and media. Their queries focused on the propriety of signs and media with regard to reality, and on the appropriateness of media with regard to the attempts of man to apprehend and comprehend reality. The validity, the nature, the scope and adequacy of the media with respect to both reality and man's symbolic competency and practical will, in short 'mediation processes', were the focus of communication critique.

However, the last decades seem to be turning all this upside down. The most perceptive theoretical analysts and philosophical critics see the world of communication being progressively absorbed, since 1942, under the tyranny of the mediatic empire such that mediation itself is eliminated: 'everything we see and hear *is* reality' goes the dictum. This blows up the notion of communication into a vast, autonomous and totalitarian world simply shaped by the rule of information technologies and 'new media'.[1] A deeper look, however, shows that this happened on several accounts, and in several forms, over the last six decades. This occurred ideologically through a figuring of communication as a political utopia that would replace the totalitarian regimes and ideologies arising amidst World War II. It was in these years that the discourse of communication as a claim to offer the real alternative was born; an enthralling utopia 'without victims' based on transparency, 'free' circulation and access by all, to all sorts of information and knowledge. It provided the hopes and effective means of man's reconciliation, which religious and secular philosophers across eras have dreamt of.

Materially, communication became a constituency of information communication technologies, whose recent explosion has become synonymous with the communication revolution. The belief is that one needs to simply make full use of all sorts of machines to secure a limpid transparency to enjoy a direct access to reality *with no intermediary*, to memorize and transmit knowledge most reliably and objectively, to engineer processes of social transformation and eradicate poverty, to bring scattered human beings together on one single public square of the world, beyond boundaries of space and time. The sphere of communication is to be definitely removed from the sphere of man's opaque symbolic productions, and brought into the sole sphere of information—of numerals, texts, images or sound[2]. Tools of storage, replication and transmission and their corporate institutionalization are the referent and subject matter of any discourse on and study of communication. Thus, a new brand of technological mystification is projected as an antidote to ignorance and values, blind faith and poverty.

Cognitively, this provides an hegemonic epistèmè which infiltrates all the disciplines and methods of knowledge construction, as also the pre-existing discourses on work management, material development, social engineering and human enlightenment. The new epistemological paradigm suggests that the relationships between all the natural, cultural and social phenomena are not an attribute, among others, of their reality, but are integrally and ontologically constitutive of their reality itself. In doing so, it not only challenges the hypotheses at the root of physics, biology, artificial intelligence, cognitive sciences, economy, 'man' management and human sciences, but as a paradigmatic rupture seeks to substitute existing mechanisms in a number of constituencies of knowledge.[3] This is fine in itself; what is not is that underlying this specific paradigm is a dangerous, relativist axiom that reality has no substance and we as individuals have no subjectivity.

Symbolically, communication has recently developed into a tautistic implosion of human speech; the individual has definitely turned into a reactor and ceases to be an actor. Lucien Sfez coins the neologism 'tautism'—a contraction of tautology and autism—as a symbolic category designed to qualify the contemporary régime of communication systems and their all encompassing industrial grounding.[4] Tautism, thus, defines our era in which everything is communication and vice versa, and nothing else. This refers to the power of the media in bringing reality to everyone without mediation and mediators, 'live' news reportage and 'reality television' being the most prominent cases in point. Never mind that the actual phenomenon at play is the capacity to turn the represented reality into the real world itself. All that appears on screens and headphones, brought through waves and cables, becomes thus a forcefully compelling Real, 'a totalitarian world'. As a consequence, men's mind entirely feed on and belong in the representation, the latter rising as man's alter ego, that is, an absolute and gratifying identity of the self with itself. The media gives the human self its being. Perhaps, therefore, as this era has progressed, an increasing quantum of analyses in communication and media theory confines itself to representation alone!

The point being brought out here is that the explosion of such systems, and systemic forces, cause the end of communication by implosion. Here is the real revolution, if any, in communication: the triad of communication, information and technique is increasingly causing the implosion of human interaction and all dialogical activities.[5] The 'electronic church' and its various congregations triumphantly claims to bring, and ultimately be, the very sole real world. New technologies can melt and weld us directly within reality through complex webs of disembodied cultural codes, information systems, consumer products and commercial transactions. Instead of signs, only signals trigger off chains of interactions.

Thus, the discourse of the communication revolution is actually an inversion within communication, an inversion of the rapport between the three levels mentioned earlier. What this 'revolution' has achieved is positioning communication as an ersatz of democracy ideologically, and increasingly politically. This allegedly vibrant 'society of communication' aloof from a withering state and abiding by rules of rational and procedural consensus turn conflicts, denials and marginalization definitely archaic.[6] For, they are alleged to be contrary to the ethos of an era of seamless interaction and information flows.[7] We realize that the 'society of communication' has become a substitute to former political structures, since industries of communication offer facilities that are the definite, secure and potent medium of democracy. Thus, embracing the term 'communication revolution' becomes indicative of a fetish'—a fetish which elevates the means of communication to the status of transformatory social agents. At worst, its discourse proclaims the revolution in communication to exemplify social transformation itself.[8]

Going beyond puncturing such myths, the writings in this section reflect upon the anatomies of arbitration by both dominant and counter-cultural practices. In doing so, its authors are guided as much by their wariness of the 'revolution' as by their critique of the economy of representation of these arbitrations themselves.

While political communications, having a long tradition as a vital cog of the modernization paradigm, has been variously reshaped by the transforming culture of 'the political'—as elaborated in the Overture of this volume—it is necessary to explicate this process of transformation—especially since the precise form of the new arrangements depends upon the specific socio-economic and cultural configurations on which it is acting. For instance, the shift from the years of Doordarshan to private channels was as much implicitly guided by the state as it was spearheaded by global capital. It provided varied permutations in which communication processes may cut across boundaries of nation, community and kinship; it is within these permutations that new figures of identity and commerce got reconfigured. How are we to make sense of the frameworks of understanding and action that people live in and live through? In 'State, Market and Freedom of Expression', Uma Chakravarti wonders what freedom of expression implies in a deregulated media environment. Focusing on three segments of television programmes—advertisements, serials and news—she argues that commercial representations have their own brand of silencing and marginalizing. This begs the question: is this mirage of pluralism, which forms the ideological kernel of the 'communication revolution', any better than either the erstwhile monopolist state media or the fundamentalist polity of censorship?

As the media become integrated with commercial culture, we ought to make sense of the frameworks of understanding and action we live in and live through. The author's approach implicitly suggests getting rid of theoretical presumptions and methodological limitations of 'impact studies'. For even today we observe the presence of a longstanding assumption that the spread of television leads to greater spread of information, which in turn allegedly contributes towards general processes of democratization of society.[9] In contrast to this standpoint, 'Forging Public Opinion' by Krishna Reddy is an exercise in understanding media's role in transforming polity. The essay addresses the transformation of political campaigns from traditional party-mediated ones to increasingly media-led ones, by looking at events in Andhra Pradesh. But the study feels that there is an intricate relationship between the transforming political campaigns and deeply felt crisis in the political processes in India, and Andhra Pradesh in particular, over a period of time. In the emerging scenario, electoral politics appears more like a market place—which, in turn, necessitates a 'new' media environment in the world of party politics. Consequently, the author also explores the implications of the changes in the political campaigns for the larger dynamics of competitive politics.

While there is a wide consensus on the argument that subnational and transnational broadcasting provide a fertile ground for political identities to be remoored, utopian concepts of the Internet as an identity-less place mark the buzz of our times. These are derived from standpoints that misconstrue human interaction in machinist terms. What has proved such techno-determinism wrong is the persistence of pre-existing and non-virtual identities playing a vital role in all forms of computer mediated communication (CMC). Nevertheless, where all forms of CMC differ from broadcasting and other centripetal media systems, is the means and ways in which identities unfold and redefine themselves during, and because of, virtual encounters. While the first part of 'Personal and Social Communication' by Bernard Bel emphasizes the impersonal and phantasmagoric aspects of electronic communication, the report on *listenaissance* aims at demonstrating its potential in fostering the construction of a 'social fabric' among people concerned with changes at the 'micro' and 'macro' levels. Bel stresses that cyberspace, like any communication space, constructs its own reality, but its reality is so incomplete, flexible (and open to manipulation) that it rarely clashes with other sources of information. It is here that the paradoxical aspect of electronic communication as a form of mediatic knowledge is revealed.

On reading this essay, some of us may be reminded of the euphoria around 'new change-agents' in the India of the early 1980s. In this context, the term macroinitiatives[10] was employed in referring to their devising new forms of political action and organizational linkages. Going beyond a narrow, organizational scope, the term referred to social interventions that sought to create alternative fulcrums of communication aimed at the production and sharing of subjugated knowledge. Over a decade later, in scrutinizing social interventions in the sphere of communication, the *democratic nature* of the emergent practice additionally demanded addressal, especially the high value of aspired democracy in the evolution of new forms of struggle.[11] Without any substantial discord, 'Is the discourse "on", "for" or "of"?' provides a radically different insight on social agents and transformatory processes. The authors, two social animators and one intellectual, start by questioning the alien construction of the term communication and its usages in rural Maharashtra. They find that there are no free flows of communication within rural society; what exists is 'miscommunication', 'vi-samvad' in Marathi, distorted communication and not samvad. This then provides different vantage points to examine the modes of producing and sharing knowledge, and their role in the construction of social ties at micro, intermediate and macro levels.

This brings us to investigate the status of knowledge—as cultural good and cognitive practice. In the guise of giving greater access to and democratizing information, global institutional regimes and the industries of communication entrench modes of domination that in some ways resemble what took place in previous epochs. At the same time, powerful nations at the forefront of technological innovation extend their empires of information, and with that of other commodities—most ironically, in the very process of making the former available to all of us. This is what Pradeep Thomas implies by, and in, 'That Persistent "Other"'. Cognisant of the cultural consequences of intellectual property rights, he explores the political economy of copyright in the media industries in India principally because they demonstrate the extent to which a global 'proprietary' agenda has become a significant aspect of the country's social and economic future.

Paradoxically, amidst the hullabaloo about knowledge society and the glut of emanating misnomers and mythologies, questions on the substantive aspects of knowledge gain a renewed credence. Some of these form the locus of 'The Political Meaning of a River' by Joël Ruet wherein, most significantly, the figure of the intellectual is itself questioned—for s/he is the prominent bearer of the knowledge and the communication of knowledge *about,* and *of,* the Narmada; for s/he has allowed the river to substantiate itself and subjectivize into a discourse, and further into an *acting,* therefore *political,* reality. The key question in the nexus of communication processes on this issue—as indeed in the writing on this issue and in our volume carrying this writing—is to know which structure of the economy of knowledge and representation do intellectuals as a group unearth!

Notes

1. P. Breton, A.M. Rieu and F. Tinland, La techno-science en question (Seyssel: Champ Vallon, 1993).
2. Lucien Sfez, *Critique de la communication* (Paris: Seuil, 1992), p. 15.
3. This is most starkly amplified in the case of Cybernetics, which projects itself not merely as a new discipline but as an avenue to renew all existing disciplines.
4. Lucien Sfez, *Critique de la communication.*
5. Georges Balandier, *Le pouvoir sur scènes,* 10 (Paris: Balland, 1992).
6. Philippe Breton, *L¹utopie de la communication* (Paris: La Découverte, 1997).
7. The information age, with all its promises, has been dismissed on arguments that 'more and more communication create less and less meaning'. An appropriate reference here is Jean-Pierre Dupuy, 'Myths of the Informational Society', in K. Woodward (ed.), *Myths of Information* (London and Henley: Routledge and Kegan Paul, 1980), pp. 3–17.

8. A. Mattelart, *Mass Media, Ideologies and the Revolutionary Movement* (Sussex: Harvester Press, 1980), p. 10. This point had been reiterated specifically in the context of video in N. Garnham, 'The Myths of Video: A Disciplinary Reminder', in *Capitalism and Communication: Global Culture and the Economics of Information* (London: Sage, 1980).
9. Most recently, Kirk Johnson, *Television and Social Change in Rural India* (New Delhi: Sage, 2000).
10. D.L. Sheth, 'Grass-roots Initiatives in India', *Economic and Political Weekly*, vol. 19, no. 6, 1984, pp. 259–62.
11. For instance, D. Slater, 'Social Movements and a Recasting of the Political', in D. Slater (ed.), *New Social Movements and the State in Latin America* (Amsterdam: Cedla, 1985), pp. 1–26.

2.1
Invasion and Intrusion

9

STATE, MARKET AND FREEDOM OF EXPRESSION:
Women and Electronic Media*

UMA CHAKRAVARTI

In the newly constituted public sphere available to women, a space created largely by the women's movement, the debate on the freedom of expression has tended to be reduced to taking sides in what may simply be called the 'obscenity' issue. It is as if 'women' have focused solely on obscenity and have had no other concerns in the context of the media's handling of the portrayal of women. The critique of representations of women and their stereotyping in the visual media, articulated by feminists in the early phases of the women's movement, has been somewhat misunderstood and exaggerated by certain feminist media scholars in recent years. Impelled by real or imaginary fears some women activists had on occasion blackened cinema hoardings for their depiction of women (often with no relationship to sequences in the film itself); their actions have been cast as puritanical, repressive in their understanding of female sexuality and supportive of censorship. Apart from making an unwarranted series of easy slides whereby feminist concern for how women are

*Originally published in *Economic and Political Weekly*, 29 April 2000.

represented in the media is being viewed as an obsession with obscenity, even the context of women's actions is being erased in this rewriting of the women's movement along a single homogenized axis of the deployment of a middle class puritanism in the field of popular culture. However, thanks to the rapidity of events in recent years the whole question of censorship and silence(ing) in relation to the visual media has acquired a complexity which is forcing us to address the more real issues we are being confronted with; these include the actions (and inactions) of the state, the workings of the market, and the appearance of new forms of cultural policing spearheaded by the Hindutva brigade through a recourse to a violent display of street power, which is unashamedly male, even as the cultural policers often include women.

I shall attempt in this essay to explore some of the complexities of the connections and the contradictions in the processes unfolding at the moment inasmuch as I understand them from the point of view of a non-media specialist, even as I am a fairly sustained film and television watcher—this makes me a very average though not typical viewer. My starting point is the shift from a state controlled electronic media, where Doordarshan was the sole player in the field with total monopoly, to the opening up of the media to private channels—a shift that we must remember accompanied the shift to the market and global capital spearheaded and guided by the state itself. I will try to examine what has actually changed as a consequence of the shift, and this attempt at trying to understand what is happening in the electronic media is not to be placed within a simplistic pro–anti censorship polarization which is particularly dangerous today given the actions of the saffron brigade.

The contemporary historical moment encapsulates within itself a complex set of processes; the existing disparate social formations in different ecological and cultural regions, overlaps in modes of production, capital formation and uneven development have now been overlaid by globalization, structural adjustment and the retreat of the state in the very limited role it had played in the field of education, health care and commitment to human resource development. Older and newer processes of development have thus created an intensely transitional moment. The series of transitions underway include actual migration and other kinds of linkages between rural and urban and between provincial and metropolitan locations. New forms of work and living conditions have contributed to a sense of alienation from roots, familiar traditions and cultures without the dislocated always being able to form new kinds of solidarities.

Is it possible that television is providing a means by which these transitions are being bridged? I have been struck by the wide range in the social and regional location of television audiences here more than in the postindustrialized West, and yet the television increasingly does produce homogenized images overriding the very real material, social, and cultural differences of its viewership; at least at the apparent level these homogenized representations seem to be working. On the basis of my lay viewing, the private channels are targeting a very narrow buying audience, which of course is large in terms of the numbers that the West normally deals with. However, from our point of view it is narrow as it is restricted to those who have access to the private channels. The homogenized images are set in a largely upper class urban 'Indian' milieu with no specifically regional identity but where the persona in the images are Hindi speaking and therefore North Indian; by implication they are also upper caste, upper class and almost invariably rich. Why and how then do the watchers, who may be located in diverse sites, identify or respond to these people who are very different from them? Perhaps the homogenized images are working because the market, which now dominates the electronic media, has created a new narrative—that of consumption. The homogenizations maybe working because they bridge the distance between specific locations and amorphous, inchoate aspirations, between the real world and the world of desire. And because the site for viewing is the home, not only is the medium domesticated but the electronic media also seems to domesticate and normalize the images and messages that it is beaming as also the legitimacy of the desire, however unreachable it may be in reality.

What is interesting are the differences in the way television in its new market driven *avataar* is positioned vis-à-vis the global, the 'national' and the local. Although the context for the market in the new dispensation is very definitely the policies of liberalization and globalization, and the consequent creation of a 'transnational consumer subject through television', in the transnational arena it is achieving this objective by working through 'local cultural specificities'.[1] The early experiments in beaming dubbed versions of American soaps failed to hold the attention of the upper class viewers and was quickly given up with the Star channel switching to home made Hindi programmes. Within the country, however, first via the beaming of the epics on television the production of a fairly homogenized viewer was facilitated which the entry of the market has consolidated. Thus the absence of cultural specificities does not appear to be a disadvantage within the subcontinent even as the global /western culture is being kept at bay by providing a cultural anchor through Indian soaps and a decisively Indian locale for the advertisements. A dual process is underway: the dynamic of the global and the local working at the level of the creation of a 'national' culture is not accompanied by a similar process within the nation, noticeable in the days of Doordarshan vis-à-vis the regional through serials such as 'Buniyaad', 'Humlog', 'Daera', Sarat Chandra Chatterjee's 'Shrikant', the Hindi serial set in a 'tarawad' in Kerala, and 'Malgudi Days'. Such regional locales have now completely disappeared on the 'national' private channels and have been replaced by a unified set of protagonists in a unified representation of a home. The 'local' is no longer part of the national; instead it is now represented by the regional channels of Doordarshan and a series of private channels operating programmes in the regional languages such as Asianet and Sun TV. These channels dub advertisements and occasionally a Hindi serial, as well as produce their own soaps, but these do not have the same clout in the advertising market that channels such as Star, Sony and ZEE TV have.

The other much flogged argument, especially when private channels were being debated, was the promise of real choice in contrast to the 'boring and sloppily made stuff' put out by Doordarshan. The promise included a multiplicity of themes and views providing the viewing public with a wider range to choose from. That promise too has been belied. Writing from a deep sense of personal frustration I find that while there is more apparent choice, there is very little real choice, as you flick from one channel to the other you find much of the same since all the channels compete along the same baseline in a desperate attempt to outdo each other. We thus have serials of the same kind, 'antaksharis' of the same kind (where the anchorpersons are indistinguishable even sartorially) and quizzes of the same kind. All the private nationally operating channels have the same biases in terms of class, caste, gender and region with their focus on urban India and the celebrated 200 million buying public. The only time the other India comes into focus is in the news during election time or in the form of disaster stories, natural havoc, or class, caste and ethnic violence. But before anything sinks in this reality too is immediately overlaid by glossy urban India via the mandatory commercial breaks which must go on regardless of the tragedies that the news might fleetingly bring to the viewers consciousness; 'commerce is clearly above tragedy' and the advertisements impose their own reality as the camera cuts from the particularities of a tragic event to the universality of consumption desires. What does this do to our sense of comprehension? Does the other India register when the camera does focus on it while every two-and-a-half minutes our senses are invaded by the ubiquitous lure of goods? Can the electronic media, under the power of the market, communicate the enormity and the complexity of the experiences that people and regions are undergoing in our country?

Within the broad framework of the issues raised in the preceding paragraphs I shall now examine more closely, but very selectively, drawing from things that have registered in my mind, the three main segments of television programmes: advertisements, serials and news (including chat shows and panel discussions) with special reference to women.

Advertisements: Shifting Portrayals

In the field of advertisements the most striking feature is the shift that has occurred in portraying women: whereas earlier women were almost invariably used instrumentally to sell goods, many of which they did not use (and this type of advertisement continues even today), now women are being targeted by the market directly. Further they are being targeted not merely as consumers of goods but as desirers and active buyers of goods. This is evocatively depicted in the saucy mobile phone advertisement where a glamorous but completely confident single woman in an expensive restaurant puts a sophisticated executive type in his place by apparently mistaking him for a waiter. The image of the successful woman whose confidence lies in her ability to be the discriminating buyer grants a new agency to women which is a new creation heralding the gender friendly globalized market. 'New relations are thus being made between consumption, pleasure and culturally specific notions of femininity';[2] in this context Malini Bhattacharya has persuasively argued that the image of the new woman in advertisements has wider meanings than the mere act of her buying a particular consumer item, and is linked to wider national and international economic processes:

> The new economic policy gives visibility to women as a target group as the slashing of excise duty on cosmetic goods shows ...The image that often appears in commercial advertisements of the inveterate consumer of goods is often a feminine image. It sends out the message of vibrancy in demand and therefore in production, creating a vicarious enjoyment of the good life even for those who can only see the images without being able to buy them, the squeeze on the purchasing power of the great majority of people is glossed over by the ubiquity of the image of the woman as consumer [and] creates implicit social consent [for the goodies provided by the globalised market].[3]

Initially women had figured in the advertisements as buyers mainly in the area of domestic goods; this was particularly so in the celebrated war for possibly one of the largest markets between companies in the soap/detergent advertisements. The message in all the advertisements was that the smartness of women lay in their ability to get the best bargain, typified in the *Lalitaji* advertisements put out by Surf.

These advertisements, and the war between Surf, Rin and Wheel, continue to play out the theme of the smart woman whose pride lies in the startling whiteness of her family's clothing but the narratives of whiteness are also subtly changing. On the one hand, the wife's choice of detergent leads to better finances for the household, enhances the husband's image in the office and makes for happiness in the family; once the wife chooses the right product the husband's shirt is so dazzlingly transformed that his boss, who never noticed him before, now not only notices him but also straightaway gives him a promotion; the wife's low self-esteem—a consequence of the husband's depressive state of mind because of being ignored by the boss—thus gets its own required boost. All in all, the market has effective solutions for every situation ranging from stagnant careers to the ups and downs of everyday marital relations! On the other hand, dazzling white makes for a better-dressed career woman herself. One advertisement that plays on the emergence of the new woman shows a woman prancing about in a dazzling white naval uniform but what is left subtly unstated is whether it is her uniform or her husband's that she is play acting in; the image is left open-ended for the viewer to fill in thus satisfying both constituencies, the working woman in a newly opened field of work and the full time 'housewife' for whom a career is still in the realm of secret desire.

The field for buying has been vastly extended beyond detergents, cosmetics and the kitchen—the longstanding domain of women's goods—to other objects but still centred on the home, the special domain of all women, whether in careers or not; advertisements of high class plumbing have moved from thieves stealing the stunning faucets to the more trendy depiction of a beautiful wife, whose sole occupation seems to be to shop, seductively pleading over the phone with her harried and hardworking husband while he is busy at work. Another advertisement for expensive plumbing fixtures has the young and attractive wife of a tubby husband packing to leave home; the husband throws things at her for her to take away along with herself in an angry fit but all ends well as the husband lets drop the crucial information that he has got her what she was fixated on—the beautiful taps. Both advertisements norm the male as the earner-provider and the female as the non-earning but persistent consumer of goods; the latter advertisements also makes domestic violence a humorous playing out of domesticity and in any case the market has quick fix solutions for every marriage whatever be its apparent ills.

The appearance of the new working woman and/or the assertive woman who knows what she wants is one situation where role reversals are brought in but always with a dose of humour; husbands now either make the tea for the working wife or claim to do so as a necessary element in the new man's ability to please and care for the woman in his life so that power relations within the home are shown to have dissolved. In these advertisements husbands are either charming fools who are caught out lying because the wife is so smart, as in the Duncan Tea advertisement or they are appliers of soothing balm upon the fraying nerves of their hysterical working wives, via the hot cup of tea. The role reversals, however, only go as far as making tea or using the washing machine to atone for clumsy actions—all of which are designed to make the wife happy while ensuring that this is done without too much exertion; as one husband puts it endearingly, *kuch paane ke liye kuch dhona bhi padta hai*, 'you have to wash a little if you want to gain a little'! Only in one advertisement does the husband attempt to make something as basic as a *chapati:* the rest of his family watches with awe his attempts to bring perfection (an attribute which is the monopoly of the male, naturally!) to the making of the *roti*. It is clear that no one will have dinner that night so it might be better for mama to deal with the *chapatis*.

The adaptation of advertisements to 'local specificities' is very evident in the incorporation of the parents-in-law into the family advertisements; the typical Indian household shifts from the joint to the nuclear depending upon the particular consumer item being marketed. Kitchen goods in particular often play on the mother-in-law–daughter-in-law relationship, often seeking to subvert through its images the power of the mother-in-law; the crucial alliance that leads to success is between the clever daughter-in-law and the gender-friendly maker of goods. No women's movement is necessary in India to counter the power of the mother-in-law as the young wife has now been emancipated by the market! Just recall the very clever visual of the daughter-in-law dancing in the kitchen to music playing through her headphones while the mother-in-law reels off a list of 40 odd *masalas* for her to grind from the next room—all quite unnecessary as we have MDH *masalas* to take care of dictatorial and demanding mothers-in-law. The market provides ingenious ways by which a *bahu* can be free as well as please the *saas* while keeping the sexual division of labour and the ideologies that go with it intact.

While the mother-in-law is often a fixture in the visuals suggesting that the traditional Indian household is part of the contemporaneous present, the advertisements also norm the nuclear family unit as father, mother and son. This is the new Indian (Hindu) household, a complete unit itself; accompanying messages that go with this happy trio are images where the object of the nurturant mother is mostly the son, very rarely a daughter. Daughters appear only to extend messages such as the washing of pretty clothes, in what have been called the cutified advertisements or in the context of women-focused goods like washing machines, microwave ovens and refrigerators; when they appear, daughters usually feature along with a son not instead of him. If one absorbs this along with the new phenomena of the routinization of the amniocentesis test among the middle classes, even at the time of the first pregnancy to ensure that the firstborn is a son, and the census data which shows that the sex ratio has fallen well below 900 to 1000 males in certain states of North India, the implications of such norming are far from idiosyncratic, they are sinister.

And finally if one goes by the advertisements of today the debate on the existence of two Indias has now been decisively resolved, as there is only one India as far as the private channels go—a vibrant, rich and glossy urban India. Undeveloped, rural India has disappeared and in its place we often have a transformed ethnicized 'countryside' where the only structures are *havelis* set against a desert backdrop and the only people are beautiful women in diaphanous clothing or men in Digjam or Siyaram suitings. Occasionally you may get a turban-clad *dehati*, a comic figure for the most part, using

Bharat Telecom to connect with his son, who has already been absorbed into urban India, or a camel-riding man exhorting the viewer to join the Cadbury chocolate eating fraternity, but that is the extent of the countryside in the world of advertisements. It appears that nobody washes clothes in rural India, not even those colourful turbans that we see in other advertisements; somehow such themes do not seem to make good copy. In sum, rural India on advertisements is invariably Rajasthan in keeping with its tourist value for foreigners. Perhaps in the view of the market, the urban Indian is as much a foreigner in India as the foreign tourist who will believe or want to believe that village India is only peopled by heroic Rajput men and beautiful Rajput women who have successfully bridged the tradition—modernity divide, always of course retaining what is best in Indian tradition—its chaste women a la the heroine of the popular film 'Des Pardes'.[4] One can then conveniently forget the reality of rural India with its caste, class and gender violence: its Bathes, and Bhanwari Devis who do not even register in the consciousness of our television viewing consuming elite, or such embarrassing politicians as Laloo Yadav, who does register but whom glossy urban India and the metropolitan media hates with a passion it normally does not display for anything or anyone else, except of course for Mayawati! Images that stay in the consciousness of this class are those of happy families, a happiness that is the result of the market catering to their every need and their every desire whether at the conscious or subconscious level.

Serials: Reflecting Family Tensions

It appears to me that while the advertisements suggest that marital tensions between young couples, or potentially conflictual relations between different generations within the family do exist, they can be solved by buying the right product and so they always fade out their visuals on images of happy families. However, the serials the same products often sponsor reflect the serious tensions that the family and the marriage system are currently facing. That marital relations are particularly under stress is evident from a number of popular serials such as 'Saans', 'Kora Kagaz', 'Heena', 'Ashirwad' and 'Palchin'. This display of anxiety strips off some of the tinsel trappings of the new ethnicized marriage ceremonies which have increased visibility in a variety of advertisements (for example the disgruntled Punjabi NRI auntie who is being thwarted from dancing the *bhangra* at the marriage of her nephew to a South Indian bride, the Pan Parag variant of the unbroken singing and dancing of Indian family festivals of the film 'Hum Apke Hain Kaun', or the *mehndied* bride trying to get at the chocolate). The recognition that the marriages are facing internal tensions from one of the partners' search for romance is a replay of the nineteenth century fictional dilemma of trying to reconcile love with the system of arranged marriages between appropriate partners, a euphemism for the endogamous marriage which still dominates the realm of marriage. Whatever the nature of class formation in our society, you only have to open the pages of the newspapers at the matrimonial columns to register the fact that endogamous marriages as a system of fortifying the boundaries of caste has not eroded even within English speaking, metropolitan, yuppie households.

The proper subject of fiction and narratives has been love ever since new genres of writing emerged in the nineteenth century, but since marriages are arranged both fiction and the visual narrative to be realistic must work with this given. The only way to resolve the contradictions arising from the compulsions of the form with those of lived experience was to fall in love with your wife without knowing she was your wife (as in Tagore's 'The Wreck', or in 'Sahib Bibi aur Ghulam'). More down to earth stories, which fill the pages of *Women's Era,* celebrate the falling-in-love-with-your-husband type of romance as the most superior and lasting sort of love, which suits the unique institutions of India. However, many films and now television serials have begun to recognize male desire as not being containable within the arranged marriage system, or not being containable within monogamous marriages. 'Heena' and 'Kora Kagaz', both extremely popular among women, played out the disruption of the marital relationship at the point of the inception of the marriage itself, the only arena where the Hindu household and the Muslim household share exactly the same social experience! This theme has the added advantage of being able to simultaneously make its female protagonist both someone you empathize with, because she is the victim of an oppressive situation, and allow her to interrogate the unfairness of the situation she is placed in. Of course the interrogation is contained within strict limits and no action is performed by our protagonists which upsets the applecart in any way. Pooja's portrayal in 'Kora Kagaz' is meant to be the story of the new woman—*vidroh ki kalam se likha hua aurat ka naya itihas* ('written with the pen of rebellion the new history of a woman') says the by-line in advertising the serial. But this new woman is carefully crafted as someone who can deal with the most oppressive situation and that too with a never fading smile. Pooja is not a weepy-waily heroine but displays a great deal of agency in upholding the 'honour' of the family of her husband and the authority of the in-laws whatever it may cost her by way of personal suffering. She alternately battles with her mother-in-law and serves her dutifully even when she knows that her mother-in-law is manipulative and wilful. Her agency is thus carefully crafted and is deployed in making highly controlled statements; her little struggles serve to merely provide a catharsis for herself and her female viewers rather than upturn the system in any way. This is a point I shall return to later.[5]

Serials located in a rural milieu have completely disappeared in the 'range' provided by private channels, whether indigenously owned or controlled by the king of media, Rupert Murdoch. So have serials that dwell on the lives of the underclass: dalits whether in the rural areas or even in the cities cannot now impinge on the consciousness of the viewer. There is no place for the documentaries that attempted to conscientize the middle classes on various themes, which one occasionally saw on Doordarshan even though the filmmakers had to often go to court to get a good viewing slot. This is not surprising given the logic of the market and the sponsors who determine what narratives will sell best with the consumers of goods. There is no question of seeking viewing time on television now unless you can get a sponsor, which is a contradiction in terms as no business house will fund an oppositional narrative of any kind. What is somewhat surprising, however, is that even the fairly huge channel watching middle class is not represented in the serials currently dominating the media; it is as if this class does not relate to its own social experience, so ubiquitous is the world of the rich. Very occasionally a serial such as 'Naya Zamana' might devote a segment of a narrative to the lives of the poor but the flattening of the images of this class is so grotesque that it is revolting to watch—perhaps this is intentional. In 'Naya Zamana' we have the full assemblage of stereotypes: the central character naturally is a *bai* who is upright and tries to live honestly. Her husband is a brutal male—we have seen no poor upright men in a long time—who whiles away his time in a drunken stupor when he is not engaged in beating his wife, or harassing his stepdaughter. The *bai*'s daughter, seduced by the lure of goods, naturally rejects her mother's attempts at surviving on honest labour and wishes to join the 200 million buying public by becoming a prostitute. While the brutal stepfather stands for the degradation of all lower class men the daughter, who 'chooses' prostitution, stands for the corruption of the youthful poor. There is no question of a range of characterizations or complexity of personalities when it comes to the poor. Such images then feed into middle class perspectives on poverty and morality which are distributed in inverse proportion among the different classes; if the poor are poor it is because the lower class male is so irresponsible. Popular perception sees no structural reason for poverty, which is firmly believed to be self-induced. The only feature that unites the poor with the others is the world of desire, as typified by the daughter of the *bai* who has exactly the same desires as the young women of other classes, so it is the market that achieves the longed for unity of social experience and thus demolishes the class divide.

News: No Place for 'Other'

In surveying the news channels, including the surfeit of chat shows, one is struck by the exacerbation of the class and regional biases that I have referred to earlier especially in the content of the latter. Chat shows invariably deal with persona who are rich and famous and obviously cater to a vicarious pleasure derived from getting an inside view at the personal lives of the 'beautiful' people featured on it. While the news itself cannot completely ignore non-metropolitan India, where a great deal of the political action lies, other features on the 'news' channels mesh the world of the advertisements with the focus on prominent people. Watching a feature on Indian management students who are making it big in the global corporate world (with starting salaries of US $82,000 for the 'brightest' of them we were told) I wondered whether other bright young people who choose to work in off the beaten track occupations like the rehabilitation of handicapped poor children would ever get the kind of visibility that management students got on this feature. Similarly while the electronic media went gaga, like the print media, over the Indian Miss Worlds—heralding the arrival of India as a beauty super power—other quiet and unglamorous achievements by rural women like Fatima Beevi never make it in the same way despite the fact that she received a UN award for her work; neither the market nor the upbeat globalizing nation are interested in these explicitly political transformations taking place in the lives of some women who are storming male bastions and so women like Fatima Beevi slip past television without being noticed.

There are other news type features that focus on contemporary controversies. A popular programme in this genre is the 'Big Fight' on Star Plus anchored by Rajdeep Sardesai. Among the controversies dealt with in the last year, four that I managed to watch were focused on issues relating to women: one took up the campaign for the Lok Sabha elections last year where certain politicians made offensive remarks against Sonia Gandhi, a second dealt with beauty contests, a third dealt with the Women's Reservation Bill, and the fourth dealt with the controversy around the portrayal of widows in 'Water'. Like everything else determined by the market these 'debates' are cut up by the mandatory commercials which must be aired even if it means that serious arguments being put forward by the personalities are cut off in the middle (by a smirking Sardesai who enjoys his role of separating his 'combatants') and they never get a chance to go on with them. The audience is then left with a series of statements that quite often do not amount to a full argument, but who cares? On the face of it the viewers get to see women debating issues, and trying to do so spiritedly: we are seeing the new women in action, whether it is Manpreet Brar arguing for beauty contests or Tanuja Chandra arguing against the disruption of the shooting of 'Water'. When these 'images' (which is what the fragments on television amount to) are juxtaposed to images of women as aggressive buyers in advertisements we can believe that women's liberation has been achieved, at least for a particular class and that women are asserting their agency. They are actors in their own right.

Only one set of images disrupted this picture of the new woman and returned us to the traditional gendered images and that was the coverage of the Kargil war. Hyped more than any other event in recent memory, although carefully timed on the media to follow after the cricket world cup so that the market investments on advertisements could be recovered and profited by, television channels outdid themselves in an orgy of blood, gore and patriotism set off by the competing nationalisms of the different channels. Television cameras manufactured images for nationalism for the first time in Indian television history by providing live coverage of action on the battlefield even as it actually provided us with carefully edited visuals. As Sonia Jabbar points out:

> The wars at Kargil or in the Gulf war shown on TV can hardly compare to what was happening on ground reality. The Stinger missiles, green luminous streaks, comet-like, lighting up the night sky during the Gulf war looked so beautiful on the small screen. Our very own carefully edited Kargil war showed only our brave jawans against the muted sound of the Bofors guns. No piercing screams of victims, no ear-splitting booms of guns whole dimensions of war edited out and presented as the real thing.[6]

While television could manufacture certain images and blot out certain realities there were other aspects of the reality of the war that they played up. Television cameras dwelt at length on body bags bringing back dead soldiers to their homes. What I found striking in these visuals, which were intended to generate a wave of sympathy and to back the war without asking uncomfortable questions, was the way war breaks down gender roles to their bare essentialities: man, the actor/hero, woman the passive victim; men guarding the borders of the nation, women waiting at home. Kargil reiterated the divide between men and women: soldiers laying down their lives, widows and mothers grieving at funerals. The agency granted to women by the market became as illusory as the joy that buying goods is supposed to bring to purse happy families.

Only one set of images of Kargil returned agency to women and this was the powerful statement made by the presence of Barkha Dutt on the war front. Breaking, for the first time, into the male domain of war reporting the NDTV bureau and Dutt pulled off a coup in television journalism. Apart from reporting while enemy shells fell all around her, heightening the dramatic impact of Dutt's presence on the war front, her unique womanly contribution to reporting from the front was a charming and moving interview with a very young officer on the complex emotions of courage as well as fear that he had experienced on the battlefield. Dutt's report from the war front, even more than mothers stating that they were ready to gift their other sons to the war, worked to provide women's consent to the war and obliterated other voices of women, voices of dissent (which we did not get to see on television) which pointed to the futility of war as a means of resolving conflicts. Dutt's reporting was visible proof of the new woman and her agency, deployed here very effectively in the arena of an endangered nationalism. While women are not yet 'actively' fighting for the nation, they are providing the much needed consent for war as epitomized in the presence of Dutt on the battle field.

Market as Censor

If we return to the issues we began this essay with, that is the debate amongst women on how to deal with portrayals of women that were not acceptable to some of them, we can see that matters have become more complex than they were a decade ago. What has been missed in the debate on the state's power to ban according to its selective notions of morality, which of course needs to be resisted, is that the market and 'civil society' too have a similar, and sometimes greater, power to silence a whole range of issues even while appearing to be pluralist in its handling of images. This is being done by privileging the urban, well placed consumer as the viewer and excising all other experiences of men and women. We can also see that a limited agency is granted to women by the market and media projecting the state's point of view to uphold the family, the market and a Hinduized and centralized nationalism, all of which are currently embedded in the dominant structures of patriarchy. Further, nationalism, state interests,[7] the religious right wing and the dominant forms of patriarchies are perfectly in harmony with globalization and the interests of the market; this heady brew is best epitomized by the indigenized, 'nationalist' pop music which is repeated ad nauseum on music channels. These channels have refined the technique of superimposing fragmented images upon each other and simultaneously providing the viewer with some coherent narratives, such as that of a new and trendy nationalism via refrains such as 'I love my India,' 'yeh mera India,' 'jahan hath mein kangan, pair mein payal aur mathe pe bindiya—it happens only in India,' 'east or west, India is the best' etc.

If we tie up this discussion on women and the electronic media by looking at what is being privileged and what is being excluded, we can approach the question of censorship and silence from a different end: in the main the state in contemporary times continues to excise images or sequences from films according to its understanding of what is obscene. But that is not the only form of censorship going on; an informal street censorship mounted by segments of the Sangh combine have struck terror in the field of culture such that film and theatre producers have taken to showing their films to Bal Thackerey, as Mani Ratnam did in the case of 'Bombay', or Advani, as Aamir Raza did in the case of his version of the 'Ramayana', before they exhibit their films or plays. Those who do not recognize the real censor board in this country are attacked as the film crew of 'Water' was. The newly constituted Hinduized and otherwise hard state can and has taken a soft line on such attacks so that it cannot be directly implicated in the silencing of voices that do not conform to their agenda of celebrating Hindu culture, or turn the searchlight on oppressive conditions under which women have lived within Hindu society. At the same time the media beams a number of vibrant images of women, happily buying, or competently dealing with their lives even under what might appear to be oppressive conditions. 'Why talk about oppression of women' says the Hindu right about the portrayal of widows in 'Water'; 'that was in the past', they assert and we might believe them if we base our understanding on the messages being beamed on television.

In conclusion, what we need to recognize is the nature of the current conjuncture where a right wing state silences women and other marginalized groups through the power of the state to send out signals as well as censor certain points of view, ways of thinking and expressing creativity, and right wing forces display their power on the street to achieve the same silencing of discussions of exploitative practices with regard to women. Simultaneously, market forces that the right wing state has consolidated systematically between 1994 and 2000 and which is continued by the state today, obliterate many points of view through the power of money to determine what messages are to be put out. The question that arises is: from the point of view of women, especially the non-elite sections among them, what does freedom of expression imply? Has freedom of expression in the age of globalization any relevance for reflecting women's real concerns?

In the context of the absences and exclusions of certain categories of people and issues that reflect their lives from the electronic media our analysis of the dominant trends in serials, news features, chat shows and advertisements, indicates that the opening up of the electronic media to private channels has not substantially altered the biases of total state control over the media. In fact it has brought in new biases. Fully capable of reflecting the state's ideologies on nationalism, militarization and nuclearization, as well as religious majoritarianism as effectively or even more so than the state controlled channels, the private channels have exacerbated the regional, class and caste biases, and the gendered representations of the earlier era of state monopoly over the media. As pointed out earlier rural India has virtually disappeared from the media, except to figure as disaster arenas in the news. On an everyday representational basis rural India, where the majority of our population still lives, has been reduced to a trope figuring in a new ethnicized glossy or comic depiction depending on the product being advertised. The continuing poverty, illiteracy, inequality and vulnerability of most sections of rural men and women has been completely erased from the screen and from the consciousness of globalized India.

How do we address the problem of these absences and exclusions? How can we reinstate these excluded people and issues back into the frame of the electronic media and how can we make the media more genuinely representative to include the social and regional diversities of India and Indian women? Creative and sustained strategies are required from women to counter the informal censorship of the right wing state now in command and the profit driven market of global capitalism, something for all of us to think about.

Notes

1. Vinod Pavarala, 'Studying Television Audiences: Problems and Possibilities', *Journal of Arts and Ideas*, nos 32–33, 1999 (April), pp. 95–106.
2. Kumkum Sangari and Uma Chakravarti, *From Myths to Markets: Essays on Gender* (Shimla: Indian Institute of Advanced Study, 1999), p. xviii.
3. Malini Bhattacharya, 'Women in Dark Times: Gender, Culture and Politics', *Social Scientist*, vol. 22, nos 3–4, 1994 (March–April), p. 11.
4. A host of films that feature the ethnicized traditional Indian family have been made in recent years; these include the vastly popular 'Hum Dil De Chuke Sanam' featuring the beautiful Aishwarya Rai, the Miss World turned actress, who is attracted to the charming but feckless non-resident Indian Salman Khan who comes to India to learn music. Instead, she finds true love

in her *desi* husband Ajay Devgan, the new man who knows how to win the new woman—with patience and sublime devotion, values traditionally associated with the Indian woman.
5. The theme of a new kind of woman who is not a passive victim of circumstances but displays agency was first popularized in soaps like 'Shanti' with Mandira Bedi playing the daughter seeking to revenge the wrongs that her father had committed upon the mother. 'Shanti' was a daily soap which was beamed in the afternoon slot on Doordarshan, a slot that was specifically meant for women. Women viewers strongly identified with the wronged woman seeking revenge by humiliating the father, over hundreds of episodes, and then getting on with her life.
6. Sonia Jabbar, 'The Art of War', *Biblio*, vol. 4, nos 11–12, 1999 (November–December), p. 5–6.
7. The complicity of the state in promoting consumerism and the interests of the market has been very striking in the last few years. Ever since the new economic policy was introduced in the budget, Reserve Bank policies have been dropping interest rates thereby making it unattractive to save. At the same time buying is made attractive by various buy-now-pay-later schemes which are flooding the market, leading to increased consumerism. Amongst the most glossy and sexy advertisements are those of automobiles. At the same time the hype about buying and participating in the good life is directly related to the expansion of dowry, a moment when all the postponed desires of a family are dramatically satisfied, via the new bride. I am indebted to Prem Chowdhry for these observations.

10

FORGING PUBLIC OPINION:
The Press, Television and Electoral Campaigns in Andhra Pradesh

G. KRISHNA REDDY

The political context of communications has undergone substantial change after the advent of modern media, and more so with the revolution in communication technology.[1] While political communications have been shaped by the transforming culture of competitive politics, media technology—be it print or broadcasting—has created its own necessities which, in turn, have shaped politics, politicians and political discourses. The changing political culture created a space for the 'mass' media to make inroads into the political sphere. Consequently, it becomes necessary to explicate this process of transformation. The transformation of the culture of politics implies changing political orientations, values and attitudes about the way electoral parties are functioning; about participation in terms of its base—class, caste, gender, etc., the norms of electoral politics, the competition for power among the parties and the procedures they observe; and about the very idea of democracy.

The entry of new social groups into the electoral arena has qualitatively affected the participatory base and brought in a new political environment of values and vocabulary which shaped the campaign agendas and strategies of almost all parties. Political articulations of caste centred discourses have been striking examples in the recent history of electoral politics in India. It has challenged all the earlier functionalist paradigms by bringing caste from the periphery to the centre in their analysis; early functionalist explanations considered caste as merely one of those traditional institutions which would undergo the modernization process. But it has come to influence the modern institutions and processes such as political parties and electoral politics substantially.[2]

Caste-based mobilization is now no more a liberal stigma. On the contrary, politics and parties addressing social cleavages on caste lines have become quite a legitimate way of representing and articulating the interests of segments of people in the electoral arena. It was made possible because of a series of attempts on the part of the lower strata to assert themselves in the political arena. Post-Mandal Commission political developments like the rise of the Bahujan Samaj Party (BSP) and Samajwadi Party (SP) in Uttar Pradesh, the Rashtriya Janata Dal (RJD) in Bihar, or other minor parties launched on the lines of caste polarization, have initiated new themes into electoral politics. The major parties like the Congress, BJP and even the left parties have been compelled to take cognizance of the caste factor and mend their strategies accordingly.

The shift from vote catching on the basis of the power brokers of the traditional rural elite who held sway over patron–client relations, to addressing clearly identifiable communities as the vote blocks in the 1990s has been evident through the way the parties—whether the parties of catch-all character or social cleavage based parties—started competing and negotiating for their share of votes among these communities. 'The assumption is that there is a collective identity which can be mobilized for votes through promises and concessions. Political parties then negotiate with community leaders as well as make other gestures to woo the community'.[3]

The transition from patronage politics to 'the politics of crisis' marks one fundamental change in the perception of the political parties about elections: elections have come to be seen increasingly in instrumentalist terms. 'Hence, parties are resorting more and more to marketing techniques, selecting issues likely to carry the widest appeal, projecting images. Few view them as occasions for raising basic issues and concerns'.[4]

The newfound cleavage-based parties and the 'old' parties both are interested only in raising questions pertaining to identities at the symbolic level without contributing to any substantial transformation of the marginal groups in terms of material gains. Yet, the politics of identitarianism introduced a crucial factor into the campaign agenda, that is 'social justice' as sharing of political power. Politics of marginal groups not only helped to develop new parties but also introduced radical vocabulary into the campaign language and in turn flouted all the rules of the electoral game. All the parties, new and old, have become victims of the changed political culture in which they have become personality centred without being internally democratic. The BSP with Kanshiram and Mayavati, SP with Mulayam Singh, RJD with Laloo Prasad Yadav, or regional parties like the Telugu Desam Party TDP in Andhra Pradesh with NTR earlier and Chandrababu Naidu later, DMK with Karunanidhi, AIADMK with Jayalalitha—all experienced the collapse of internal networks and democratic structures. In a way, democratic politics with enormously expanding active participation of varied sections is followed by more manipulative and symbolic politics.

In plebiscitary politics, the leader becomes all pervading and politics more symbolic and image based. Institutions other than parties, which deal with public consciousness such as media, play a central role as parties become dependent on them in various ways in the absence of their own networks and contact with the people.

The atrophy of the party organization and the rise of the leader-centric parties have promoted a new breed of politicians who characterized the culture of new politics. The politicians who joined the different ranks of parties are devoid of past political experience and are out of contact with people at the grassroots. The only qualification they have is their close connection with the leader of the party. They generally hold the view that politics is just another 'vocation' and profits must be reaped out of it to the best of their abilities.[5]

Ashis Nandy quotes Arun Nanda of Rediffusion, the advertising agency that marketed Rajiv Gandhi during the 1984 Lok Sabha elections when the Congress won the elections: 'He had a good product to sell.' And further Nandy notes that 'his [Nanda's] concept of goodness derives from the idea of saleability, and that saleability in turn is connected to a particular form of indefinability. This indefinability invites the buyers to project their own ideologies, stereotypes and desires onto the product being marketed; it also allows the sellers to change the content of product overnight in response to public demand.'[6]

It is this change in the culture of politics that has created the necessity on the part of politics and political actors to explore new ways and means of approaching the voter environment. It created the space for new modes of political campaigning and brought in the mass media in a big way. Political parties have substantially changed their organization of campaigns by relying more and more on media experts and market managers, ad-men and professionals. The change in the political culture has necessitated new modes of political communications, but the advancement of mass media with its technological innovations, the extent of reach and its newly acquired power dynamics has transformed competitive politics as much.

Transformation of Election Campaigns

Traditionally, the political campaigns were predominantly party mediated and more interpersonal in their communication. The organization of the campaign was shaped by the party network, which was in close touch with the people at local levels. Issues were more or less identified through party channels. 'Formerly, it [campaign] was more a bottom up than a top down process; candidates or their surrogates travelled from village to village in jeeps, addressing local crowds by voice or loudspeakers.'[7] However, it should not be mistaken for a truly democratic practice as it was much bound by caste hierarchies.

Earlier, the election campaigns were more decentralized in its organization. There was a plurality of sources of information—party networks, opinion makers, caste networks, gymnasia and newspapers to a lesser extent. For instance, according to Sirsikar the 1967 general election was essentially heterogeneous in the sense that the electorate used to be mobilized through a variety of institutions.[8]

It must be said that so long as the *Congress system*[9] existed on the basis of politics of patronage, party networks were active and thus these traditional forms of campaigning were found to be useful. The twin factors—the collapse of patronage politics and ensuing crisis, and the advent of modern media and its permeation into politics—have affected the field of political campaigns phenomenally.

Modern campaigns are predominantly media driven and technology oriented. During the last 20 years multivariate communications has gradually given way to the increasing concentration of sources of communications in the modern mass media because of advancement in technology. Modern media does not replace the traditional forms but it coexists and assimilates them. Thus modern forms come to acquire monopoly over the information systems and knowledge forms.[10] It creates its own necessities; accordingly the institutions such as political parties have to mould their campaign strategies when they resort to modern communications.

One can discern the corresponding relation between the top-down and centrally controlled campaigns in the Congress Party and the TDP and increasing monopoly of the modern media such as the print and electronic media over the communication processes. The mass media is gaining control over all flows of information owing to the rapid strides in information technology. There has been convergence between the political parties' exigencies and the advancement made by the mass media. On one hand, the modern media necessitates the political parties to make use of the readily available resources of public power that are invested in the press and television. On the other, the media facilitate the central control in the parties over the campaigns through its wide networks and reach.

The growing media networks fit well with the conditions that the parties have been experiencing—that the parties are leader dominant without grassroot networks. Thus, the political ambience and the transforming nature of communication practices suit each other. Rudolph rightly observes that, what political parties used to do through their networks, they now seek to do the same through mass media.[11]

The Telugu Press and Politics

The association of the Telugu language press and politics has been intensely felt in the politics of media in Andhra Pradesh (hereafter AP). The changes that occurred in the media during the emergence of the TDP with the involvement of *Eenadu* are seen as one of the pioneering efforts on the part of the regional language press in the country.[12] First, the media have been actively involved in the political developments of the state. Second, the Telugu language press has become intensely competitive. Third, the notion of non-partisanship in the reporting particularly among leading Telugu dailies has become suspect in the 1990s.

Two crucial factors contributed to the enormous growth in the language press, both of which occurred during the 1970s.[13] First, the rise of political consciousness of different sections and concomitant political changes like the rise of regional forces; and second, the technological advancement in the field of communications. There has been a phenomenal increase in the growth of newspapers from four dailies per 1,000 people in 1961 to 10 dailies per 1,000 people in 1991 (Table 10.1). In both respects, *Eenadu's* approach to its rise is exemplary and the rest of the language papers were forced to follow suit.

The formation of Andhra Pradesh based on the linguistic principle marks the beginning of the consolidation of the regional elite. These elites were albeit accommodated in the power structure at subordinate levels. The green revolution gave new economic power to the agrarian classes. This triggered new socio-economic forces in the rural sector which called for a new political equilibrium. Political stability

Table 10.1
Population Change in Andhra Pradesh and Newspaper Change in Telugu, 1961–91

	1961	1971	1981	1991
Population (millions)	36.0	43.5	53.6	66.5
Literacy (% of total pop)	21	25	30	38
Urbanization (%)	17.5	19.4	23.3	27.0
No. of literate (millions)	7.6	10.9	16.1	24.9
Telugu daily circulations ('000)	158	237	439	664
Telugu dailies per '000 people in Andhra Pradesh	4	6	8	10

Source: R. Jeffrey, 'Indian Language Newspaper: 4–Telugu: Ingredients Growth and Failure', *Economic and Political Weekly* (1 February 1997).

received a setback. The years 1967–71 were the period when Indian polity underwent the process of readjustment. The assertion and counter assertion of the elite came to an end with Mrs Gandhi's emergence as a strong leader at the national level.

The Andhra economy acquired a new momentum in the 1970s. As it picked up, the agrarian elite started investing in the industrial sector. The investment in industry in the 1970s started coming from the agrarian surplus generated by the peasant castes particularly *Kammas* from coastal Andhra. This linkage between the agrarian and industrial capital gave rise to a new regional elite which was more sophisticated and articulate than the agrarian classes.[14] They became more entrepreneurial and started investing heavily in agro-industries, cinema and the Telugu press. It was, in fact, during this period and context that the Telugu press became more assertive, if not aggressive. *Eenadu*, that was launched in 1974, was the culmination of these changing trends in the Andhra society. *Eenadu* played a significant role in the origin, development and success of the regional party, Telugu Desam.

Eenadu was instrumental in bringing about some significant changes in the world of Telugu journalism. This paper made several departures from the early traditions with a massive network and electronic teleprinters spread across all the districts and had reporters in every nook and corner of the state. It gave extensive coverage to local news by introducing local editions. Another important aspect of the organization was its own distribution system and transportation.[15] Thus, *Eenadu* was the only paper, which managed to reach all the parts of the state sooner than others. With these measures it emerged as the largest circulated daily touching about 200,000 in 1980.

The phenomenon of *Eenadu* in the mass media indicates the changing context of politics in general and the politics of Andhra Pradesh in particular. The press that had stood for *Vishalandhra* movement in the early part of the twentieth century articulated the sentiment of greater Andhra in the 1950s and 1960s. This earliest phase expressed forcibly the ideas regarding the formation of a separate regional identity for Andhra Pradesh. However, by the 1980s, the context completely changed. The regional elite who were in the formative stage in the early part grew into fuller stature. This phase saw the gradual transformation of the rural gentry into a rich industrial class, although they still retained their economic and political hold in the villages. This new regional bourgeoisie exploited all the possible avenues and grew quite assertive insofar as the media was concerned. Not only did they venture into media directly but also transformed it into a very articulate, vocal and aggressive industry. The phenomenon of *Eenadu* represents this underlying trend.[16] This whole process was further buttressed by the new technology that was used in a highly advantageous manner. Thus, a section of the press has come to play a significant role in the consolidation of the regional elite in the power structure.

There are at least three instances where *Eenadu* was intensely involved and openly took a partisan role in favour of the TDP and still managed to be legitimate in its anti-establishment position. First is *Eenadu's* deep involvement with the origins and emergence of the TDP. The association of *Eenadu* and TDP marks an important beginning in AP politics. Media and politics are brought closer on the regional plank. The rising regional forces which sought to look for a political organ to articulate and further its interests found a political vehicle in the form of *Eenadu*, which in its turn has given a powerful voice to its interests. *Eenadu*, having taken a plunge into politics on the platform of regionalism is bound by it in its subsequent expansion and growth in the industry. Thus *Eenadu* and TDP, having been born out of this new political formation, have become so identical in their base and growth. It is not surprising to say that the social composition of readership and *Eenadu* and the social base of the TDP are not very different.

Second, *Eenadu* played a crusader's role in bringing back N.T. Rama Rao (NTR) into power after the unlawful overthrow of NTR's government by Governor Ramlal at the behest of his own colleague in the cabinet, Nadendra Bhaskar Rao in 1984. *Eenadu* took up the cause of restoring 'democracy' in Andhra Pradesh.[17] Third, by 'spearheading' the anti-arrack movement in 1993, *Eenadu* set the ban on arrack and this topped the campaign agenda of the TDP much ahead of the other parties in the 1994 Assembly elections.

The TDP's promise to ban arrack was lent credibility through the columns of *Eenadu*. During this period *Eenadu* ran a special column *Saarapai Samaram* ('waging war with arrack') for about two years. Jeffrey notes that *Eenadu* was instrumental in spreading the movement across the state, in what was otherwise confined to just a pocket of villages around Dubagunta (where the movement originated) in Nellore district.[18] However, what is crucial to understanding the politics of media is the way *Eenadu* appropriated the anti-arrack movement. Originally, protests were not aimed at the state banning arrack. Local protests asked the state machinery to help them in controlling the arrack consumption locally. This was a better option than the state doing it with its centralized machinery as the government itself admitted later when it planned to lift the ban partially in 1997, justifying that a strong mafia network had developed around the arrack ban. It was *Eenadu* which deflected the issue on to the banning of arrack by the state by making it a statewide issue. The locals lost the initiative. Thus, TDP could make it a major campaign issue in the 1994 elections, whereas the Congress failed to capitalize on it as it was in power and late in realizing this political potential.

On all the three occasions, *Eenadu* explained its position in terms of taking up a just cause on behalf of the Telugu people. Interestingly, on all the occasions *Eenadu* chose the TDP as the legitimate spokesperson of the problems of the people. When Chandrababu Naidu gradually lifted the ban on Indian-made foreign liquor in 1997, as it was felt to be a burden on the states exchequer, *Eenadu* made a surprising u-turn from its earlier position and subtly supported the government to reintroduce liquor in the state.[19]

Two other notable examples of the newspapers with sharp political positions were *Udayam*, which was established in 1984, but was later bought by the Congress Member of Parliament (MP), Magunta Subbarami Reddy and *Vaartha*, established in 1996, by Girish Sanghi of Sanghi industries. Both the newspapers have taken pro-Congress positions on different occasions. *Vaartha*, particularly, has thrown its mantle behind the agitation launched by the Congress against the Chandra Babu Naidu government's decision to hike the power tariff in the early part of 2000; the agitation came to an end abruptly after the police fired at the demonstrators in Hyderabad. In the 1999 Lok Sabha and Assembly elections, when the Congress promised free power to the farmers, *Vaartha* ran a series of articles to prove the possibility of free power for agriculture[20] for and created an impact in the Telangana region where the lack of power was felt more intensely. Congress secured substantial support in the 1999 elections and gained a decisive majority in the state elections of 2004.[21]

Ostensibly the Telugu press is acting in the name of the 'larger interests' of the people and legitimizing their respective political biases. However, one could discern two reasons for this, which are intricately linked to the political process set in the state since the emergence of regionalism. As the media became a more profitable industry, a new crop of entrepreneurs started to invest in it. But as the competition grew among them there was also a clamour for revenues through advertisements and circulation which in turn forced them to compromise on various political issues.[22] Ramoji Rao of *Eenadu* expanded into other media-related industry such as film production with Ramoji film city and *Eenadu* Television that now runs 11 channels in different languages like

Gujarati, Bengali, Hindi, Urdu, Marathi, Kannada, Oriya across the country. It has thus acquired a gigantic presence in the world of information.

The second is the interest shown in the local issues by this new media. Issues such as the Dalit movement, anti-arrack agitation, Dandora demand for categorization as Scheduled Castes, Telangana subregional agitation, caste specific mobilization among Backward Castes, anti-power tariff agitation in a great way influenced the campaign agendas of the elections in the 1990s. The Telugu press particularly *Eenadu* and *Vaartha* played a prominent role in framing the agendas in these elections.[23]

It is instructive to note that *Eenadu* that started special tabloids to cover all the corners of the state first recognized the significance of articulating local issues through newspapers. Gradually it increased the number of editions to 10 by 1997 and its circulation touched a whopping 722,771 in July 1999 (Table 10.2). After *Eenadu* other newspapers also started local tabloids which have become a major source of information to the local people and has found instant empathy.

Vaartha, with its big capital backing, started with an unprecedented 10 editions simultaneously and at present has 12 editions. With its recent origins, *Vaartha* has acquired a significant standing. The strength of *Vaartha* lies in opening the space for local dynamics both in terms of organization and the techniques of reporting. The reporting as well as editorial staff is predominantly drawn from the lot of journalists who are associated with political activism of various hues. It is interesting to note that *Vaartha* had drawn its main staff at the time of its launch from the just closed *Udayam*, which in fact highlighted the local protest movements in the 1980s.[24]

A senior academic notes that '*Vaartha* has been trying to capture that political space which hitherto has not been adequately represented in the Telugu press. It has been its conscious effort to harness this resource to out beat *Eenadu*.'[25] Thus, it has acquired a prominent place in the Telangana region, as it was sympathetic to the demand for separate statehood for Telangana. There was a phenomenal rise in the circulation of *Vaartha* from 150,000 to nearly 300,000 before and after the demand for separate Telangana. It is not

Table 10.2
Agencies and Circulation of *Eenadu* Daily Newspaper

Year	Agencies	Total circulation	
1974	32	12,730	(Visakhapatnam edition: 10 August 1974)
1975	143	12,824	(Hyderabad edition: 17 December 1975)
1976	502	60,317	
1977	602	70,980	
1978	1,057	150,811	(Vijayawada edition: 1 May 1978)
1979	1,384	202,149	
1980	1,412	197,350	
1981	1,262	197,605	
1982	1,749	271,647	(Tirupathi edition: 20 June 1982)
1983	2,142	337,329	
1984	2,125	374,891	
1985	2,445	288,491	
1986	2,305	281,940	
1987	2,262	263,529	
1988	2,275	289,655	
1989	2,554	315,326	
1990	2,405	311,346	
1991	2,454	308,834	(Ananthapuram edition: 24 February 1991)
1992	2,785	350,547	(Karimnagar edition: 30 March 1992) (Rajahmundry edition: 24 September 1992)
1993	3,808	442,573	
1994	4,624	558,463	
1995	4,851	567,798	
1996	4,998	604,112	(Suryapet edition: 27 March 1996) (Guntur edition: 7 April 1996)
1997	5,373	665,885	(Nellore edition: 19 March 1997)
1998	5,826	588,916	
July 1999	6,289	722,771	

Source: Eenadu Pathikella Akshara Yatra (1974–1999), Published by Quality Cell, *Eenadu*, Hyderabad, 10 August 1999.

uncommon in this part of the state for people tend to identify *Vaartha* with the Telangana issue and *Eenadu* as an integrationist. Furthermore *Vaartha* runs weekly columns on Dalits, gender, caste, etc., to articulate the issues related to specific groups. What is significant about *Vaartha's* representation of local groups is not spearheading the cause on behalf of the subaltern groups but appropriating them for expanding its own sphere. Thus the variation and differentiation between *Eenadu* and *Vaartha* lies no more than in the issues they represented, regional in the case of the former and local in the case of the latter.

What is normally neglected by the analysts regarding media politics is the nature of political fault lines drawn between newspapers. The political stands and the corresponding biases that the newspapers take are undoubtedly context specific. In essence both *Eenadu* and *Vaartha* remain pro-establishment newspapers so long as the respective governments to which they owe loyalty remain in power. However, we cannot at the same time undermine the strength of the local movements for it drew the mainstream media to take cognizance of these otherwise neglected social spaces. Interestingly, most of the time, it is the anti-establishment papers like *Vaartha* that appropriate these constituencies; of course, the danger of *Vaartha* converting into pro-establishment always remain an open question. It is interesting to see what remains with the spaces created by the local movements autonomous of mainstream/dominant politics—whether they get appropriated and become victims of the process or they thrust fresh compulsions on the media.

Whatever the claims of any newspaper may be, what comes out clearly is that the Telugu press sees the potential gains of moving closer to the local issues. The engagement of the Telugu press has been substantial, not just in terms of reporting, but also in involving itself in the political developments and shaping the discourses around it. Thus, Jeffrey notes that 'Members of India's elites in the 1990s, deplored the newspaper revolution—vulgarity titillating the semi-literate and harked back to former times when serious editors edited serious (and scarce) newspapers for serious (and scarce) reading.'[26] This comment reflects the problem of unintelligibility between the elite and the masses that so characteristically shaped politics in India and also got reflected in the world of media.

Television and Politics

Television in India started playing a prominent role in politics since the mid-1980s. It was Rajiv Gandhi who tried to get a maximum mileage out of the government-owned Doordarshan. The fact that the misuse of Doordarshan and the opposition's contest for space in television was one of the major campaign issues in the 1989 elections indicates the growing importance of the role of television in politics. Since then the autonomy of Doordarshan has been regularly appearing in the manifestos of almost all major parties in all the elections during the 1990s which resulted in the Prasar Bharathi Board in 1997. Ironically, the Board was set up without much autonomy. After all the fact of the matter is that no ruling party—be it the Congress or National Front or NDA coalition or the present UPA—would be willing to forego its controls over such a coveted instrument of public power.

The battle for control over the airwaves increased with the entry of satellite-run private television channels in the early 1990s following the Gulf War. There was increasing competition among the channels for expanding their popularity through a variety of programmes—including political, social, financial and news-based programmes. Doordarshan has also been pushed to the defensive in this competition, as private channels started making a dent into the monopoly of Doordarshan.[27] The 1990s experienced a total transformation in communications as television expanded phenomenally with the emergence of cable networks, which enabled people to have easy access to all the television channels.

During the 1980s, Indian soap operas like '*Humlog*' (1984–85), '*Buniyad*' (1986–87), '*Ramayan*' (1987–88) and '*Mahabharat*' (1988–90) gained phenomenal success on television.[28] They played vital roles in building large blocs of followers from the public for Indian television. This attracted the attention of politicians, advertisers, markets and others who dealt with the masses towards the power of the television. It is not surprising that television gradually acquired centrestage of all the processes including discourse construction.

Figure 10.1
The Rapid Growth of Cable Television in India

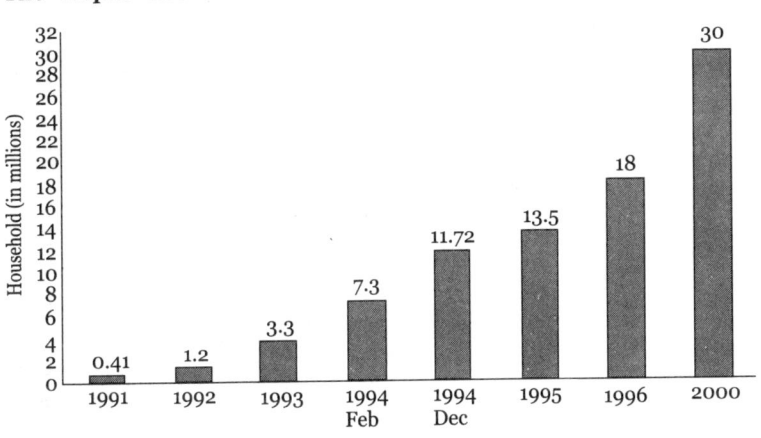

Source: Arvind Singhal and Everett M. Rogers, *India's Communication Revolution: From Bullock Carts to Cyber Marts* (New Delhi: Sage, 2001), p. 112.

In the 1990s, television in India underwent yet another change with the advent of satellite-based private channels. There was a phenomenal growth of the regional language television channels that were able to compete with the national channels. The Sun TV network in Tamil Nadu with its presence in all the South Indian states and *Eenadu* television network in Andhra Pradesh with 11 language channels across the country emerged as leading regional players. With Star, Sony and Zee networks as major figures, around 40 private television networks are presently operating. The rapid growth of cable television operators facilitated the fast expansion of private channels (Figure 10.1).

Doordarshan increased commercialization towards the late 1980s, when Rajiv Gandhi's government increasingly pursued the pro-liberalization policies. It was slowly eschewing its development agenda which was the major justification for the government to hold control over television.[29] Doordarshan's advertisement revenues grew to as high as US $133 million during 1993–94. But since then Doordarshan has entered into a pitched battle with the private channels. By

330 G. Krishna Reddy

Figure 10.2
Advertising Revenues of Doordarshan

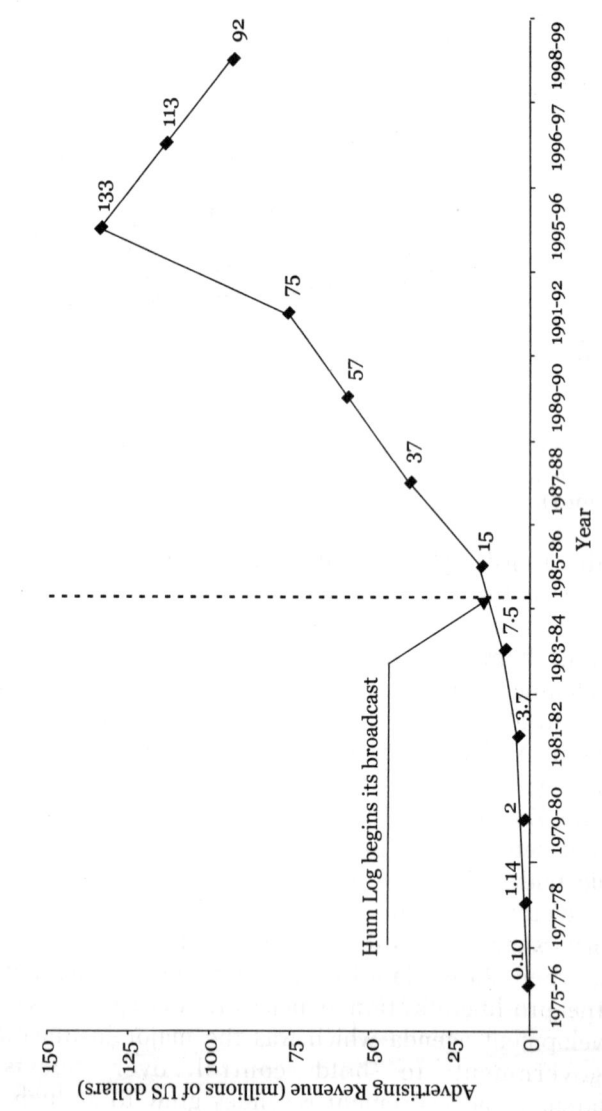

Source: Arvind Singhal and Everett M. Rogers, *India's Communication Revolution: From Bullock Carts to Cyber Marts* (New Delhi: Sage, 2001), p. 112.

1998–99, the advertisement revenues of Doordarshan have come down to US $92 millions (Figure 10.2) as its market share has been eroded by the big private television networks in the country. This profile is important to understand how high are the stakes that are involved in the media industry. For its own growth, the public and private television channels got entangled with the prospects of the economic reforms which would do a lot of good to it, a point that can be buttressed by the way television in India conducted the debate around the politics of economic reforms in the 1990s. The issue of economic reforms has been a major point of debate in the elections in Andhra Pradesh particularly since the 1994 Assembly elections. Despite the resistance from various sections of people, all the parties and media tried to build a consensus around the economic reforms.[30]

At the regional level, the proliferation of private channels in Andhra Pradesh started around the same time as the other television networks at the national level. It was the regional *Eenadu* newspaper group which expanded into *Eenadu* television network and has come to be one of the biggest television players in the country in terms of its reach, popularity and revenues. Its advertisement revenues topped the list among the regional channels (after Sun TV networks), drawing Rs 55.1 crore ($12.45 m) in 1999 (Table 10.3). Incidentally *Eenadu* television network was launched only on 27 August 1995.

Another important Telugu television network is Gemini TV which is part of the Sun TV conglomerate. It was launched in February 1995. A sister concern of Gemini, Teja was launched recently to serve as an entertainment channel with cinema music and news based programmes. Gemini's advertisement revenues was Rs 23.6 crore ($5.32 m) in 1999 (Table 10.3). The third important private channel was Citi cable, originally launched by Ramakrishna who was allegedly killed in the local feuds over distribution of cable operating areas. The channel was later bought by Zee TV network as part of its regional language expansion.

Each passing election witnessed a spurt of television channels in Andhra Pradesh that explains how intricately the prospects of the media industry are linked to the political markets.

Table 10.3
Aiming Sky-high! I Advertisement Rates and Airtime Utilization (1999) of Regional Channels

	Actual spots sold (number) a	Card rates (Rs per spot, approx) b	Discounted rate per spot (Rs approx) $c = b*0.56$	Adv revenue (Rs m) $d = (a*c/10,000,000)$†	Available spots (number) e	Airtime utilization (%) $f = a/c$
Asianet	64,795	13,268	5,904	383	525,600	12
Sun TV	135,163	12,053	5,363	725	525,500	26
Surya	7,196	6,003	2,670	19	525,600	1
Udaya	79,778	8,914	3,967	316	525,600	15
Vijay TV	149,306	5,949	2,647	395	525,600	28
Eenadu	106,566	11,619	5,170	551	525,600	20
Gemini TV	79,734	6,661	2,964	236	525,600	15
Jaya TV	5,291	7,692	3,424	18	525,600	1
Lashkara	7,272	6,697	2,980	22	525,600	1
Raj TV	225,511	5,169	2,300	519	525,600	43
Total	860,611	8,315	3,700	3,184	5,256,000	16

Source: Ogilvy & Mather, ETIG, cited in *The Economic Times*, 'Entertainment 2001-2002', An ET Intelligence Report, N.A.

Note: †Industry sources indicate that discounts on card rates average 56 per cent. The above list might not be complete and some smaller channels might have been left out, especially cable channels. In this scenario, the discounts on card rates would be lower than 56 per cent. The above table also includes sponsorship earnings for the channels.

For instance, in the recently concluded 2004 elections, three major television channels were launched. TV9, a complete news channel owned by Sreeni Raju who runs a software company and belongs to one of the most enterprising and dominant community, Rajus, has become enormously popular. It has surpassed the other major channels—ETV and Gemini TV in ratings. Two, ETV launched its news-based channel ETV2 just before the election. Another TV channel launched was CTV, converting a cable television network into a state-of-the-art satellite television channel. A family belonging to the Kamma community owns it. Interestingly two dominant communities Kamma and Raju in the state own 90 per cent of the media establishments, print as well as electronic.

It is important to look at the growth of regional media in comparison to the national channels. Like the regional press, regional television also asserts its identity and acts through the local idiom. The success of regional media in India has something to do with the way it associated itself with the rise of local politics. One media expert comments on the success of regional television: 'The southern channels continue to maintain a distinctive identity, are local and target specific in their concern and language of communication and are willing to experiment with forms that are derived from the folk subconscious.'[31]

Television set the campaign agendas in the 1990s election with its overwhelming control over communications. Mass media particularly the press and electronic media have moved from the *channel* that disseminates information to *the source* of information with its authority over communications. The TDP amply recognizes the power of mass media in modern day politics more than any other party in the state. A comparative analysis of the media management in the campaigns under NTR and Naidu indicates an emphatic stress on the role of the media in winning elections.

There was a fundamental shift in the TDP's campaign strategies so far as media and communications were concerned, from NTR's regime to that of Naidu's. The two documents on the campaign methods issued by the party in 1983 and 1999 amply prove the point.[32] NTR's campaign strategy was multivariate in using the communication forms ranging from holding public meetings, which was given greater importance to modern communication means like cinema, audio-video cassettes, etc. There was a special emphasis on amalgamation of folk arts like *Burrakathas* and *Harikathas* with modern communication forms performed by skilled cinema artists.

While it is true that television gained enormous control over the communication processes by the time of Naidu, campaign strategies singularly centred around the modern media during Naidu's period in the TDP. The management of media, time management and the surveys carried out by independent agencies for political information such as the support base were given greater emphasis. The urgency about the elections was suggested to the party leaders and workers. It implied that the party must be always election oriented. Interestingly a senior leader in the TDP admitted that there was nothing wrong with the party relying on the media for information.[33] Naidu using Doordarshan or hiring private Telugu channels to beam his messages during his tenure as the chief minister was rather frequent. Publicity of his policies on electronic media itself acquired a strategic place in the governance with a huge machinery of communication experts designing it constantly. The public spending on publicity is said to have gone up steeply.[34] The figure was often shown by the opposition as Rs 300 crores ($0.06 bn) annually in a resource crunch economy and in a regime ostensibly committed to austerity. The campaigns, unlike NTR, became a permanent feature of governance. Thus electronic media had become integral to his 'permanent campaign'.

An intermediary functionary with a longstanding association with the TDP stated that 'the training that the TDP imparts to the cadres is managerial type. It does not enable party workers to develop any longstanding association with people. It does not inculcate commitment towards the party programmes nor to the political work. Party is presently filled with mercenary like cadres who are merely interested in the fringe benefits that they obtain from the TDP, being ruling party nor are they capable of organizing mass protests, if the TDP has to sit in the opposition.'[35] Though it may appear a little farfetched, the comment echoes the general state of affairs in all the parties. What marked the TDP differently from the other parties was its centralization and the total dependence on the manager-like leader, Chandrababu Naidu who often called himself the Chief Executive Officer of Andhra Pradesh Inc.

Much before election time, Naidu gathers information about the party's prospects in different constituencies. There are mainly four channels that the party makes use of: police intelligence, district level bureaucrats, independent private agency and local level party committees, among which the police intelligence report and district collectors play a crucial role in selecting the (political) candidates for elections.[36]

It has been widely understood among the rank and file of the party that media channels have been the crucial source of information. Thus it is not uncommon for the activists and leaders in the TDP at the local level to maintain a record of their activities with photographs and reports in the local edition of the newspapers. They use this record as an evidence of their service to the party in claiming a stake with the leadership for appointments in the various committees, and even in the selection of candidates in the elections for various local bodies. The bio-data of the politicians has to be endorsed by the media reports. The Congress party started replicating this practice as well. From the perspective of the media this development has actually made even the mofussil reporter indispensable in the power circles.[37] Media and other exogenous networks, it must be noted, become vital sources of information for the centralized leadership with weak party networks as the TDP.

Among other changes, the 1990s also witnessed media organizations competing for the audience/readership by evolving new programmes. Increased interest among the new groups in political developments generally traced to the emergence of the TDP and later on to the rise of local movements like Dalit movement, anti-arrack, Dandora movements brought the people closer to politics. The Telugu channels developed a variety of programmes based on political themes, reports, news and discussions. After entertainment it is politics which occupies prime place on television. Programmes like 'Prathidhwani' (echo), 'Netibharatham' (Today's India), 'Dear CM', 'Idandi Sangathi' of *Eenadu*, *Gemini* and *Teja* channels air weekly discussions on current problems in politics, especially the local problems and offer pungent critiques of the government's policies. It is now a practice in all the television channels that the prime time news is usually accompanied by commentaries on the issues central to the public debate.

The intervention of these political programmes of the television channels into the public discourse is substantial even during the non-election period. Political parties keenly follow these debates on media and respond to them. Very often a key politician is invited to air the interests of their respective parties and usually the programmes are debate based. This of course, is apart from the daily briefing given to the press after a day's session of the Assembly proceedings.

The expansion of television has brought profound changes in the way electoral politics is looked at. Operating in the milieu of marketing politics, it opened up a plethora of avenues for the political parties and politicians. Big advertisement agencies like Rediffusion, Mudra, Rashtriya Madyam for the Congress, Market Missionaries, Solutions, Ad-Dict for BJP entered the elections scene during the 1990s to market the product parties and even sometimes the individual politicians.[38] In the 1998 elections, Telugu Desam Chief Chandrababu Naidu evolved his own style of image management devised largely by treasurer P. Prabhakar Reddy, a noted businessman. He was quoted as saying 'electronic media is our priority. We are also planning 35 mm films for theatres.'[39] The entry of advertisement agencies combined with electronic media has substantially altered the economics and politics of elections.

The emergence of the television, as stated earlier, created necessities of its own in gearing the political parties to put in their best in handling electoral debates on television, which have become a predominant way of highlighting issues in the elections that eventually shape the campaign agendas. The media dominated electoral dynamics necessitated primarily two aspects: Parties have developed media expertise by drawing skills from the market resources. A new breed of politicians with media and market skills have become prominent in the parties and have come to be called 'spin doctors'.

Another important aspect which has acquired prominence in the media driven elections is psephology. Though psephology has its origins as a political practice independent of the media, the television has surely augmented this practice and taken it to new heights. This hitherto academic exercise has acquired a significant place in the elections since the 1990s. Psephology has now become predominantly a media event as the surveys are done by market agencies like ORG-MARG, MODE, CMS, SOPHRES, etc., hired by or in collaboration with media like *India Today, Outlook, Week, Sunday*, etc. Even the state owned Doordarshan conducted similar surveys. These discussions very often come to shape campaign issues, by framing some issues as primary and dropping out others.

Telugu channels regularly feature the discussions on the poll predictions. In fact, *Eenadu, Vaartha, Deccan Chronicle* and other regional newspapers hold their own surveys on the state elections and are taken seriously. *Eenadu* television, *Gemini, TV9* and *Citi* cable organize intense debates over the issues and the prospects of parties, which become a staple diet for the public.

What does psephology in the elections signify? Psephology as a wide practice with huge amounts of finances involved is a result of uncertainties that the political parties have been experiencing owing to their unstable support bases and voter volatility. Yogendra Yadav remarks,

> when the political process fails, the market steps in. The fact is that today the routine processes of democratic politics have ceased to function properly. Politicians know less and less about the people because there is no party mechanism. The channels of information from the ground are thin and getting thinner. So you need an objective survey if you want to know the truth. When political organizations fail, you have to pay for an election forecast.[40]

The spectre of election perhaps is less fearful for the political parties and a matter of bounty for the media with psephology doing the rounds.

More importantly, some issues are made more primary than others, leading to a politics of exclusion. It could be discerned in the manner in which questions are asked in the surveys. For instance, the large-scale suicides among small farmers was not seen as an issue of significance in the recent elections in the state, when it actually has become a crucial factor. Neither the media nor the surveys could gauge the intensity of the situation.[41]

Similarly the question, 'Who is the most preferred prime minister?' became the most discussed aspect in the elections of 1998, 1999 and 2004. The political campaign of the parties increasingly centred around personalities like Sonia Gandhi, Vajpayee, Jyoti Basu. The question of the foreign origins of Sonia Gandhi acquired prominence particularly in the BJP and the TDP campaigns and surveys in the 1998, 1999 and 2004 elections. The surveys reinforce a certain type of stereotype which helps to prime the issues in the campaigns. The BJP and the TDP's much taunted slogans like the 'feel good factor' and 'India shining' in the 2004 elections could be fine examples of this type. Ironically, the spin doctors went awry with their assessment of the ground reality of poverty, drought, etc., in the elections where the TDP and the BJP lost thoroughly.

The division between the channels on political lines, though not very sharp, is significant. Generally, the Congress party places its campaign advertisements overwhelmingly on *Gemini* or *Teja* while the TDP focuses on *Eenadu* television. However, one must be cautioned that this kind of preference to a particular channel by political parties is hazy and cannot be quantified.

Media intervention in politics can be understood at two levels. One, the sharp polarization of the print media on party lines shows the intense competition in AP. Partisanship is the hallmark of political reporting here. Two, while competing for new constituencies the media along with political parties build a consensus over crucial issues like the economic reforms for their prospects. Both conflict and consensus building thus become integral to media and political establishment as well.

Finally, the structures of media and of politics in AP increasingly resemble each other in terms of competition. In their race to expand the base of audience/readership and support for the television channels or newspapers, and parties respectively, they are increasingly focusing on local issues in the local idiom. That is where the convergence between media and politics is more evident. The act of convergence being one of appropriation of local cultures and groups, both media and the political parties help each other in shaping the campaign agendas which seek to rebuild consensus over the new political culture.

Conclusion

The conventional exposition that campaigns are generally individualistic and concerned only with particular political parties during electioneering simplifies the complex phenomenon they really are. The campaign structures are drawn from a combination of the immediate electoral context and the long-drawn political process. Campaigns in their immediate context are a strategy created and designed by a party or a candidate to impress upon the voters. As a structure, the campaign's operations in terms of form and content is intricately linked to the competitive politics and the compulsions that it experiences as participation of diverse social groups expands, as in the case of Indian politics. It is because these new groups raise new demands that often the system may not be able to cope with such demands. Failing to meet them results in erosion of the credibility of the ruling elite. Thus the terms of competition undergo significant changes with the different groups exerting pressure on the system, and so do the electoral processes. With the ensuing uncertainties, electoral politics get increasingly symbolic and manipulative. Consequently, the campaigns come to be dominated by modern media in terms of both form and content.

In a way, the crisis in competitive politics engendered by the decline in party grassroots networks has resulted in the politics of crisis which is characterized by the growing symbolic politics, in turn helped by the modern media. Modern media has come to substitute the loss of party networks and the earlier organized politics of the parties.

The scenario in AP presents an emphatic case where the transforming nature of competitive politics was felt more profoundly than elsewhere. The rise of the TDP signified two features of competitive politics. First, the transforming culture of politics that changed the orientations and value patterns about the way the electoral politics could be viewed. The TDP also represents the percolation of political competition downward to the regional level but at the same time it faced a stiff challenge with the incorporation of larger social sections into the polity.

Second, the transforming culture of politics necessitated the parties to resort to new forms of communication which facilitated their image centred politics. The advancement of communication technologies has helped the mass media's abilities to monopolize communication forms. Thus, television and the print medium have come to play dominant roles in politics. Evidently one can see this in the transformation from the multivariate nature of traditional communication forms to increasingly centralized communication structures.

The modern media has become the main source of information for the parties in the absence of grassroots organization. Identification of issues and moulding the public opinion has become the prerogative of the media. Thus the parties adapt themselves to suit the new media environment by improving their media expertise. The TDP particularly under Naidu has become managerial and laid newfound emphasis on the media skills; so also is the Congress party, though to a lesser extent.

The intense competition, the reduction of the whole political process to electoral practices and the constant intervention of the media into political debates have extended the campaign period virtually beyond the elections. This has resulted in a continuous campaign on the part of political parties whose prospects have become uncertain with the increasing volatility in their support base.

There is a convergence of the interests between the media industry and the political parties in an increasingly 'market like' politics, which determines the nature of the campaign structure in its form and content. Both media and the parties are in search of their constituencies. Television channels and newspapers both compete for their audience and readership respectively. The competition among the media is akin to competition between the political parties. It is this convergence that helps both associate so closely with each other in the present day campaigns.

Local issues moved to the centre of politics replacing national issues with the rise of the lower strata through 'local' movements by the 1990s. Now it is imperative on the part of the media and the parties to appropriate the rising social groups by shaping the campaign agendas on the lines of local issues. Simultaneously, the modern media and the party organization are increasingly getting centralized. Thus, the modern campaigns have come to be localized in terms of its content and centralized in their form.

Finally, to sum up, political parties, in the absence of grassroots networks, cannot translate the local/regional issues to the generic levels. By building public opinion around the issues projected in the elections, the media brings the masses into the system and integrates them in the electoral processes which hitherto was done by organized party politics. The capability of mass media to both create a uniformity in opinion making and build opinion suits the exigencies of the political parties in the present day political scenario.

Notes

1. Duncan Watts, *Political Communications Today* (Manchester: Manchester University Press, 1977). See especially, Arvind Rajgopal, *Politics After Television: Religious Nationalism and the Reshaping of the Indian Public* (Cambridge: Cambridge University Press, 2001) for an illuminating analysis of the political persuasion of voters which changed after the advancement of television in the Indian context. For a detailed description of the communication revolution in India, see Arvind Singhal and Everett M. Rogers, *India's Communication Revolution: From Bullock Carts to Cyber Marts* (New Delhi: Sage, 2001).
2. M.N. Srinivas (ed.), *Caste and Its Twentieth Century Avatar* (New Delhi: Viking, 1996).
3. Sarah Joseph and Gurupreet Mahajan, 'Elections and Democratic Process in India', *Economic and Political Weekly*, vol. XXVI, no. 34, 24 August 1991, pp. 1953–54.
4. Ibid., p. 1955.
5. Ashis Nandy, 'The Political Culture of the Indian State', *Daedalus*, vol. 118, no. 4, 1989, p. 21.

6. Ibid.
7. L.I. Rudolph, 'The Media and Cultural Politics', in Subrata K. Mitra and James Chiriyankadath (eds), *Electoral Politics in India: A Changing Landscape* (New Delhi: Segment Books, 1992), p. 86.
8. V.M. Sirsikar, *Sovereigns Without Crowns: A Behavioural Analysis of the Indian Electoral Process* (Bombay: Popular Prakashan, 1973), p. 153.
9. Rajni Kothari, *Politics In India* (New Delhi, Orient Longman, 1970).
10. Craig Calhoun, 'Indirect Relationships and Imagined Communities: Large-scale Social Integration and the Transformation of Everyday Life', in P. Bourdieu and James S. Coleman (eds), *Social Theory for a Changing Society* (New York: West View Press, 1991).
11. Rudolph, 'The Media and Cultural Politics', p. 86.
12. R. Jeffrey, *India's Newspaper Revolution: Capitalism, Politics, and the Indian Language, Press 1977–99* (New Delhi: Oxford University Press, 2000).
13. Ibid.
14. Sanjay Baru, 'Economic Policy and the Development of Capitalism in India: The Role of Regional Capitalists and Political Parties', in F.R. Frankel, Zoya Hasan, Rajeev Bhargava, Baveer Arora (eds), *Transforming India: Social and Political Dynamics of Democracy* (New Delhi: Oxford University Press, 2000).
15. *Eenandu Pathikella Aksharayatra: 1974–1999*, Hyderabad, Quality Cell, 10 August 1999.
16. G. Haragopal and G. Krishna Reddy, 'Regionalism and the Press: Emerging Trends in Andhra', Paper presented at the national seminar on Nation Building, Development Process and Communication, Delhi, 3–7 December 1988.
17. Interestingly, when Naidu had unseated his father-in-law NTR from power in August 1995 by turning 177 MLAs to his side, the media particularly *Eenadu* was conspicuously silent. See G. Krishna Reddy, 'New Populism and Liberalisation: Regime Shift Under Chandrababu Naidu in A.P.', *Economic and Political Weekly*, vol. XXXVI, no. 9, 2 March 2002, pp. 871–83.
18. Jeffrey, *India's Newspaper Revolution*.
19. Focus group interviews with activists—15 women, youth and elders in Malapalle and Madigapalle of Kodurupadu village which was one of the major villages where anti-arrack movement was strong. Some of them were also interviewed individually. In the course of interviews, they often endorsed this view and expressed disillusionment, 24 November 1994, Kodurupadu, Nellore district.
20. *Vaartha* reports on debate over free power supply to the farmers during August and September, 1999.
21. Reddy, 'New Populism'.

22. R. Jeffrey, 'Monitoring Newspapers and Understanding the Indian State', *Asian Survey*, vol. XXXIV, no. 8, 1994, (August).
23. Interview with Laxmaiah, a Senior Journalist who worked for *Vaartha*, 14 February 2000, Hyderabad.
24. Interview with Surender Raju, who worked for *Udayam* and *Andhra Jyothi*, 2 January 2000, Hyderabad.
25. Personal conversation between F.D. Vakil and the author, 15 January 2000.
26. Jeffrey, *India's Newspaper Revolution*, p. 13.
27. Sevanti Ninan, *Through the Magic Window: Television and Change in India* (New Delhi: Penguin, 1995).
28. Anand Mitra, *Television and Popular Culture in India: A Study of Mahabharat* (New Delhi: Sage, 1993).
29. Ninan, *Through the Magic Window*.
30. K. Srinivasulu, Ravindra Shastry, G. Krishna Reddy and Channa Basavaiah, *Electoral Politics, Political Parties and Public Policies: A Study of the 1998 Parliamentary Elections*. Report submitted to SAP (UGC), Department of Political Science, Osmania University, 1999.
31. Shashi Kumar, 'The Shadow of Chimera', *Gentleman*, 1999 (June), p. 65.
32. 'Campaign Methods', A Pamphlet issued by The TDP Office, 1983 and 'Campaign methods', (excerpts from a brochure containing campaign materials issued by the TDP Office), 1999.
33. Interview with Ummareddi Venkateshwarlu, Member of Parliament, a senior leader and in charge of party affairs, 23 February 2002, Hyderabad.
34. Personal conversation with a senior bureaucrat in the government of Andhra Pradesh, 15 July 2001, Hyderabad.
35. Interview with Inayatullah, State Urdu Academy Member and Member of the TDP Sircilla Assembly Constituency Coordination Committee, 10 July 2001, Hyderabad.
36. A number of TDP functionaries at the district level expressed this view during this interview in Karimnagar, 11 January 2000.
37. Interview with T. Srinivas Reddy, Sub-Editor, *Eenadu*, Karimnagar edition, 10 January 2000, Algunoor, Karimnagar District.
38. *India Today*, 2 February 1998.
39. Ibid.
40. Quoted in *Outlook*, 14 February 1996.
41. P. Sainath, 'Andhra's Electoral Earthquake', *The Hindu,* 12 May and 'McMedia and Market Jihad', 1 June 2004.

References

Baru, Sanjay, 'Economic Policy and the Development of Capitalism in India: The Role of Regional Capitalists and Political Parties', in Francine R. Frankel, Zoya Hasan, Rajeev Bhargava and Balveer Arora (eds), *Transforming India: Social and Political Dynamics of Democracy* (New Delhi: Oxford University Press, 2000).

Calhoun, Craig, 'Indirect Relationships and Imagined Communities: Large-scale Social Integration and the Transformation of Everyday Life', in P. Bourdieu and James S. Coleman (eds), *Social Theory for a Changing Society* (New York: West View Press, 1991).

Haragopal, G. and G. Krishna Reddy, 'Regionalism and the Press: Emerging Trends in Andhra'. Paper presented at the seminar on Nation Building, Development Process and Communication, Delhi: 3–7 December 1988 (Mimeo).

Jeffrey, R., 'Monitoring Newspapers and Understanding the Indian State', *Asian Survey*, vol. XXXIV, no. 8 (August) 1994.

———, *India's Newspaper Revolution: Capitalism, Politics, and the Indian Language, Press 1977–99* (New Delhi: Oxford University Press, 2000).

Joseph, Sarah and Gurpreet Mahajan, 'Elections and Democratic Process in India', *Economic and Political Weekly*, vol. XXVI, no. 34 (August) 1991, pp. 53–54.

Kothari, Rajni, *Politics In India* (New Delhi: Orient Longman, 1970).

Kumar, Shashi, 'The Shadow of Chimera', *Gentleman*, June 1999.

Mitra, Anand, *Television and Popular Culture in India: A Study of Mahabharat* (New Delhi: Sage Publications, 1993).

Nandy, A., 'The Political Culture of the Indian State', *Daedalus*, vol. 118, no. 4, 1989.

Ninan, Sevanti, *Through the Magic Window: Television and Change in India* (New Delhi: Penguin Books India Ltd, 1995).

Rajagopal, Arvind, *Politics After Television: Religious Nationalism and the Reshaping of the Indian Public* (Cambridge: Cambridge University Press, 2001).

Reddy, Krishna G., *Press and Politics: A Study of Eenadu in Andhra Pradesh Politics—1980 to 1985*, an unpublished M. Phil Dissertation. Jawaharlal Nehru University, New Delhi, 1989.

———, 'New Populism and Liberalisation: Regime Shift Under Chandrababu Naidu in A.P.', *Economic and Political Weekly*, vol. XXXVI, no. 9 (March) 2002, pp. 871–83.

Rudolph, L.I., 'The Media and Cultural Politics', in Subrata K. Mitra and James Chiriyankadath (eds), *Electoral Politics in India: A Changing Landscape* (New Delhi: Segment Books, 1992).

Singhal, Arvind and Everett M. Rogers, *India's Communication Revolution: From Bullock Carts to Cyber Marts* (New Delhi, Sage Publications, 2001).

Sirsikar, V.M., *Sovereigns Without Crowns: A Behavioural Analysis of the Indian Electoral Process.* (Bombay: Popular Prakashan, 1973).

Srinivas, M.N. (ed.), *Caste and Its Twentieth Century Avatar* (New Delhi: Viking, 1996).

Srinivasulu, K., Ravindra Shastry, G. Krishna Reddy and Channa Basavaiah, *Electoral Politics, Political Parties and Public Policies: A Study of the 1998 Parliamentary Elections*. A Report submitted to SAP (UGC), Department of Political Science, Osmania University, Hyderabad, 1999.

Watts, Duncan, *Political Communications Today* (Manchester: Manchester University Press, 1977).

2.2
Interaction and Appropriation

11

PERSONAL AND SOCIAL COMMUNICATION:
Two Instances of Electronic Mail

BERNARD BEL

Paul@nowhere (1998)

I have forgotten the circumstances under which I got acquainted with Paul. Indeed, there is no such thing as a 'circumstance' in cyberspace, the space of electronic communication. Everyday millions of mail boxes get filled with messages relating to the current professional and personal activities of their owners. Incoming mail materializes as a rather enigmatic list of senders with brief 'subjects', some of which (such as 'undelivered mail' or 'reduce your debts') immediately call for discarding the message. Most requests are examined for one or two minutes, prompting replies like 'yes', 'no', or the sceptical and enigmatic 'Hmmmm'. Part of the mail eventually gets forwarded to potential interested people, discussion lists, etc., a privileged way of building and maintaining networks of professional and personal contacts.

This essay does not deal with the technical know-how required for an extensive use of simple tools like the electronic mail. Commercial providers and printed media claim that Internet lets you 'travel' at a mouse click, which may be true when travelling 'without luggage' and aimlessly. Achieving something concrete with the Internet demands training plus a fair knowledge of 'nethics'—the net *savoir-vivre*.

The email (electronic mail), which is now growing at a high rate as a commodity of the middle class, is an efficient tool for making one's place in the global communication 'market'. None the less it requires skill to seize valuable opportunities and discard a great amount of junk information. To some extent, socializing in cyberspace is as difficult as doorstep selling, except that whilst electronic doors open for sure they may also close at light speed. It takes hardly more than one second to trash a message.

Meeting people via electronic mail might resemble the encounters a blind person would experience in a city crowded with other blind people. The contact is based exclusively on verbal communication. Notifications of gender, ethnic and cultural background are at the discretion of communicants. Many times when I received messages from, say for instance, a Finnish person I had to reply whimsically: 'Sorry, Jukka, I don't know whether you're a man or a woman.' And Jukka would reply: 'Does it really matter?' without providing the information.

Nothing matters, indeed, in an idealized global space of communication aimed at eradicating social prejudice on gender, ethnic difference, academic status and so on. But written communication cannot bypass discriminations embedded in natural language. For instance, I find it hard to communicate on the Internet in my native language (French) because of the difficulty of making a consistent decision on polite versus familiar forms *tu/vous*. Hierarchies encapsulated in linguistic structures seem to be more problematic than the absence of diacritical marks.

When I write to companies or research institutions in North America, often I receive an answer starting 'Hi Bernard...' and signed 'Nick' or 'Linda'. I would never expect this from French professional circles, and I confess that it makes my professional life a little more enjoyable!

Paul is a male US citizen. All the rest is the matter of default assumptions. I decided from the start that he may look like my wife's uncle Paul whom I never met and had only seen photographs of. The two Pauls can easily merge since the former is a verbal, and the latter a visual construct.

English is assumed the default language and America the default place of cyberspace. Domains like 'edu' and 'org' are US-centric, others such as 'in' (India) relate to countries. The heterogeneity of space may be put in contrast with the homogeneity of time and discourse styles. 'Hi Bernard.' Cyberpeople pay little attention to the place in which they live. They would only become aware of distances if they had to calculate postage fees or spend money on sending faxes.

Default attributes of persons are not the same depending on the communication medium. If Paul had my postal address, the day I get a letter from him he would become another person who does not fit anymore with paul@nowhere. Several Pauls might coexist in projected spaces. Cyberspace, like any communication space, constructs its own 'reality', but this reality is so incomplete, flexible (and open to manipulation) that it rarely clashes with other information sources.

In the beginning I was not able to grasp idiomatic expressions used by Paul. I asked friends who know American English. After a couple of years his language has become reasonably decipherable. Cybertalk transcends speech barriers but in the same time it imposes a unified language. I had a bitter experience of this a few years ago, when I entered into a controversy on a discussion list. Someone had a vigorous argument with a friend of mine who signed off the list. His opponent came up with the statement that my friend was 'mad'. I reacted strongly, tension rose and the offender eventually got sacked from the list. However, a British member of the list sent me a private message saying that 'mad', in colloquial American English, would mean 'angry' rather than 'crazy'. I contacted the list moderator, also a British scholar, who broadcasted a warning against the use of local expressions leading to such misunderstandings. At present I have the feeling that Internet 'speaks' two languages: Oxford English in 'serious' academic discussion lists, and American slang everywhere else, including professional forums such as the ones dealing with technology.

Paul's colloquial language is evocative of all kinds of images, again inferred by default reasoning. He once asked me to send documents in the hypertext format so that he would be able to read them on his electronic pad 'while I walk my dog...' The exquisite transitivity of the verb 'to walk one's dog' reveals a lifestyle in which there are mainly 'actors' and 'instruments'. No stray dogs around, no time for tea breaks! Ever seen anyone 'walk a dog' in India?

Paul seems to be a graduate in physics. He probably introduced himself in the first message before he became my cyberfriend. But these old messages have long since been trashed. The initial introduction rarely matters. There is no picture of Paul and myself with a date materializing a precise event legitimizing our friendship. On the Internet every interaction takes place 'here and now'. 'Here' is a vague statement, as suggested above, but 'now' refers to the Greenwich Mean Time (GMT) universal clock whose accurate signature is attached to every message. So what? It all ends up in the trash.

Paul recently perfected his way of reading my mail. In winter he cannot read while walking his dog. Instead he uses the Macintosh speech manager to read messages aloud while he is preparing breakfast. Which synthetic voice has he selected as mine? I would not dare to ask.

The breakfast scene confirmed that Paul is a middle-aged unmarried man. He goes to a dance course and gets dates with women who seem to behave like European women of my (our?) age. I cannot visualize such scenes. By sympathy I grant him the friendship of people I know and appreciate. Thus, Paul's emotional space strangely overlaps my own. While I had a date with his tango teacher he probably fell in love with the Ladakhi shepherd woman I enthusiastically described in a holiday report.

We often talk about music. He plays the piano. When he is not walking his dog or frying eggs, he is indeed driving a car:

> The idea of understanding music fascinates me. I think I am getting
> my lab experience in my car playing my little tiny piano which is
> now amplified.

This image would also be difficult to situate in the Delhi traffic.

Paul and I have set up implicit rules regarding which thoughts are worth sharing on the Internet. We never attempted any description of ourselves, people we live with, nor even places we live in. We feel satisfied with imaginary pictures. He must live in one of the houses I have seen on American television series—indeed like my wife's uncle Paul who was certainly enough of an eccentric to play the piano while driving a car, if he hadn't owned a bicycle and a violin.

We never talk about politics or public events, and our discussions on the diversity of cultures almost always take us back to musical statements. My cyberfriend seems to have a very regular life. He talks with a man playing organ in a church. I concluded he must be a Christian like 'all' North American men. Here lies a contradiction: my default assumptions are based on a conformist point of view whereas almost every message suggests an eccentric character.

I once received a very cryptic message from Paul. From the GMT time signature I made it out that he had written it around Saturday midnight, a time which is not appropriate for an American male citizen to write mail nor play piano at the wheel of his car!

Sharing this four-year experience of friendship in cyberspace, I would like to stress an important and paradoxical aspect of electronic communication: it opens a tremendous space for free exchange of views but it also tends to activate implicit rules inhibiting provocative speech. After all, most personal electronic mail is processed at leisure time after sorting out professional tasks. For this reason there is little commitment and hardly any regularity in this type of interaction. Paul and I sometimes keep silent for months.

Perhaps some day a message to Paul will be returned with the mention 'undelivered mail', meaning that he changed his Internet provider, and the whole relation will end up being trashed as junk. Paul and I could 'trash' each other at any time for reasons the other one will never know. Our friendship, therefore, remains 'virtual'. However, is it not the case with many human interactions, except that most of them get reinforced—and biased—by visual and physical exchange?

Let Paul have the last word:

> I had thought to share information about [your music software] with
> a beautiful woman I had composed a song for (with my little piano,
> my hands and my heart). I suddenly got terrified of high technology
> and I meditated. Then I thought that I was taking her to see Disney
> Interactive and I became less terrified by high technology.
> [...]
> Ethical dilemmas aren't supposed to be easy and I thought God was
> giving me one. Well, He easily gave me an ethical 'undilemna.'
> Perhaps he doesn't always play the role of the great puzzler in the
> sky and I can have a little relief.
> The pitch to the woman and those who would make music to call their
> own creation for a woman is that high technology doesn't replace the
> human heart, it only assists it in interacting. The song I wrote her
> jamming on top of Jobim was 'Sad is to Live in Solitude.' So, happy
> is what interaction is all about. Maybe India will become a
> Disneyland someday with just enough dreamers.

Mmmmmmh...

liste-naissance@yahoogroupes.fr—The Birth of a Virtual Community (2002)

On our return to France after several years spent in India, my wife and I decided to get in touch with persons promoting 'gentle' birth attendance and baby care, as they had been sensitized to these issues in rural India (Bel 1998). A few clicks on a search engine unveiled a galaxy of English websites dedicated to birth activism, and for a while we took part in several discussion lists such as *Online Birth Center News*. In spring 1999 I collected the email addresses of half a dozen French activists (mostly midwives and doctors) and decided to set up a small bilingual discussion list dedicated to birth activism. The current agenda of the list included the support of the unique free-standing birthing centre in France, *Maison de naissance de Sarlat*[1] which was under the threat of closure by a court decision, and facilitating contacts for the preparation of a *Midwifery Today* conference in Paris.

The same group of people exchanged ideas about ways of bringing together individuals and non-profit societies involved in birth activism over the entire country. Many French activists who had not yet been exposed to the North American birth movement were still sceptical, or even contemptuous, with respect to the Internet. Electronic mail, in particular, was loaded with the presumption of carrying unchecked information distributed by persons whose identity could not be traced accurately. The reference to North American activists even fuelled a rumour that the growing action group might be connected to some unknown cult organization trying to take the control of a vanishing birth movement in France.

In January 2000 the discussion list was set up in its final operational mode. It was operated by a list server run by voila.fr, which (due to market transactions) was taken over by egroups.com and finally handed over to yahoo groups.com.[2] The technical features of this list server are manifold, notably: (*a*) it has a customizable public procedure for admitting new subscribers; (*b*) all messages are archived in a searchable database; (*c*) subscribers may interact with the server to change their mailing address or subscription mode.

List activity

The growth rate of *liste-naissance* has been roughly exponential with a doubling of its membership every year. In Spring 2002 it counted 118 subscribers. The list is advertised on various web pages, among which are the Naissance.ws portal (see *infra*) and directories of discussion groups.

The average traffic over the past 15 months has been 30 messages per day, covering up to approximately five simultaneous discussion threads. There is no more growth of traffic despite the absence of moderation or restrictions in the number of dispatched messages. Apparently, there is a self-regulation of simultaneous discussion threads depending on the average time an active member may spend reading or writing new messages.

About 20 per cent of the list members who contribute more than one message per week could be designated as 'active writers'. Within this group it is possible to distinguish a small kernel of 'permanent writers' taking part in nearly all discussion threads. Typical active writers are birth activists (including men) or/and women who can invest a longer time when staying at home during their pregnancy or in the care of small children.

The sets of 'active' and 'permanent' writers change over time due to family or professional constraints, and indeed a variable personal commitment to the list. It is quite common to read a message by a member who remained silent for several weeks and declares that s/he is now busy reading hundreds of messages piled in her mailbox.

It would be impossible to categorize sets of 'active' writers, except by naming them one by one and browsing the database of personal presentations. It is felt that the very diversity of the group, the non-intervention of moderators, the absence of an ideological framework, advocacy or guidelines on the topics and contents, play a crucial role in its growth and social impact.

From time to time, an active writer broadcasts an appeal to silent members asking why they do not take an active part in discussions. This yields a relatively large number of replies. Many 'passive readers' feel happy to read discussion threads without writing. A few of them point out that, before they have set up their mind to compose a message, another member already wrote the very thing they wanted to say.

An unmoderated discussion list works in a way that is very close to a permanent semi-public forum. It is 'semi-public' in the sense that there is no restriction for becoming a member and taking part in discussions, except that applicants must introduce themselves through their individual experience with birthing and parenting. Professional status and enrolment in non-profit societies, trade unions, etc. are of little relevance. Even midwives or birth activists would be prompted to tell their personal stories rather than professional and social commitments. Members are expected to expose who they 'are' rather than what/whom they 'represent'.

People who sign off the list are not supposed to motivate their departure. A few of them feel like sending a farewell message. Signing off is often the result of the lack of time and an uneasy feeling of piling up hundreds of unread messages in their mailbox. When time is the unique reason, members are advised to change their membership status to 'web only' so that they no longer receive messages but still can read them in the server's archive. Thus, a small number of occasional writers are 'web only' members who keep reacting to selected discussion threads.

Sociological profiles

List members belong to a broad category of Internet users in French-speaking countries, mainly France, Belgium and the Quebec province in Canada. (In France, about 33 per cent of the population has been in touch with the Internet.) The list does not have a sociological profile of its own, despite a convergence of motivations in membership. During the year 2001, many applicants were women in the age group 25–30 who introduced themselves with stories of their hospital births, declaring that they seek moral support, an exchange of information and advice for making better birth plans in the future. A typical situation is the expectation of a vaginal birth after a caesarean section (VBAC). Men are also invited to take part in discussions. Currently, 10 per cent of the list members are men whose wife or partner is directly concerned with the list issues. A few list members are midwives unsatisfied with the compulsive medical thinking about birth in hospitals, some of whom have started attending home births under a liberal status.

It might sound extravagant to define *liste-naissance* as a group of 'oppressed' people (mainly women), given that most members belong to the middleclass of developed countries who can afford personal computers and spare time for the Internet. However, oppression here is less the matter of economical status than the feeling of being victims of unnecessary medical interventions and unethical procedures with respect to the attendance of childbirth.

This applies to professional attendants as well (see Bel and Bel forthcoming). The social role of midwives in the hospital environment is increasingly perceived as one of subordination to medical doctors and technology (DeVries and Barroso 1997). Liberal midwives are indeed more autonomous, but the very fact that they interact with less than 1 per cent of families opting for home births results in a *de facto* marginalization. In France, it is not uncommon to ostracize supporters of home birth as members of a *'secte'* (cult organization) whose *guru* would be the midwife.

Thus, discussions on the list highlight the perception of families being victims of an oppressive techno-medical system—the 'birth machine' (Wagner 1994)—in the face of which any sort of individual response is exposed to a strong social rejection. Indeed, criticizing the medical system *per se* is commonsensically perceived as a refusal of the 'comfort' and 'security' allegedly provided by the medicalization of childbirth (see discussion in Tew 1998; Bel and Bel forthcoming). The disavowal of analgesic epidurals, for instance, is ridiculed in much the same way opponents to nuclear power are said to yearn for a return to the days of oil lamps and horse carts.

In sum, many list members introduce themselves as powerless, voiceless and isolated individuals with a strong desire to reverse the alienating process of putting their destinies into the hands of professional medical caregivers, under circumstances critically significant for the healthy pursuance of their family lives.

The Flesh and History of Individual Members

After setting up the list on a public list server, moderators had to face attempts of semi-anonymous subscriptions. It was decided that membership must be nominative, and each applicant was further prompted to send a personal presentation exposing her/his personal motivations for joining the list. Presentations were also asked to all current list members and the ones who did not comply with the new rule were signed off by moderators.

Presentations are circulated on the list and membership is approved the following day if no objection has been raised. This procedure discards about 50 per cent of the applicants who never send their presentations.

Presentations are stored in a database that is accessible via a simple link on the web. Making it easy to retrieve personal presentations (and edit one's own) was essential for the perception of *liste-naissance* as a community of 'real' people. Unlike my 'virtual' friend Paul, people become 'real' when they have both a full name and history. This encouraged list members to talk about the significant events of their daily lives, indeed everything directly linked with pregnancy, childbirth and parenting, but sometimes off-topic stories and statements contributing to a more accurate picture of their personalities and expectations.

A radical change occurred in October 2000, when a dozen list members met for the first time in Paris after attending a conference. No pictures had been exchanged beforehand, and all were eager to discover the faces of persons who had already become their close friends through regular communication via the list. This physical recognition might have been the starting point of the kernel of 'permanent' active writers that is giving an impetus to the entire group.

The Memory and Flesh of *liste-naissance*

With the rapid growth of the list after fall 2000, more and more list members sought 'real-life' contacts with others living in the same area. New contacts are often reported to the list, thereby enhancing the awareness of a 'social fabric' of parents concerned with pregnancy and childbirth. The earlier social fabric (or 'birth culture') has been torn apart by many factors: the increasing medicalization of childbirth, the dislocation of joint families and alienating lifestyles imposed by housing and job constraints in cities.

At the local scale, some non-profit societies and informal groups play an important role in reconstructing the social fabric of birth. At the global scale, the discussion list may be viewed as an attempt to interconnect existing pieces of the fabric and isolated individuals. 'The list is my family!' said a member.

Because of its heterogeneous, non-ideological and transient nature, *liste-naissance* might not be perceived as a 'birth community' with aims similar to those of North American networks, for example, [to] augment collaborative marketing efforts for birth professionals and create pockets of activism to promote birth change and the midwifery model of care (Yula and Heffelfinger 2000). Far from these objectives, *liste-naissance* does exist as a 'body' with two essential features: *memory* and *flesh*.

The memory of the list is basically its archive. The list server has its own in-built search engine for 'introspective' tasks. However, due to the growth of this extensive memory, and because its access is restricted to list members, it is also necessary to build up a comprehensive replica of it 'at the surface'. This is achieved by publicly accessible web pages tracing the most significant discussion threads, technical points and personal testimonies, notably birth stories.

The 'flesh' of *liste-naissance* grew in list-related encounters that took place after the first historical meeting in October 2000. In August 2001, a group of 60 adults and children met during three days in a summer camp near Forcalquier in the south of France. The organization was reduced to minimal tasks, that is sharing expenses and material work. There was no agenda for this meeting. The group sat in a circle and worked as a 'free speech forum' with no moderator and no time limitation—much like the list in 'real time'. Participants had introduced themselves and listed the topics they felt like discussing during the encounter. All sessions lasted for two to three hours and were tape recorded. Each session started with a collective decision on which of the pending topics should be examined in priority.[3]

The Forcalquier summer camp in 2001 was evaluated as a great success. It had a deep impact on the perceptions, sometimes even personal histories, of couples who had taken part in its work. Several expecting parents who had come with a sensation of hopelessness felt empowered and experienced beautiful home births a few months later. Evidently, the fact that whole families had been invited to participate—not only pregnant women 'plus the father of their child'—contributed to casting a family-centred, rather than woman-and-midwife perception of childbirth and care of the new born.

After summer 2001, several encounters on the same organizational pattern took place, notably one near Charleroi (March 2002) and another one in Forcalquier, France (summer 2002). It has become obvious that a (heterogeneous) community of friends—an 'organic body'—is growing within the (heterogeneous) 'virtual' community of inquiry embodied by the list.

The Time-space Structure of a Mailing-list Community

An unmoderated discussion list with its archive and database of presentations is characterized by a manifold reappropriation of communication space and time, as illustrated below.

Communication Space:

- *Where:* There is no need to decide on the place of a meeting and make travel arrangements for remote participants. The place is 'everywhere' in cyberspace. Members are often warned against geocentric normative statements since membership is not restricted to a small territory.
- *Up to where:* Although space is not located, it is precisely delimited by membership, with the possibility for each member to examine its content (the presentations of list members).

- *From where:* Every member may decide 'where to sit' with respect to the current discussion thread: being active as a writer, a reader, or selectively discarding messages. With simultaneous threads, a member may even sit in several places, or move from one to the next at different moments.
- *Focus:* A message may be written as an answer to a particular person's statements, or explicitly addressed to all. It is up to writers to adjust the scope of their communication by designating the potential addressees of their messages. This includes off-list exchange in narrow groups and the creation of subgroups.
- *Growth:* Off-list subgroups may in turn evolve as self-standing discussion lists. During the past year, *listenaissance* prompted the creation of several related lists. Once it has grown to a critical size, the 'swarming' or 'hort cutting' of a discussion list may be viewed as a spatial expansion bearing witness of its vitality. In physical gatherings with limited material resources, it would be much more difficult to imagine similar migrations of individuals or groups.

Communication Time:

- *When:* Members may react to messages or start a new discussion thread at their convenience—including messages that were broadcast and discussed before their admission.
- *Up to where:* Members may expose their point of view *in extenso* without being interrupted. The persuasiveness of their assumptions does not depend on message length, physical appearance, gender, speech fluency, etc., although it could be argued that rhetorical and stylistic abilities (including French spelling and grammar) do make a difference.
- *From where:* Discussion threads are persistent over years thanks to the storage of messages, and message databases (both on the list server and in recipients' mailboxes) may be searched via electronic queries. It is

of great relevance to be able to trace a discussion thread from its very beginning and come back to the point at which a reader may have felt frustrated or offended by the turn of the debate. Previous messages are generally explicitly quoted for the sake of clarifying viewpoints. 'Rewinding' time to accurately review a discussion thread would be impossible in a physical gathering.[4]
- *Focus:* Electronic communication makes it possible to achieve an immediacy near to that of real time speech or Internet *chat*. However, since messages are preserved they may as well claim a permanent validity, as it is the case with press articles, essays, reports, pamphlets, etc.
- *Growth:* Participants in a discussion thread sometimes feel the need to break the linearity of time (leading to oblivion) and retain a trace of the discussion in a public web page. Thus, the list opens itself to the outside world while retaining its temporal-discursive dimension. This is particularly noticeable in the way technical information is made available to outsiders. Instead of storing a definitive statement in response to a particular question (for example, 'Are episiotomies any better than tears?'), the page reflects the actual discussion that took place on the subject. In addition, it invites readers (outside the list) to contribute with their own comments and pieces of information. This process may be viewed as one of 'hort cutting' a fragment of communication from the space-time boundaries of the list to another space and time of communication associated with web content.

From the 'Micro' to the 'Macro' Level: The Conditions for Social Mobilization

Electronic communication is both praised and decried because of its adequacy to prompt immediate action lacking reference to established power/information structures. Due to its speed and accuracy in sharing material among individuals and heterogeneous groups of people, it is typically the space of innovative, self-organizing and short-term activism.

In its early days, *liste-naissance* was meant to coordinate action groups and work as an observatory of the birth movement in France. It quickly became clear that focusing on individual, rather than group membership, had created the need for a separate list dedicated to information exchange. One of the list members created *lettre-naissance* with the set-up of an announcement list. She only receives messages, checks their relevance to the field, and broadcasts them via the list. The subscription to *lettre-naissance* (currently several hundred members) is anonymous and unrestricted.

Because of its insistence on individual commitment, and despite its 'global' existence in cyberspace, *liste-naissance* may be viewed as a means of communication between persons working at the 'micro' level of their nuclear families and close friends. Indeed, a few members are also active in non-profit societies at the local or global scale, but there is little reporting about this medium-scale activism in mainframe discussions. Further, there is no action group, agenda or strategy emerging from a consensus within the community of *liste-naissance*. For instance, while a few list members would support actions in favour of improving hospital care in childbirth (similar to the Changing Childbirth movement in the United Kingdom), others estimate that it makes more sense to exert one's own freedom by opting for home births, and a third subgroup feels best supporting the creation of free-standing birthing centres.

After a year of running the list, a few members came up with the idea of creating a non-profit society on French territory, or rather a federation of existing societies, as it was felt that the Internet would have a federative effect facilitating the coordination of local actions. This idea was quickly discarded because a federation already does exist and (arguably) claims to coordinate goings-on. In addition, the very fact of founding a non-profit society would imply setting up a hierarchical system run by elected representatives, which was felt inconsistent with the operation of the list.

The discussion focused on the actual meaning of the word 'citizenship' (*citoyenneté*) that has become trendy in France owing to the early anti-globalization movement (the protests in Seattle against the World Trade Organization (WTO) in 1999, ATTAC, etc.). A better English wording for 'citizenship' in this context would be *active democracy,* here meaning a system of non-hierarchic, self-organizational empowerment of citizens, in contrast with *formal democracy* whose basic operation consists of delegating power to elected representatives. The list itself (and list-related events) embodied the idea of active democracy in its ability to prompt the emergence of provocative ideas and innovative thinking about childbirth and educational issues.

We claim that the concept of *active democracy* is distinct from that of *participatory democracy* recently taken up as a motto by almost all French political parties. The latter evolved from the experience of *Participatory Action Research* (PAR) carried over three decades ago in South Asian countries:

> The argument essentially is that praxis and the methodology of PAR releases the creative energy of people, brings out the knowledge system and sets in motion an ecologically sound socio-political dynamics within each culture which can lead to a new kind of transitional pathway to sustainable development. It could also be the precursor of a new kind of state structure which should be participatory, pluralist, truly democratic, and supportive of the emerging 'seeds' at the micro-level. This support system also helps in the further multiplication of the process in a non-alienating manner. These do not follow the conventional socialist or capitalist state formations nor the traditions of institutions of the 'representative' parliamentary democracy or bureaucratic type. It promotes a new kind of committed leadership both external and internal; and an open state system based on freely communicated knowledge with the micro-level organisations providing a countervailing force. In other words PAR looks to a better sharing of power, a better balance between the state and people's organisations and of course between people and nature.
> (Wignaraja and Sirivardana 1998: 334–35)

The problem with the participatory process is that it is more consensus-oriented than inquisitive of irreducible confrontations between the different levels of reality experienced by actors involved in the same event. For instance, the 'micro' reality of birthing parents, the one of professional attendants and the 'macro' reality of scientific studies. Who are 'the people'? In the European birth movement, a typical participatory strategy has been the emergence of parent groups in support of strategies ultimately manufactured by professional birth attendants, for example the undebated focus on midwife-managed birthing centres (Bel and Bel forthcoming).

Active democracy may better be related to the *cooperative research methodology* (Maid et al. in this volume) which is both self-educational and productive of a 'culture'. Thus, it is more an informal (and constructively 'chaotic') dynamic process of empowerment and conscientization, than a formal informational framework aimed at structuring a fair distribution and delegation of power.

Producing a 'birth culture' cannot be dissociated from the construction of a 'social fabric of birth', which further requires the integration of all levels of reality, including scientific facts. A typical example of cooperative action using Internet resources would be the *Réseau des Marraines d'Allaitement Maternel*,[5] a self-organized network of breastfeeding women exchanging information and moral support.

Indeed, the growth of *liste-naissance*, once witnessed by the mass media, is likely to induce changes in the vision of childbirth at the 'macro' level. However, the necessary confrontation and integration of different levels of reality need to be worked out in a way that consolidates isolated efforts. For example, on 14 March 2002 a group of list members attended a seminar organized near Charleroi (Belgium) by *Carrefour Naissance,* a non-profit society. In the afternoon, a free-running discussion took place in an audience comprising parents, midwives, students and teachers of midwifery. Many questions relevant to the notion of individual responsibility in childbirth were raised and passionately debated by the audience. The entire discussion was recorded. The organizers felt that a transcription of the debate should be edited and displayed on a website, as it could serve as the starting point for more interactions between parents, birth activists and providers of midwifery/obstetrical care. In addition, on the same web page readers are invited to resume the debate in a specific discussion list with a public archive.[6]

This example highlights a process by which a particular event at the 'micro' level (a 'point in space and time') may provide rich informational material that is further exploited at the 'macro' level of the Internet (both global and time-unbound), with the possibility of promoting new discussion groups at the 'micro' level of a discussion list. Much in the same way, in April 2000, two years of discussions on *liste-naissance* had provided enough text material and links to set up an Internet portal dedicated to 'citizen' approaches of childbirth. Since its inception, the Naissance.ws portal[7] has become the reference for Internet resources on 'free and responsible' childbirth in French. Its home page contains links to more than 30 reference sites indexed by its internal search engine. It also links to articles, bibliographies, related websites, non-profit societies, and excerpts of discussion threads on *liste-naissance*. Bilingual list members have been invited to take part in translating documents for a better accessibility to French readers.

Thus, the Naissance.ws portal may be seen as a 'window in the global world' reflecting local and multifaceted visions of childbirth and progressive parenting in French-speaking countries. It has also been used as a showcase in public events such as the Eco-Festival exhibition that brought together more than 3,000 visitors on 7–9 June 2002.

Legal Aspects

The Naissance.ws portal is a collective emanation of the *liste-naissance* group. A consensus is sought on the list whenever a new website is candidating for a link on the portal's home page and indexing on its search engine.

When it came to finding an advertisement-free space for hosting the portal, *liste-naissance* was introduced as an 'unregistered non-profit society' so that it could become a member of the fraternet.org society offering low-cost web hosting to non-profit societies. The entire legal responsibility of the portal's content lies with the webmaster of the portal, as s/he alone is able to modify the web pages, taking advice from the list.

The webmaster is also the 'owner' of *liste-naissance* and *de facto* (according to French law) responsible for the content of messages exchanged on the list.[8] In view of this, a management committee keeps an eye on the archive to delete any message that might turn out to be prejudicial to the list in the future, that is as new members join the list.

These points are of great significance because they underscore the need for a clear connection between the 'virtual' and 'physical' existence of the mailing list and its website, in compliance with the current regulation on electronic communication.

Conclusion

Using the same communication tool—electronic mail—makes it possible to construct a great variety of patterns of human communication. Users may work out different patterns, depending on the communication context and their level of self-implication in it. In other words, the tool itself does not decide on the quality, depth and durability of the exchange. Nor do its alleged limitations, as these can be worked around by other means. For instance, the excessive 'immediacy' of electronic mail in discussion groups is defeated by message archiving, while its 'impersonality' is neutralized by the ritual of personal presentations. Thus, there exist solutions to all limitations, once these have been clearly spelled out, much in the same way there exist solutions to problems in 'real life' conflicts once there is a real desire on both sides to overcome them.

It remains that constructing a sustainable framework for social mobilization via the Internet (websites, discussion lists, etc.) implies a clear strategy for articulating the 'micro' and 'macro' aspects. There are steps in which encounters of 'physical' people need to take place, although these are not meant to facilitate the building or strengthening of uniform groups with consensual views on problems and solutions. The heterogeneity of the virtual community must therefore be positively taken into account in every type of action emerging from its work.

Notes

1. <http://www.ctanet.fr/naissance-liberte/>. Our support, though, proved insufficient, as they lost the court case in September 1999.
2. The current home page of the list is <http://fr.groups.yahoo.com/group/liste-naissance/>
3. Links to reports and photographs of all *liste-naissance* encounters may be found on <http://naissance.ws/events.htm>.
4. In summer camp discussions, we try to compensate the elusiveness of speech by sharing indexed sound recordings of the entire encounter. The new MP3 format has made it possible to store 10 to 20 hours of high quality sound on a single compact disc. Excerpts of the discussions may be later transcribed and published on web pages.
5. <http://www.reseau-mdam.org>
6. See <http://users.swing.be/carrefour.naissance/Articles/refl/TextDebat14mars2002.htm> for the full text and links.
7. <http://naissance.ws>
8. Evidently, any member using the list to broadcast illicit or defamatory messages might be banned on a majority decision by other members. It never happened so far.

References

Bel, Andréine, 'Three viewpoints on the praxis and concepts of midwifery: Indian *dais*, cosmopolitan obstetrics and Japanese *seitai*'. On-line document <http://www.bioethics.ws/dais/daicomp.htm> down loaded April 1999.

Bel, Bernard and Andréine Bel (forthcoming). 'Birth Attendants, between the Devil and the Deep Blue Sea', in B. Bel, B. Das, V. Parthasarathi and G. Poitevin, (eds), *Communication Processes 2: Dominance and Defiance* (New Delhi: Sage, forthcoming).

DeVries, Raymond G. and Rebeca Barroso, 'Midwives among the machines: Recreating midwifery in the late 20th Century', in H. Marland and A.M. Rafferty, (eds), *Midwives, Society and Childbirth: Debates and Controversies in the Modern Period* (London: Routledge,

1997), pp. 248–72. On-line version <http://www.stolaf.edu/people/devries/docs/midwifery.html>

Jitendra Maid, Pandit Padalghare and Guy Poitevin, 'The Micro-Dialectics of Communication' (in this volume).

Tew, Marjorie, *Safer Childbirth? A Critical History of Maternity Care* (London: Free Association Books, 1998).

Wagner, Marsden, *Pursuing the Birth Machine* (Camperdown NSW, Australia: ACE Graphics, 1994, original 1930).

Wignaraja, Poona and Susil Sirivardana (eds), *Readings on Pro-Poor Planning Through Social Mobilisation in South Asia. Vol. I: The Strategic Option for Poverty Eradication* (New Delhi: Vikas, 1998).

Yula, Cynthia and Katie Heffelfinger, 'How to Build a Birth Network', *Midwifery Today*, 56, *Building a Birth Community*, 2000, pp. 10–14.

12

COMMUNICATION FOR SOCIO-CULTURAL ACTION:
'Is the Discourse "on", "for" or "of"?'

JITENDRA MAID, PANDIT PADALGHARE, GUY POITEVIN

The concept of communication is far from being univocal or possibly universal. All around the world, for instance, a number of grassroots action groups (Weid and Poitevin 1981; Sheth 1984) and so-called new social movements (Laclau 1985; Escobar and Alvarez 1992; Amin 1993) share a somehow iconoclastic approach to those conventional theories and usual practices familiar to experts in the field of modern mass media (Habermas 1995: 58; White 1995: 34–36, 241–47). They look for alternative modes of communication geared to processes of people's sociopolitical organization, networking and empowerment (His 1996; Sen et al. 2004). They challenge the common illusion that the immense possibilities arising from new technologies of communication necessarily provide safe avenues for democratization (de cuéllar 1995: 103–27). They ground their agency on two basic axioms: a recognition of the common man's creative potentiality, and the denunciation of social communication marketing. They share the view that communication is too serious a matter to be abandoned to professional practitioners and consultant agencies. Their experience is that the more one professionalizes in the mass communication systems, the more one moves away from the voice of the man in the street. Their intervention as social actors is motivated by a common concern, namely with challenging structures of unilateral communication and information. Their objective is to break the monopoly of dominant minorities which one-sidedly create and impart knowledge. Their aim is to help those kept away from the centres of knowledge creation, deprived of access to information, and alien to processes of decision making speak for themselves and count as full fledged social partners.

Restoring a Democratic Mode of Communication

As a whole, four main perspectives can be identified as motivating and shaping the objectives and methods of sociocultural action at the grassroots level. They specifically distinguish processes of grassroots communication from techniques of mass communication.

First, the basic aim is to promote voices till now purposely silenced, through facilitating processes of self-expression and sharing of knowledge. This goes with a positive appreciation of cultural singularities and indigenous knowledge (de cuéllar 1995: 52–78, 211–13). For a number of members of local action groups, the option mainly results from the experience of failure with top-down communication patterns where there are 'transmitters' who know and 'receivers' who swallow. Some of them realize with bitterness that they have been subjected as youth to authoritarian indoctrination, as political militants to ideological brainwashing, as 'social workers' to the vested interests in modernization of private or state agencies, and that they have accordingly subjected others to the same through dogmatic postures and propaganda campaigns. They wish to no longer repeat the same blunders in their own practice. Many would recognize themselves, in one way or the other, in the following testimony: 'I was committedly involved in an underground movement. I have been in prison. But the Great Evening never came. Precisely because I imposed a vision of things on the others.'

Second, there is the persuasion of the distinctive characteristics—richness, creativity and greatest diversity—of the modes of grassroots communication. This goes with a higher appreciation, on account of their greater relevance, of those modes of communication where human relations retain the foreground. Significant attention is being given in this regard to the specificity of oral modes of expression (Poitevin and Rairkar 1996; Poitevin 2000a, 2001b). The category of 'orature' has been framed against the concept of 'literature' to circumscribe the distinctiveness of 'letter', namely technologies of writing, and the rule of written texts (Poitevin 2000b, 2001a).

Three constitutive dimensions conceptually differentiate 'orature' as a distinct régime of cognition, expression and symbolic communication. The first component is the actual context in which the sociocultural action is performed as a singular act of expression and communication. This dimension is so determinant that the key to deciphering the import of the event may reside in the performance itself with all its extra-linguistic features and other concrete modalities of communication. Second, in the course of the performance, the social actor adjusts and transforms if needed his/her speech according to the reactions of the audience. Effective social performers are those gifted with the capacity to interpret the will of the majority and possibly carry it further. The third dimension is that of semiosis as production and transmission of meaning through signs. At this level, rhythm, lyrics, intonation, tunes and melody (singing and even dancing are common elements of effective grassroots agency) are pregnant with a metaphoric potency which transforms the language, and forcefully expresses what ordinary speech cannot verbalize. These linguistic tools and strategies of communication specific to popular oral traditions are essential constituents of effective processes of grassroots communication.

Third, strategic options direct local action groups towards committing communication processes to serve the dynamics of social and cultural transformation (Chatterjee 1993). This goes with a wish to restructure systems of human relations along lines of wider responsibility of all partners and greater accountability of those vested with authority and power through transparency of control systems (Mattelart 1980). Communication cannot be conceived as a category for itself in a social vacuum; that is to say substantively defined in isolation from given political and organizational processes. Democratization is the political category against which action groups conceive of it, though not as a panacea, by transcending restrictive notions of democracy in terms of state formal institutions and the rule of administrative procedures. Emphasis is placed instead on micropolitical dynamics and everyday initiatives directed against entrenched circles of power (Orbe 1998). Such active citizenship cannot but be rooted in local forms of communication, building up an organized strength of people raised against top-down, institutionalized flow of information and knowledge (White 1995: 167–81). There is a circularity between the emergence of specific modes of communication and a concept of democratization defined as the dialectic interplay of integration in the mechanisms of collective choice, on the one hand, and, on the other hand, a capacity to resist and reshape.

Fourth, the firm persuasion is that the creation of knowledge really conducive to the progress of mankind is a function, in the last instance, of the intensity and openness of the forms of social communication obtaining at any level of the social fabric. This goes with the theoretical assumption that culture is a process of constant osmosis through exchange and sharing (Martin 2001). In brief, culture is synonymous to inventive participatory communication. Communication means the capacity to discuss, comment and modify messages.

Base Action Group: A Communication Setup

In the remote villages and hilly tracts (talukas of Velhe, Mawal, Wadgaon, Ambegao, Junnar) of the western Ghats as well as in the flat and drought-prone eastern parts (talukas of Shirur, Dhound, Indapur) of the same district of Pune (western Maharashtra), a score of local action groups have operated under the name of '*Garib Dongari Sanghatna*' (GDS: *Organization of the Poor of the Mountains)* for the last two decades. They comprise of villagers—men and women, the latter in a greater number, youth and children, middle-aged and elders—from the lower social and economic strata of neighbouring villages. They belong to any caste—most of them are Maratha since a great majority of the population belongs to this caste—while others belong to Scheduled Castes, Scheduled Tribes and nomadic communities. They presently number about 100 volunteers. None of them is in any way formally qualified for 'social work', but everyone is expected to progressively become more knowledgeable and competent as agents of social and cultural transformation. None of them would consider himself or herself as the 'staff' of a non-governmental institution with particular programmes or domains of social work, but as one from the marginalized sections of the village community acting on his/her own initiative, together with fellow villagers, out of a will to social and cultural transformation. As a response to the felt local needs and challenges, they spontaneously volunteer to act collectively and intervene as per their capacity to act and their level of social perception. To this effect they hold regular monthly meetings for evaluation, planning and self-learning. Along with an increasing experience of social and cultural intervention, a continuous self-learning process aims at enhancing a capacity of social critique and reflexive consciousness regarding the dominant systems of symbolic communication.

The one among them with more experience and personal authority is considered the 'main animator' of the group with a function of coordination more than leadership. The number of members in each group varies from a couple to 10 or 15, each at a different level of intervention capacity. The groups themselves, in the course of time, sometimes grow, sometimes diminish, some new groups emerge, some disappear, depending upon the clarity of motivations of the members and their personal evolution. Some members develop a stronger sense of accountability to local communities and accordingly take up wider responsibilities; they may try to raise new groups in nearby areas or specific study groups concerned with particular tasks. Some do not stand the trial of time and constant group evaluation, they then discontinue. This is considered a sign of group maturity. Representatives of each local group attend a monthly general coordination meeting.

The methodological perspectives are that of a pedagogical process, on the basis of practices of social transformation, of social, political and cultural awareness originally termed 'conscientization' by Paulo Freire (Freire 1972; Weid and Poitevin 1981: 39–66). The objectives are an organization of the deprived and oppressed sections grounded on a prior collective, critical understanding on their part of the structural causes of underdevelopment. These causes are embedded in and operate through, dominant systems of symbolic and social communication, whether traditional or modern or both.

A critique of the discourse of 'liberal democracy' becomes in this regard a particularly important point of departure in a series of steps of social critique focusing on the systems of communication control; the reason is that liberal democracy is blindly assumed to be a school of democratic freedom and equality.

1. Liberal political and economic democracy gives but a formal and abstract freedom to those deprived of economic power, choice and actual participation in decision-making processes at any level, cultural, social, economic and political. It is still as much a chance as a challenge as it opens a space of communication for the marginalized to possibly make their voice heard.
2. An effective citizen's democracy is a matter of grassroots processes of communication as it means a meaningful participation in the decision-making processes at the local as well as the state and national levels. This implies that the disprivileged are (a) listened to and no more made use of and manipulated; (b) capable of expressing their own needs with a sense of emergency, priority, self-respect and the conscious authority of knowledgeable and assertive citizens; (c) feel confident and competent to articulate and claim alternative policies in respect of basic needs and rights; and (d) prove capable of organizing themselves to fight for their own rights, resist oppressive practices of any kind, define, claim and enforce alternative schemes, policies, laws and regulations meeting the every day needs of the many.

3. Many short-cuts towards development and social transformation are advocated under the auspices of development communication studies with the assistance of the powerful resources of modern information technology associated with the catchword of development: *ad hoc* welfare or palliative economic schemes designed by alien agencies, top-down planning and management by elites, enlightened control let alone dictatorship by political interests, crash development policies and modernization ideologies, etc. All prove short of a genuine democratization on account of various communication failures or misdeeds which are not a matter of snags in the technology of information.
4. Collective empowering of the deprived is best achieved through cooperative self-learning procedures, that is to say, through making the sharing of knowledge between all those concerned the avenue toward appropriate knowledge creation. Multilateral exchange or communication of knowledge is an effective way towards counter balancing the hegemonic control of dominant symbolic systems of communication and their agencies.
5. This self-education through communication is antithetic to formal teaching and unilateral guidance by outside experts. It is an analytical and critical thinking process set in motion from within the community through attempts of collective self-learning reflecting upon attempts of autonomous cultural action. It is an awakening process, immediately conducive or directly geared to a committed practice of transformation. This education qualitatively differs from a mere transfer of information which communication usually happens to be equated with.

Cultures of Dominance, Breaches of Communication

Confronted with these perspectives on issues of people's communication processes and practices of development communication, the volunteers of *Garib Dongari Sanghatna* observe that they used to face a number of challenges and handicaps raised by prevailing modes of social communication, which actually proved to work as breaches of communication.

> Though the word samvad, 'communication', is not known in our villages, people use other expressions and words which convey the same meaning. It is obvious that if we do not speak with each other how could we understand one another? But in our society, if we raise the questions: Who is speaking with whom? How is he/she speaking? What will he/she speak? How is he/she behaving? All answers are predetermined by the norms of established social structures which offer a ready made framework for different prescribed patterns of social interaction.

The first wide breach of communication is between villages and cities as a result of education. The gates of education are open to all in India and students flood educational institutions. But the framework of education being essentially class-ridden and geared to aims of social reproduction, this type of education creates chasm in the society far from facilitating communication.

Nowadays the youth have developed the idea that village means 'inferiority', 'debasement', 'impossible progress', 'habit of bearing hurdles'. Rural youth are not willing to utilize their intellectual and physical skills to improve the villages from where they come. For employment or education they go to cities where they become urbanites. They do not even look back to the village from where they come. And if by chance they happen to go and visit their own village, they behave in a self-important way to show their superiority and express their feeling that people living in villages are very unfortunate. In reality, these youths remain alien in urban areas. They become rootless by a double rift of communication and belonging.

> In the school, the teacher tells the students: 'Listen and accept!' In the village, the social and political leader talks and the villagers listen. People listen to and obey

those who have both wealth and information, but share neither. People give honour and listen to those who enjoy social prestige. In this society people have imbibed such ideas that 'one has to obey teachers and elders,' 'no genuine knowledge without a guru, a master,' 'knowledge comes with physical punishment.'

People are proud of a culture which gives honour and status to elites and high castes. This cultural power is a comprehensive culture of dominance which has the strength of welding together social and political power. To keep the role of social leadership, Brahmins become social workers. This is the situation in the villages. At the state level, the same thing happens through such mottos as *swadhyaya parivar*, that is, moral and religious 'rearmament' of 'teacher groups', or the Balasaheb Thackeray Shiv Sena movement. At the national level, the same thing happens through shankaracharyas and mullahs. That is why when the communication media are in the hands of the members of higher castes, they try to impose their cultural patterns which repress and exploit the deprived.

The effectiveness of social communication depends on the personality, sex, age, caste of the individual as well as his position and authority in the society. Let us take the example of government servants: we see that they cannot take a clear stand regarding their superiors. Let us take the example of the farm owner and the farm labourer: we see how the landowner enforces his ideas to safeguard his own interest and that the farm labour accepts them as he has no choice, for the sake of his own survival. Farm labour accepts subservience for fear of losing the job. For similar reasons, government servants in the lower cadre are always afraid of transfers or dismissals and keen to oblige their boss.

In short, this is a one-way communication. This method of communication reinforces the rigidity of the existing social system. To 'keep the honour' of the superiors, people have imbibed the tendency to behave according to prevalent value systems and observe traditions and customs, *ritirivaj*, caste rules and habits, all that goes under the name of *niti-dharma*.

If we turn towards rapport in the family, it is a pattern of disharmony. Educated youth tend to belittle others: they insult their old and illiterate parents. They do not communicate with their parents. We came in contact with some educated boys when we were collecting grindmill songs. We enquired whether in their family women knew grindmill songs. They emphatically told us that nobody in their family knew such songs. But when we visited one house and discussed with the mother of the boy, we discovered that she knew many. Her son was shocked to know that his mother could remember and sing a number of grindmill songs. He then felt guilty because he did not know anything about his mother. This is only typical of a general attitude.

If we consider the way a husband and wife mutually look at each other, we see that the man by right needs a 'servant' to serve him while the woman needs an 'owner' to exercise power on her. We can imagine the kind of relationship which prevails between a husband and wife through the words that they use when they address and call each other. A wife calls her husband 'owner', *malak*, 'master of the house', *ghardhani*, 'manager', *karbhari*, 'they', *te*, 'god bride-groom', *navardeo*, etc. A husband calls his wife: 'family', *kutumba*, 'our people', *mandali*, 'she', *ti*.

The rule of the family system states that there is the one who 'tells' and the other who accepts. The head of the family 'tells' and the other members of the family accept. The mother-in-law 'tells' and the daughter-in-law listens. The husband 'tells' and the wife listens. The father 'tells' and the children obey.

The son is considered the future support of the family. 'The lamp of the lineage' or 'the stick for the old age' are idioms used for the son. Parents educate and shape a son in such a way that he will support them in their old age and live his life according to their wishes. If a son behaves against the wishes of his parents, for example, if he marries without their consent, then the parents do question his attitude with the following terms: 'Have we given you birth to bear such misbehaviour on your part? We repent from having given you birth.' Children have no authority to take their own decisions. They have to obey parents unless they prefer to bear the wrath of society.

When we consider such examples, we naturally come to

the conclusion that society lacks communication. What exists is 'miscommunication,' *vi-samvad*, distorted communication and not *sam-vad*. Where nobody communicates on an equal footing how can we call it *sam-vad*? Under that word, one tries to cultivate a culture of subservience, and through that to maintain one's own ascendancy over each other. Everybody tries to subjugate someone else. We see only grounds of divide, imparities and conflicts in that culture.

In such a cultural environment, two correlated consequences follow. On the one hand, the deprived tend to become status quoist, dependent and passive, submissive and subservient. They behave like sheep. On the other hand, as a result, the existence of a number of deprived groups and communities raises serious concerns in some quarters among the better-off sections. Social workers and non-governmental agencies are bound to crop up and come forward for the upliftment of the so-called 'poor', those that all the systems of social and symbolic communication of which they are the beneficiaries and have the monopoly have actually 'marginalized'. Government agencies feel obliged to chalk out welfare schemes for the 'destitute'. NGOs and the government make up their mind and resolve to work for the progress and development of social sections which on account of their 'culture of poverty' condemn themselves to lag behind and remain backward for their fault only.

The fact is that people who conceive of themselves as community leaders, 'social workers',[1] *karyakarta*, educated elite feel that 'others do not understand anything', that society is 'stupid and ignorant', that those 'backward' are naturally reluctant to listen, cooperate and change their traditional customs. They intervene under the illusion that 'society will develop if they listen to me.' That is why they are always lecturing, taunting and advising people about ideals to be followed. If society ignores them, they stigmatize that society as adamant. They show off a great concern for the upliftment of 'the poor' and 'the backward'. Pretentious and self-conceited, they deem themselves different. This is the reason why society hardly allows them to come close or does not enthusiastically respond to their initiatives. Society never feels in affinity or communication, *su-sam-vad*, with them.

The communication gap only widens and may become unbridgeable. Moreover we disagree with their attempts and concepts of development.

The process of development is elusive because it carries assumptions and objectives alien to the basic needs and expectations of the deprived. Development as we understand it would not really start as long as there is no wide exchange of ideas. If we want development we must have mutual communication between the government and people based on equality, confidence and friendship.

> Inside the Mulshi dam area (Pune District, Maharashtra), on the slopes of the mountain, is a village called Pomgao, where the agriculture depends on rain water. In the village, there is only one well which provides drinking water, but it dries up in summer and people have to walk a distance to fetch water from the dam. The Govt. has sanctioned a tap-water scheme which will cost thirty lakhs rupees [$67,720], the cost of which is supposed to be reimbursed later on by the villagers on the basis of water taxes. The scheme is prepared with no consideration for the ideas of local population: it is based on lifting the water from the dam and will provide only drinking water. People have an alternative scheme in their mind. A stream flows near the village and a much less costly tank can be built on it. The water from that small percolation tank can be used also for the fields. The percolating water will feed the well which will then not dry up in summer. In irrigated fields, people can take cash crops like vegetables. This will provide them with an opportunity of increasing their income and paying the increased water taxes. But the government or local leaders do not listen.
>
> There should be at the start an awareness that common people have some knowledge. We GDS animators do not consider the people as stupid and ignorant. Local communities can determine themselves their own 'ideal development' programme. Somebody from outside should not impose it on them. Local collectives are themselves conscious of what is proper or improper.

This is our conviction. The communication between local population and those from outside, experts and officers, should take place on an equal footing. They can talk with each other and behave with each other without any assumption that one is superior and the other one inferior. We are engaged ourselves in creating an atmosphere conducive to a dialogue and behaviour taking place on a basis of full equality between all those concerned in the respect of the variety of competence, experiences and roles.

GDS' activities consist in analysing together with the people established ideas and structures. Through such discussions the limitations of the thoughts and structures prevalent in the society are brought to the notice of the participants of the discussion. In other words we are trying to develop a concept of culture which will give opportunity, dignity, self-respect to the oppressed and empower them as per their resources and capacities. This is possible only where and when the deprived start speaking up for themselves with full knowledge of their case.

Communication Begins as a Capacity to Speak Up

No one is voiceless, but many are silenced. In such circumstances, how do we promote the 'voices from silence'? What could be the conditions of the possibility for recovering a capacity to speak up? How can the first word be genuinely uttered in the speaker's own name so as to break the inbuilt compulsion of imposed silence? Communication starts as a social training to speak up on one's own name.

Let us immediately discard in this regard a very common and trivial misconception. Artificial plays, group games, technical gadgets are designed by experts in communication techniques in a number of books for the use of graduate social and community workers (Weid and Poitevin 1981: 101–3). The latter are naturally anxious to draw people out of their inhibitions and obtain from them successful cooperation and implementation of programmes of poverty alleviation, social welfare and the like entrusted to them by a funding agency. These communication tools hardly meet the needs of social actors who are not facing handicaps of a psychological nature to be overcome by simulation techniques. Those who tried to make use of them were soon disillusioned.

Adequate strategies ought to directly address the social constraints which impose silence. As these constraints are embedded in patterns of social and symbolic communication, these inhibiting patterns, their cause and their forms are to be discovered, denounced and dealt with.

Dynamics of Democratic Communication

The following are particular examples of strategies of sociocultural action meant to initiate and restore elementary forms of democratic communication processes on the part of the marginalized.

> One difficulty may be that 'many are the cases where the nature of what peasants or inhabitants of a neighbourhood want to express disturbs us in several ways.' It is therefore advisable to be listening to what the groups really want to express or for that matter repress, even if this is disconcerting and throws wide open the gaps prevailing between the cultures, the classes and groups within the same city, the same area or the same country. A preliminary step consists in fully acknowledging the extent and nature of the gap, and on the part of the communicators eschewing anxiety about possibly unwanted demands and claims.
>
> Listening is not a passive, descriptive, detached or impersonal attitude especially when cultural gaps are wide and communication forms alien. The latter call for an effort of decoding. This undoubtedly is not a matter to be left only to semiotic treaties, linguistic surveys and the like. This endeavour requires a patient apprehension from within of the meanings

of symbolic forms, mindsets and behaviour. A genuine knowledge of 'the other' means an understanding of the significance of those forms with regard to systems of social rapport.

Two elementary attitudes are required on the part of animators–facilitators as basic foundations of their entire practice. First, links of personal acquaintance and confident relationship, spread over a period of time, are an unavoidable initial moment towards free speech on the part of the marginalized. Second, a conscious discipline of self-imposed silence should remain a permanent rule.

When a rural animator of GDS arrives in an area that he doesn't know, the first instruction that he is given is not to haste to do 'social work', but to just observe and establish personal relations with members of the community. He should simply get accepted by the community. This can last for months so that he feels at ease with the people and the people at ease with him.

Then, he can gather some of the inhabitants from the community in a free circle to discuss local issues that some people feel ready to take up. The small circle is a fundamental model for having a dialogue of a different nature, as opposed to traditional modes of information and forms of knowledge dissemination. This said and done, the fact of getting together in a small circle of concerned citizens, does not solve everything. There are women, for instance, who continue to hide their face behind their sari. At this stage, each one should introduce oneself and tell one's name. This may look trivial but it is not.

To make one's voice heard in a small circle of fellow villagers, for the first time, is already a fundamental step. Then each one would be drawn out as to speak as much as the other, no more, no less. The animator-facilitator should pay attention to silencing those who talk too much, and to stimulating the expression of those who do not dare to speak. This requires tact, authority and the knowledge of how to keep one's own mouth shut. As a rule, an animator-facilitator who does not know how to keep his mouth shut, may mainly prove counter-effective through unknowingly maintaining habits of passivity, dependency and inhibition as a result of his own untimely intervention. A pedagogy of self-imposed silence is the best way to obtain that those hitherto voiceless start voicing their own experience and be duly recognised.

Village sketch is used to facilitate a self-reflexive insight of the structures of social and symbolic communication by villagers themselves.

This is a typical example of our effort to make villagers realise the patterns of their everyday rapport of communication and/or isolation. Presently, we are organising a training meeting for local animators of the Poor of the Mountain from different villages. As an observation exercise, we start by requesting them to draw a map of their village. Each one has to draw on the map of his/her village in particular what will reveal the social structures, social relations and all forms of social communication or discrimination (e.g. meeting places, footpaths, distance between settlements or houses, the relative position of the latter, the signs of social differentiation, land distribution, cropping patterns, etc). The drawing and the minute study of each one's map in the group help animators to understand hierarchical and unequal forms of social relations, economic structures, cultural specificities, symbolic and linguistic forms of differentiation, etc. The skills expected to be acquired with this exercise are, in particular, a capacity of minute observation, the ability to discover the social and cultural import of each detail, a deep insight into the rapports of communication or exclusion which prevail. Others would bother themselves with statistical surveys: their results do not give as much to learn and understand as does an insight of the symbolic significance of the forms of every day rapport, and the structures of relations.

Reactivating spontaneous and traditional forms of communication among the marginalized and displaced communities often helps liberate a wish of self-expression, reappropriate a smothered heritage, liberate a repressed capacity to speak up, and retrieve one's self-esteem. Documenting, building up and thus revalourizing this collective popular memory helps individuals and collectives rediscover their historical roots and own with due appreciation and evaluation their patrimony. This is particularly the case with elder women recalling with pride grindmill songs (Rairkar 1993), elder story-tellers narrating again myths of yesteryears (Poitevin 2001b, 2001c) in front of young generations, traditional midwives giving detailed accounts of their expertise in midwifery, peasants explaining their traditional knowledge in respect of farming techniques, water conservation, herbal medicines, etc. and the way these traditional systems of knowledge are being learnt, capitalized, transmitted and improved. These systems are embedded in specific forms of social relations and symbolic communication.

Facilitating individuals' initiatives within their own environment is an effective step towards free self-assertion:

> To make village women, especially young women used to keeping silent in public, speaking up, is not easy. We sometimes may tell them: gather village children who don't go to school, and improvise some class for them. The main objective is not to teach the children to read and write. The objective is to help women break their shackles with an initiative which is not beyond their personal resources and that the village may appreciate. Then, further on, they will gain assurance and be capable of gathering young girls and conducting group discussions with them. The capacity to speak up is only progressively acquired and this progress cannot be dissociated from concrete initiatives. What matters to us is to create simple conditions in which people can start expressing themselves and acting on their own with some self-confidence, initially getting bold enough to speak about common things with common words, then later becoming capable of further assertive steps.

The strategy of those intervening from outside should aim at creating new spaces and at times promoting expressions of one's feelings, wishes, suggestions, dissatisfactions and initiatives, leading those hitherto deprived of such opportunities towards a free self-expression within a group (Poitevin and Rairkar 1993). Self-expression is a point of elementary or basic strategy. The voiceless should recover their capacity to articulate their smothered subjectivity. This is especially important with regard to women.

> The problems of deserted women are not individual or personal issues. Systems of social communication offer explanations for this. While establishing personal contacts between scattered and desperately isolated deserted women, the objective is to create a collective consciousness among such women through giving them a chance to come together and share their feelings. This leads them to understand that they are victims of social evils and that society is wrong in putting the blame and dishonour on them. We arrange personal meetings, group discussions. We have prepared on the issue and staged a street play in public squares, bus stands, market places using folk forms of expression. We may occasionally take the help of court and legislation, though the court offers only a very limited scope as it does not address at all the wide issue which is one of forms of personal and social communication. Through study groups and collective debates, we try to act at the level of every day relationships and systems of social relations. We bring together both the parties with their families for exchange and discussions. Such debates help solve individual problems while proving conducive to tackle issues of sociocultural transformation as they question the whole structure of symbolic communication.

The following general question may eventually guide a critical insight of communication processes and their dynamics: 'Is the discourse "on", "for" or "of"? Do the speakers speak for themselves, or do a few speak for the many?' In this regard, the small local group, in which the criteria of self-evaluation can be commonly agreed upon to measure the progress, is the milieu par excellence of initiation and training to effective practices of basic communication on an equal footing.

The small group of people from neighbouring villages meeting regularly generates soon the perception in the members that 'I carry also some weight in the society' on account of the discovery of one's capacity to think for oneself and act collectively with others. In-born but hidden potentialities come to the surface in individuals and the latter gain confidence in their capacity to achieve some change in their immediate environment despite a low social status. The group generates its own strength to the extent it cares for the weak to regain daring and strength through appropriate pedagogical efforts.

The pedagogical dimensions and needs that a basic action group can secure for its members are the following: finding the ways towards adequate information input as per the needs at a particular moment, learning communication skills enabling to articulate one's convictions and overcome fear, training in intellectual skills to observe and analyse, discovering through practices appropriate organisational methods, enlarging one's social insight through focussing on structural constraints, increasing reliance on one's hidden cultural resources and ability to act with success, etc.

Communication is an operational asset. Analytical tasks, evaluation, decision, intervention are most effective when carried out collectively. Cooperation and self-reliance in any substantial issue (theoretical perspectives, management, relations with superior authorities), and transparency are the key elements which the effectivity of the group depends upon.

Moreover, in the absence of external directive control, permanent collective self-learning and group evaluation are the necessary safeguards to disintegration and apathy. Their opposites are external guidance by experts with regard to the internal life of the collective, and advocacy by alien intermediaries with regard to the interests and objectives of the organisation. Both the practices would spell the end of an approach based on internal processes of communication and thwart the aim of a concrete initiation to active democracy.

Local groups are the best asset for self-learning attempts, that is to say, learning through collective brainstorming performed within small groups. This learning based on intense and systematic processes of personal interaction proves the most effective foundation of sociocultural action and cultural transformation. The programme 'Self-Learning Workshop' conducted by GDS for rural animators-communicators from all over the state of Maharashtra on the basis of the experience of GDS grassroots groups gives a pattern for such attempts. The experiment has given the participants great satisfaction over the last 12 years mainly because it meets needs of information (which could possibly be obtained elsewhere). It is increasingly found relevant and appropriate by the trainees on account of its practical initiation to democratic communication processes for social transformation at the grassroots level. The pedagogical structure of the training method makes a radical effort to break with all the 'miscommunication' challenges which stand as handicaps.

The full course consists of nine six-day, intensive and residential sessions held every alternate month in a Centre located in a common village with no environmental attraction to divert the attention, and offering austere, village-like accommodation. Nine sessions are required as the attitudes and skills to be generated through group dynamics and sharing of experience demand time to mature. The first sessions are dedicated to extended sharing of personal bio-data to build up attitudes of collective trust, introspective questions of personal identity and motivations, and queries to clarify the purposes of one's action as social agent.
The group usually comprises of twenty five participants. They are expected to come and attend, each time, after having prepared, on their own, a written report on any subject of their choice, relying on their intellectual

capacities, direct observation, personal experience and reading, as per their level of concern and commitment. Information and knowledge are secondary though important aims of the workshop. Each participant is to present his view and critical understanding of the social issues which he finds relevant, at that moment. Every participant progressively learns how to clearly and analytically articulate his/her own thoughts and submit them to the group scrutiny. Thought provoking discussions are expected. They are meant to develop a capacity of social critique. Participants get some new insight and new direction to the extent they are open-minded and accept the suggestions and questions of their companions. Absolutely free brainstorming is the basis of the intellectual progress. No experts are called to be passively relied on as upon an alien or elder authority from whom the last word would be expected as there is no such word.

Among the criteria of evaluation, besides the capacity to raise proper analytical questions, is a concern for the equal participation of all, the discipline of speech in formal sessions, the quality of listening in small study group, the respect for each one's experience especially of those who feel shy to intervene, the control over a fruitful use of time, the exploration of various modes of communication besides usual forms of speech especially through acting, role-play, mime, poetry, story-telling, singing, dancing, free physical expression in 'cultural programmes', drawing, posters, etc. We insist on transparency of the communication processes which should take place on an equal level. Nobody is big or small, every participant is rich of his/her own experience to share on equal footing with others, differences in literacy and formal education making no significant differences. The group of twenty-five as a milieu for the interplay of various dynamics of communication stands as the source and means of knowledge and sharing.

At the end of each six-day session a substantial report is prepared and circulated among the trainees who comment upon it in their own local group. The report becomes the basis for further discussion in the next session besides being used by the local group as an extension of the self-learning training. This spreads the benefit of the sessions, checks their impact and helps in creating chains of groups of like-minded social agents. The participants are enthusiastic about the experience and education that they get in the workshop. They help later to prepare and select the beneficiaries of further courses. A network of like-minded groups is progressively created at the level of the whole state.

The local group must be able to extent its democratic dialogue as to reach out to administrative officers.

Sometimes we invite officers to attend meetings of the organisation. We do not treat them as higher up people. We treat them at par with everybody. We do not allow them to make lectures and speeches about schemes. We take the precaution to warn them in advance that they have to come and discuss with the people, listening to them first, instead of lecturing them. In these meetings we sit in a circle on the ground, and officers have to sit likewise on the floor, in the same circle. The level of communication is equal and common, and not hierarchical. At the time of demonstrations, we also as a principle oblige the officers to come out of their office and meet the people directly, for complete transparency of the discussion.

Four Crucial Concerns

(1) Technical Means Offer Risks of Gadgetization

In view of a fear of gadgetization of the technical tools of communication, a controversial question is that of the alternate, exclusive or combined use of the traditional and modern forms of communication.

The standardization and miniaturization of modern technologies may wipe out locally specific forms to the benefit of a certain standardization. One is afraid to find the same communication technologies everywhere. Means of communication tend to be centre staged on account of their fascination and attractive sophistication. While increasingly becoming the focus, if not the aim in the operations of communication, they accordingly prove a handicap to actual people's communication. The latter tends to be perturbed, diverted towards other ends let alone controlled by rules of technical performances and market constraints.

Among the tools most questioned at the grassroot level is the video. The experience of many is that it is hardly democratic and does not significantly help to mobilize people. Its fascination is a matter of worry because it stands as a substitute to direct and actual communication between persons.

If video can keep a record of events and words (in any case for a limited period of about 10 years), can it really build up a lasting, collective and inspiring people's memory? If such is the case, how and on what conditions?

One positive impact on the common man of an elementary familiarity with video shooting and production is that this enables him to demystify the television itself. The peasant who sees himself on the screen realizes how the journalists themselves can tell lies. Moreover, he gets a sight of his own social appearance in the world at large, and of his everyday existence as in a mirror. The mirror effect opens the way towards a perception of self and feelings of self-esteem and self-confidence. Instead of being watched as a source of magic, video may give a chance to a democratic process.

(2) Ways from Micro Communication to Macro Processes?

Local communicators and catalysts of sociocultural transformation processes are particularly sensitive to the connection between local processes, overall policies and national politics. The passage from personal, micro and local processes, forms and networks of communication to impersonal, macro, regional, national and global institutions, channels and systems of communication is, on the one hand, strongly felt as a necessity, but, on the other hand, the ways and the modes of the nexus are unclear and problematic. Moreover when market and power—social, political and cultural—vested interests succeed in spreading their hegemonic control over systems of symbolic communication, the challenge becomes a dramatic one.

The issue is to be raised at various levels and in different terms. When a group has a specific experience to share and does it among its members, it really performs an effective work of communication. But when it wants to circulate its experiences among other such groups in the hope of building a network or weaving links of sustainable coordination, the result is often a reduced and lifeless product: there is no more communication but circulation in writing of dry information. Moreover, when the intent is to reach out to, and secure a decisive impact at, the level of public opinion, the challenge is still more serious and of a different nature as one does not know how to move from grassroots exchange to mass circulation.

(3) To Macro Communication through Mass Media?

An important aspect of the passage from the micro to the macro is the access to media of mass communication: 'How to reach the mass media, and contribute to the general political debate?'

This raises two elementary issues: training in mass media communication and the marketable quality of the product. Considering the modes and levels of operation of grassroots groups, and the nature of their strength and human resources, both the issues remain problematic. The controversy is confusing and inconclusive, first of all, for want of adequate parameters of reference with regard to the basic aims and needs of grassroots communication actors with regard to mass media. The following points may help clarify the discussion but do not provide a satisfactory answer.

The lack of training on the part of the communicators often leads to a 'poor communication for the poor'. As a result, popular newspapers may end up being used 'only for wrapping meat', and video materials lie on shelves for nobody due to lack of demand, want of network for their circulation and marketing constraints.

More significantly, 'poor communication' should not basically be defined in terms of only technical expertise. 'Quality' does not mean only technical quality, it means also 'relevance' to be assessed with reference to the aims and objectives of sociocultural action.

Reciprocally, with regard to the common viewers, there is the urgent need of a counter culture in respect of visual literacy. A colossal task of critical initiation is to be undertaken. Unfortunately, barring a few experiments by city based groups active among student youth, action groups seem totally unaware of the strategic importance of this wanted cultural action of the first order.

(4) From Hijacking to Cooperative Reappropriation

The rediscovery of the relevance of popular oral traditions as effective modes of symbolic communication with deep roots in the subconscious and the history of local communities, leads towards queries about the propriety of their reappropriation. Local communities, academic institutions, cultural agencies, political parties, tourism industries and ministries, commercial companies, etc. use them with a number of opposite purposes: as emblem of social distinction, as ground of assertive identity, as ethnic commodity, as means to maintain control, instigate rebellion or serve material gains. This raises ethical challenges when traditions are hijacked by people other than their natural heirs and turned into strategic tools for alien aims. Some non-governmental development organizations utilize these traditions to disseminate modern messages and induce people to implement their projects taking advantage of the popularity of traditional forms of expression.

In view of this present context, action groups should find time and competence to reflect upon the epistemological conditions of legitimacy of this reappropriation and apply their mind to the anthropological and methodological issues that such practices imply. The question may be stated as follows: how can local communities in a deeply modified sociocultural environment claim for their oral, cultural patrimony the capacity of strengthening present identities at the level of material development as well as social transformation? (Poitevin 2001c). How can the pitfalls of communalist obscurantism, political manipulation, confusing empathy, anachronic reading, archaic identification, commercial exploitation, fanatic nationalism, segregated identity, etc. be avoided?

In our perspective of a reflection geared to social action our answer is that of a cooperative research (Poitevin 2002: 352–54, 368–69), that is, of a process of communication at the level of knowledge creation itself.

Conclusion

Four lessons may be drawn from previous testimonies and reflections.

First, social transformation, democratization and production of knowledge on man and society are not functions of communication technology. One of the most dangerous illusions imparted by prevailing discourses on new technologies of communication, is the naive belief that these technologies would, *on their own,* open wide channels of free circulation of information and universal exchange of knowledge in the 'global village', revitalize political activity, expand the boundaries of social interaction and enhance social responsibility. It is the other way round. Only citizens with an increased sense of social commitment, a will to global political responsibility and a capacity of critical insight can painstakingly avail, in a significantly relevant manner, of the potentialities of present technologies of communication for monitoring processes of democratic structuration and innovative sharing of knowledge.

Second, 'social work' and 'social action' emerge, equivalently, as two distinct operational concepts and patterns of social communication. The process of democratization implies a clear cut operational divide between two types of social agency, namely, 'social work' which aims at modernization, improvement, change, development, welfare, uplift and the like of the 'poor' and 'destitute', on the one hand (White et al. 1994; Servaes et al. 1996), and, on the other hand, 'social action' which aims at self-assertion, social equity, dignity and the like, of the 'deprived' through political restructuration. In India, the prevalent neoliberal discourse of 'social work' presumes an external intervention by outsiders with a superiority in terms of means of articulation of needs and management skills of welfare projects (PRIA 1991). This approach and practice reinforce hierarchical orders and unequal class relations as they imply top-down forms of social relations, enhance attitudes of dependency and maintain the *status quo*. They smother processes of democratic communication. Against this, the discourse of 'social action' focuses on the capacity and responsibility of any citizen to intervene on its own initiative. This attitude aims at building a proactive democracy at any level, from knowledge creation to economic planning.

Third, the circularity of active democracy and grassroots communication has a component of revalourization of various forms of oral language. This points to the significant fact that democracy mainly belongs in orality (Ong 1982). Democracy is a matter of faith in the spoken word, of public debate and public opinion enlivened and enlightened by a play of questions endlessly linked up. Democracy means constant and collective assessment of viewpoints in the public square.

In modern societies, the evolution towards advanced stages of modernity has gone hand in hand with the development of writing technologies and the hegemony of the written word. This nowadays reinforces the power of the dominating elite classes which can master the production of written texts and impose their control through scriptures (in religious spheres), nation state constitutions (in political domains), judicial codes (in civil society), legislation (in national territories), literary standards (in language systems), etc., and legitimize these canons through investing them with a universal value. The written word brought about homogenization through general norms. Against these trends, oral forms of communication remain singular, local and spontaneous. Every one has equal access to his/her mother tongue and remains free to utilize the language in his/her own way to speak out his/her mind. If the written word is an argument of legitimacy and strength of the powerful then the spoken word is a claim to counter authority by the weak.

Fourth, orality points to more than the spoken word as it is a matter of rhythm and auditive prosody. Oral modes of directly human—non-technically mediated—communication represent a comprehensive régime of cognition, expression and communication which we defined as a system of intertwined rhetorics to be called 'orature' as opposed to 'literature' (Poitevin 2001a). This régime does not rest upon fixed written signs but on the various and flexible capacities of the human voice: lyrics, intonation, melism and tunes. The oral transmission of meanings through voice and personal physical presence transcends the limits of the verbalized through incorporating in varying proportions in the acts of social performance, three main communication strategies: language or speech acts use the words of a lexicon and a linguistic system, intonation or speech inflections use the lyric resources of poetry and the prosodic tools of a particular intonation system, tunes or melodies avail of the expressive potentialities of musical structures (Bel et al. 2000).

The rhetorics of 'orature' may suffer from 'technical' deficiencies with regard to norms ruling over systems of 'correct' communication. But this deficiency is possibly a blessing in disguise as this rhetoric infirmity is more than compensated by the symbolic potency of the gesture of the body, the intonation of the voice, the rhythm of the utterance, the rhyme of the verses, the tune of the song and the melism on particular words. The written sign is miserably deprived of all this. 'Orature' is coined to refer to this sophisticated, composite texture of intertwined rhetorical systems of expression and symbolic communication from which popular communication processes significantly draw their strength. A study of 'orature' would significantly help us to properly appreciate the full power of the communication potentialities vested in the human body as opposed to those credited to technical media of communication. Such studies are unfortunately missing but urgently wanted to give a proper account of the regime of expression and symbolic communication specific to processes of democratic transformation.

Note

1. The word 'worker' *karyakarta*, practically applies indistinctively to all kinds of social interventionists: local political volunteers, corporators, volunteers of neighbourhood groups of youth such as those who manage the Ganpati festival for instance or other festivals for that matter, muscle men in slum areas, those also who are trained 'social workers' such as MSW graduates or those with only practical training, people otherwise called 'field workers', on the whole all those involved in the activities of a voluntary action group or any type of social organization whatever its domain, from culture to politics, from arts to development.

References

Amin, S., 'Social Movements at the Periphery', in P. Wignaraja (ed.), *New Social Movements in the South* (London/New Jersey: Zed Books 1993), pp. 76–100.
Bel, Bernard, Geneviève Caelen and Hema Rairkar, 'Say it in singing! Prosodic Patterns and Rhetorics in the Performance of Grindmill Songs'. Contribution to the Seminar on Linguistic and Inter-Disciplinary Approaches as Critical Resources in Development, 12–14 July 2000, Mysore: Central Institute of Indian Languages.
Chatterjee, Ashoke, 'The Problem' *Seminar, Communication and Chang, 408*, 1993 (August) pp. 12–15.
de Cuéllar, Javier Pérez (ed.), *Our Creative Diversity. Report of the World Commission on Culture and Development* (Paris: Unesco Publishing, 1995).
Escobar, A. and S. Alvarez, *The Making of Social Movements in Latin America: Identity, Strategy and Democracy* (Boulder, CO: Westview Press, 1992).
Freire, Paolo, *Pedagogy of the Oppressed* (Harmondsworth: Penguin, 1972; New edition, New York: Continuum, 2000).
Garnham, N., 'The Myths of Video. A Disciplinary Reminder', in F. Inglish (ed.), *Capitalism and Communication: Global Culture and the Economics of Information* (New Delhi: Sage, 1990), pp. 20–55.
Habermas, Jürgen, *Postmetaphysical Thinking* (Cambridge: Polity Press, 1992).

Habermas, Jürgen, *Moral Consciousness and Communicative Action* (Cambridge: Polity Press, 1995).
His, Alain (ed.), *Communication and Multimedia for People. Moving into social empowerment over the information highway* (Paris: FPH, 1996).
Laclau, E., 'New Social Movements and the Plurality of the Social', in D. Slater (ed.), *New Social Movements and the State in Latin America* (Amsterdam: CEDLA, 1985), pp. 27–42.
Mattelart, A., *Mass Media, Ideologies and the Revolutionary Movement* (Sussex: Harvester Press, 1980).
Martin, Denis Constant, 'Pratiques culturelles et organisations symboliques du politique', in Daniel Cefai (ed.), *Politiques culturelles* (Paris: PUF, 2001), pp. 117–35.
Ong, Walter J., *Orality and Literacy: The Technologies of the Word* (London and New York: Methuen, 1982).
Orbe, Mark P., *Constructing Co-Cultural Theory: An Explication of Culture, Power, and Communication* (New Delhi: Sage, 1998).
Poitevin, Guy, 'L'appropriation de la figure de Sita dans les chants des paysannes du Maharashtra', in Françoise Mallison (ed.), *Constructions hagiographiques dans le monde indien* (Paris: H. Champion, EPHE, 2000a). See online: *Sita's exile* <http://www.ccrss.ws/sita.htm>.
———, 'Popular Traditions, Strategic Assets', *Madhyam*, vol. XV, no. 2, 2000b (December), pp. 42–44.
———, *L'orature n'est pas la littérature*, 2001a Online: <http://iias.leidenunivnl/host/ccrss/orature.html>
———, 'Myth and Identity: The Narrative Construction of Self in the Oral Tradition of Vadar Communities', *Indian Folklore Research Journal*, vol. 1, no. 1, 2001b (May), pp. 81–122.
———, 'Folklore and Creativity', *Folklife, The Advent of Asian Century in Folklore*, vol. 1, no. 5, 2001c (April), pp. 14–25.
———, *The Voice and the Will. Subaltern Agency: Forms and Motives* (New Delhi: Manohar, 2002).
Poitevin, Guy and Hema Rairkar, *Indian Peasant Women speak Up* (Hyderabad: Orient Longman, 1993).
———, *Stonemill and Bhakti* (New Delhi: D.K. Printworld, 1996).
PRIA, *Voluntary Development Organisations in India* (New Delhi: Society for Participatory Research in Asia, 1991).
Rairkar, Hema, 'Songs of the Grindmill', *Seminar* 408, 1993 (August), pp. 30–33.
Sen, Jai, Anita Anand, Arturo Escobar and Peter Waterman (eds), *World Social Forum Challenging Empires* (New Delhi: The Viveka Foundation, 2004).
Servaes, Jan, Thomas L. Jacobson and Shirley A. White (eds), *Participatory Communication for Social Change* (New Delhi: Sage, 1996).
Sheth, D. L., 'Grass-root Initiatives in India', *Economic and Political Weekly*, vol. 19, no. 6, 1984, pp. 259–62.

Weid, Denis von der and Guy Poitevin, *Roots of a Peasant Movement* (Pune: Shubhada-Saraswat Publications, 1981).

White, Shirley A., K. Sasanandan Nair and Joseph Ascroft, *Participatory Communication. Working for Change and Development* (New Delhi: Sage, 1994).

White, Stephen K. (ed.), *The Cambridge Companion to Habermas* (Cambridge: Cambridge University Press, 1995).

2.3
Interrogation and Contestation

13

THE POLITICAL MEANING OF A RIVER:
Intellectuals and the Economy of Knowledge around the Narmada

JOËL RUET

Today's activist movements have various terrains—the local, the less material 'national opinions', the highly diffuse 'global' and its opinions together with their institutions. Being set in these *various* networks of groups and sympathies, knowledge has reached a rather ambiguous status. Indeed, 'knowledge in the fight' is always construed mostly through two main systems. In this 'information age' approach, the fact that information is not given per se, but produced specifically to a political agenda is occulted. On the other hand, we have the text-culture-ideology of the 'global village', that revolves around an implicit myth of commonality of issues, stakes and struggles all over the world, whatever the cultural specificities. This needs being explored and mythologies, be they in the intellectual or political terrain, must be unearthed. For we know since Foucault how knowledge conveys power, the economy of knowledge production and dissemination is central. Economy of knowledge, in as much as it articulates communication processes in a play with different stages, would form the analytical locus of this contribution, its illustrative focus being the intellectual and the flows of information which constitute the backbone of a series of political struggles against dam projects on the river Narmada, or what we call the (anti-dam) 'Narmada Movement'.

Communication processes at stake are far from being reified and are dynamically embedded into power structures, ideologies and solidarities. That way, communication constitutes the politics and reveals the nature of politics with respect to Narmada. In this essay, the first section deals with the general signification of politics using political philosophy that will serve as our base throughout this reflection. In the next section we analyse the communication networks as structures of power that revolve around the anti-dam protests. That is to say, communication as simultaneously revealing and shaping politics. In the final section we recall the centrality of the tribals in Indian democratic communication.

Autonomy/Heteronomy of Politics, and the Organic Intellectuals: Gramsci via Balibar

The Narmada debate, apparently, is about facts. These are known but, sadly enough, differently known by different 'experts'. Indeed, so-called 'facts' but also counter-facts and communication by 'experts', involve their situational subjectivity, on the first place of which is their ideological position on the aims and contents of development policies. For this reason, we will propose political philosophy as a framework of further analysis, and first examine in detail what is to be understood by the concept of politics.

Whose Narmada: 'Facts' for Describing or Ascribing?

The foundation stone of the first large dam over the Narmada was inaugurated in 1961 by Nehru, opening a new series of the 'temples of modern India', as he called them. A project comprising a total of 29 large dams (out of which the culminating Sardar Sarovar was initially planned for a height of 138 m), complemented with countless small works, had become the new destiny of a river. Irradiating modernity, the dam as a temple has its worshippers: it is to provide electricity, water for cities, as well as for irrigation. Numerous governmental progress reports, as well as mind boggling laudative declarations of otherwise discredited politicians, just pile up. The question of the beneficiaries is hardly addressed, however, as often seen in the Indian 'mythology of the public' (Ruet 2002b), and as recalled with figures by Racine (2001) or Arundhati Roy's essays.[1] Urban beneficiaries are not every city dweller, but those actually connected to water and electricity networks, that is, the few residential colonies unaffected by the plague of recurring cuts (see Ruet 2002a, 2004). On the rural side, due to the persistence of a large socio-economic divide, beneficiaries of any rural project usually are the rural rich (Shiva 1992; World Bank 2001). On the opposite side of the social ladder, Racine (2001) recalls that, and on the overall post-independence dam policy, 62 per cent of the affected population was constituted by tribals and scheduled castes (when they represent only 24.5 per cent of the total population). Worse, tribals alone are 47 per cent of the affected population[2] (for 8.5 per cent of the total population). Is it that tribals have this tendency to live where dams have to come, or just the reverse? Though provocative, this latter statement nevertheless throws light on some postcolonial aspects of the Indian psyche: in an unequal society, the oppressed of yesterday is better careful not becoming the oppressor of tomorrow. No one less than the former President of India, R.K. Narayanan, once declared, referring to colonial times that, unlike 'the British imperialists [who] had gone around the world damming rivers and damming peoples, [we should] take every possible care to see that the impact of dams we build is not ruinous to our tribal brothers and sisters'.[3] This opens up a key feature of the debate: how many people are affected by the Narmada projects? In 1979, the number of families was officially estimated to be of 6,000.[4] Today's official figures vary between 40,000 and 41,500 families, depending on the sources. They happily climb to 1.2 million people for the 'total project', according to the activist Medha Patkar. It is to be noted here, that 'officialese' (bureaucrats, developers) enjoy the softness of 'family' statistics, while activists handle the roughness of the appalling immensity of masses.[5] The units used—family versus people—already tell a lot. Looking at these figures, the standpoint we adopt from here necessarily goes beyond the quarrel of experts: arguing on the level of water, the number of megawatts, the surface to be irrigated, just looks like missing the point. These may be arguing elements, but the rhetoric, the debate, the political stake is about people.

In the actual vastness of approximates, in the odd fakeness of polished and precise estimates, where have the people disappeared? Communicative logics have gained the stage and become the master of the play. How can people from both the sides, beneficiaries as well as evicted ones, express their very existence as citizens, where the numbers are unknown (whatever be the numerical value of this number) or unacknowledged? Further, how can the fighting armies of the 'pros' and the 'against' be reconciled from such a diverging basis? How are these figures created? Used? Represent an emerging political reality? The pragmatic question is therefore ultimately on the positionality of people as a meaning and criteria of Indian politics.

Political Philosophy: A Politics For and By the Alienated

Balibar (1997), in his political philosophy, analyses politics as the articulation of three concepts (related to three ethical dynamics):

- the autonomy of politics (related to the ethical figure of emancipation), which address the aim of politics: the change for the alienated;
- the heteronomy of politics (meaning the conditions in which the transformation takes place), as politics embedded into historical heritage, processes and material conditions. That way, the heteronomy of politics arises also from the structures of power, where we will locate the nature and political significance of the discourse and of the means of communication;
- and as a reminder the heteronomy of the heteronomy of politics (ultimately related to the human dimension

of the politics: the civility), which we will not address here.

Balibar underlines the first essential concept of politics, its *autonomy*, as the fact that politics first refers to a universal to be sought, more than to institutions or powers. This is the underlying definition that we shall keep for the analysis of the existence of communicative processes and hence of politics in India. Choosing this definition will also have the advantage that it strongly relates to the conscientizing objective of the groups we analyse. Further, for them, the issue at stake is really to build a political process whose essence is to seek for an *autonomous*, normative goal. In the meantime this process occurs in the very context of a whole history of debate on developmentalism. Looked at that way, the Narmada project as a part of the developmentalist debate does constitute a heteronomy that we cannot neglect in this process of political construction. Balibar details: 'The autonomy of politics [in this sense that it represents a process with no origin or aim but itself, or what we shall call the citizenship] is not conceivable without the autonomy of its subject, and this autonomy in turn is nothing else than the fact for the people to "make" himself, in the same time as the individuals who compose the people grant themselves fundamental rights'.

As an enabler of such a process, autonomy of politics solely can allow the existence of the communicative networks we are trying to unearth. Looking at the Narmada problem under this philosophical perspective will thus mean, inter alia, a *dépassement* of the mere politics of vested interests.[6]

In order to *do* (and thus to think) politics, the practical (as well as theoretical) question that emerges is on the nature of the class that will bear the historical legitimacy of politics-as-a-universalism. In Marxian and Balibar's philosophy, this legitimacy is carried by the class which will be the guarantee against inequality. De facto as well as in action, this responsibility is borne by the class struggling against inequality in the access (by everybody) to identified rights beyond vested interests. The *sense* and the *perception* of the universal is carried and represented by the identity of the class that perceives itself, feels itself as the representative of this universal.

Autonomy in Front of the Dam: The Right to Live

Let us now take the risk to operationalize political philosophy. Name one of these rights, for instance, the right to live in India, and there comes the meaning of this theory in analysing dams in India. This allows specifying the definition of the 'right to live'. Especially, one can disentangle between the right to live in traditional land deemed to be submerged on one hand, and the right to get electricity and water through a dam on the other hand, and we no longer get the usual stakeholders opposed face-to-face in the discourse of the state and the activists in the Narmada case, which is only the surface of things, but rather an analytical situation where all parties actually articulate and construct systems of proof around their own conception of the 'right to live in India'. The way to dialectically clinch the debate, is with the concept of the 'universal class' projected, in subjectivity, as an *actual*.[7] Then, the most 'shareless' people are the evicted people. The articulation and the defence of their rights is the key issue of the existence of politics (in a universalistic conception) in India.

The actuality of the struggle of the alienated class is central and this can practically be studied by no other means than through the very processes around which it revolves. But this, however, leads to what Balibar theoretically articulates as the second concept of politics: its heteronomy. If the people 'makes' itself, it does so within an economically, socially, culturally *given* environment. How does, on one hand, the necessary autonomy of the consciousness and action of the universality as politics, and on the other hand, this heteronomy to the given, relate? In the Narmada context, what is the given, from where can politics start and convey a universalistic dimension? If structures change and follow a path, then, for Marx, the political practice is already inscribed within a process. And, as Balibar specifies, 'politics is therefore not the simple change of conditions, as if it were possible to isolate them, and to abstract oneself from them to gain power on them. But it is in fact the change within the change, the differentiation of the change'. In the 'interstice', in the tiny place between the materialist structures and the progressive norms, is an area of undetermination and invention. There *is* and revolves politics.

The technical means in 'operationalizing' this theory, we believe, necessarily implies at a first level the identification of an objective to serve as a reference in the external analysis. That may be stylized either as 'stop the dam', 'ensure a real rehabilitation', 'ensure availability and transparency of information' or any other one as long as it is (*a*) formulated and commonly shared, and (*b*) acknowledged as a feature towards benchmarking the 'result' of action. The analysis of these mottos in the anti-dam movement actually constitutes the central second section of this essay.[8] But, more importantly, a second level is needed, which is the specified ethical perspective on politics, lies at the root of the action, and that only is able to colour the process as *political*.

In Search of an Organic Intellectual for the Narmada

Let us now detail in which perspective we will consider the effectivity of the political desalination of the Narmada dweller. If he/she has to 'emerge at the surface of history',[9] there have to be intellectual relays, to provoke and convey (towards the state and the political sphere) this consciousness of their own existence as a class, homogeneity and function. In Gramsci's political philosophy, the function to involve the productive forces is carried by the intellectual. The intellectual is the mediator between the various classes and the state seen as the apparatus of the hegemonic class. This mediation is twofold and not exempt with a certain amount of ambiguity. At the same time, according to Gramsci, the intellectual carries and transmits the hegemonic functions of the leading class, but thereby puts the other classes in its contact, thus conscientizing them. If we follow this analytical scheme, our question articulates as follows: what is the role of intellectuals in the Narmada fight; how do they relate to global intellectuals, to the local class; how do their communicative channels shape the class consciousness? How do they shape the class' perception (and therefore surfacing) of the people's historical function? And, importantly enough, can the existing (urban traditional) intellectuals be able on his own to produce a differentiated change in this process? Or, on the contrary, is there for the Narmada class any need of organic intellectuals, more strictly defined as having emerged out of a kind of 'specialization of some partial aspects of the primitive activity of the new social type to which the new social class has given birth' (Gramsci)? In that respect, communicative actions by tribals reflexively drawing upon their cultural practices might serve such a purpose and, given the initial conditions, *in relation* with intellectuals from an original urban background. In other words, the process lies in the relationships and dialectics between different degrees of intellectual activity.

If we practically look at how conscientizing the alienated class *as a class* and as a class-understanding-its-ascribed-position-within-the-Indian-society (as well as the possibility to evolve this ascription), then the a priori definition of this intellectual we are looking for can be quite open as far as his means and techniques, ways of expression, and modes of communication are concerned. The modes can actually vary all the more so that the process itself will actually be the determining factor: for Gramsci, 'the relationship between intellectuals and the world of production is not immediate, as it is the case for fundamental social groups'. He specifies that it is 'mediate' (in the sense of mediated). Different elements generate this mediation, relevant from the whole social fabric. However, Gramsci qualifies the role of the organic intellectual as the one of a 'builder, organizer, permanent persuader' (ibid.: 244).

We can now analyse communication processes that revolve around Narmada within a set perspective: the connection between the urban intellectual and the information-flows, the extent of emergence of the tribal intellectual, and the type of dialectics between them, if any.

Intellectuals in the Networks of Knowledge: The Dam within the Heteronomy of Global Activism

Everyone has his own story to tell about Narmada and each one serves a specific communication strategy. There is nothing as one single story about the Narmada. There are at least the official version on the one hand (with again its several variants[10]), and various forms of different activist group's stories on the other hand (with its sometimes naïve alterations or approximates[11]). Besides, we shall see in the next section that the discrepancies between the stories of the nongovernmental organizations (NGOs) receive more profound antagonisms. Since our aim is to articulate the discourse and its communicative processes to the people, with reference to the ethical concept of politics that we have taken as a yardstick, we need not balanced and compare the details of each type of story here. We even need not assert the 'superiority' in terms of 'truth' of one over the other, for there is no objective criteria to be retained. Instead, we will rather analyse the mechanisms of truth-making of the Narmada Bachao Andolan (NBA) story. However, since (a) the anti-dam movements themselves situate the meaning of their action into political representation and (b) the public position has been criticized at length, we will address in this section the communicative relevance and political significance of the 'antis',[12] in the perspective set up by Foucault.

Intellectuals in the Networks of Knowledge

For Foucault (1980), 'truth ... is produced only by virtue of multiple forms of constraint. And it induces regular effects of power'.

As far as the Narmada is concerned, typically, the questions are: does the number of protesters prove the truth of a cause? How do the various protagonists/story tellers such as government officials and NGO activists, acknowledge each other's degrees of legitimacy in stating figures? How does this depend upon the debated issue such as the number of oustees, the rehabilitation schemes, the technical characteristics of the dam, its electricity generation, its irrigative capacity? In short, how is any 'truth' produced, stamped as 'scientific', transmitted, consumed, and under whose control?

As an illustrative example, the concept of development conveys the centrality of the state in the process, and any communication about the benefits of these forms of development serves as a legitimation and reinforcement of this political centrality of the state.[13] In contrast, for Kothari, the concept of *rights* refers to social movements and the dynamic of struggle as a system of autonomous truth-making. Potentially all three different systems (development, participation, rights) of truth-making exist in the case of Narmada, borne by different 'story tellers'. In that respect, knowing the very context of the evolution of the social and political thinking, practices and means of justification in India at the time of the Narmada will be central to understand where lies the politics—the differentiated change—in the anti-dam protest.

Who Appropriates the Story? NBA's vs Global Activist's Dam

Let us now recall *the particular* story that the NBA propels, in order to exemplify the nexus between communication and intellectuals. We will be, in that respect, much more concerned with the ways and means the NBA uses to develop and expand its story. Central to it is a foundation myth. It mentions the origin as the federation, in the 1980s and around the totemic figure of Medha Patkar, of several formerly distinct NGOs. The 'NBA coalition', to simply become the NBA, was born, working on resettlement policies for the tribal people. It was soon after radicalized (in 1988), again around the central figure of Medha Patkar, to be reborn as an anti-dam movement this time, radically contesting the very idea of resettlement to contest the displacement itself.

On the NBA's website, the principles are for making truth adopt an 'authority principle' communication system. Take an example. In a press release dated 2 April 2001 (NBA 2001),[14] beyond the contents, articulates a justification process through referring to the 'eminent writer' Arundhati Roy, and the 'noted film-maker' Jharana Jhaveri. Further in the text appear a 'retired Justice', an 'advocate in the Supreme Court', an 'ex-commissioner', a 'national secretary', a 'secretary general'. When titles and official identifications are missing, we get a socialist 'leader', and a 'noted' theatre activist.

Indeed, this communication strategy is addressed to the multilateral agencies, and therefore aims at showing how the movement, despite dealing with the rights of uneducated and alienated people is however directed by 'serious' people. The movement adopts this self-projection to show its being at par with their interlocutors in the multilateral agencies, postgraduate students from the best schools in the world. This is the way to take in confidence these 'bearers of knowledge' that constitute the staff of the World Bank, and lead them to carry counter-inquiries. Here is a process of *'justification of the equals'* targeting the *'rehabilitation of the subalterns'*. And actually these arguments partly work and make the NBA action succeed in bringing multilateral agencies to reassess the situation. This is this kind of communication that leads, for instance the UN Commission on Human Rights to depute a 'Special Rapporteur' (*The Hindu,* 11 August 2001). The special rapporteur can address the 'landless and the alienated', through the medium of the 'eminent activists.'

The second communicative strength of the NBA movement derives from its ability to catch the attention of the middle class and politicians in Indian metropolises. An illustration of this is the 'rally by Narmada's children' (*The Hindu,* Wednesday, 22 August 2001), where 70 tribal children from affected villages from Madhya Pradesh met school children in major towns of Madhya Pradesh and Gujarat on the way to Delhi, to finally camp on the highly symbolic India Gate facing the presidential palace. Here again the symbolic value of this location, when the rally camps at the window of the guardian of the nation, carries an element of justification. On yet another symbolic mode, calling on the figure of a leader of the national consciousness, the 'noted activist' Baba Amte gave his blessings[15] at the departure of the rally, the press recalls, while the children gained an extra legitimacy in the sense that they are 'students' of an NBA-run school, and that they 'represent children of 245 villages affected by the Sardar Sarovar Project'. Again, 'personalities' were present, and 'pledged solidarity with them'. But the ultimate significance of communication is also reflected in the feedback by the media, which impacts on the minds of the urban middle class. Within three days, the children lose their central status, regained again by the personalities. *The Hindu* (Saturday, 25 August 2001) declares that 'it was Ms. Arundhati Roy who virtually led a spirited protest march and addressed a public meeting in support of the 70-odd tribal children from the Narmada Valley who are in the capital these days'. The very fact that she addressed a public meeting has taken precedence, in the press' eyes, over the long march of the children, who just happen to be here, these days, in 'our' town. The figures, too, had in-between endured their fate, since *The Hindu* reports 40,000 people declared as affected by the UN report, while Roy declares them to be 'four lakh [400,000] oustees'. It seems facts do not matter in the Narmada case.

What the 'anti' story does not mention is that the mythic birth has also come out of other NGOs parting from the NBA views that no kind of relocation could be acceptable. NGOs like ARCH-Vahini,[16] that work in relationship with the state, have further constantly devoted their line of argument around bettering the resettlement conditions through a mix of pressure upon and cooperation with the state. This different conception of the right to be fought for (right to stay in the traditional living place at any cost, that is conveyed by the anti-dams, versus right to be properly resettled somewhere else) shapes the whole representation and ground of the vision of the world supported by the respective proponents. Out of this, the universalistic vision of the Narmada politics is no longer necessarily coevolved. Neither self-labelling nor self-advertising oneself as a 'pro-people' movement, will be enough to prove the point. The 'pro' dimension, as well as the proof of the universalistic change, really have to be constantly provided and reassessed.

Politics as Institutions and Social Processes: The Economy and Location of Communication

The messages by the intellectual and the debates around them come on the stage as an ensemble of activities, more like constellations of varying and often seemingly distant, social

The Political Meaning of a River   417

processes. Messages encompass other dimensions and protagonists and communication translates the problems. In particular, we argue that the key modification that communication operates in the Narmada case, is about the location of the struggle. In that respect, the fight for Narmada has three 'places', the play has three stages: 'the valley', 'Delhi', 'the global contestation'. This change in location alters the nature of the problem itself.

Anti-Dams, Stage I: 'The Valley' as a Starting Point, off Delhi

The starting space of contestation—in both terms of geographical location and mediatic environment—is well recorded in Patel (1997), an activist of the Gujarati NGO, ARCH-Vahini. He insists that the initial coverage by press and written media and the consequent first legal successes has been really instrumental in providing the initial impulsion to make tribals conscious that something can happen out of their action. While at the beginning of the 1980s only registered landowners were deemed to be rehabilitated, a faux pas of the Government of Gujarat, soon infirmed by the Gujarat High Court, led the tribals to see that courts might support their claims. From 1984, their claims started involving rehabilitation for all. Throughout this period was a slow but progressively increasing awareness campaign and recognition that a problem exists, mostly through isolated journalist 'friends' in metropolitan cities of India. Singh (1997a and 1997b) details that, in the 1980s, work of several NGOs had started in the valley through information campaigns and local public meetings, and he situates the 1989 Harsud (Madhya Pradesh) demonstration as the turning point of the NBA strategy. By that time, according to Singh, and 10 years after the Narmada Water Disputes Tribunal verdict of 1979,[17] Harsud had demonstrated that the 'NBA received widespread support from environmental and social movements in India and abroad'. It was high time for the struggle to go beyond the valley, and to capitalize on the 'NBA's broad-based support, in the valley as well as among intellectuals and activists nation-wide'. Singh actually describes well how 'Delhi' (understand: the political parties system) had initially failed to become a really structured place of the Narmada fight in the summer of 1990. Counter-marches, counter-sittings in Delhi by Gujarati organizations and politicians had soon left the political parties unanimously supporting the dam, cutting across otherwise usual divisions.

Anti-Dams, Stage II: Delhi through Global Communication

By mid-1988 only some activists 'and the people' (*sic*, Parasuraman 1997) realized that the government had no clear idea about relocation. A new series of rallies was conducted and opposition to the dam got evolved as a strategy. For the first time within the activist movement, the environmental and larger economic considerations came to the fore. The divorce with ARCH-Vahini was consumed, and soon the state governments would set up a line for refusing any negotiation with anti-dam movements. A common attempt to work at a collective solution had failed. The NBA developed a decidedly non-cooperative movement. As a result, in early 1992, all the 33 villages concerned by the submergence zone of the Sardar Sarovar were no longer accessible to government officers or project developers. Equally, in Madhya Pradesh, there were 34 non-accessible villages, 99 with difficulties to access, for only 60 without resistance (NCA 1992).

The double-level communication of the NBA (global positioning as seen from its website, but also urban rallies in India) has been made possible through, and maybe only through, a well orchestrated lobbying on multilateral government agencies and an objective alliance with 'global' NGOs (that is, western NGOs adopting global communication processes as well as a political stand that they project as of global relevance). It is this *détour* which has allowed the NBA shifting the attention *from* the *location* of the valley to a national and global scene, for instance with the march organized in July 2000 in the Nimad region in Madhya Pradesh. The latter saw 400 personalities, *joined* by 10,000 displaced people, as the press recalls. As one can see, out of the journey from valley to Delhi, the primacy had again been reversed in press records, in spite of the logic of numbers: the 400 were joined by 10,000, and not the reverse as one would have actually expected.

It seems, in the 'anti' story, the resident educated urbanites deserve priority in mention compared to the huge number of those who made a long journey. In the anti-dam story, the Valley is indeed a first step only, which was soon to lead to another strategic choice on the ways to expand it: Delhi (the legal politics) versus the world and its global influential politics. At the turn of 1990, the latter option had won, with its accrued role for communication as a protagonist in truth-making.

Anti-Dams, Stage III: The International and the Role of the Environment Defence Fund (EDF)

How did the international connection start and develop? Patel (1997) mentions that, in 1984, John Clark (from Oxfam-UK) 'mounted an intensive campaign in close collaboration with ARCH-Vahini. He enlisted the support of many international NGOs which became aware for the first time of the problem of displacement of tribals in the Narmada Valley. The issue became a "cause célèbre" in the World Bank, as John Clark put it'. This has practically led the World Bank compelling the government of Gujarat to revise and upgrade the resettlement and rehabilitation schemes that were planned for oustees from the project. One shall definitely wonder at the instrumentality of a western NGO putting this case at the very time when the World Bank was starting considering its own policy in the matter, finally taking stock after 15 years of worldwide critiques against its dam projects. Narmada was, so to speak, the emerged part of a large iceberg of accumulated, constructed knowledge, collectively constructed by activist networks in the whole world. The World Bank also entered in the business of renegotiating resettlement schemes, and communicated around it as a way to modify its dam policy while safeguarding its essential features. This was to lead to a new policy granted by the government of Gujarat by December 1988.

How did this divergence arise? We have one account of it. According to Patel (1997), in June 1988 'the Environment Defence Fund, a US-based environmental organization which had until then lobbied for the World Bank in concert with

Oxfam-UK and supported the resettlement and rehabilitation demands of the tribals, suddenly changed course'. It seems that here the chronicle matters, since Patel mentions that 'the Maharashtra and MP organizations had still not declared their opposition to the project' and that 'when they did so in August 1988, their opposition was as sudden as it was total. They declared that the project was environmentally disastrous and economically ruinous'. For Patel, these 'rumblings against the project' had come from 'metropolises of Bombay, Delhi, etc'. What is lacking is the NBA version of the facts, when the 'anti-dam' mythical story actually starts around this troubled period.

Anti-Dams, Stage III Today: 'Medha Speaks in DC', the Self-justification of the EDF

The international campaign will go on around an alliance between the NBA and the EDF. In 1991, the NBA, Medha Patkar and Baba Amte are the co-winners of the 'right livelihood award', in 1992, Medha wins the Goldman Environmental Prize. In 1989, the EDF takes her to the US to give a talk before the House of Representatives, qualifying the project as a 'planned ecological disaster' (Patkar 1989). The World Bank ultimately cancels its support to the project in 1993. In 1994, 1999, she travels again to the US. By that time, the fight had become largely 'symbolized' and NBA has adopted lines of presentation in tune with global debates. The website of the right livelihood (www.rightlivelihood.sc) mentions that the NBA 'has succeeded in generating a debate across the subcontinent which has encapsulated the conflict between two opposite styles of development: one massively destructive of people and the environment in the quest for large-scale industrialization; the other consisting of replicable small-scale activities harmoniously integrated with both local communities and nature'.

This vision is largely simplified, romantic, and deafeningly silent about... the tribals! However, references tell a lot: this new debate supposedly generated by the NBA is actually the old socialist Gandhian vision, sometimes accidentally articulated to the naïve essentialized perception of nature (in that latter case eschewing the possibility of its social construction and its acception as such[18]), and the whole range of progressive fights at the same time. These debates are historically and sociologically situated, in a marginal progressive India, in a today diminishing part of the urban 'elite'. Politically situated, such a presentation ultimately glorifies an unspecified 'local', despite using the global means of the international awards.

Beyond processes, one can wonder if unlimited association with orientalist western NGOs does not loosen the credibility of NBA's proposed alternative: 'an energy and water strategy based on improving dry farming technology, watershed development, small dams, lift schemes for irrigation and drinking water, and improved efficiency and utilization of existing dams' (www.rightlivelihood.sc). But the fight has definitely gone beyond, when Medha advocates (as the unsaid and unreferred part of a very intricate and subtle network of Indian debate around this issue) for the need to 'redefine "modernity"'. This goes much beyond the tribals.

Still, how can we characterize this statement in its historicity, and unearth its discursive archaeology? A very echoing critique of development and of the Indian state has been raised by Kothari (1984: 219), who poses that 'the linkage between (progress) and "poverty" has become so organic and almost irreversible'. He actually advocates for the fact that 'the "grassroots" movements and non-party formations ... have to be seen as part of the democratic struggle at various levels, in a radically different social context than was posited both by the incrementalists and by the revolutionaries, at a point of history when existing institutions and the theoretical models on which they are based have run their course...and when large vacuums in political space are emerging thanks to the decline in the role of the State and the virtual collapse of "government" in large parts of rural India' (ibid.). But he does not militate so much for a simple critique as for a very refoundation of politics, as a concept and a practice. 'It is an attempt at redefinition of politics in another sense too, namely redefinition of the contents of politics. Issues and arenas of human activity that were not so far seen as amenable of political action—people's health, rights over forests and community resources, even deeply personal and primordial issues are involved in the struggle for women's rights—get defined as political and provide arenas of struggle' (p. 219–220). In political philosophy's terms, the focus of the autonomy is expanding; the differentiated change rebels against the material strength of the parties, seen as historically dated and a call for their dépassement is made.

The NBA of the 1980s looked to be in tune with this hope of a renewal. What is, however, interesting is to note the progression of the idea. If the concept of non-party politics has not, far from it, submerged the classical system, it has thoroughly evolved and sought for allies outside India. If Kothari sees well the historicity of this new avatar of politics, by stating that 'the rationale and historical specificity of the non-party (groups) is of course clear', we can in effect note that he refers to struggles within Indian only: Assam, Jharkhand, tribal Northeast and Andhra Pradesh, among others. Few years after, the extension of the fight has taken place on new rights and even more radically beyond India.

By doing so it also has been immersed within a larger system of truth-making. When Patkar (1989) mentions about the project, rehabilitation issues are no longer discussed and environmental aspects of the project come first. For environment is everything but objective and, given in itself, one has to wonder which agenda is pursued in such matters. Das (1992), analysing the functioning of EDF with respect to the internationalization of the Narmada campaign, details how involving 'local' or 'third world' activists has 'contributed towards the consolidation of the notion among US environmental groups involved in the MDB[19] movement that (and, from here, Das quotes the EDF[20]) 'third world organizations are sharing common goals with the US groups'. Ultimately, the movement such as perceived in the western World has gradually taken the shape of an ecological movement, mostly for intra-US communicative reasons. However, these interventions are at the very source of the cancellation of the World Bank support. This is then striking to see that the major 'external' development in the Narmada case has ultimately derived from what resembles an exercise of self-justification within the arena of US based NGOs.

The Political Meaning of a River 423

Global Struggles as a New Heteronomy

Conversely, the NBA has been ready (or instrumental) to embrace all sorts of mottos and have its own relays. In 2000, 'Narmada Solidarity Coalition of New York' protests and demonstrates against the Supreme Court of India. By 1999, when Patkar gives a talk at Asha for education, the event is cosponsored by no less than Amnesty International, ASM Diversity Committee, Campus Womens' Center, Center for South Asia, East Timor Action Network, Indian Graduate Students Association, LCA Free Thinkers, Madison Treaty Rights Support Group, NOW-Madison Chapter, Student Action for Indian Volunteerism and Aid, UW-Alliance for Democracy, UW-Greens, WISPIRG, WORT 89.9 FM. Independence movements, educationists, environmentalists, a radio and so on. NBA has its global victory: an image and communication channels that move the whole global world of activists. This success was confirmed at the 2003 Asian Social Forum in Hyderabad (*The Hindu*, Friday, 3 January 2003). At that time, *The Hindu* details the need, according to Medha's statement, to 'broad base the struggle to fight not just globalization but casteism and communalism'. The archaeology of knowledge of such a sentence encompasses a whole century of colonial construction in India, post-independence debates and institutions, socialist thinking on imperialism and critique of neoliberalism. Actually, this discourse is embedded into a whole series and history of fights in India and beyond India. There is no longer a simple fight against a dam, nor a fight conveying a particular process of transforming the society with an associated vision of it. There is on top of that, a materialistic result of a history of struggles, which encompass the dam. It articulates in a precise combination of elements: (*a*) a Gandhian socialist identity, (*b*) a globalized mode of communication, and (*c*) an anti liberal-globalization symbolism. The dam that allows and crystallizes politics is ultimately drowned in the historical and material heteronomy of the latter. Isolated from its context, Patkar's above mentioned statement is a pure formal, symbolic, conceptual, communicative stanza. What makes it understandable and operative finds its roots far beyond the dam. Medha has gone from the valley to *the* global.

And indeed, we have mentioned that the fight for Narmada has three 'places': 'the valley', 'Delhi', 'the global contestation', out of which the former and the latter are more of a mythical order. Indeed, the former faces difficulties in taking off, as we will analyse now, while the latter takes place in a completely altered mode compared to the valley reality. And indeed two tensions arise, respectively symbolized by the evolution over 20 years of the *focus* and *kind* of intellectual involved. The focuses have grown and multiplied, most likely because the economy of knowledge has more and more revolved around mechanisms of truth making through foundations, public philanthropy, doctoral studies, 'independent' studies and awards. The EDF example is telling, and the multiplicity of channels has led to the multiplicity of truths around Narmada, at least to a multiplicity of levels of truth. Second, the type of the intellectual at play has evolved over three periods. While the first non-party intervention was already a politico-intellectual one (the Kalpavriksh report in 1983), the present 'urban intellectual' commitment is both of a higher magnitude, and of a much higher institutionalization, when 'DC' and 'NY' are taken to the fore. Similarly, the backgrounds have diversified, rights fighters and social workers to policy makers, academics, information people, film makers. Concerning the remains of the second phase which had seen the local involvement of the tribals, its reality today has to be reassessed.

All together, the third place of the Narmada, the 'global contestation', is highly symbolic therefore highly 'effective'; but nevertheless its 'efficiency' with respect to a non-symbolic local problem is questionable. There is undoubtedly a political success here, which no *party* could have realized. And in that case, the processes at stake today in India do not give any legitimacy in this field to the political parties. However, the success of the NGOs has been limited in terms of location of the fight. And indeed, the intellectual a la Foucault is not directly in an immediate relation to the world of production, though Foucault, however, gives the clue for his indirect and subtle articulation within the production process: the critique of the truth makers (people and institutions). In this problem is the core of the evaluation of the Narmada action:

where is the intellectual challenging through communicative means the public, state, truth-makers? We will see that this is, in many respects, the figure of the global (urban) intellectual, armed with very specific communication means. This will in turn lead to the following question: can the global intellectual relate to the local Narmada's alienated class, and how?

The Narmada Without an Organic Intellectual?

The task to relate to the people, for the urban intellectual, is actually uneasy in the valley. Parasuraman (1997) mentions that concerned tribals in 'inaccessible villages' do not generally go beyond the third standard in elementary school (and even so, quite exceptionally) while usually no adult can read. However, some unexpected results had initially generated hope.

ARCH-Vahini, or the Wish to be More Than 'Representative': Reactive to the Tribals

Parasuraman (1997) recalls the origin of the movement and states that 'people had little or no information about the project'; 'it was only after the activists arrived in the valley that some consciousness was generated'.[21] Something rarely mentioned in the western media, especially after the opposition strategy had been adopted by the 'antis', was that resettlement policies concerned only those few who had land records in hand. This not only questions the fate of landless people, but also the future of those numerous tribals de facto cultivating public forest land whom the state (initially the colonial, but this was maintained after independence) considers as encroachers. In that context, some undeniable success had been reached by both NBA and ARCH-Vahini. Indeed, Singh (1997a) mentions that, at Harsud, 'The NBA had succeeded in uniting the oustees throughout the valley (from poor tribals to rich farmers and traders), overcoming the entrenched prejudices and divisions that had so far governed the polity and economy of the region'. Parasuraman (1997) adds that, in Gujarat, 'Young men and women were in the forefront of the emerging movement to demand better compensation. A new set of young leaders emerged under the initiative of the activists. They composed songs on health care, education, self-sufficiency, self-respect, tribal independence, and assertiveness'. 'By 1987, about two years after the activists had entered the villages, people started questioning the officials and persuaded them to come to their villages to talk about the project and Resettlement and Rehabilitation issues'. 'The village committees prepared [for the Government] comprehensive household data on land possessed, location, and extent of submergence'. Actually, this is quite interesting to see that, what at that time was an information and rehabilitation movement, and not yet an anti-dam movement, had first of all developed a popular basis and did convey a universalistic approach. Indeed, Parasuraman (1997) details that, among other demands, 'extension of rehabilitation and resettlement benefits to those affected by colony, canal, sanctuary, and compensatory afforestation programmes' were raised. This undoubtedly constitutes a practical success, detailed by Baviskar (1995), but not followed with a second step either in acts by the state or as a consequence by the evolution of the movement.

Patel (1997), an activist from ARCH-Vahini, describes a process of learning-by-doing for the activists themselves, stating that they knew nothing about administrative practices, rules, laws, Forest Acts and so on, by the beginning of their fight. Though from an urban origin, they have developed a Narmada-specific political action. They therefore gained the legitimacy of not only putting to the fore the issues, but of doing so from within, and from knowledge gained around and articulated with their political demand. Patel details that, from 1986 onwards, tribals from Madhya Pradesh and Maharashtra evoked the same claims of resettlement for all, with demands 'made village-wise and collectively'. Patel recalls the whole details of that fight but, what we find interesting in our questioning, is that for this major step Patel credits the tribals themselves and not his own organization. And from there we get just another narrative compared to what the 'antis' give. Indeed, he recalls that the whole process of credible rehabilitation for all was deemed to be stuck due to lack of available land in 1985, the tribals responded 'in a most unusual way' by giving the activists 'a list of landowners in the command area who were ready to sell about seven thousand acres of land'. And, Patel comments, 'Once again, the tribals had taken the initiative at a critical juncture'. Of course, this may not prove much on their actual action compared to NBA except the fact hat they choose to communicate and to make their truth revolve around the tribal rather than on the principle of authority (intellectual, artists, noted activists, and so on).

From this juncture, one question arises: was it possible to go on in this way of creating a tribal consciousness and a tribal action as a collective? This may well be impossible to know, just because it is impossible to know what would be the 'change in the change' and, ultimately, the NBA/ARCH-Vahini's clash revolves around respective conceptions of the world to be won. Are these articulated around 'different tribals'? Are the Gujarati tribals ready to be relocated in Gujarat, while the Madhya Pradeshi and Maharashtrian tribals (under the organization called Narmada Dharangrast Samiti) would not be ready to go to Gujarat (INTACH 1994). Patel indeed recalls that according to the Tribunal Award of 1979, tribals could either get relocated in Gujarat or in their own state if such was their choice. The Indian administration, and especially the Forest Department, bears a high responsibility in leading the Madhya Pradesh and Maharashtra governments to 'push all the oustees to Gujarat', Patel mentions. While ARCH-Vahini considers the Gujarat policy of December 1987 as 'a revolutionary policy', the NBA has declared it a paper policy. Still, the issue that remains is about what 'the tribals' really think of it, and of how they can either *be made* to think about it, or *by themselves* think about it. According to Patel, in the Gujarat new model, 'the tribals' central role has been to identify land, to have the prices of land fixed through the formally appointed Land Purchase Committee (LPC) of which (ARCH-Vahini is) a permanent member body, and to make sure that land parcels of two hectares are allotted to each family'. According to him, 'the tribals have taken the initiative to form groups of their own to identify land, to press for the fixation of a just price, and to oversee the final allotment'.

These latter examples amply illustrate, we believe, the difference at stake between the intellectual involved in party politics, like Gadar, the revolutionary singer of People's War Group naxalites[22] or again their Telugu poet, Sri Sri, aiming at a large long-reaching conscientization, and the intellectual engaged in non-party politics, concerned with the present and looking for direct outcomes of action. Exemplary of the second category, beyond Medha Patkar of the mid, 1980s, is Niyogi, from Chattisgarh Mukti Morcha, the liberation front to which Kothari explicitly refers. This format of non-party involvement conveys the old Gramscian idea of the possibility to integrate not only the political society, but also civil society in the function of direction, which is the only one legitimate, where the function of domination alone is not. This idea may have been short-lived in the Narmada case, though not fully unlived. For politics as autonomy can never practically be measured or even assessed, three practical questions will remain: was there (is there still) any specific way for the Organic Intellectual to emerge in the Narmada?

In terms of instrumentality, what can be, if any, the modes of creation of the tribal organic intellectual? In the Narmada case, no intellectual in the 'superior' strata could straightforwardly emerge from among the tribals. Still, thanks to the necessary intervention of the urban intellectuals, the (though minoritarian) intellectual part of tribal activity has increased: vision changes and meetings structure the shift towards a higher share of the intellectual in day-to-day life. Indeed, according to some testimonies,[23] the tribals concerned with the NBA movement started raising questions and making critical statements. They include, at different levels and with varying degrees, questions pertaining to the fact that Medha Patkar has not favoured the emergence of tribal spokepersons, that the decisions concerning the movement have been top-down, radical and refuse negotiations, especially at a time when tribals perceive a relative defeat of their struggle. Besides, rumours about the possibility for the movement turning political have sown doubts in the minds of tribals who have long been taught to be defiant towards party politics.

Equally, misunderstandings have developed out of blurred alliance policies, ranging from objective support by nationalist sympathies to ultra leftist groups, contributing even more confusion. In some extreme cases, observers declare, some wonderings have emerged about the leadership qualities of a leader who proposes to be drowned as a last recourse policy. These extreme measures, though Gandhian in inspiration, are rather considered by the tribals as a sign of weakness and failure. These elements show that, out of the objective, material conditions of the struggle, and whatever can be won on that side, the gradual construction of a struggle is even more grounded on social links and representations.

In other words, and in the case of the Narmada, the economico-corporatist only represents the categorial economic stakes (as an heteronomy of politics), while the ethico-politic has to be, we believe, the functioning of the Indian democracy. This reconciliation only will allow restoring the ethical aspect of the autonomy of politics: the figure of emancipation, the practical aspect of it residing in the subtle intermeshing of the processes of communication.

If the NBA fight has an ambitious spectrum, is it for such a universal claim articulated to an alienated class? Nothing is as sure as this. When Medha Patkar has claims in reassessing modernity, she is much more connected to other intellectual figures in India than to the tribal. Not that this is not historically relevant for the tribal, but that the NBA has not succeeded in creating and actualizing this connection and this relevance where politics resides. On the contrary, INTACH (1994) reproduced an open letter from a tribal to the Madhya Pradesh Chief Minister. The letter is a long, non-romanticized, account of the diversity of agricultural production, of the stability it provides in times of low market prices, on the amount of money it can also procure. It recalls a documented list of all goods and services, including non-material, that the tribal way of life procures once articulated to an external market but in a way independent from it. The way the fight is stylized matters: whether it is around 'stop the dam', 'ensure a real rehabilitation', 'ensure availability and transparency of information' is not neutral.

In that context, the whole issue of the symbolic dimension of the Narmada lies in integrating this claim as well. In Baba Amte's words 'Narmada will linger on the lips of the nation as a symbol of all struggles against social injustice.' However, if this symbol is deemed to be used in socialist Gandhian or naïve global NGOs contexts only, without connection to the Narmada as a location and the Narmada people as a collective, then the local has lost its flavour, its identity, its meaning. It is just another denial.

Conclusion: Substantive Aspects of Knowledge and the Heteronomy of Narmada Politics

The substantive aspects of knowledge articulated around the Narmada, its varying forms, its producers and dynamics, matter in shaping or not a political identity of the tribals. Can the sole participation of outside intellectuals create politics in the sense of Balibar? At different levels, the analysis shows a contrasted picture. At the global level, of course, the continuum between Indian (urban) and 'western' intellectuals seem to prove the vitality of a global politics: the perception of the universal is transboundary. However, the relative inability to bring up rural organic intellectuals raises the question of the actuality of politics understood as the universal struggle *for* but also *by* the alienated class.

A practical problem will always reside where the theory names the differentiated change: do the evolving perceptions already reveal such a change and, therefore, a success? All depends on what is the teleological criteria adopted, and where the benchmark is put. In particular, since social struggles develop on experience accumulated over years, some amount of success can still be seen despite the direct goals not being attained. Conversely, a more pessimistic vision would analyse the same context quite differently. This question might actually be clinched by the political context in today's India: if, for progressive circles in the country the urge of the day is to fight against radicalization and communalization of politics, then the short-run experience might not give enough time to enjoy nor appreciate the long-term progress provided by too minor successes.

Even worse, given the castiest and class background of India, it is not even sure that the very perception, by the concerned class itself, of what its (the universal) 'rights' are, is not constrained too much by the social conditions. Politics is actually a process when thought of as universal by citizen-looking people. Or in other words, when it relates to a 'politics of human rights articulated to a philosophy of democracy' (Raynaud 1999, on Balibar, 1997). As a limit, the definition itself of the intellectual matters. But, we argue, the philosophy of the praxis, in the sense that it relates to *processes*, can provide a measure of the degree of progressiveness in the so-called Indian democracy. In that latter respect, different testimonies prove that, in some circumstances, tribals are willing to speak and act. If we believe that the Indian democracy is more directly endangered than the global environment, or if we only believe that the global NGOs will not necessarily address the former while they would anyway focus on the latter, supported or not by the 'Global South NGOs', then there is an urgency to shift back to the figure of the tribal, and look for inspiration from the several tribal movements in the past.

Anyway, and as it stays today, the Narmada fight, over 20 years and more, has seen a mind-boggling diversity of people to comment, a diversity of media. Groups have emerged, some have disappeared. The role of urban support groups in India has changed, to becoming paradoxically marginalized today with respect to the battalions deployed by the US economy of knowledge. If at any point of time, Hoshangabad, Bhopal, Rajasthan, Delhi, Bombay and other places have mattered, to further engender 'the' NBA, the Narmada has now become a hub with much longer spokes for politics, for scholars, for social movements of all kinds. It has become a metaphor of changes of political activism in India and beyond. It may have, in the process of emerging as a mediatic figure, paradoxically lost its original clarity and substance.

Notes

1. Racine quotes the figures of 15,000 sq km of irrigated land and 2000 mw of electricity generation for Madhya Pradesh based dams, to be added to the 21,000 sq km and 1450 mw of the Sardar Sarovar project, situated in Gujarat.
2. As far as the Narmada project is concerned, the proportion of tribals in the affected population is of 100 per cent for the submergence zone in the state of Gujarat, 100 per cent for the zone in Maharashtra, and 30 per cent for Madhya Pradesh. Source: *The Hindu*, 16 December 2000.
3. *The Hindu*, 11 December 2000.
4. Under this socio-economic contexts, a family can represent five persons on an average.
5. With an average family size of five persons in India, family figures are always much lower than people numbers.
6. However, these will also be covered by the concept of heteronomy of politics and, for they are part of the Narmada world, the communication around these interests will be at the heart of the communication processes we will study.
7. That is, as a subjective criteria, and not as a truth a la Foucault, related to the objectivity of power. This subjective criteria as well as the way it objectively connects to materialism is further discussed later on.
8. The discussion of the 'right' analytical and 'political' objective is left for a later stage in this essay.
9. Quoted from the Cahier n°12, on 'The question of the intellectuals, the hegemony, politics', Cahiers de prison, Gramsci. (Page nos in quotations from Gramsci's works refer to the edition by Tosel, 1983).
10. Among several other documented publications on the whole project, D'Souza (2002) shows well the appalling inefficiency of the state, its failure to catch the social consequences of the project, its many withdrawals, compromising, or voluntary neglect of important aspects or even public information, like the Morse report, released by the World Bank in 1992. He, in other words, analyses what Patel (1997) calls the 'historically proven low credibility and ineptness' of the Indian state.
11. In their 'communiqué' dated 6th August 1999, for instance, the French 'Friends of the Earth' ('amis de la terre'), so-called 'testify' around what can at best be seen as pleasant ideas and sympathetic categories. Indeed fact, they took part in an NBA rally in village and tribal areas. Despite the evident language barrier, despite the fact that the political meaning since of such rallies is to be understood in its rootedness in the long term action, despite the fact that they had followed the rally for just a very few days, this NGO claimed having 'verified', received 'testimonies',

'without the intermediary of the NBA', what '*the* people directly concerned have *re-*affirmed'... Where the very heart of the problem is that nobody knows who, or how many are the affected people, anyway, the friends of the earth have 'transmitted their support to the local populations'. Source of the quotes: www.amisdelaterre.org

12. Further, though out of scientific ground, the author feels sympathetic for such an involvement and recalls a conversation with one NBA leader, before being invited to join the 'anti' rally. Having explained that, with a technical background and a past of training in 'loving dams', the author wanted to join and see with both an open and critical mind, the reply had been that he should 'therefore all the more join', *because* he was a product of a dam-loving education.
13. In our case, an illustrative example can be taken from the power Supreme Court of India today has in these matters.
14. 'Eminent writer Arundhati Roy and film-maker Jharna Jhaveri visit affected villages and demand that there can be "No Construction without Completion of Rehabilitation First". Citizens Forum—Independent Fact-Finding Committee from New Delhi investigates rehabilitation process and suspected human rights violations in Man Project Chittaroopa Palit and Urmila Patidar still held in jail for the 12th day', NBA Press Note, http://www.narmada.org/nba-press-releases/april-2001/in.jail.for.12th.day.html
15. In another rally, that this time was bringing 'urban intellectuals' to the tribal villages, and it which we participated, a meeting with Baba Amte was organized. After a long while, he came and lay under trees on a 'charpai', from where he addressed the urban crowd in a truly Gandhian set-up, filled with self-absorption and pious respect.
16. Along with a growing mobilization of the RSSS (Rashtriya Swayam Sevak Sangh), they had started their work right from the early 1980s.
17. Explicitly providing for reallotment of agricultural land for oustees, it never followed in action.
18. For a detailed panorama on the political philosophy of nature, see Giri (2003).
19. Movement for monitoring Multilateral Development Banks.
20. See EDF (1989).
21. Based out of the 1987 reports of the Multiple Action Research Group, New Delhi.
22. The CPI(ML)PW stands for the Communist Party of India (Marxist Leninist) People's War.
23. This refers to personal communication with rural animators representative of action groups active in rural Maharashtra and in contact with tribal activists of the NBA as well as other tribal communities in the submergence zones.

Bibliography

Balibar, Etienne, *La crainte des masses* (Paris: Galilée, 1997), p. 456.
Baviskar, Amita, *In the belly of the river* (New Delhi: Oxford University Press, 1995).
Dalal, Sucheta, 'The Narmada dammed', Guest column, 23 October 2002, www.rediff.com.
Das, Maitreyi, 'The Internationalization of the Narmada Dam: Do Western Environmental Groups have a Role in Third World Ecology Movements?', working paper, Harvard University, 1992. http://www.hsph.harvard.edu/hcpds/wpweb/92_01.pdf
D'Souza, Dillip, *The Narmada Dammed: An Inquiry into the Politics of Development* (New Delhi: Penguin, 2002).
EDF, 'Summary of Objectives', prepared as a funding proposal for the Mac Arthur Foundation, Washington DC.
Foucault, Michel, *Power/Knowledge* (New York: Pantheon Books, 1980).
Gramsci, Antonio, *Cahiers de prison*, vol. 3 (Paris: Gallimard, 1978, 1983).
Giri, Saroj, 'Sifting through the ecological debate', Ph.d dissertation, Jawaharlal Nehru University, 2003.
INTACH, 'Sardar Sarovar Project, the Issue of Developing River Narmada', *Current Environmental series* no. I, (New Delhi: INTACH, 1994), p. 44.
Kothari, Rajni, 'Non-party Political Process', *Economic and Political Weekly*, vol. 19, no. 5, 1984, pp. 216–24.
NCA, *Rehabilitation Sub-Group 18th Meeting Report*, Narmada Control Authority, 1992.
Parasuraman, S., 'The Anti-Dam Movement and Rehabilitation Policy', in Jean Drèze, Meera Samson and Satyajit Singh, (eds), *The Dam and the Nation: Displacement and Resettlement in the Narmada Valley* (New Delhi: Oxford University Press, 1997), pp. 26–65.
Patel, Anil, 'Resettlement Politics and tribal interests', in Jean Drèze, Meera Samson and Satyajit Singh, (eds), *The Dam and the Nation: Displacement and Resettlement in the Narmada valley* (New Delhi: Oxford University Press, 1997), pp. 66–92.
Patkar, Medha, 'A Critique of the World Bank financed Sardar Sarovar Dam with special reference to Environmental and Social Problems', before the Subcommittee on Natural Resources, Agricultural Research and Environment, Committee on Science, Space and Technology, Washington DC, 24 October 1989.
Racine, Jean-Luc, Le débat sur le Narmada: l'Inde face au dilemme des grands barrages, *Hérodote*, 3ème trimestre 2001, Paris.
Raynaud, Philippe, Les nouvelles radicalités–de l'extrême gauche en politique, *Le Débat*, n°105, mai-août, Paris.
Roy, Arundhati, *The Cost of Living: The Greater Common Good and the End of Imagination* (New York: Random House, Inc, 1999),

Ruet, Joël, *Against the Current: Organizational Restructuring of State Electricity Boards* (New Delhi: Monohar Publisher, 2002a).
——, 'Mythologie Indienne', *Courrier de la planète*, no. 70, 2002b, p. 19–21.
——, *Power Cuts for Sale? Ownership and Organisational Reform of State Electricity Boards in India* (New Delhi: Academic Foundation, 2004).
Shiva, Vandana, *The Violence of Green Revolution: Third World Agriculture, Ecology and Politics* (London: Zed Books, 1992).
Singh, Satyajit, 'Introduction', in Jean Drèze, Meera Samson and Satyajit Singh (eds), *The Dam and the Nation: Displacement and Resettlement in the Narmada Valley* (New Delhi: Oxford University Press, 1997a), pp. 1–25.
——, *Taming the Waters: The Political Economy of Large Dams in India* (New Delhi: Oxford University Press, 1997b), p. 270.
Tosel, André, 'Introduction', *Gramsci : textes, Collection essential* (Paris: Editions Socials, 1983), pp. 9–40, 388.
World Bank, *India Power Supply to Agriculture*, report no. 22171–IN, Volume 1, Summary Report (New Delhi: World Bank, 2001), p. 40.

14

THAT PERSISTENT 'OTHER':
The Political Economy of Copyright in India

PRADIP N. THOMAS

Critical media theory in India is yet to grapple with issues related to the political economy of copyright and intellectual property rights (IPR). Given the turn towards cultural studies, it is tempting to assign copyright to the realm of culture. However, it is becoming clear that the turn towards cultural critique, that initially allowed for new ways of conceptualizing and understanding the place of the 'superstructure', has ossified and become the exact mirror image of what it once set out to redeem. It has led to numerous cultural determinisms via valorizations of culture, an obsession with meanings at the expense of understandings of how meanings are intimately linked, and in part, generated by structures, a pre-occupation with the autonomy of audiences and cultural processes, signification and subjectivism resulting in numerous celebrations of the particular. These trends have accelerated in the wake of the celebration of many a 'post' theory that has tried to capture the essence of the 'new' as against the tired 'old'. One can argue against this turn and make a case that the neglect of structural persistences—poverty, the globalization of capitalism and markets, deepening inequalities between rich and poor, new symbiotic relations between market and class—are just too important to be ignored. While issues related to IPR can and do need to be seen in terms of a contestation over cultures, meanings, knowledge and representations—there is no getting away from the fact that the current global IPR regime is essentially about markets, monopolies, enclosures and the refeudalization of the economy. While people do make meanings, this is always done in context and influenced by that context. There are realities such as the market that loom large in any consideration of intellectual property (IP). The 'life science' industry which has played no small role in globalizing IP has a palpably real presence in and as the 'market'. So are the copyright industries. Given the real presence of economic power in our world today, we cannot obfuscate this reality or marginalize questions related to political economy to the side lines.

In a recent article, Graham Murdock, has argued against 'over-valuing the new' and has highlighted some of the questionings that key media and cultural theorists have raised about the blind spots in contemporary cultural critique.[1]

'Cultural globalisation theorist's reluctance to engage with questions of class is part of a more general aversion to political-economic analysis.'....James Curran has noted, their accounts repeatedly fail to 'engage critically with economic power'... Stuart Hall has lodged the same reservation against postcolonial theory, arguing that instead of 'generating ways of thinking questions about economic relations and their 'effects', as the 'conditions of existence' of other practices, rejecting the deterministic economism that supposedly underpinned theories of cultural imperialism has led instead to 'a massive, gigantic, and eloquent *disavowal*'.

This essay, while cognizant of the cultural consequences of IP, essentially deals with the political economy of IPR, in particular copyright, in India.

IPR Harmonizations in India: The Current Situation

The range of policy changes that have recently been administered to India's IP regime are a clear indication of the extent to which a global 'proprietary' agenda has become a significant aspect of India's social and economic futures. The pace of accommodation with the Trade Related Agreement on Intellectual Property Rights (TRIPS) treaty has accelerated during the last two years. India had become a signatory to the Paris Convention and the Patent Cooperation Treaty on 7 December 1998 and had earlier become a signatory to the Berne Convention and the Universal Copyright Convention. Recent legislative changes that will have a direct impact on IPR in India include the following: the Patent (Amendments) Act, March 1999, the Copyright (Amendment) Act, December 1999 which conforms to the Berne Convention on Copyright and Related Rights, the Trademark Act, 1999, the Geographical Indications of Goods (Registration and Protection) Act, and the Designs Act, 2000 that is in compliance with TRIPS agreements on Industrial Designs and the Protection of Plant Varieties and Farmer's Rights Act (2001) (The Indian Plant Act) in line with the International Convention for the Protection of New Plant Varieties (UPOV Convention). Other bills that have recently been, or are yet to be debated in parliament include the Information Technology Bill, 2000, the Semiconductor Integrated Circuits Layout-Design Bill, the Patents (Second Amendment) Bill that has been pending since 2003, the Convergence Bill that has been pending since August 2001 and that addresses regulatory issues related to the convergence of communication, IT and broadcasting, and the bill on Biodiversity intended to create local affinities with the Convention on Biological Diversity (CBD).[2]

India's gradual accommodation to the regulatory requirements of TRIPS, which in itself is representative of a set of concerns related to the management of global knowledge, has to some extent been the outcome of constant, external pressure exerted by the World Trade Organization (WTO) and its dominant partners, aimed at opening up every conceivable sector of the Indian economy to external investments. The WTO which is the successor to the General Agreement of Tariffs and Trade (GATT) was established on 1 January 1995. It is the pre-eminent lobbyist for global free trade, in goods and services, a generator and administrator of global trade agreements, supporter of proprietorial versions of IP via TRIPS and the General Agreement on Trade in Services (GATS) and also significantly involved in adjudicating trade disputes.

External pressure also includes the threats of sanctions inspired by the US Trade Representative's Section 301. In fact India features in the 'Special 301' 2004 annual review. The 2004 review,[3] after commending India's progress in matters related to the harmonization of its IPR law with global standards, nevertheless point to the gaps that remain. 'Piracy of copyrighted materials (particularly software, films, popular fiction and certain textbooks) remains a problem for US and Indian right-holders. India has not adopted an optical disc law to deal with optical media piracy. Cable television piracy continues to be a significant problem.'

Economic liberalization has had a positive effect on the fortunes of a host of local companies particularly in the information technology (IT), computer and entertainment sectors. Digital rights management is the source of billions of dollars worth of revenue for the copyright industries—revenues that are bound to grow given the intense, disaggregated, cross-media, cross-multinational corporation (MNC) and cross-product marketing strategies that accompany leisure products, the Hollywood film in particular. IPR, and in this case 'Copyright', needs to be seen from the perspective of the winners—MNCs and to a lesser extent local industrialists on the one hand, and on the other hand, the losers, consisting of the growing population of people who do not have the means to buy into or contribute towards the global market.

Contesting Copyright: Issues and Approaches

At the heart of the current debate on copyrights are three issues/contestations: (*a*) an economic one related to the fact that IPR generated revenue worth billions of dollars for the USA and other developed countries. 'The economic value associated with intellectual property rights accounted for $327 billion and 5.5 million jobs in the United States in 1991',[4] and in particular, the many public hand-wringings over piracy; (*b*) a technological issue related to the translatability of information across and between technologies—copyright in a digital world; and (c) the contentious maze of moral issues related to differing interpretations, use and consequences of IPR in general and copyright and patents in particular, held by governments, corporations and trade bodies on the one hand, and public domain activists and indigenous groups on the other. From a social perspective, issues related to the ethics of IPR reveal the vast gap that exists between what are largely 'proprietorial', private, understandings of intellectual value, and those that are firmly linked to the public domain and that promote the social value of IP over and above its economic value.

There are also less public but equally unresolved issues—for instance the issue of 'authorship', a concept that was developed by the enlightenment scholar John Locke in his treatise on the 'natural rights of man' and given legal status through the Copyright Act of April 1710, enacted in the UK that gave protection to individual authors against print piracy. The original understanding of authorship, meaning reward for an individual's creative labour, that evolved during a period when trade was conducted within limited boundaries is no longer valid. Today 'authorship' does not accrue to the individual or to the collective authors of traditional texts, software and other cultural products but to their corporate employers. The migration of rights originally invested in individuals to corporations, and the attempts to legalize such translations, have been primary strategic means employed by corporations in their bid to take control over the knowledge economy.

In fact every lingering trace of this original understanding of authorship has been removed from the TRIPS agreement of 1 January 1995, which remains the most comprehensive multilateral agreement on IPR to date. While tightening and consolidating the global IP regime, the TRIPS agreement has dispensed with the 'moral' obligations of IPR.[5] The TRIPS agreement categorically states that 'Members do not have right or obligations under the TRIPS agreement in respect of the rights conferred under Article 6*bis* of that [Berne] Convention, i.e. the moral rights (the right to claim authorship and to object to any derogatory action in relation to a work, which would be prejudicial to the author's honour or reputation), or of the rights derived there from'. When placed against Article 6*bis* of the Berne Convention for the Protection of Literary and Artistic Works, the clause reveals the extent to which IPR has become an extension of corporate rights. Article 6*bis* affirmed that 'Independently of the author's economic rights, and even after the transfer of the said rights, the author shall have the right to claim authorship of the work and to object to any distortion, mutilation or other modification of, or other derogatory action in relation to, the said work, which would be prejudicial to his honour or reputation'.[6] One of the consequences of such interpretations is the negation of the social, public value of IP, its value as a socially accessible good rather than as private property. Miller reminds us of that tradition—'It is central to the legal history of both copyright and patents that although each of them creates a property interest owned by the holder, their primary purpose is the promotion of the public interest by encouraging the creation and widespread availability of socially useful information'.[7]

'Authorship', however, continues to be a problematic concept, especially in the context of new, digital technologies of reproduction. Digital technologies have unfixed the singular location, fixed materiality and objectivity associated with products related to the previous generation of technologies. The appropriation and transformation of digitally manipulated material, access to 'sampling' technologies, intertextual mixing and matching and net-based peer-to-peer sharing of popular culture has further complicated the notion of authorship. The issue of 'illegal appropriation' is of course the reason for the continuing attempts by the recording industry in the USA to silence net-based, peer-to-peer music sites, popularized by Napster and sites such as Kazaa and Gnutella. The original, legal basis for copyright protection to cover the expression of ideas rather than the ideas themselves is under threat in a digital world. Given the depth and breath of the current intellectual land grab and the corporate appropriation of knowledge—by way of gene banks, code banks and restrictive copyright and patent laws—ordinary people cannot be expected to know when and why they are in breach of

IP laws or for that matter their own rights to IP. The cultural theorist Rosemary Coombe in her book *The Cultural Life of Intellectual Properties: Authorship, Appropriation, and the Law*, has an answer to that particular quandary. She supports transgressions against the dominant IPR through 'appropriations' of popular culture. The logic that she uses to support her position is founded on a public domain perspective that affirms that human beings, as heirs and creatures of culture, are indebted to ideas and meanings that circulate in the public sphere—ideas and meanings that antecede any subsequent 'expression' of the idea or meaning for which authorship, and originality, is claimed. In support of her position that '...cultural distinction is socially produced',[8] she argues that trademarks for instance, that have their origins in a particular context, are open to the play of meaning available in that context and cultural environment, and thus susceptible to legitimate appropriation. As she explains, 'Increasingly, investment in a mark's signalling function is recognised to create an entitlement to control and appropriate surplus expressive value. The underlying argument is that trademark owners created this value through their investments and should garner any and all available rewards....This, of course, is...the Lockean assertion that one should have the benefit of one's own efforts'. However, 'the choice for assigning the benefits of surplus signifying value should at least consider public economic and expressive interests. One could argue that if the public creates meaning for *Barbie* in excess of the signifier's capacity to signal Mattel's toy, they have done the sowing, and thus they should do the reaping: in short, authorship of such meanings might be seen to reside in the public sphere'.[9] Coombe's perspective on IP and appropriation is similar to the view expressed by Henry Jenkins III in his account of 'textual poaching' of popular culture in the USA.[10]

Coombe's theory of cultural appropriation relates to recent work on IPR and daily life, especially issues such as piracy and contestations in both the informal and formal economies over mediated knowledge. In this approach, taken up by Lawrence Liang and others belonging to the Alternative Law Forum, Bangalore, short circuiting the enclosures around global knowledge, breaching the barriers against access, and making the impermeable permeable is not a 'venal sin' but merely the means by which the excluded resist, contribute to and benefit from modernity and the knowledge economy. In a (5–7 April 2004) WACC-sponsored workshop held in Bangalore 'IPR and the Media: Emerging Paradigms', Liang dealt with the many ways in which piracy reproduces itself organically—in the centres of power, right under the noses of the copyright police, exemplified by pirated circulations of Hollywood releases often within hours of its premier in the USA, along with the ways in which the excluded engage with the system by tapping into it in the most innovative and resourceful ways, leading to the remaking of modernity by people on the 'periphery' into what he calls a *jugaad* modernity'.[11] This approach of sympathizing with piracy as a form of resistance culture is not far removed from James Scott's celebration of the 'infrapolitics of subordinate groups', everyday resistance that is the means of negotiating entry into hitherto excluded zones.[12] In my view, such examples are also, quite significantly, stories about the ways in which people survive in economic spaces of their own creation that are nevertheless linked to (although not always recognized by) the global economy. The over-pricing of knowledge in a context characterized by poverty and low incomes remains a factor that has contributed to piracy in India, a fact that has been noted in the 'Study on Copyright Piracy in India' sponsored by the Ministry of Human Resource Development.[13] 'In India, an application computer software, on the average, is sold at US $250, a good quality audio CD is not available below Rs 200 [$4.5]. The text books for professional course such as engineering, medical and management remain beyond the buying capacity of many students. Under such circumstances, piracy provides the natural escape route for all those who cannot afford to buy the originals'.

Coombe's cultural studies perspective on copyright and her advocacy of 'direct action' and counter-hegemonic strategies relate to but are sufficiently different from the political economy perspective on copyright, particularly that of Ronald Bettig's *Copyrighting Culture: The Political Economy of Intellectual Property*.[14] Bettig takes the view that current IPR and copyright laws are intrinsically linked to the

'... expansionary logic of capital'[15] and that the seamless incorporation and extension of every new technology and its products within this logic merely results in the reinforcement of the dominance of the intellectual property regime. Bettig illustrates the manner in which the cultural industries in the USA, through their intersectoral ownership of the media, their connections to the political elite and their global lobbying power have invested in and control global understandings of IPR. His comments on the manner in which Hollywood has extended its control over IP, raises parallels with the current situation in India where the appropriation of film rights has been complemented by attempts by large media players to establish themselves in every conceivable media sector through which these rights can be exploited. As Bettig has observed 'The control of intellectual primary material, in particular copyrights in television programe and motion pictures, facilitated Hollywood's capture of new cable and video technology. Rather than undermining the oligopolistic structure of filmed entertainment distribution, these technologies have become means for perpetuating concentrated ownership and control of communications and information industries and for heightening barriers to these sectors'.[16]

Bettig's pessimism, although understandable, does not provide a platform for another understanding of IPR, a platform which is explored by Robert Boyle and defined in his *A Politics of Intellectual Property: Environmentalism for the Net*.[17] Calling for a political economy of intellectual property, the author explores the means for a politics of IP and a strategy of bringing IP into the 'public domain', rather like what the environmental movement has achieved. He notes that the

> '....public domain is disappearing, both conceptually and literally, in an IP system built around the *interests* of the current stakeholders and the *notion* of the original author, around an over-deterministic practice of economic analysis and around a "free speech" community that is under-sensitized to the dangers of private censorship. In one very real sense, the environmental movement *invented* the environment so that farmers, consumers, hunters and birdwatchers could all discover themselves

as environmentalists. Perhaps we need to *invent* the public domain in order to call into being the coalition that might protect it'. Boyle's analysis suggests that together with the 'appropriations' of popular culture, there have to be organized, inter-sectoral attempts to legitimise such appropriations and validate other IP orders.

Copyright in India

All copyright laws have a dual function—to protect the claims of authorship expressed through a variety of media, and to prevent piracy, the unlawful copying of copyrighted products. The Indian Copyright Act, 1957 is itself an amended version of the Indian Copyright Act of 1914 which was modelled on the U.K. Copyright Act of 1911. The 1957 Act confirmed to the Berne Convention and to the Universal Copyright Convention. This Act was amended in 1983 in compliance with the revised Berne and UC Conventions effected in 1971 (Paris). The 1957 copyright act provided protection for 'original' works of a literary, dramatic, musical and artistic kind, inclusive of architecture, art, cinema and sound recording. The act was amended on a number of occasions to enable a correspondence between domestic and international laws on copyright. With the advent of new technologies of copying—audio-cassettes, video-cassettes and recently digital media—the incidence and scale of copyright piracy has increased, in certain instances, quite dramatically. The music industry in India has estimated that in 1997, 175 million out of the 580 million cassettes sold were unauthorized duplications.[18] In response to these developments, the Copyright Act, 1958 was amended in 1984, 1992 and 1994. The 1984 Amendment, for instance, specified that video films be treated on par with cinematography for the purpose of copyright. The 1992 and 1994 Amendments have progressively included copyright matters related to cable television and computer software. The amendment effected in 1984 recognized the reality of audio-visual piracy and offered provisions to control piracy. The most recent amendment in 1994 has enabled compatability between domestic laws on copyright with TRIPS requirements, in particular the extension of the notion of 'literary works' to cover computer programmes, along with an increase to the protection period from 50 to 60 years. The 1994 amendment also vested copyright societies and the Copyright Board in India with powers to handle copyright infringements. It also mandated the establishment of expert benches in the High Court on IP and enforcement cells at the state level. Furthermore it established conditions of 'reciprocity', meaning the granting of copyright protection for foreign authors (corporations) on par with that granted to nationals.

At first glance the Indian Copyright Act seems to have balanced private and public interests in the area of IP. For instance, Section 52, explains legitimate infringements of copyright law—in the context of private study and research, performances organized in the course of study at an educational institution, in front of a limited audience and in a not-for-profit situation. While such provisions do provide the space for non-commercial uses of copyrighted material, it is impossible to predict with any accuracy if these provisions will survive the emerging versions and visions of international proprietorial law, or whether it will become a victim of the attempts to harmonize and homologize global IP law with domestic law. The standardization of trade-related practices—for instance, the extension of 'Most-Favoured-Nation' status—requires all WTO signatories to treat non-domestic service suppliers on par with domestic players, offer them the same level of tax breaks, preferential treatment, etc. Point 4b, Article 6 entitled 'Domestic Regulation' in Part II, General Obligations and Disciplines, Trade in Services[19] is the infamous 'not more burdensome than necessary to ensure the quality of the service' clause, which can be invoked by IP holders in the developed world, or for that matter in India, to restrict public, limited uses of cultural material in the interest of commerce. Interestingly enough, Section 63B of the Indian Copyright Act, 1994 reserves the strictest of penalties for those involved in using pirated software, penalties not reserved for any other form of copyright infringement covered in the Act. 'Any person who knowingly makes use on a computer of an infringing copy of a computer programme shall be punishable with imprisonment for a term which shall not be less than seven days but which may extend to three years and with a fine which shall not be less than fifty thousand rupees [$1,128] but which may extend to two lakhs rupees [$4,514]....'[20] Furthermore the accent is on 'enforcement' and 'violation' of copyright rather than, for instance, on the means to reward 'creativity' and 'innovation'. Such statutory provisions suggest that the Indian Copyright Act as it stands today is little more than an extension of global copyright law and TRIPS.

This accent on enforcement is in turn reflected in the overall strategies employed by the premier Indian software trade lobby—the National Association of Software and Service Companies (NASSCOM) that has, on a number of occasions, acted as an anti-piracy enforcement agency and has conducted anti-piracy raids along with the Business Software Alliance and the police. The relationship between employers, employees and copyright in the section 'Copyright of Software: Frequently Asked Questions' in the NASSCOM website is explained in the following manner—'In the case of a programme made in the course of an author's employment under a contract of service or apprenticeship, the employer shall, in the absence of any agreement to the contrary, be the first owner of the Copyright'.[21] Since, 'agreements to the contrary' are invariably the exception rather than the rule, the ownership of copyright is bound to remain with corporations rather than with any group.

The amended Indian Copyright Law assumes that copyright law related to software exists solely to benefit the business community and no other sector. N. S. Gopalakrishnan, from the National Law School, Bangalore[22] suggests that since the benefits of software are bound to accrue primarily to business communities that we must '...consider keeping computer programmes outside the domain of the private property monopoly rights regime. It appears that the jurisprudence of considering intellectual property as 'common property' is going to pay better dividends to the average Indian computer developer, researcher and user in the days to come, when compared to the short term benefits of a few million dollars investment and export (earnings) by big companies in India in return for the heavy price that we (will) have to pay in terms of private property rights'.

It would seem that controversies over the copyright of computer programmes are bound to remain since programme makers use source codes and mathematical algorithms that have in some cases been patented, notably in the USA. In the context of the anti-trust rulings against Microsoft, the question—would the Windows platform, with its many derivative features including the graphical system of windows, menus, etc., get to its position of global dominance if copyright laws had been strictly enforced at the time these programmes were developed?—reminds us of the collective origins of much that exists in global culture today. Anne Branscomb,[23] rues the fact that useability has been compromised because of competing standards. 'By encouraging differential user interfaces, the law impedes the adoption of widely shared conventions, frustrating users, unnecessarily requiring programmes to reinvent the wheel, pushing up development costs, and inhibiting the compatibility that encourages a competitive marketplace. The challenge is to devise a legal system that encourages standardized user interfaces while rewarding human labour that leads to innovation and progress.'

The Cultural Industries and Copyright in India

The cultural industries in India—the press, broadcasting and film along with the telecommunications and computer hardware and software sectors—are key proponents of IPR. To a large extent, this turn towards enforcement has been a by-product of global media and IT ownership of and involvement in the media and IT sectors in India.[24] Monopolies in the leisure industry are the norm—the latest being the Sony-BMG merger that was completed on 1 August 2004. This merger between Sony Music Entertainment (11 per cent market share) and Bertelseman Music Group (12 per cent market share) has led to a single company controlling nearly a quarter of the global music business, a third of all releases and to the strategic positioning of this company to take advantage of the online, legal music download market. Local media monopolies owned by family-based business concerns—the Tatas,

Ambanis, Modis, and media houses that have cross-sectoral interests such as the Times of India Group (print, FM Radio)—too benefit from strict copyright enforcement. Most, if not all media, public relations and IT sectors in India are characterized by monopolies—in satellite and cable broadcasting, FM Radio, cellular telecommunications, software and hardware. Monopolies also exist at the state levels, for instance Eenadu in Andhra Pradesh and the Sun Group in Tamil Nadu. In response to competition from foreign players, in particular Murdoch's Star India, some of the larger media houses, including Living Media, Zee Telefilms, Eenadu, Bennett Coleman & Company have formed a lobby—the Indian Media Group. There are five major players in the cable industry—Siticable owned by the ZEE TV empire, IndusInd Media owned by the Hindujas, Hathway Cables owned by the property tycoons the Rahejas, Sumangali Cable Vision owned by Kalanithi Maran of Sun TV and the network owned by Harsh Goenka of RPG.[25] While 80 per cent of the business outsourcing market continues to be in the hands of independent companies such as WNS Global Services, Tracemail, ICICI OneSource and others, the recent entry of global IT services such as IBM Global Services, Electronic Data Systems and Accenture is set to change this situation. IBM alone has signed ten strategic outsourcing deals during the 2000-2004 period.[26]

An equally powerful, although relatively unknown emerging industry is the entertainments industry. The March 2000 FICCI-Arthur Anderson report on the Indian entertainments industry estimates revenue figures of Rs 8,445 crore ($1.8 bn) in the year 2000 and predicts that it will reach Rs 33,984 crore ($7.5 bn) in the year 2005, out of which Rs 14,692 crore ($3.2 bn) will come from film exports alone.[27] With an average yearly production output of 800 films in regional languages, the Indian film industry produces annually more films than Hollywood. Film and film-based spin-offs such as film music have become the basis for a multi-million dollar, regional languages based satellite and cable television industry. There are three potential growth areas in the entertainment sector in India—first an overseas market for Indian film, music and entertainment software. There is a booming film export business to the Middle East, Europe, North America and Southeast Asia. In the year 2000, $800 million was spent by overseas Indians on Indian movies, serials and music. Indian movies earned over Rs 400 crore ($95 m) in the international market and it was expected that film exports would grow over 80 per cent by the year 2003. As Rao[28] observes '...the entertainment industry...is expected to see in five years, film exports grow from Rs 400 crore ($95 m) to Rs 1,000 crore ($230 m), cable and satellite advertising from Rs 1,366 ($325 m) to Rs 2,050 crore ($480 m), music from Rs 1,700 crore ($400 m) to Rs 3,000 crore ($690 m).... Entertainment software is expected to export $20 billion by the year 2008 and employ 15 million people'. Second, animation, specifically the outsourcing of products for global studios. Leading companies included the Mumbai-based Unilazar Group and the Chennai-based Pentafour, and finally, investments in domestic broadbanding by multichannel companies who are poised to take advantage of the demands for entertainment in the domestic market. Today regional media moghuls like Subhash Chandra of Zee TV, Kalanithi Maran of Sun TV and Ramoji Rao of Eenadu are creating new regional entertainment pipelines via satellite television and cable television. Their ambitions are linked to providing a host of services including internet, telephony, video-on-demand and other services. Others like Adlabs-Mukta, Time Cinemas, Ultra Digital Cinema, Real Image, Broadband Pacenet have invested in digitizing film theatres. In fact the front runner, Adlabs-Mukta is the first integrated film company in India and is involved in film and film processing, multiplex cinemas, film production and digital cinema—in other words in production, processing, distribution and exhibition. There are 6000 production houses in India involved in creating software for this thriving, growing market.[29]

With such concentrations of ownership by local and increasingly global firms and the prospect of huge revenues for government (through taxes) and the private sector, there is bound to be greater attempts at tightening the IP regime in India. That process has already started with the moves by the Ministry of Human Resources Development to increase royalty fees to performing artistes and place limits on 'remixes'.

IP Futures in India: Copyright in a Global Market Economy

In the context of broadcasting in India, and from the perspective of copyright, the most potentially lucrative cultural products are those associated with the Indian film industry and its spin-offs, particularly video, DVD, music and television programmes derived from, or based on Bollywood, and the film industry in South India. With a 27,000 feature film database and an average of 800 productions per year, this cultural industry is a potential and actual source of revenue for both government and the private sector. The collective administration of copyrights in the popular cultural sector in India is currently enforced by three societies—the Society for Copyright Regulations of Indian Producers of Films and Television (SCRIPT) for cinema, Indian Performing Rights Society Limited (IPRS) for musical works, and the Phonographic Performance Limited (PPL) for sound recordings. These societies represent larger industry interests. For instance, the PPL has been constituted by the Indian Music Industry (IMI), an organization that represents 75 per cent of national and regional music labels. While audio and video piracy was a reason for the establishment of these interest groups, it can be argued that a combination of factors—the exposure of the relationship between the Indian film industry and money laundering, lax copyright enforcement, outdated copyright legislation and the sheer scale of policing cultural piracy—prevented the emergence of a viable copyright culture.

India's negotiations at the Uruguay Round of GATT had included a commitment to the progressive liberalization of trade in the audio-visual sector. Hollywood had lobbied hard to reverse the 20 year-old quota policy that restricted the annual import (100 films) and distribution of Hollywood films in India. It had urged the US government to enforce Section 301-based trade sanctions against India for content piracy. The US-based International Intellectual Property Alliance had in 1995, estimated trade losses to the US service industry as a result of piracy in India alone in the region of US $119 million out of which $58 million was incurred in film, $10 million in recorded music, $26 million in entertainment software and $26 million in the book trade.[30] In the year 2000 alone, estimated global piracy-related revenue losses to US motion picture companies was estimated to be in the region of $2.5 billion. The issue of piracy was turned into the means by which the Motion Picture Association of America (MPAA), representing the seven major film and television producers in the USA inclusive of Walt Disney Company, Sony Pictures Entertainment, Inc., Metro-Goldwyn-Mayer, Inc., Paramount Pictures Corporation, Twentieth Century Fox Film Corp., Universal Studios, Inc., and Warner Bros, made a determined effort to enter the Indian market. With a potential audience of 200 million, that includes cable and satellite television viewers, and box office returns of US $6 million for the Hindi version of *Jurrasic Park*, US $12.5 million for *Titanic* and a similar amount for local blockbusters such as the Hindi-language *Dil To Pagal Hai*, the Indian film market was perceived as a potential source of revenues for Hollywood. In fact as Sidhva[31] has noted, Hollywood planned to carve 10 per cent of the Indian film market by 2000, through the consolidation of a production, distribution and exhibition strategy, the latter aided by the establishment of multiplexes in Mumbai. The influence of Hollywood needs to be seen not merely in terms of the reach of its products, but the way in which it has influenced the content of popular film throughout the world. One can, for instance, argue that the stereotype of the 'angry young man' in the Hindi film industry, who uses violence to avenge violence and to settle scores, has its roots in Hollywood films of the 1970s and 1980s and characterizations by actors such as Charles Bronson and Sylvester Stallone.

The entry of Hollywood into the Indian market led to renewed attempts to highlight the issue of copyright violations, and strengthened domestic concerns and initiatives linked to creating an environment favourable to TRIPS and IPR. Market entry was created in a number of ways, both fortuitous and planned. The haphazard entry of satellite and cable television in the early 1990s provided the right opportunity for the global cultural industry to gauge potential revenues in the Indian cultural market. Within the space of five years, 1990–95, News Corporations Star TV Network, Time Warner's

CNN and Cartoon Network, Viacom's MTV, Sony Entertainment and Disney among numerous others had become established players in Indian broadcasting. However, the relationship between the satellite broadcasters and the local cable fraternity that is in excess of 70,000 today, was strained from the very beginning, because of a conflict of interests and objectives, perceived loopholes in the existing Copyright Act and lax enforcement which resulted in large-scale violation of copyright by cable companies. Cable operations in India, for the most part, remain small, and is very much a cottage industry, in spite of the attempts to consolidate 'content and carriage' shares by large groups like Star TV's Siticable, the Raheja group owned Hathway Cable and Datacom in which the Star TV network has a 26 per cent stake. In 1999, nine Hollywood studios including all those represented by the MPAA, filed suits against two of India's largest cable television networks for the infringement of copyright. The Delhi High Court's ruling favoured these studios and led to the enforcement of penalties against these cable firms. The local film industry too has initiated a number of civil cases against copyright pirates–cable pirates, VCR and VCD pirates. However, given the nexus between the film world, the cable networks and organized crime, it has been difficult to enforce copyright regulations nationally or to restrain cable releases of international and domestic films prior to their official release in theatres. The extent of the problem is particularly visible in India's film and finance capital, Mumbai in which the cable business in the most lucrative parts of the city, is run by family members associated with the right wing head of the Shiv Sena, Bal Thackeray.[32] While the government, along with the film industry, have recently been involved in trying to clean up the industry and give it a new image, the links are institutionalized and involve local and national politicians.

Piracy, although an issue of concern for both international and domestic players, needs to be seen in perspective. In the emerging environment of IP, the issue of piracy has the highest priority. Other equally pressing concerns, such as the predatory pricing of cultural products, barriers to cultural appropriation of products conceived in the public domain, the protection of collective authorship, among other issues of concern to ordinary consumers, are rarely, if ever, debated, or treated with the importance that they deserve. As Parthasarathy[33] has observed, the international furore over the case of Napster and piracy has deflected attention from the ways in which the international music business has used that pretext to charge higher prices for their products. The big four in India, BMG, EMI, Sony and Universal, protected by the umbrella body, the Recording Industry Association of India (RIAA), have recently increased the price of their products. 'In India, the international foursome has, almost in unison, doubled the price of Western music cassettes in the last three years from around Rs 75 to Rs 125–Rs 150 and CD's can cost over Rs 500 a piece for 8–10 songs'.

The tightening and strengthening of copyright enforcement with respect to domestic cultural products, film in particular, has also become part of MPAA's New Delhi-based India-wide operations. It would seem that such a prioritizing will, in the long run, also ensure the protection of Hollywood films in India. The reason for MPAA's involvement in copyright protection of local film products becomes clearer when seen against the investments made by one of its members, Sony Entertainment TV, that was launched in October 1995 in the Indian subcontinent and has bought rights to 300 Hindi films, and secured exclusive rights for cultural and sporting events in India. Sony also hosts top-rated show *Aahat,* currently has access to and owns 1500 hours of exclusive programming, has invested millions of dollars in dubbing Hollywood films into Hindi and in the making of local feature films, and is also involved in making profits from its Sony music label. Similarly, another member of MPAA, Twentieth Century Fox, part of News Corporation is also poised to break into the film market with 20 productions per year. With such investments at stake, India can look forward to the active involvement of the MPAA in the matter of copyright enforcement. There has also been a similar scramble for film rights by local firms. The Mumbai-based Eros Network for instance owns rights to over 1000 films. Sippy films, producers of the Bollywood blockbuster *Sholay* have major plans to brand the film and licence its merchandizing, and companies like B4U and Star TV have invested vast sums of money into the ownership of film rights. There is of course a major commercial reason for copyright enforcement and that has to do with the global cross-sectoral marketing of products. These developments, and the emergence of strong contenders in the domestic software and entertainments business, along with the entry of global players and North-South alliances supportive of copyright protection, have led to the emergence of a new culture of IP in India consonant with the global IP regime. The prospects for merchandizing has also been explored by international branded satellite channels such as MTV India and Cartoon Network.

Enforcement is being carried out on a war-footing all over India and government anti-piracy cells, private security firms and national and international organizations like the National Association of Software and Service Companies (NASSCOM), the Indian Performing Rights Society Limited (IPRS), the Phonographic Performance Limited (PPL) and the Business Software Alliance (BSA) are involved in a variety of enforcement actions. In fact the government has established cells for copyright enforcement in 23 states, has published a book, *A Handbook of Copyright Law* to be used by government agencies, has organized training programmes at the National Police Academy and National Academy of Customs, Excise and Narcotics and created a Copyright Enforcement Advisory Council to coordinate these efforts.

The wave of global media mergers and acquisitions, including the star-crossed merger between America OnLine's and TimeWarner in 2001 that led to the creation of a $165 billion strong company, has been spurred on by the need for companies to maintain their strategic advantage in a new media environment, to invest in 'content and carriage', in futures that guarantee economies of scale, by the desire to create near complete monopolies controlling every aspect of a media product—from production and transmission to its distribution and marketing—to take advantage of the knowledge capital that is the basis for rights to intellectual property and to exploit the many opportunities for marketing these rights through the ownership of a range of media channels. Every Disney-based film is more than just a film for it is conceived as an opportunity to synergistically market a commodity. So a film like the *Lion King* is marketed through numerous media channels—film viewings, theatre performances, video, DVD, CD-ROMS, web-sites, computer games, posters, cassettes and CDs and is further marketed through the sale of branded toys, sponsorship of activities in primary schools, kids meals at fast food chains, clothes and other accessories. In other words, copyrights and patents have become the basis for the exploitation of content over many media and non-media sectors. In this context Coombe's[34] remarks on the intellectual commodification of 'celebrity' in the context of Hollywood, is a reminder of another potential revenue source in India, a country in which the cult of celebrity and revenues from celebrity are already a source of huge revenues for MNCs and local businesses. 'It [IP protection] is no longer limited to the name or likeness of an individual, but now extends to a person's nickname, signature, physical pose, characterisations, "singing style", vocal characterisations, body parts, frequently used phrases, car, performance style, and mannerisms and gestures, provided that these are distinctive and publicly identified with the person claiming this right'. The South Indian film star Rajnikant's attempt to copyright a specific hand gesture in his below-average film *Baba* is one example of new copyright manoeuvrings in the Indian film industry. Some features of copyright and the entertainment industries in India are discussed below.

- Copyright in the entertainments industry in India primarily involves the protection of film and derivative products. From a public perspective, access and affordability are key concerns. While the national broadcaster, Doordarshan (DD), does have rights to film and archival material and can theoretically at least, provide universal access, it has increasingly become commercial in its focus and operations. DD will, in its present context and focus, have predominantly commercial reasons for exploiting copyright.
- Given the reality of convergence, both domestic and global players in the Indian entertainment market are bound to use the protections afforded by copyright law to exploit their products over a range of media.

- While access to film shows are affordable for the majority of people in rural and urban areas, new ventures such as multiplexes, new synergistic ownership patterns, and new partners from money-rich Hollywood could lead to higher prices and to the edging out of access to poorer sections. With the imminent arrival of global, Direct to Home television, the space for 'pay-per' channels has increased. It would seem that the current low prices enjoyed by customers of satellite and cable television will change in the light of commercial pressure for increased revenues.
- The copy of popular television formats, such as 'Who Wants to be a Millionaire'(licenced to the UK-based Celedor)—*Kaun Banega Crorepati* (Star TV), *Sawal Dus Crore Ka* (Zee TV), *Koteeswaran* (Sun TV), has brought in major audiences and revenues. Formats or quiz programmes and dramas are a potential source of revenue and in the context of attempts to take over parts of the entertainment market in India by global players, could well become a copyright issue in future. For an update on the continuing problems with copyright infringement in the Indian film industry see Desai (2005)
- With the development of niche markets, the copyrighting of material presently in the public domain could become the norm and could affect folk and traditional music. With the involvement of global players in the music business in India, copyrights for specific niche markets such as Indian classical music, Hindustani and Carnatic, could become part of global empires.
- The public consequence of a restricted IP regime will particularly affect software use in the context of another development. With the accent on the development of business software that can bring in revenues, very little time and effort is being devoted to the development of socially beneficial software. The e-commercialization of the net may lead to similar consequences—the shutting out of the net to those who cannot pay for the privilege.

The Cultural Politics of IPR in India

While these mobilizations have acknowledged threats to culture, culture has been perceived in the classic anthropological sense, as 'a way of life', in terms of constraints to the existence and continuity of village traditions, local consumption habits, relationships, and knowledge systems. This tradition is, for example, represented in Aboriginal mobilizations over IPR in Australia. Their understanding of 'Indigenous Cultural and Intellectual Property' privileges the concept of 'heritage'[35]—heritage seen as literary, performing or artistic works, scientific, agricultural, technical, ecological knowledge, items of movable cultural property, human remains and tissues, immovable cultural property and the documentation of indigenous heritage in archives, film, etc.[36]

While there is an urgent need to protect heritage and to counter threats, it would seem that there is also the need to relate the understanding of culture as a way of life, to the mass-mediated versions of culture that are a consequence of the globalization of the mass media and the information economy. One could argue that the cultural environments in which we live consist of the cultures that we live by and the cultures that we live in. Both these cultures are threatened by the emerging global IP regime, that on the one hand, appropriates traditional knowledge systems, and that on the other, imposes proprietorial understandings of culture that ordinary people cannot appropriate or give public meanings to. One could therefore argue that notions such as 'collective rights' and 'common resources' can be equally applied to IPR in the context of our cultural environments.

So what can be done to mobilize people in India on larger understandings of IPR? There are a couple of initiatives that can be explored:

- The French followed by the Canadians have tried to advocate for a 'cultural exception' clause in the matter of audio-visual trade. The genesis of this clause goes back to the Uruguay Round of the GATT negotiations that almost derailed in 1993 as a consequence of the EU's 'Television Without Frontiers' policy that supported the idea of quotas on Hollywood exports to the EU. This clause explicitly privileges national jurisdiction on the issue of trade in culture and makes a case for trade in 'culture' to be treated differently from trade in goods and services. While there are obvious limitations to such an exception especially in contexts like India where this clause may well be used to protect local cultural empires at the expense of the cultural rights of ordinary citizens, it nevertheless also provides a strong foundation for the exploration of non-commercial understandings of domestic IP rights. The recent initiative created by concerned citizens in South Korea—the Coalition for Cultural Diversity in Moving Images (CDMI) towards the mobilization of support for the protection of the indigenous film industry in South Korea, is an example of the internationalizing of issues related to 'cultural exception'.[37]

- From a practical perspective and from the point of advocacy, a grassroots strategy linked to expanding the concept of culture to include audio-visual and virtual culture could possibly be the means for introducing copyright and other IP issues into the public domain. Since indigenous groups are already involved in 'heritage' related issues, the introduction of copyright issues—universal access, the social benefit of copyright, public investment in 'shareware' software, limits to proprietorial understandings of copyright, the time frame for copyrights—and other issues, can become an aspect of larger, anti-WTO, anti-globalization advocacies.
- In the urban context, the media can play an important role in highlighting the public, social nature of copyright issues. At the moment, much of the debate is restricted to the dominant terms of copyright and is more often than not, on issues related to the perceived transgressions of global copyright laws, particularly piracy. There is, for instance, need for a real debate on WIPO's Copyright Treaty and cognizance of suggestions such as that made by the UK Government Commission's[38] report that recommends that countries in the South not ratify the WIPO Copyright Treaty.

We believe developing countries would probably be unwise to endorse the WIPO Copyright Treaty, unless they have very specific reasons for doing so, and should retain their freedom to legislate on technological measures. It follows that developing countries, or indeed other developed countries, should not follow the example of the DMCA (Digital Millennium Copyright Act) in forbidding all circumvention of technological protection. In particular, we take the view that legislation such as the DMCA shifts the balance too far in favour of producers of copyright material at the expense of the historic rights of users. Its replication globally could be very harmful to the interests of developing countries in accessing information and knowledge they require for their development. Similarly we have concluded that the EU Database Directive goes too far in providing protection for assemblages of material and will restrict unduly access to scientific databases required by developing countries.

- And last but not least, there is also the need for extensive studies on the culture and political economy of piracy in India—piracy as big business and piracy as economic survival and as entry into the world of modernity and the knowledge economy.

Notes

1. Murdock, G., 'Past the Posts: Rethinking Change, Retrieving Critique', *European Journal of Communication*, vol. 19, no. 1, 2004, p. 29.
2. 'India Prepares to Meet TRIPS Obligations', *The Hindu*, 24 February 2001, p. 10; Lal, C.M., 'The Indian Film Industry and Copyright Laws', pp. 1–6, http://www.indiaip.com/main.articles.; Cullet, P., 'Farmer's Rights in Peril', *Frontline*, vol. 17, no. 1–14, 7 April 2000, pp. 1–5, http://www.frontlineonline.com.; Rangnekar, D., 'To Balance Regulation and Compliance', *Frontline*, vol. 17, no. 9–22, 25 December 2000, pp. 1–6, http://www.frontlineonline.com

3. Special 301 Annual Review 2004, http://www.ustr.gov/reports/2004/special301-pwl.htm#India
4. Monberg, J., 'Identities, Commodities and Information Flows: Intellectual Property Rights and the Construction of Emergent Electronic Social Spaces', in S.J. Drucker and G. Gumpert (eds), *Real Law @ Virtual Space: Regulation in Cyberspace*, (Cresskill, NJ: Hampton Press Inc., 1999), pp. 267–86.
5. An Overview of the Agreement on Trade-Related Aspects of Intellectual Property Rights (TRIPS, Agreement), 1999, pp. 1–20, http://www.wto.org/wto/intellec
6. Berne Convention for the Protection of Literary and Artistic Works (Paris Text 1971), 1999, p. 1, http://www.law.cornell.edu/treaties
7. Miller, S.E., *Civilizing Cyberspace: Policy, Power and the Information Superhighway* (New York: ACM Press, Reading: Addison-Wesley Publishing Company, 1990), p. 360.
8. Coombe, R., *The Cultural Life of Intellectual Properties: Authorship, Appropriation, and the Law* (Durham/London: Duke University Press, 1998), p. 61.
9. Ibid., p. 67.
10. Jenkins, H. III, *Textual Poachers: Television Fans and Participatory Culture* (New York: Routledge, Chapman and Hall, 1992).
11. See Liang's paper as well as papers by other participants at the Voices For All website http://www.voiceforall.org/ipr/voices_ipr.htm. See also the InfoChange website, http://www.infochangeindia.org/Intellectual_Pro_Rts_04.jsp and the WACC web-site, www.wacc.org.uk for articles on IPR. Read his article, 'Global Commons, Public Space and IPR', *Media Development*, 1/2003 (first issue), also available on the WACC website.
12. Scott, J.S, *Weapons of the Weak: Everyday Forms of Peasant Resistance,* (New Haven: Yale University Press, 1990), p. xiii.
13. Ministry of Human Resource Development, Government of India, *Study of Copyright Piracy in India,* Chapter IX, pp. 2–3. http://www.education.nic.in/htmlweb/cr_piracy_study/cpr.htm
14. Bettig, R., *Copyrighting Culture: The Political Economy of Intellectual Property* (Colorado/Oxford: Westview Press, 1996). Also see his paper 'Copyright and the Commodification of Culture', of *Media Development* Intellectual Property Rights and Communication, 1/2003. This paper has subsequently been published in the Hyderabad-based *The ICFAI Journal of Intellectual Property Rights*, vol. III, no. 1, 2004 (February).
15. Ibid., p. 195.
16. Ibid., p. 36.
17. Boyle, R., 'A Politics of Intellectual Property: Environmentalism for the Net?', 1997, http://www.wcl.american.edu/pub/faculty, p. 14.
18. 'The Indian Music Industry–Piracy', http://www.indianmi.org, pp. 1–2.

19. Part II: General Obligations and Disciplines, Article II, http://www.wto.org/wto/services
20. The (Indian) Copyright Act, 1957, http://www.scatindia.com
21. Intellectual Property Rights, http://www.nasscom.org, pp. 1–13.
22. Gopalakrishnan, N.S., 'Computer Software Protection, the Dunkel Draft Text and the Indian Copyright Law', 1993, pp. 1–8, http://www.iprlawindia.org. originally published in *The Academy Law Review*, vol. XVII, nos 1–2, 1993, p. 6.
23. Branscomb, A.W., *Who Owns Information: From Privacy to Public Access*, (New York: Basic Books, 1994), p. 176.
24. The NASSCOM Strategic Review 2004 estimates the value of the hardware, software and services industry in India for 2003–2004 at US$ 7.42 billion.
25. For a more detailed reading of media ownership in India and its consequences for public life see P.N. Thomas, 'The Political Economy of Communications in India'. in S.R. Melkote and S. Rao (eds), *Critical Issues in Communication: Looking Inward for Answers, Essays in Honour of K.E. Eapen* (New Delhi: Sage, 2001); 'Copyright and the Emerging Knowledge Economy in India', *Economic and Political Weekly*, vol. XXXVI, no. 24, 16 June 2001, pp. 2147–56; and 'Media Ownership and Communication Rights in India', in Pradip N. Thomas and Zaharom Nain (eds), *Who Owns the Media: Global Trends and Local Resistances* (London and Penang: ZED/Southbound/WACC, 2004). On the Sony-BMG merger see comment by S. Eralp, 'Sony Merger Unsafe at any Volume', *The Guardian*, 10 June 2004, p. 21.
26. See S. Sengupta, and S. Singh, 'BPO: Slip slidin' away', *BusinessWorld Online*, April 19 2004, http://businessworldindia.com/apr1904/indeptho1.asp, pp. 1–5. and S. Singh, 'IBM in India', in *Business World Online*, 10 May 2004 at http://www.Businessworldindia.com/may1004/coverstory 01.asp, pp. 1–7.
27. S. Dutta, 'Real Life, Reel Woes', *Business World*, 15 January 2001, http://www.businessworldindia.com/archive
28. S.L. Rao, 'India's Rapidly Changing Consumer Markets, *Economic and Political Weekly*, 30 September 2000, p. 3571.
29. V. Kohli, et. al., 'It's Showtime Folks', *Business World*, 10 January 2000, pp. 1–7, http://www.businessworldindia.com/archive; V. Kohli-Khandekar, 'Adlabs: The Big Picture Company', *Businessworld*, 10 November 2003, http://www.businessworldindia.com/Nov1003/indeptho4.asp
30. R. Mansell and U. Wehn, 'Institutional Innovations for the Governance of Information Services: Enforcing Intellectual Property Rights and Protecting Security and Privacy', in R. Mansell, and U. Wehn (eds), *Knowledge Societies: Information Technology for Sustainable Development* (Oxford: Oxford University Press, 1998), p. 212.

31. S. Sidhva, 'A Target for Hollywood', *Financial Times*, 11 July 1996, p. 6.
32. S. Anandan, 'A Different Television War', *Outlook*, 22 May 2000, pp. 1–3, http://www.outlookindia.com.; S. Raval and S. Aiyer, 'Return of the Dons', *India Today*, 1 January 2001, http://www.india-today.com
33. A. Parthasarathy, 'Napster Case is no Music to Indian Ears', *The Hindu*, Int. Ed. 25 February 2001, p. 13.
34. Coombe, *The Cultural Life*, p. 90.
35. T. Janke, 'Proposals for the Recognition and Protection of Indigenous Cultural and Intellectual Property', in A. Pattel-Gray, (ed.), *Communications from Down Under* (London and Queensland: World Association for Christian Communication (WACC) and centre for Indigenous and Religious Research (CIRR), 1998); and B. Leavy, 'Indigenous Heritage and Intellectual Property Rights in Communication' in A. Pattel-Gray, (ed.), *Indigenous Communications in Aotearoa New Zealand, Australia and the Pacific* (London and Queensland: WACC and CIRR, 1998).
36. Chapter 1: Indigenous Cultural and Intellectual Property Rights, http://www.icip.lawnet.com.au
37. See B. Grantham, *'Some Big Bourgeois Brothel'—Contexts for France's Culture Wars with Hollywood* (Luton: University of Luton Press, 2000), for a contextual explanation of the key issues related to the French culture-Hollywood clash of interests. The URL for the CDMI website is http://www.screenquota.org. For a take on AV trade and the media in India, see P.N. Thomas, *Economic and Political Weekly*, vol. XXXVIII, no. 33, 16 August 2003, pp. 3485–93. 'GATS and Trade in Audio-Visuals: Culture, Politics and Empire', Also see the Media Trade Monitor website for global information on AV Trade and resistances to it at http://www.media trademoniter.org/node?From=20
38. Report of the UK Commission on IPR: *Integrating Intellectual Property Rights and Development Policy* (2002), http://www.iprcomission.com, p. 108. WIPO plays an important role in extending the copyright remit on behalf of broadcasting industries. A news report (10 June 2004), by the civil liberties organization IP Justice reaffirms this role of WIPO 'From 7–9 June, in Geneva, Switzerland, WIPO's Standing Committee on Copyrights and Related Rights is debating a text that would create copyright protection over broadcast signals for 50 years, more than twice the current length of protection permitted under the Rome Convention, which allows counties to give broadcasting corporations 20 years of exclusive rights. A 50-year term far exceeds the economic lifespan of a broadcast and the time necessary for a broadcasting corporation to recoup its investment in the programming'. See http://www.ipjustice.org/WIPO/Top_10_reasons_WIPO.html

References

Bel, Andréine, 'Three Viewpoints on the Praxis and Concepts of Midwifery: Indian *dais*, Cosmopolitan Obstetrics and Japanese *seitai*, On-line document <http://www.bioethics.ws/dais/daicomp.htm>, 1998, downloaded April 1999.

Bel, Bernard and Andréine Bel 'Birth Attendants, between the Devil and the Deep Blue Sea', in B. Bel, B. Das, V. Parthasarathi and G. Poitevin (eds), *Communication Processes 2: Dominance and Defiance* (New Delhi: Sage, forthcoming).

Desai, Rachana, 'Copyright Infringement in the Indian Film Industry', *Vanderbilt Journal of Entertainment Law and Practice*, Spring, 2005, pp. 259–78. Also available at http://law.vanderbilt.edu/jelp/archive/vol7no2/DesaiCopyrightInfringementintheIndianFilmIndustry.pdf

DeVries, Raymond G., and Rebeca Barroso 'Midwives Among the Machines: Recreating Midwifery in the late 20th Century,' in H. Marland and A.M. Rafferty (eds), *Midwives, Society and Childbirth: Debates and Controversies in the Modern Period* (London: Routledge, 1997), pp. 248–72. On-line version <*http://www.stolaf.edu/people/devries/docs/midwifery.html*>

Maid, Jitendra, Pandit Padalghare and Guy Poitevin 'The Micro-Dialectics of Communication' (in this volume).

Tew, Marjorie, *Safer Childbirth? A Critical History of Maternity Care* (London: Free Association Books, 1998).

Wagner, Marsden, *Pursuing the Birth Machine* (Camperdown NSW, Australia: ACE Graphics, 1994; original 1930).

Wignaraja, Poona and Susil Sirivardana (eds), *Readings on Pro-Poor Planning Through Social Mobilisation in South Asia. Vol. I: The Strategic Option for Poverty Eradication* (New Delhi: Vikas, 1998).

Yula, Cynthia and Katie Heffelfinger, 'How to Build a Birth Network', *Midwifery Today*, no. 56, 2000, Building a Birth Community, pp. 10–14.

IN LIEU OF AN EPILOGUE:
Beyond Disciplinary Elusiveness

EDITORS

This volume was propelled by the desire to expand the canvas of research in communication within India. In doing so, we also realized the need to interrogate the precarious position of established producers of knowledge who have defined and limited this discipline. Many of the significant weaknesses in research seemed to be connected with the generalized, functionalist explanatory frameworks, on the one hand, and the unidimensional, often shallow interpretive frameworks on the other. To strike a balance between the two was not our task. We do not feel that the study of communication has failed existing, especially institutional, research; rather their marshals and foot soldiers have not reflected deeply enough about the conceptual and methodological assumptions and implications about the objects of their pedagogy and writing. In conventional research, as also in streams of trendy writings in the late 1990s, it was commonly perceived that crucial, real world questions were being unaddressed. Resultantly, the gulf between intellectual inquiry and various spheres of communication had widened to the point where fundamental doubts could be raised about the relevance of their academic and quasiacademic concerns.

The disparity between the research themes, methodological moorings and theoretical preoccupations that have mobilized established writings and the critical concerns of civil society are noticeable in this anthology. The range and substance of what we might now call post-impasse communication research is a cause for celebration. But it is also time to take stock of the progress made along the lines suggested at the outset, as also where precisely this anthology has got us and, furthermore, what any steps need to be taken to guarantee the renewed sense of collective distinction that has been achieved.

That most contributors sought to work across conventional disciplinary boundaries is not the point; what is worth realizing is that such perspectives have helped them to define, address and fill the glaring gaps in this field of inquiry, and in the process, open newer sites of investigation and rejuvenate existing debates. The fresh and exciting work comprising this volume conveys a congruence of concerns and methods, sufficiently striking to justify the emergence of a critical research agenda. In identifying what effectively distinguishes this agenda, the variety of substantive concerns and crosscutting intellectual influences have played a seminal role. Whereas former influential standpoints ignored, in more or less deliberate ways, recognizing the notion of communication as a complex, this is precisely what the styles of research that have come into prominence now take as their central task. Since diversity implies choice, and some sort of choice is the key to effective intellectual action, the trends in this volume are significantly more attuned the urgent needs of the contexts—disciplinary and political—that these actor-contributors find themselves in.

Our concern has been with a critique of communication as dominance, and consequently with an overall attempt to turn it, not upside down but, inside out. We thus found it worthwhile to excavate the diversity and complexity of the many communication revolutions around us. Recognizing the multidimensionality of communication as a concept helped us in understanding where we stand—as writers, consumers and citizens—in the so-called knowledge society. There is need for reconceptualizing how communications exist in new and different relationships with socially diverse people—often fragmented, often in conflict. This inspired the contributors to convey their particular vision of 'the political', a vision which is grounded as much in the world outside their writings as in the writings themselves.

The volume also suggests looking beyond and beneath mediums—unlike what the trend in the study of, say, the 'old' and 'new' Media, or of audio-visual and informatic media. What we require is to reconceptualize how communication processes—across allegedly watertight technologies—exist in relationship with the diverse social demography and particular political economy of India. Equally, there must be a thrust on rigorously examining the anatomy of the technoindustrial configurations of the media, and thereby to evolve a historically informed theorization of mediums—not in themselves but as expressions of the ways in which institutions and human relationships manifest themselves. In doing so, we have demonstrated the efficacy of a renewed understanding of communication as a concept, as also the vast potential communication research holds as a social science constituency.

This led us to explore how politics is understood in communication processes and how it is theorized in communication studies. Government communication policy remains based on an image of democracy either being indigenously produced and worthy of support, or else being something which needs to be more efficiently delivered through market mechanisms. On their part, industry lobbies and academic hubs of the new ICT project often share a similar tenor in presenting communication facilities as a potent medium of democracy and empowerment—sometimes even as a substitute to political and politicizing processes. Clearly, critical communication research has a lot more to do to aid us in demonstrating the hollowness and hypocrisy in all this. Moreover, the precise nature and scale of the transition to a market economy itself need further documentation and analysis. The whole landscape of communication is transforming so fast, and at so many different levels, that there is now substantial backlog of research and policy studies which urgently need our attention.

In pondering over the extent to which the media industry reflects our priorities and aspirations, we often wonder about the status and possibilities of preindustrial forms of social interaction and symbolic expression. Are they waning, or are they being substantially transformed, or for that matter superficially appropriated? While there are many queries unanswered in this direction, what is clear is that 'the traditional' or 'the local' have their own limits to reflect progressive ideas. This then forms the basis of inquiries in the next volume.

For now, further beginnings are needed in identifying and radically redefining preexisting avenues and concerns to remoor the contours of and debates on communication— together with appropriate agendas pertaining to the teaching of communication as a social science constituency, both pedagogically and institutionally. Not only should these be undertaken from a different vantage point than in the past, and those few that are in vogue today, but we ought to locate research within the specific historical and political contexts of our society, itself undergoing transition at various levels and speeds. If we refrain from looking at our distant past, historical present and emerging future in tandem, the precise nature of these oft talked about transition(s)—viz., towards a market economy, knowledge society, federal polity, globalized culture et al.—will remain unattended or/and, at best, grossly misconstrued. What will prevail is either more of the blind euphoria on the magical wands of the present, a rejection of ideas from everywhere except the past, or a poor mimicry of standpoints from outside these contexts.

ABOUT THE EDITORS AND CONTRIBUTORS

The Editors

Bernard Bel is a research engineer currently working at *Laboratoire Parole et Langage, Université de Provence*, a speech research laboratory of the French National Centre for Scientific Research, Paris. Earlier, he was a member of the *Groupe Intelligence Artificielle*, Marseille II University. Between 1994 and 1998, he was deputed to Centre de Sciences Humaines (CSH), New Delhi, to carry on projects in musicology and sociocultural anthropology. He has published numerous articles on both subjects and is currently involved in social activism for an improvement of birth practices in French-speaking countries, both as the webmaster of the Naissance portal http://naissance.ws and the secretary of Alliance Francophone pour l'Accouchement Respecté http://www.afar.info.

Jan Brouwer recently retired as Professor of Cultural Anthropology from the North-Eastern Hill University in Shillong. He is presently Professor of Anthropology at the University School of Design, University of Mysore and Honorary Director at the Centre for Advanced Research on Indigenous Knowledge Systems (CARIKS), Mysore. He has many published works to his credit and is currently working on the concept of autonomy and death as a social relation. Email: ikdfcar@eth.net

Biswajit Das is Associate Professor at the Department of Sociology, Jamia Millia Islamia, New Delhi. He has over two decades of teaching experience and specialized research in communication studies, during which he was also a visiting fellow at the Universities of Windsor, Canada and Hawaii, USA. His research has been supported by various foundations and institutions in India and abroad such as Indo-French Scholarship, Shastri Indo-Canadian Institute, the Indian Institute of Advanced Studies and the Charles Wallace Trust. Email: biswa@sify.com

Vibodh Parthasarathi, an independent communication theorist and policy consultant based in New Delhi, maintains an interest in the political economy of communication and comparative media practice. His work has gained support from the Charles Wallace India Trust, Charles Leopold Mayer Foundation, Commonwealth Fund for Technical Cooperation, India Foundation for the Arts, and the Netherlands Fellowship Programme. He has also taught at government and private universities in India, besides dabbling in documentaries. 'Crosscurrents—A Fijian Travelogue', his last documentary, explored the many faces of 'reconciliation' after the decade of coups in the tiny Pacific nation. His current research includes tracing the history of the music industry in twentieth century India. Email: vibodhp@yahoo.com

Guy Poitevin (1934–2004) was born in Mayenne (France). After studying to become a priest and graduating in philosophy and theology, he taught for twelve years in a seminary in Western France. He settled in Pune in 1972 and later became a naturalized Indian citizen. Along with his wife Hema Rairkar, friends and associates, he set up the Village Community Development Association (VCDA, http://vcda.ws) in 1978 to support socio-cultural action in remote rural areas, and the Centre for Cooperative Research in Social Sciences (CCRSS, http://ccrss.ws) in 1980 for the purpose of carrying out theoretically related activities. Besides numerous articles, he has written several books in English and French, including translated works from Marathi.

The Contributors

Uma Chakravarti is a feminist historian who has taught history at Miranda House, University of Delhi, for four decades. She has been associated with the Womens' Movement and the Movement for Democratic Rights. She is the author of *Social Dimensions of Early Buddhism* (New Delhi, New York: OUP, 1987), *Rewriting History: The life and times of Pandita Ramabai* (New Delhi: Kali, 1998) and *Gendering Caste: Through a Feminist Lense* (Stree, 2003).

Maitrayee Chaudhuri is with the Centre for the Study of Social Systems, Jawaharlal Nehru University, New Delhi. She works in the area of globalization, culture, media and gender studies. Her earlier works include *The Indian Women's Movement: Reform and Revival* (New Delhi: Radiant, 1993) and the edited anthologies *The Practice of Sociology* (New Delhi: Orient Longman, 2004) and *Feminism in India* (New Delhi: Women Unlimited/Kali, 2004; London: Zed, 2005).

Shanti Kumar is Assistant Professor of Media and Cultural Studies in the Department of Communication Arts at the University of Wisconsin, Madison, USA. He is the co-editor of *Planet TV: A Global Television Reader* (New York: New York University Press, 2003) and the author of *Unimaginable Communities: Television and the Politics of Nationalism* (University of Illinois Press, 2005). He holds a double masters degree in Mass Communication and Journalism from Osmania University, and in Media Studies from Texas Christian University, and a Ph.D. in Mass Communications from Indiana University, Bloomington. His research and teaching interests include television and new media technologies, global media studies and postcolonial theory. He has served on the Advisory Committee of the Centre for South Asia, at the University of Wisconsin, Madison.

Deep Kanta Lahiri Choudhury is Visiting Professor at the Centre for Jawaharlal Nehru Studies, Jamia Millia Islamia, New Delhi. He completed his Ph.D. under the supervision of Professor C. A. Bayly, University of Cambridge. The thesis, entitled 'A Social and Political History of the Telegraph in

India, circa 1830–1920', was awarded the Ellen McArthur Prize by the University of Cambridge for excellence in social and economic history. He was Research Officer at the Wellcome Unit for the History of Medicine, University of Oxford in 2002–4. His publications include 'India's First Virtual Community and the Telegraph General Strike of 1908', *International Review of Social History*, Special Supplement XI; 'Uncovering Labour in Information Revolutions 1750–2004', Amsterdam, December 2003; 'Treason of the Clerks: Representation and Sedition in the Telegraph Strike of 1908', in C. Bates (ed.), *Beyond Representation* (New Delhi: Oxford University Press, forthcoming); 'Sinews of Panic and the Nerves of Empire: The Imagined States' Entanglement with Information Panic, India, c. 1880–1912', *Modern Asian Studies*, 2004 (October).

Jitendra Maid was born in Shirur in 1971, graduated in commerce and studied journalism in the University of Pune. He has been in contact with the Centre for Cooperative Research in the Social Sciences (CCRSS) since 1990. He started helping Hema Rairkar to document grindmill songs in the Mulshi area and later in other parts of Maharashtra. He also collected myths of Parit, Vadar and Mang communities and helped in the final editing of the compilation of monographs. Given his skills and interest in street theatre, he takes the responsibility to teach girls from the hostels run by the Village Community Development Association (VCDA). Jitendra has been active in the organization of self-learning workshops under the guidance of the late Guy Poitevin and Hema Rairkar. He is also involved in the implementation of a network called Jan Hit Vikas Chalval (Movement for the Development of the Benefit for People) over the entire state of Maharashtra.

Pandit Padalghare, the son of a small peasant in Mulshi taluka, in Pune district, joined the *Garib Dongari Sanghatna* at the age of 18. At that time his family had only one crop of rice and their financial condition was weak. But these conditions improved, notably when a percolation tank was built in their isolated village, enabling them to harvest two crops of rice and grow marketable vegetables. Currently, Pandit is a principal animator of the organization. He is responsible for the Shirur taluka in the eastern side of Pune, and shares with other principal animators the responsibility of the self-learning workshops.

G. Krishna Reddy is Associate Professor at the Department of Political Science, Osmania University, Hyderabad. He obtained his M.A. and M.Phil. from Jawaharlal Nehru University, New Delhi and Ph.D. from Osmania University. He has contributed articles on regime politics in Andhra Pradesh to journals like *Economic and Political Weekly, Indian Journal of Federal Studies,* etc. He was part of the LOGO-Link project on rural governance, at the Institute of Development Studies, Sussex University. Presently he is working on media, identities and social movements.

Joël Ruet holds a Ph.D. in Economics, and is an Alumni from the *Ecole des Mines,* Paris. He is currently Marie Curie Fellow in London School of Economics and Associate Researcher in CERNA, Paris. He also teaches in Jawaharlal Nehru University, New Delhi. From 2000–2004, he was the Head of the Economics Department, *Centre de Sciences Humaines,* New Delhi. His works cover reform of the electricity and water sectors in various countries, and socio-economic study of the public sector in India.

Dipankar Sinha is Reader in Political Science, University of Calcutta, and Honorary Adjunct Fellow, Institute of Development Studies, Kolkata. He also held positions in Kalyani University and Scottish Church College, Kolkata. Sinha's writings focus on the development–communication linkage, in both global and local contexts, in postcolonial societies. His publications include *Communicating Development in the New World Social Order* (New Delhi: Kanishka, 1999) and *Media Culture* (in Bengali) (Kolkata: Dey's Publishing, 2003). His current research explores the role of communication in globalization from various vantage points.

Pradip N. Thomas is currently Associate Professor at School of Journalism and Communication, University of Queensland. He was formerly Director, Global Studies Programme, at the World Association for Christian Communication (WACC), London. He has published widely on issues related to communication rights, the political economy of copyright, audio-visual trade, media ownership and control, communications and development and communications for social change. His latest publication is a co-authored volume (with Zaharom Nain), *Who Owns the Media: Global Trends and Local Resistances*, (Penang/London: ZED/Southbound/World Association for Christian Communication, 2004).